CAN THE WELFARE STATE COMPETE?

Also by Ian Gough and published by Macmillan

THE POLITICAL ECONOMY OF THE WELFARE STATE

Can the Welfare State Compete?

A Comparative Study of Five Advanced Capitalist Countries

Edited by
Alfred Pfaller
Friedrich Ebert Foundation, Bonn
and
Ian Gough
Senior Lecturer in Social Policy
University of Manchester
and
Göran Therborn
Professor of Sociology at Göteborg University

First published 1991 by
THE MACMILLAN PRESS LTD
Houndmills, Basingstoke, Hampshire RG21 2XS
and London
Companies and representatives
throughout the world

ISBN 0-333-48755-9

A catalogue record for this book is available from the British Library.

Printed in Great Britain by
Antony Rowe Ltd
Chippenham, Wiltshire

Reprinted 1993, 1994

12 11 10 9 8 7 6 5 4
03 02 01 00 99 98 97 96 95

Contents

List of Tables vi

List of Figures viii

Preface x

1 The Issue 1
Alfred Pfaller, with Ian Gough and Göran Therborn

2 The Competitiveness of Industrialised Welfare States: A Cross-country Survey 15
Alfred Pfaller, with Ian Gough

3 The United States 45
Alfred Pfaller

4 The United Kingdom 101
Ian Gough

5 France 153
Xavier Greffe

6 The Federal Republic of Germany 187
Michael Krüger and Alfred Pfaller

7 Sweden 229
Göran Therborn

8 Welfare Statism and International Competition: The Lesson of the Case Studies 271
Alfred Pfaller, with Ian Gough and Göran Therborn

Notes 299

Bibliography 311

Index 333

List of Tables

2.1 Synthetic index of welfare statism for 16 OECD countries, 1979–83 18
3.1 Selected OECD countries' shares of exports in R&D intensive manufacturing, 1970–84 (%) 53
4.1 UK: output, employment and productivity 104
4.2 Manufacturing industry in four countries, 1979–87 105
4.3 UK: balance of payments, 1973–88 (% of GDP) 106
4.4 UK: indices of cost competitiveness in trade in manufactures, 1973–88 110
4.5 R&D expenditure in five countries 113
4.6 UK: public expenditure and taxation, 1975–87 125
4.7 UK car industry: selected statistics 130
4.8 UK: telecommunications industry: selected statistics 133
4.9 UK: employment and unemployment, 1979, 1983 and 1987 136
4.10 UK: social expenditure, 1973–87 139
4.11 UK: income distribution and redistribution, 1976, 1979 and 1984 142
5.1 France: external and domestic competitiveness: main indicators, 1979–86 (1979 = 100) 154
5.2 France: main results of foreign exchange, 1980–6 (billion French francs) 155
5.3 France: export/import ratios, 1977–86 157
5.4 Comparative levels of productivity, 1950, 1973 and 1984 159
5.5 Sectoral labour productivity growth in selected OECD countries 160
5.6 France: ranking of the products according to the relative export/import ratio and to relative costs 165
6.1 Ratio of exports/GDP in West Germany, 1970–85 188
6.2 Development of unit labour costs in selected OECD countries, 1970–88 189
6.3 R&D expenditure as percentage of GDP in selected OECD countries, 1986 191
6.4 Hourly compensation for workers in the motor vehicles industries of selected OECD countries, 1975, 1981 and 1986 (USA = 100) 212

6.5 The financial weight of the West German welfare state, 1970–85 217

7.1 The sum of stock exchange values as % of GDP in selected OECD countries, 1984 230

7.2 Exports of goods and services as % of GDP in small developed European economies, 1980–5 232

7.3 Indices of total hourly labour costs for manufacturing workers in selected OECD countries, at current exchange rates, 1966–85 (Sweden = 100) 234

7.4 Social expenditure in Western Europe in % of GDP, 1980 235

7.5 Public social services employment in selected OECD countries as % of the population between 15 and 64 years, 1985 236

7.6 Distribution and redistribution of income in selected countries, around 1980 (family equivalent income as distributed among persons, Gini coefficients) 237

7.7 Relative disposable income per consumption unit in Sweden, 1984–5 (all manual workers = 100) 238

7.8 Sweden's economic performance 1950–73 in international comparisons 240

7.9 Sweden's economic performance during the 1974–85 crisis in international comparisons 241

7.10 Labour market performance in Sweden and OECD countries, 1973–84 (employment change net of unemployment growth in % of the number of employed in 1973) 242

7.11 Decomposition of the change of unit labour costs in Swedish manufacturing industry relative to ten OECD countries (cumulative % change between 1974 and 1976) 249

7.12 Relative costs, prices, and margins per produced unit in Sweden related to OECD competitors, in common currency (1980 = 100) 249

7.13 Commitment to one's job and to the organisation where one works in selected OECD countries, early 1980s (survey answers in %) 268

8.1 Policies introduced in the 1970s and 1980s in five industrialised countries in order to strengthen national competitiveness 273

8.2 Retrenchments in welfare statism in five industrialised countries in the 1970s and 1980s 275

8.3 Some indicators of competitiveness for five industrialised countries 292

List of Figures

2.1	Social expenditure and manufacturing export performance in the 1980s	21
2.2	Tax load and manufacturing export performance in the 1980s	22
2.3	Synthetic index of welfare statism and manufacturing export performance in the 1980s	23
2.4	Social expenditure and manufacturing export performance in the 1970s	24
2.5	Changes in the tax load and manufacturing export performance in the 1980s	25
2.6	Change in social expenditure in the 1970s and manufacturing export performance in the 1980s	26
2.7	Social expenditure and productivity growth in the 1980s	28
2.8	Social expenditure and manufacturing productivity growth in the 1980s	29
2.9	Synthetic index of welfare statism and manufacturing productivity growth in the 1980s	30
2.10	Social expenditure and manufacturing productivity growth in the 1970s	31
2.11	Changes in social expenditure and manufacturing productivity growth in the 1970s	32
2.12	Social expenditure and total factor productivity growth in the manufacturing sector in the 1980s	33
2.13	Tax load and competitiveness rating in 1986	35
2.14	Changes in the tax load in the 1980s and competitiveness rating in 1986	36
2.15	Tax load and economic growth in the 1970s and 1980s	38
2.16	Social expenditure and economic growth in the 1980s	39
2.17	Social expenditure and economic growth in the 1970s	40
3.1	Economic growth, inflation and unemployment rates in the USA, 1961–86 (%)	46
3.2	The US trade balance, 1960–86 (% of GDP)	47
3.3	Selected OECD countries' shares of world manufacturing exports, 1965–80	51

3.4 Indices of average real hourly earnings of production workers in manufacturing, selected OECD countries, 1960–81 (1960 = 100) 52
3.5 Gross fixed capital formation in selected OECD countries, 1960–86 (% of GDP) 55
3.6 Percentage of the American population that would have been officially poor without transfers and that actually was poor, 1965–86 91
4.1 UK: trade balance in manufactures and other items, 1978–88 (% of GDP) 108
4.2 Labour productivity levels in seven countries, 1960–86 (US$ of 1980 per employed person) 108
6.1 Number of motor vehicles produced in selected OECD countries, 1970–87 (thousands) 209
6.2 Car exports of selected OECD countries, 1960–87 (thousands of units) 210
6.3 Annual production of motor vehicles per employed person in the German and Japanese automobile industries, 1970–81 213
6.4 Persons registered as unemployed in West Germany, 1970–89 (thousands) 219

Preface

The relationship between the nation state and the internationalising tendencies of market processes formed the starting point for this study. For some years it had occupied a small research group in the Friedrich Ebert Foundation in West Germany. Michael Dauderstädt, then a member of this group, wrote a proposal for a project on 'Societies in International Competition: Consequences for the Welfare State' which was eventually awarded a grant by the Volkswagen Foundation. When Michael left for Portugal, Alfred Pfaller, his close companion in the search for the world economy's hidden dynamics, made the project his own. At a conference at the New School for Social Research in New York he persuaded Ian Gough and Göran Therborn to participate in it. Both had had for a long time a professional interest in the welfare state. Later, Xavier Greffe and Michael Krüger joined the team to undertake the French and German case-studies respectively.

Can the welfare state compete? It is fair to say that all of us preferred the answer to be positive. It would be abnormal if our sympathies with the beleagured idea of social and economic citizenship for all did not show in this book. But we were aware that the cause of the welfare state would not be served by covering up real problems with words. And problems do exist. There is a growing tendency for the majority to secure their success in the internationalising markets at the expense of a minority who remain excluded. Although we recognise the economic logic pushing developments this way, our analysis has strengthened our confidence in the inherent competitiveness of the welfare state. But it is not an unconditional confidence. Under today's economic conditions two social virtues are tested more severely than in the easier days of the long post-war boom. They are discipline and solidarity. If the idea and practices of a welfare state are to regain their appeal and effectiveness at the end of the twentieth century these virtues will have to be more firmly institutionalised than they are at present.

That is, roughly, the message of this book. Our thanks are owed most of all to the Volkswagen Foundation who financed the research and to the Friedrich Ebert Foundation who provided all the logistical support for the research team. We also thank Renate Keitel, Lisa Vogel and the student-workers of the Friedrich Ebert Foundation for their technical assistance. We would also like to thank many unnamed interviewees in the various countries we investigated.

ALFRED PFALLER
IAN GOUGH
GÖRAN THERBORN

1 The Issue

Alfred Pfaller, with Ian Gough and Göran Therborn

A GENERAL SUSPICION . . .

'For the West, East Asia's growing success poses a challenge, just as Europe's expansion in the 16th and 17th centuries posed a challenge to China.' (*Financial Times*, 30 June 1988, p. 14) 'The type and model of growth which have sustained the development of the Western economies have been profoundly challenged since the early 1970s, both because the limits and drawbacks of the model itself have been realised and because economic activities have been redistributed among the continents and countries.' (Chaigneau 1981, p. 201) Quotations like these may unduly dramatise the turn of events in the past two decades, but they are indicative of a perception which has become widespread in the industrialised countries of Europe and North America. The challenges referred to imply that responses are called for. And we have reasons to suspect that such responses might bring about societies with more poverty and less quality of life for many of their members, even though these societies will be at least as prosperous as they were in the 1970s. We have reasons to suspect that the Western industrial (or for that matter 'post-industrial') societies might see themselves unable to provide for the material well-being of every citizen with the same effectiveness as they used to. Abstractly spoken, social and non-economic objectives in general might be sacrificed to the overriding priority of efficient production for highly contested markets.

In the 20 to 30 years following the Second World War Western societies – some more, some less – had come closer than ever before to a state which could be described as prosperity for all. The result of prosperity for nearly all citizens had two basic ingredients: full employment at relatively high minimum wages and a system of arrangements which assure socially acceptable standards of living to citizens who for one reason or the other are excluded from the labour market or do not otherwise earn sufficiently high incomes. These arrangements include transfer payments to those unable to work and the guaranteed provision of certain essential elements of a 'decent' standard of living and of reasonably good life perspectives, like nutrition, health care, education, or public space for the 'enjoyment of life'. In fact, more and more has the ultimate responsibility been placed with the state that regardless of adverse contingencies no citizen falls too far below the national average in his or her material well-being. This is in essence the principle of the modern Western welfare state. The formalised public programmes of income-maintenance, health insurance, education etc., to which the term 'welfare state' often refers, are the most visible manifestation of this principle. But deliberate full-employment policies, tax incentives for company pension funds, mandatory work safety and anti-pollution standards, minimum-wage legislation or the protection of jobs against displacement by adverse market conditions are as well part of the broader welfare state syndrome. Formal programmes involving public transfer payments are to some degree but substitutes for other policies or for private programmes. Referring in the most general way to the use of state power and responsibility towards the ends of protecting citizens against economic adversities and ensuring a certain standard of prosperity to all we shall use the term 'welfare statism'.

Welfare statism is the way by which the capitalist industrial economy has been made compatible with overriding social objectives – in some countries. Most important perhaps, the economy has to some degree been put at the service of the meta-economic human goal 'enjoyment of life'. As such one can call it with the Swedish economist Assar Lindbeck 'a triumph for modern civilisation' (Lindbeck, 1988, p. 21). True, this is not the whole reality. Welfare statist arrangements are also being used as a means of featherbedding politically influential groups at the expense of the rest of the society. And welfare statism has fulfilled throughout the post-war years important functions for the system of capitalist production, for instance the efficient reproduction of manpower, the formation of human capital or the stabilisation of demand. In this fundamental respect it is the welfare state which has been put at the service of the economy. And its advance has had certainly much to do with its functionality within a certain economic system.[1]

What we see at stake is that part of welfare statism which goes beyond its (declining?) functionality within the capitalist economy, the part that serves predominantly the values of equality and enjoyment of life in relative freedom from want.[2] Our suspicion is based on the general notion that international competition towards the end of the 20th century poses a challenge to the Western welfare states which is in fact different from the challenge international competition has always posed to all countries. In the following we shall first try to substantiate the claim that international competition has set stricter limits to the pursuit of non-economic objectives. Then we shall reflect on the implications this has for welfare statism. As a result we shall present a more differentiated statement of our suspicion that international competition could harm welfare statism.

...BASED ON THE CHANGES IN INTERNATIONAL COMPETITION

In the past ten years or so Western policy-makers and academics alike have given much more attention to the issue of countries' international competitiveness than they used to. Whatever the intellectual quality of this increasing public concern is, it indicates that more weight is attributed to considerations of competitiveness in the mind of the public and hence in the policy-making process as a whole. If a social practice is being considered as harmful to competitiveness it should be expected to be less easily defendable and tolerated than was the case when competitiveness mattered less. This heightened public awareness of the importance of being competitive reflects real changes with regard to countries' insertion into the broader international economy:

1. Countries have become more exposed to foreign competition on their domestic markets as natural and artificial trade barriers became less effective. Enterprises' ties to their home countries have become looser, as it becomes possible to set up production abroad more easily. All this means that products, production processes and locational conditions which previously just were as they happened to be are now subjected to critical international comparisons. Countries are forced to adjust one way or the other to the newly revealed comparative reality. It can affect their exchange rate. But it can also affect their industrial structure, as some lines of production, some ways of producing things and some locations may prove no longer viable in the new competitive world. Even if the necessary adjustments are perfectly feasible in economic terms and do not imply any losses in general welfare, the need for them may not be recognised right away. And it is most unlikely that they are accepted without

resistance by those who are directly affected. As a consequence, protracted non-adjustment may cause serious balance of payments problems with all their macro economic entanglements. For instance, unwillingness to accept the loss in real incomes which results from a necessary downward adjustment in the terms of trade could tie the pursuit of monetary stability to the maintenance of an overvalued currency. This, in turn, leads (a) to a permanent conflict between balanced foreign accounts and economic growth and (b) to a generalised problem of competitiveness. The transition to a more open economy means that certain aspirations can only be met, certain practices only be continued further if concessions are made in other respects, for example with regard to the exchange rate. Society is forced to make choices, either in a rational, explicit or in an implicit, uncontrolled fashion.

2. New types of competitors have arisen. Some offer many goods much cheaper than producers in the 'old' industrialised countries are able to. Some are coming up with superior productivity and superior innovativeness, setting new standards for the others to match. Both pose challenges which go beyond the ones of increasing exposure. They demand major adjustments also from those countries who have been heavily exposed to foreign competition for a long time. To increasingly efficient low-wage competition high-wage producers can only respond by stepping up improvements in productivity and product quality and by getting out of the contested markets. To make up for the unavoidable losses of market chances and hence jobs, the high-wage countries of the West would have to expand activity in areas where they can fend off or are not threatened by low-wage competition. But, of course, these (still) 'natural' high-wage markets are highly contested, too, as every country of the industrialised North would like to place an increasing part of its labour force there. To be successful you don't just have to be good, you have to be better than the others.[3] Even if one is confident that economic growth will prevent in the long run international competition from remaining a zero-sum game, the standards of best international practice have to be met. And these standards are changing all the time, not only in the sense of advances in product and process technology but also in the sense that ever better ways are introduced to organize for efficiency and innovativeness.[4] Competitive advantages which immunise against low-wage underbidders get lost quickly and even the basis from which they can continuously be re-created is shifting. A fundamental requirement for continuing competitiveness despite high wages, high

environmental costs, high taxes and high real estate prices is, therefore, the readiness to adopt superior new practices and to abandon old practices when they prove to be inferior. Relevant practices concern, first of all, enterprises. But there is widespread awareness today that broader aspects of societal organisation and culture are concerned as well.

3. As a consequence of the changes outlined under points 1 and 2, countries that are used to being in the global top league of technological competence and prosperity now face the danger of relative stagnation while others advance. There is even the possibility of absolute decline in prosperity, as parts of the national industry retrocede under the impact of foreign competition whereas new investments go elsewhere. What is at stake in international competition is not the balance of trade, even though the issue is sometimes presented as one of trade surpluses and deficits. Ultimately the competition is about where growth is taking place and income being generated. Which nations will in future have the wealth-creating capacity to supply goods that are marketable despite high costs? This is the decisive question. The countries which supply to the world market the bulk of these goods will also be the ones which provide for the bulk of the market. Since it is these countries where the future purchasing-power is concentrated it will also be up to them to provide the most attractive markets for services and non-tradables of all kinds.

Three points summarise our reflections on international competition: (1) Products and production processes have become more subject to international comparison. (2) International standards have changed, and meeting them has become more difficult. (3) More is at stake in international competition.

TWO CONCEPTS OF COMPETITIVENESS

Considering how these changes could affect the welfare state we have to distinguish between two broad lines of reasoning. One says that welfare statism is from an economic point of view something like a costly luxury which countries could afford as long as they were, for a variety of reasons, immune against the competition from countries who did not have this luxury. But this immunity is eroding on two fronts: (a) countries with low welfare state costs become more and more competitive in terms of productivity and product quality so that the cost advantage of a low welfare state burden, like the one of lower wages, becomes ever more important; (b) old industrialised countries with high productivity and innovativeness have started to reduce the welfare burden on their companies. As a consequence other industrialised countries are forced to follow suit if they do not want to lose out in this underbidding competition.

But there is another line of reasoning. According to this, welfare statism has become more and more of an obstacle to higher productivity and innovativeness. That is to say, welfare statism itself is – as a productive liability, so to speak – eroding the basis which, according to the first line of reasoning, has made it possible as a consumptive 'luxury'.

The first view sees welfare statism in danger because of too much competition. The second one sees competitiveness in danger because of too much welfare statism. According to both views, countries might have to cut back their level of welfare statism in order to stay competitive. But we should be aware that there are two different concepts of international competitiveness involved. One concept denotes simply the ability to sell products in an internationally contested market. This ability derives from the relative price and the relative quality of the product in comparison with foreign products. It is a concept which is appropriate for enterprises. For them, cheap inputs, including cheap labour, are a competitive asset because they facilitate competitive pricing. For a country things are different. Just as it would not make sense to call an enterprise competitive that only stays in the market at the cost of low or no profits, so it does not make sense to consider it a competitive advantage of a nation if its labour force receives permanently lower incomes than foreign labour forces. It would be more appropriate to say that this nation cannot afford its members higher incomes because it is not competitive enough. 'The competitiveness of a nation refers to its ability to achieve high factor incomes when exposed to international market forces.' (Pfaller 1987, p. 113) This ability is derived from superior productivity and qualitative excellence. We could call it the 'underlying' competitiveness of a country or a nation, whereas the actual chance of selling on the world market, regardless of the achievable income, might be called 'performing' competitiveness.[5] In the first of our lines of reasoning introduced above it is then insufficient underlying competitiveness which may force a country to reduce costly welfare statism in order to safeguard its performing competitiveness. The second line of reasoning, in turn, says that welfare statism has come to cause a decline in underlying competitiveness.

PERFORMING COMPETITIVENESS: AUSTERITY OF ONE SORT OR ANOTHER MAY BE CALLED FOR

Let us consider the situation of a country whose performing competitiveness in the world market is no longer sufficient to avoid, at full employment, excessive trade deficits and whose high costs of welfare statism are considered a major competitive disadvantage. Reducing welfare statism is one out of four basic adjustment alternatives which would improve – at given comparative productivities and product qualities – the national producers' selling chances. The other alternatives are: (a) currency devaluation; (b) reduction of other costs, most of all wages; (c) redistribution of the costs of welfare statism away from enterprises and onto households. The choice is basically a matter of societal preferences. As such it is subject to the conflict between diverging interests and the decision reflects the power behind them. Our hypothetical nation could decide against a reduction of welfare statism because it attributes a very high priority to values like 'economic citizenship for everybody' and 'quality of life'. But it has to be willing and able to bear the costs this decision implies in the face of stronger foreign competition. All three adjustment alternatives mean that somebody has to bear additional costs. In the case of currency devaluation this 'somebody' is all those who consume directly or indirectly (in the form of inputs into finished products) imported goods. If they try to defend their real income this adjustment alternative may turn out inflationary and ineffective. If non-wage labour costs, from employers' social security contributions to statutory sick payment and restrictive dismissal procedures, are to be reduced but the level of welfare statism thus financed be maintained, others will have to pay. For example, the state could take over the social responsibilities from the employers, increasing taxes (except on enterprises) or cutting other expenses, like producers' subsidies or defence outlays. This is to say, either some groups' disposable incomes are reduced or society affords itself less public goods of the non-welfare sort. The most direct way of assigning the higher costs which increased competition might attach to the maintenance of a given level of welfare statism is the reduction of money wages so as to give enterprises the additional pricing margin they need.

In either case, adjustment means that fewer goods and services are made available for consumption outside of welfare state arrangements. Economically this is feasible, if society should opt for setting priorities thus. But a more or less painful setting of priorities will be required in our hypothetical case. Since there is no good reason to postulate an absolute preference (a completely inelastic demand) for welfare statism we should expect some dismantling of welfare statism as a probable outcome. Moreover, it is not unlikely that society will have difficulties in setting priorities at all, because each avenue of adjustment is blocked by vested interests. In such a case there would be a series of abortive attempts at adjustment, recurrent balance of payments crises and general inflationary pressure, followed eventually by a more drastic (and almost certainly not impartial) attack on the structure of vested interests. In any case, it is important to realise that social underbidding by less welfare burdened foreign competitors does not undermine the *economic* basis of welfare statism but maybe the *political* one. The economic problem is not that nations then can afford less welfare statism, but that they can afford less welfare statism *cum* individual consumption.

UNDERLYING COMPETITIVENESS: EFFORT, EFFICIENCY AND TRADE-OFFS

A very different problem is addressed by the claim that the modern Western welfare state has become harmful to a country's underlying competitiveness, that is, to its ability to achieve for its citizens high wages and high profits in the international market place. This claim has been made in so many words over and over by economists, social scientists, politicians and business representatives in the last decade and a half. It constitutes today a widely held belief among Western conservatives. Even in the centre-left camp (Social Democrats, American liberals) the suspicion has gained ground that there might be quite a bit of truth to it. Looking for the rationale that supports this claim we actually find a rather disorderly conglomerate of arguments of different comprehensiveness, on different levels of abstraction and of different mutual compatibility. There are wholesale social psychological arguments which denounce the immobilising entitlement mentality which predominates in modern welfare states, their preoccupation with security, consumption and distribution instead of economic performance.[6] There are also arguments of a more narrow technical type which attribute the anti-competitive effect of modern welfare statism to a variety of socio-economic mechanisms which can be at work independently of each other, but which could also add up in their dysfunctional effects. For example, it is reasoned that welfare state security weakens work discipline because the threat of unemployment loses much of its effect as a reinforcing sanction. On this technical level, a distinction can be made between the negative effects welfare statism is said to have:

(a) on investment, that is on the effort society devotes to the formation of productivity-increasing and quality-improving physical and human capital and to the creation of technological expertise;
(b) on allocative efficiency, that is, on the readiness and the ability to shift and reshift resources, including manpower, into those economic activities for which the international market provides the highest rewards;
(c) on human performance, in other words on entrepreneurs' and employees' motivation to work, to innovate, to be efficient, and to co-operate.

Even though concrete welfare state arrangements can very well be dysfunctional on either one of the three accounts, several points can be made that the welfare state ideals of full economic citizenship and quality of life are not essentially incompatible with the successful pursuit of maximum productivity and optimal product quality.

A. The resources needed for income maintenance, the non-commercial supply of goods and services and the guarantee of certain qualities of life do not need to be provided at the expense of capital formation; they can be provided at the expense of individual consumption. This is not a matter of the magnitude of the welfare state costs but of their appropriate allocation.
B. By guaranteeing incomes independent of specific ways of earning them a comprehensive welfare state can facilitate continuous adjustment to changing market conditions. The real issue is not welfare state rigidity versus free market flexibility but rationally versus irrationally organised economic security.
C. Social arrangements which are based on the communality of interests have proven more successful in maximising commitment to efficient and high-quality production than those which rely exclusively on the contractual exchange of effort against pay and on the control which is necessary to enforce the terms of the contract.
D. Knowledge and human capabilities are probably the most important competitive assets of today's highly industrialised nations.

Societies which fully prepare their human potential, so to speak, for a high-efficiency, high-quality and high-innovation economy should, therefore, have an advantage over societies which leave human capital formation largely to the limited resources the individual is able and willing to mobilise to this end.[7]

Yet, there are also trade-offs. One is between more consumption now and more consumption later. Another one is between the consumption of more marketable goods and services on the one hand and more non-commercial value, as is for example attached to security, leisure time or freedom from adjustment stress, on the other. Choices here are, at least in principle, a matter of societal priorities. A sacrifice of commercially valued prosperity is in order as long as the choice is made rationally, meaning in full recognition of the trade-off involved, and as long as the trade-off is not unnecessarily harsh, in other words as long as there are no more efficient solutions available. The real problem again is society's capability to arrive at rational solutions. If the road towards competitive welfare state adjustments is blocked for one reason or the other, cutbacks in welfare statism may in fact be the only *feasible* way to improve conditions for the country's international competitiveness (cf. Pfaller, 1987).

Of still another sort is Mancur Olson's argument about the universal evolutionary trend towards increasing political influence of distributional coalitions who bring about public decisions in their own favour against the common interest of the society (Olson 1982). In such an Olsonian world welfare statism must be, to an ever larger degree, an outflow of particularistic 'rent-seeking'. But we should note that the argument is not one on the welfare state's inherent dysfunctional economic consequences but rather one on its distortion in the actual political reality.

Supposedly, countries who score high on Olsonian sclerosis are likely to fall back in competition with less sclerotic countries. However, this insight does not readily serve as guidance for a policy to strengthen competitiveness, because what matters are not symptoms like featherbedding welfare statism but the 'virus' of interest group power. As long as this power is not significantly weakened, we should not expect much dismantling of welfare statism either, regardless of all the rhetoric against it and regardless also of the negative effects it might in fact have on countries' international competitiveness. On the other hand, the taming of interest group power would free the way not only to a more efficient market process, but also to a more rational organisation of society's meta-economic pursuits and hence to more efficient welfare statism. In turn, if we disregard Olson's evolutionary thesis and focus only on the various perceived dysfunctionalities of welfare statism we should expect that increasing competitive pressure will – whether really warranted or not – induce society to cut back on it.

OUR STUDY: THE POLITICAL AND THE ECONOMIC QUESTION

Various lines of reasoning on international competition and welfare statism lead us to expect increasing strain in the relationship between the two. Either, welfare statist achievements are threatened by adjustment pressure or competitiveness is endangered by effective resistance to adjustment, which in the long run might well undermine welfare state legitimacy the more thoroughly. To find out whether, to what degree and in which way empirical evidence confirms the reasoned suspicion is the purpose of our comparative investigation. Our primary concern is the question: how well does the welfare state survive in the new competitive world that has emerged in the 1970s and 1980s? This is a political question and refers to the strength of the pressure resulting from the changed economic environment as well as to the strength of welfare state resistance to this pressure. It is a question of supreme importance, because it concerns the fate of fundamental societal and human values which might recede before the overwhelming imperative of economic performance. Welfare statism is – in essence and despite all its distortions – the organisational backbone of a civilisation that in the past 30 years has proceeded to subordinate the economy to meta-economic human values,[8] and the question is how much room there is still for this civilisation in the new competitive world.

As a secondary concern, we are also interested in the questions: how much and what sort of welfare statism can a country afford in the 1990s without doing harm to its international competitiveness? The two concerns are partially, but only partially related. If the degree of welfare statism we can observe today in some Western and Northern European countries is, in fact, fully compatible with continued high competitiveness, dismantling should be less likely. But welfare statism might be reduced anyway. As already mentioned, other avenues of adjustment which are more compatible with full-scale welfare statism may be blocked politically. Or policy-makers' and public views on what is required for the sake of competitiveness may simply be mistaken. Such mistaken views may be promoted and exploited by those who benefit from cuts in welfare statism. This is to say, the observation that such cuts are applied on behalf of competitiveness does not automatically warrant the conclusion that welfare statism is in fact bad for competitiveness. On the other hand, if we observe that in the political reality the welfare state resists the pressure of dismantling, this does not entitle us to discard the claim of it being anti-competitive. The stubborn welfare states may fall behind in international competition, but so slowly that conclusive evidence is not readily available.

THE DESIGN OF THE INVESTIGATION

In accordance with our primary interest – what does international competition do to the welfare state? – the investigation concentrates on the political pressure towards cuts in welfare statism which originates in public concern for the country's international competitiveness. To this end we direct our attention first to the debate which has been going on – or not – in various countries on the issue of international competitiveness. We identify the demands made on policy-makers and the policies actually implemented on behalf of competitiveness. Next we study how the demanded and the implemented policies could and did affect welfare statism. In order to prepare for this we review what has actually happened to welfare statism in each country since the mid-1970s. We then have two blocks of empirical information, referring:

(a) to the political processing of the challenge of international competition and
(b) to the evolution of welfare statism.

This puts us in a position to ask two questions, the answers to which should supplement and consolidate each other: (1) What of (a) has affected the welfare state? (2) What of (b) can be attributed to (a)? The information block (b) should also help us to discover indirect pressures which originate in international competition but which do not manifest themselves readily in the observable political response syndrome to the competitive challenge. Such indirect pressure could take the form of a non-response to changed economic circumstances which increase the need for welfare state services. Or changes in welfare statism could respond to economic constraints which at the surface have nothing to do with international competition but which nonetheless could be shown to be an offshoot of competitive pressure.

The main focus of the analysis has welfare statism as its dependent and international competition as its independent variable. But how can we gain insights into the effects of the independent variable 'welfare statism' on a nation's competitiveness – our secondary cognitive interest? Obviously we need empirical information on the evolution of countries' competitiveness and on their degree and kind of welfare statism. But in addition we need reasonable criteria for linking the two types of information. This third ingredient is the most problematic one. Statistical association derived from the observation of a sufficiently large number of cases is one criterion. We shall apply a very simple form of it in the following chapter. But statistical association, however measured, can at best provide a strong suggestion that there is a causal link between different variables. Moreover, information on the 'typical' cases, which shape most strongly the statistical measure of association, may be less relevant than the one on the exceptional cases, because the latter could tell us about the conditions under which our variables are covariate and under which not. In highly complex macro-systems like societies and national economies, a specific relationship between *A* and *B* is almost always dependent on specific configurations of variables C_1 to C_n. Thus, a statistical association of *A* and *B* might just reflect the relative frequency of alternative such configurations. A strong association (for example, a correlation coefficient close to unity) means that most cases of the sample have a configuration which is conducive to the togetherness of *A* and *B*. In other words, from a given frequency distribution of configurations results a certain probability that we find: if *A* then *B*, or if more *A* then more *B*. But all this does not tell us anything yet about the nature of the configurations.

What we need are insights into the mechanisms which relate welfare statism to competitiveness. Deductive reasoning, to which we have referred earlier, is important. But we can also make use of the empirical information we shall report in the following country studies. By reviewing the pertinent national debates we hope to learn about the anatomy of the various countries' problems of competitiveness and to get a differentiated picture of the ways welfare statism is involved in them. Comparing the different country experiences should additionally improve our judgement (a) as to the relative importance of the various hypothetical welfare state influences in the determination of competitiveness and (b) as to the configuration of conditions on which such influences depend. This must be seen, first of all, as an attempt to discover the appropriate structure of the issue, as an exercise of selecting among the many possible statements on the relationship between welfare statism and competitiveness those which prove to be relevant in the light of the reported evidence. At the present state of blurred conceptualisation of the issue we do not consider it sensible to apply a pre-structured set of hypothetical statements and to test them in a formal manner.

Our approach to both questions – what does competition do to the welfare state? and what does welfare statism do to competitiveness? – calls for the review of relatively complex clusters of concrete information. Searching for the unknown structures of interwoven economic and political processes, we cannot afford starting on a high level of abstraction. This would just imprint the inadequateness of our pre-understanding on the whole research design and hence on the range of possible answers to our questions. Therefore, case studies form the most important part of our investigation. Ultimately, the selection of cases (France, the Federal Republic of Germany, the United Kingdom, the USA, and Sweden) is arbitrary from a heuristic point of view. It is perhaps relevant that four of the five selected countries account for almost three quarters of the industrialised Western nations' combined Gross National Product. The fifth, in turn, excels through the uniqueness of its highly developed welfare state, which might provide for a contrast to the other countries' experience.

However, before we go into the details of country-specific information we shall review the whole available cross-country evidence with regard to one relatively simple question: have countries with less welfare statism been economically more successful in recent years than countries with more welfare statism?

2 The Competitiveness of Industrialised Welfare States: A Cross-country Survey

Alfred Pfaller with Ian Gough

THE QUESTION POSED AND THE METHOD TO ANSWER IT

Are advanced capitalist countries who have a fully-fledged expensive welfare state in general less competitive than those who score low on welfare statism? The case is far from obvious as the highly developed Northern and Central European welfare states have throughout most of the post-war period been among the most affluent countries of the world – while being strongly exposed to international competition (cf. Katzenstein, 1985). However, there is contradictory evidence. too. The USA and the United Kingdom, for instance, emerged in certain respects as above-the-average performers in the wake of their anti-welfare policies. The economies of Sweden and West Germany, two of the most notorious welfare states, have for a long time been among the least dynamic ones in the industrialised world.

Scientific surveys also have rendered inconclusive results. The relationship most frequently investigated is that between the share of the national product claimed by the government (an important corollary of welfare statism) and the growth of the national product. Saunders (1985), Cameron (1982) and Marsden (1983) found that relationship to be negative over certain periods. Others using different measures, different methods of calculation and different samples come to the opposite conclusion (cf. McCallum & Blais, 1984 and Korpi, 1985). Attention has also been given to more specific relationships. Feldstein (1980) and Koskella & Matti (1983) found a negative impact of publicly provided social security on saving and hence supposedly on investment, a major condition of economic growth. These findings are supported by those of Cameron (1978 and 1985) about the negative correlation between the government's share of the national product and capital formation.

But again, other inquiries have produced contradicting results (cf. Aaron, 1982).

A different theoretical proposition which has been tested is the one which suggests that workers' discipline and effort on the job, and hence productivity, decreases with the workers' general income security. Weisskopf (1987) found that this link between the essence of welfare statism and inferior economic performance depends on the absence of consensual worker–management relations as they exist in several advanced capitalist countries and as they seem to be facilitated by 'corporatist' structures of decision-making. Such consensual relations, in turn, are more likely to prevail in welfare statist settings (cf. Wilensky, 1981 and 1983).

Altogether, the very facts as to whether welfare states have done less well than other countries seem to be quite difficult to establish. Unsatisfactory as this may appear it is a useful finding in itself. It points to the non-existence of a straightforward and simple link between welfare statism and comparative economic performance.[1] In the light of these results a universally negative effect of the former on the latter must even seem very unlikely. It is equally unlikely that we can produce with an additional cross-country survey less ambiguous and inconclusive results. But our purpose in the following is foremost a descriptive one. We intend to document, as general background reference for our ensuing analyses, the apparent pattern of the relationship between the advanced capitalist countries' differences in competitiveness on the one hand and welfare statism on the other. Rather than insinuating a specific simple relationship (like a linear regression) and expressing its descriptive strength (or the deviation of reality from this 'ideal' pattern) in the form of a numerical value, we shall present, first of all, the complete information. The most adequate form of doing this is through scattergrams. They may suggest general patterns of co-variation, but they also show the 'exceptions'.

THE INDICATORS OF WELFARE STATISM

Like many comparisons ours requires to start with a certain simplification in the description of reality. As far as welfare statism is concerned those indicators which are evenly available for all or most advanced capitalist countries leave out of consideration important aspects of the reality they are meant to characterise. Our principal indicator provides comparative information on the amount of money devoted to formal welfare state programmes of income maintenance, health care, education and so on.[2] But we should suspect that this 'social expenditure' indicator does not adequately represent the degree of welfare expenditure, let alone 'welfare statism' in a country, because other significant portions of government spending, especially subsidies granted to producer groups, are also the result of welfare state considerations. Therefore, we shall also look at the sum of all taxes and mandatory contributions to public and semi-public welfare state institutions (social security systems and health care systems like the German *Krankenkassen*). In comparison this sum can be considered as an indicator of the welfare statist burden on the economy.

A more basic difficulty is that formal programmes are only one way of fulfilling the principle of welfare statism. Effective full-employment policies are another, very important one. In various respects, sustained general affluence achieved through successful management of the national economy can guarantee to most citizens a 'decent' standard of living with less recourse to special public welfare state programmes. Such programmes are then just another way of achieving the same result. Yet our indicator which measures publicly spent resources would make a big difference between functional substitutes of this kind. For instance, a country which spends much on unemployment benefits could score higher on welfare statism than one which somehow assures to every member of its workforce a market income close to the national average. In order to catch at least partially the important outcome dimension of welfare statism – instead of considering only the input dimension – we have constructed a synthetic index of welfare statism. It ranks each OECD country we want to consider on a scale of 0 to 100 according to (a) social expenditure in 1981 and (b) average unemployment in the years 1979–83. The scale is created by awarding the highest performing country 100 and the lowest 0, and ranking every other nation in between. The welfare statism score is then an average of these two scales, that is social spending and full employment are accorded equal weights. The result is presented in Table 2.1.

COMPARATIVE EXPORT PERFORMANCE AND WELFARE STATISM

Equally complex is the measurement of countries' competitiveness. What we have ultimately in mind is the ability of national economies

Table 2.1 Synthetic index of welfare statism for 16 OECD countries, 1979–83 (rank order in parenthesis)

Sweden (1)	87	Belgium (9)	50
Norway (2)	73	Switzerland (9)	50
Austria (3)	68	Italy (11)	43
Germany (4)	66	Japan (12)	42
Netherlands (5)	58	USA (13)	31
Finland (6)	56	Canada (14)	30
France (6)	56	United Kingdom (14)	30
Denmark (8)	55	Australia (16)	29

to provide a comparatively high per capita income while being exposed to foreign competition. This concept of competitiveness is different from the one of a firm's competitiveness: low factor costs enhance the latter but they may indicate a low national competitiveness the way we understand it. High national competitiveness, in turn, allows high national factor incomes, most of all high wages. Comparatively high national wages indicate in the long run that the country is very competitive. In the preceding chapter we referred to this notion as 'underlying competitiveness'. Still, wages and other national factor costs can be so high that they handicap the selling chances of national products *vis-à-vis* foreign competition, thus impairing the country's 'performing competitiveness' (using the distinction introduced in Chapter 1). The ability to keep factor prices adjusted to the conditions of the world market is also part of a country's competitiveness. To keep them lower than necessary can be part of a successful strategy of gaining market shares, a strategy which pays dividends in form of higher national incomes later. But in the long run, overpricing and underpricing are restricted by the limits of sustainable trade imbalances. Chronic deficit countries will have to adjust their factor prices (wages and others) downward in terms of foreign currency, surplus countries are bound to adjust them upward. Yet at any given moment there can be considerable deviations from the factor price level which would correspond to the countries' 'true' competitiveness.

We can approach the measurement problem from another angle. Competition in the most immediate meaning of the word is a struggle for the capture of purchasing power, or in other words for market share. Thus, the competitiveness of countries can be expected to show in their world market shares. Ideally this concept includes all foreign markets and the respective home market. But because of the importance of trade restrictions of all kinds it is probably more revealing to look at world exports only rather than at world production shares. Of course, it would not make sense to compare export shares directly, not even on a per capita basis. National economies differ in their degree of international specialisation as countries differ in their degree of physical and cultural isolation. Besides, export shares reflect the historical buildup of export capacity, something we are not primarily interested in. More adequate for our purposes are the changes in market shares over the time period under consideration here.

One has, however, to be careful in taking declining market shares as an indicator of declining competitiveness, even if one regards the ability of orientating production to the faster growing and more rewarding market segments as part of competitiveness. Early leaders are more or less bound to cede market shares to catching up latecomers. But in our sample of highly industrialised countries this caveat can perhaps be neglected. Even to the United States it would apply mostly in earlier decades.

Another problem is that increasing market shares do not necessarily indicate an ability to earn a higher income in the international market place. They may just reflect a restructuring away from home market orientation to export orientation so that the shares in foreign markets increase while the share of the home market decreases. Besides, as already noted, market shares may increase as a result of reduced factor costs due, for instance, to a real devaluation of the national currency. Price adjustments with ensuing export increases may be required as a means of reducing a trade deficit, that is, as a way to move to a situation which corresponds to the country's 'true' competitiveness. Reducing the international price of domestic production factors may also be a means of getting more of these factors productively employed and remunerated accordingly. This is the essence of export-led growth. When factors get scarce, however, selling more sooner or later means producing more per factor employed. In the long run it is more and more the ability to produce more than others which allows a country to sell more than others. Market shares reveal this ability. But they are also instrumental in bringing it about as selling prospects stimulate investments in productive capacity. Therefore, our export share indicator does have a lot to do with the development of countries' underlying competitiveness, even though over periods of five years or so it may also reflect a good deal of exchange-rate and trade-policy manoeuvrings.

Before we proceed then to compare the changes in market shares of countries which score differently with regard to welfare statism we have to specify the markets we are considering. Since we are interested in competitiveness as far as it is influenced by social and political factors we shall disregard export performance which is predominantly owed to the countries' endowment of natural resources and to the prices these resources achieve in international markets. We shall confine ourselves to manufactured goods. It is on them that the prosperity of the industrialised countries ultimately depends, even though raw material bonanzas can still raise national incomes considerably and even though services have come to contribute a higher percentage to Gross National Product than manufacturing in almost all countries.[3] But, of course, by looking at manufacturing exports only we are registering as a decline in competitiveness what may actually be a shift towards raw materials exports such as took place in the Netherlands and in Great Britain after their respective discoveries of large natural gas and petroleum reserves.

Despite this additional shortcoming we consider our manufacturing–export share indicator as a valid enough starting point for our comparative analysis of competitiveness. Different indicators may later provide for the necessary correction. Figure 2.1 then presents a first comparison of the various highly industrialised capitalist countries (except Luxemburg and other 'mini states')[4] with regard to welfare statism and competitiveness. The vertical position in Figure 2.1 indicates how large a percentage of its Gross Domestic Product (GDP) a country spent in 1979 on public welfare state programmes ('social expenditure' as reported by the OECD). The horizontal position shows the growth of its manufactured exports in the subsequent seven years.

It seems that in general the countries with relatively low social expenditure have been the more competitive ones in the 1980s. This impression is reflected by a negative correlation coefficient *R* of −0.31. But no association can be detected any more if one removes Japan and Canada, both exceptional exporters, from Figure 2.1. Figure 2.2 repeats our previous comparison with the tax load indicator of welfare statism. Australia and Finland are omitted because of lack of data. The vertical ranking of the countries is now somewhat different from the one in Figure 2.1 (in particular for Italy and Denmark). But the weak negative association of welfare statism and competitiveness appears as more or less the same – also in our statistical measure, which is now −0.36.

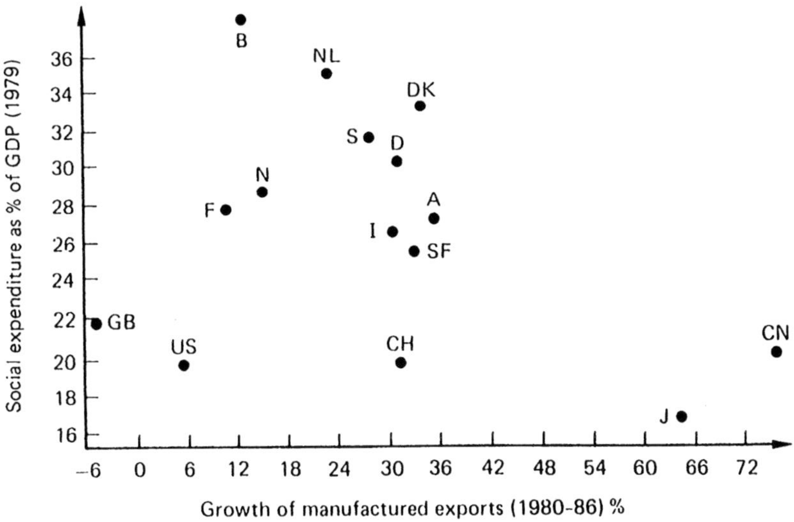

Sources: OECD, 1985a; GATT, 1987
A : Austria CN : Canada F : France J : Japan S : Sweden
B : Belgium D : Germany GB : Britain N : Norway SF : Finland
CH : Switzerland DK : Denmark I : Italy NL : Netherlands US : USA

Figure 2.1 Social expenditure and manufacturing export performance in the 1980s

Let us now consider our synthetic index of welfare statism, which does not only take into consideration public money spent for welfare statist purposes but also citizens' chance of earning an income on the market. Figure 2.3 compares countries' score on this index with the growth of their manufactured exports. It shows on both extremes of the export performance spectrum two countries with a relatively low score of welfare statism. The central range, in turn, is populated by six countries with widely differing welfare scores. The same holds for the group of four countries in the lower middle bracket of export performance. The correlation coefficient of −.11 reflects the total lack of a persistent relationship between the two variables.

Is the pattern of association between welfare statism and export performance which we find for the 1980s found in earlier times? Figure 2.4 repeats the comparison of Figure 2.1 with the social expenditure values of 1973 and the export growth from 1973 to 1980. It shows a broad inverse relationship between welfare statism and competitiveness. All low export performers with the exception of

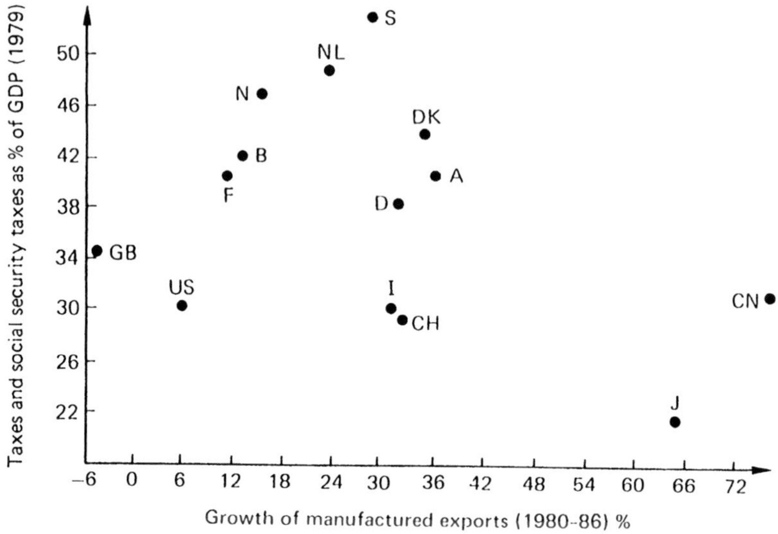

Sources: Bundesministerium der Finanzen, 1980; GATT, 1987

Figure 2.2 Tax load and manufacturing export performance in the 1980s

Canada are countries with high social expenditure. And all of the stronger export performers except Italy are countries with low or medium social expenditure. The statistical measure of association is −0.54, considerably stronger than for the 1980s. A comparison of tax load and manufacturing export performance according to the pattern of Figure 2.2 renders an even clearer inverse relation for this time period (correlation coefficient of −0.65).

Our data so far would suggest that welfare states have improved in competitiveness since the end of the 1970s. While high welfare-state expenditure seems to have been a competitive handicap in the time period after the first oil shock this does not appear to be the case any more in the 1980s. But perhaps those welfare states (countries with a high vertical position in Figures 2.1 and 2.2) which have improved in competitiveness are those which have expanded least their social expenditure and/or their overall tax load. Of the six low-performing welfare states of the 1970s Belgium and Norway remained in the low-performers' bracket in the 1980s. The Netherlands improved its relative position somewhat. Denmark, Germany and Sweden switched unequivocally to the 'standard' performers' bracket. They increased their social expenditure share of GDP 5.8, 4.0, and 7.4 percentage

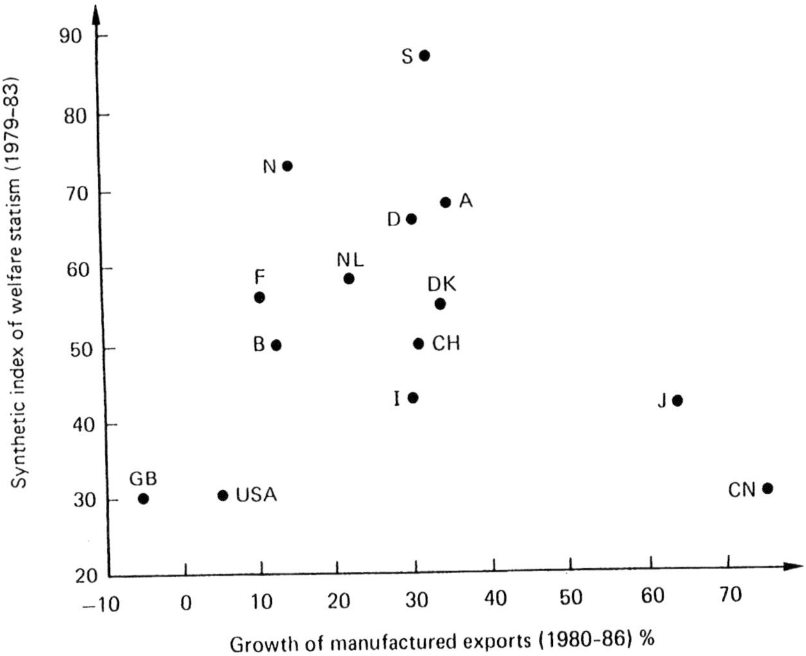

Sources: GATT, 1987; OECD, 1988b, 1988c

Figure 2.3 Synthetic index of welfare statism and manufacturing export performance in the 1980s

points respectively. For the Netherlands the value is 3.2, for Belgium 10.2 and for Norway 3.0. Again, not a clear message at all! At the lower side of the welfare state scale the USA and Great Britain experienced a significant deterioration in export market shares, as France did in the centre part of the scale. Social expenditure shares of GDP went up in the three countries 2.1, 2.5, and 6.4 percentage points respectively. These additional figures seem to undermine further the notion that shifts in manufacturing export performance between the 1970s and the 1980s are related to inverse shifts in social expenditure levels.

But another consideration can perhaps help to reconcile the finding for the 1980s with the broad pattern of the 1970s. In Britain, Norway and the United States exports of manufactures faced in the 1980s very particular exchange-rate handicaps – in the first two countries because of their oil bonanza and in the US because of its combination

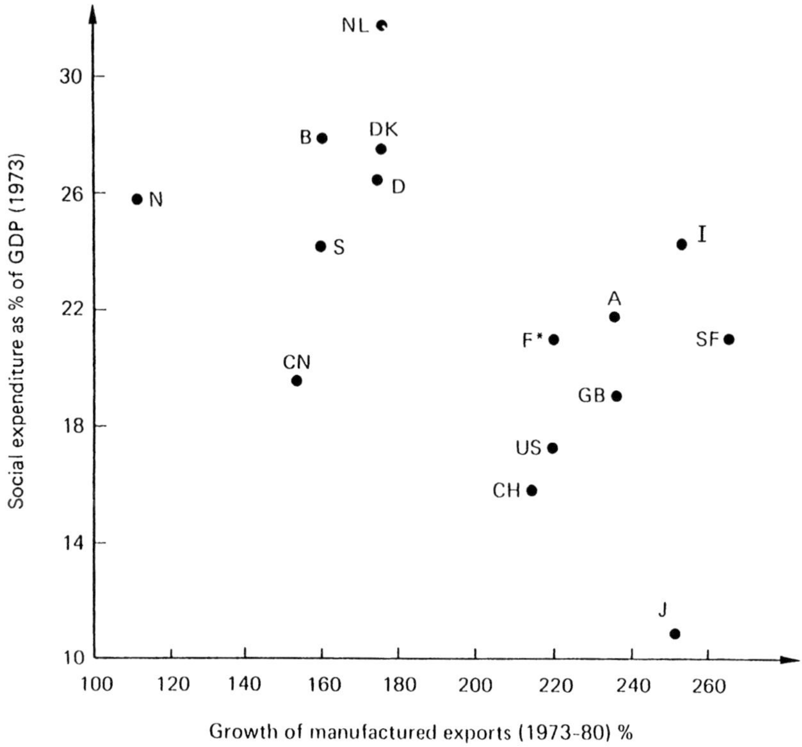

Sources: See Figure 2.1

Note: Value extrapolated from the ratio of social expenditure over total government expenditure in 1975

Figure 2.4 Social expenditure and manufacturing export performance in the 1970s

of fiscal deficit and restrictive monetary policies which led to huge capital inflows (see Chapter 3). If we remove all three countries from the diagrams in Figures 2.1 and 2.2, there is at least no weak performer any more at the lower end of the welfare scale. We may also note then that, apart from Norway, it is precisely the most 'expansionist' welfare state Belgium which did not move up in export performance and that, apart from Britain and the US, it is the welfare expansionist France who fell back drastically.

Pursuing further the notion that competitiveness might be related to the expansion (rather than the level) of welfare statism we shall look simultaneously at the development of both variables. Figure 2.5

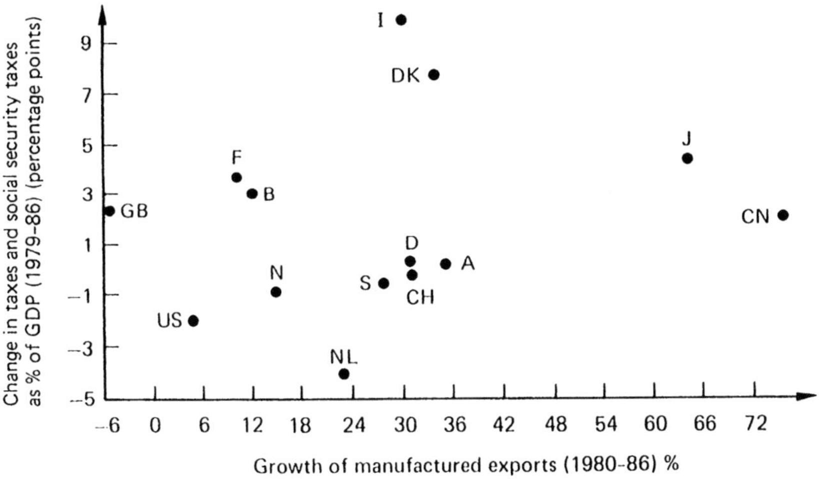

Sources: Bundesministerium der Finanzen, 1980; Globus Kartendienst Td–6781; GATT, 1987

Figure 2.5 Changes in the tax load and manufacturing export performance in the 1980s

shows the results for the period from 1980 to 1986 (using the tax load indicator of welfare statism). We see that the two most radical welfare expansionists, that is, the countries with the highest score on our tax change measure, are both among the 'standard' performers. The moderate expansionists are split between the two brackets of the 'super' performers (those who started from a low level are placed here) and the weak performers. And if we disregard the two handicapped exporters of manufactures, USA and Norway, we find all the 'consolidators', i.e. the countries with a tax-change score lower than one, in the bracket of the 'standard' performers with the Netherlands (who consolidated on a very high tax level) tending towards the weak performers' side. The correlation coefficient is now positive – but only 0.23.

If we replace, for the same period, the tax-load indicator with the social expenditure indicator countries are ranked differently. The extreme expansionists are France, Canada, Italy and Austria. They are spread over the entire export performance spectrum. So are the moderate consolidators (USA, Finland, Japan). The extreme consolidators (Denmark, Sweden, Netherlands, Germany and Norway) are concentrated in the standard performers' bracket. The statistical

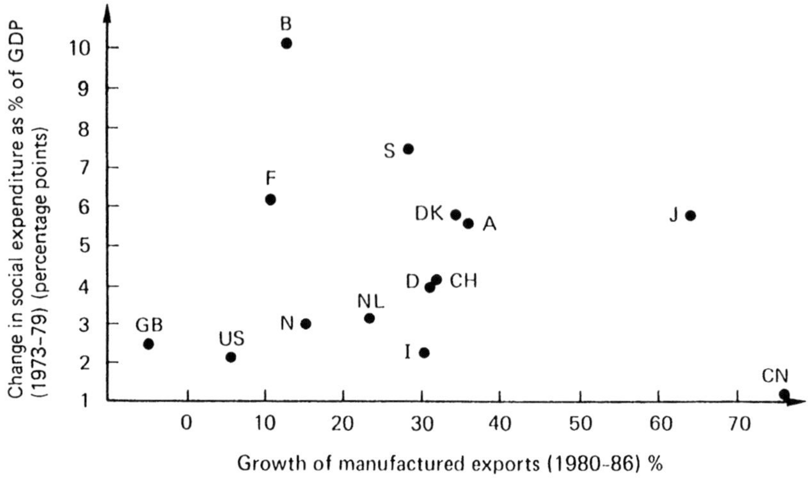

Sources: See Figure 2.1

Figure 2.6 Change in social expenditure in the 1970s and manufacturing export performance in the 1980s

coefficient of 0.13 indicates a non-correlation, as does the one for the 1970s, which is −0.1. In other words, we get nothing which would support the suspicion that competitiveness is systematically affected by the concomitant pace of welfare state expansion.

But maybe the expansion of welfare statism shows effects only after a certain time lag – when economic agents have fully adjusted to the changes. Figure 2.6 places countries vertically according to the increase in their social expenditure share of GDP between 1975 and 1981. The horizontal position indicates, as in Figure 2.5, the growth of their manufactured exports in the 1980s. The first impression here is one of a general positive relationship between the two variables with some exceptions (most notably Belgium as expansionist on an already high level and Canada as consolidator on a moderately low level). But if we allow again for the exceptional circumstances of Britain, Norway and the USA we find all the moderate expansionists as well as most consolidators in or close to the bracket of the 'standard' performers. The more radical expansionists are divided between weak performers and the 'super performer' Japan, who expanded from a very low level. Statistically, we have a clear non-correlation (−0.12).

PRODUCTIVITY AND WELFARE STATEISM

Our search for a systematic relationship between welfare statism and competitiveness remains without convincing results. But before we take this as proof of the absence of such a relationship in reality we should allow for the possibility that our indicators present a distorted image of the reality we are investigating. We can use different indicators of competitiveness which are less sensitive to exchange rate disturbances and adjustments. Instead of looking at market shares as the measure of apparent competitiveness we can look at the determinants of a country's ability to earn high factor incomes in international trade. As already noted, the development of export shares in the manufacturing sector can, over a seven year-period, understate and overstate this ability. Behind it is the ability to offer goods which achieve a relatively high price in the international market place and to produce a relatively large quantity of such goods per person and unit of capital employed. Both aspects are implied in the concept of productivity. The more marketable value the economically active people of a country produce the higher is the income, including the wage income, they can obtain in the market. Whether they actually will is, of course, also a matter of adequate pricing. Productivity refers, so to speak, to the competitive potential of a country.

We shall look then for the relation between welfare statism and productivity. As with market shares, however, we are not interested in that part of productivity which is owed to the historical accumulation of (tangible and intangible) capital. We are interested in the gains and losses of productivity during the time period under consideration here. In Figure 2.7, which includes for the first time Australia (AUS), the horizontal position shows for each country how much more value per employed person was produced each year from 1979 to 1986 in the private sector of the economy, that is to say neglecting public administration and the armed forces for example. The vertical position indicates, as in former figures, the level of social expenditure at the beginning of the period. There is a slight positive relation (R = 0.2) with evidence of a backward-sloping association in the upper half of the diagram.

We should, however, take a closer look at our productivity indicator. Obviously, it does not just measure the performance potential of an economy. At a given state of endowment with physical, human and organisational capital, productivity tends to decrease with employment and to increase with unemployment. For it is often only in

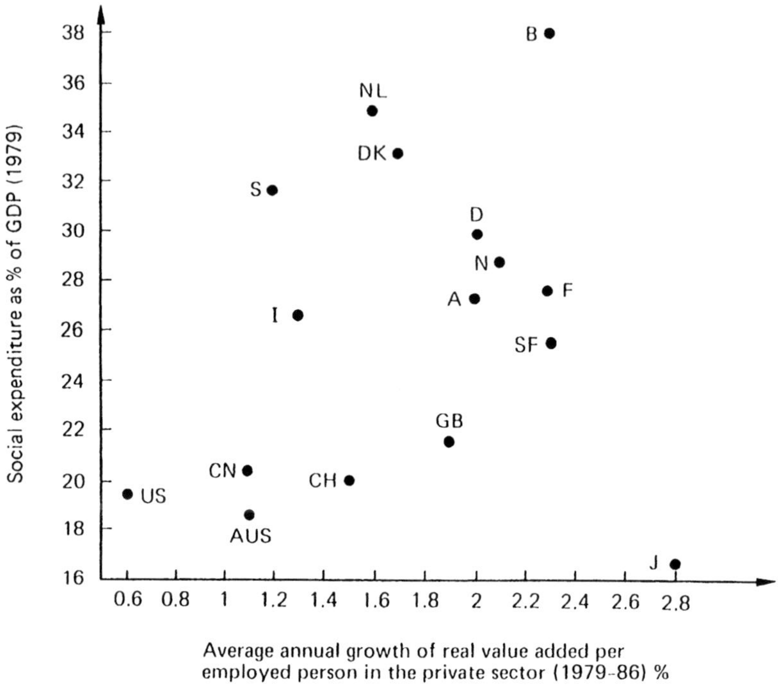

Sources: OECD, 1985a, 1988a

Figure 2.7 Social expenditure and productivity growth in the 1980s

low-productivity jobs that otherwise redundant members of the workforce can find employment. If, for example, rigid high wages prevent many unemployed finding work in ill-remunerated service jobs, average productivity per *employed* person will be higher than if this were not the case. If a country provides work for many additional job-seekers (for example, baby-boomers or immigrants) this depresses its overall productivity growth. Eliminating low-productivity jobs boosts productivity even if output decreases.

One way of taking these considerations into account is to look at the manufacturing sector only and to disregard services, which provide the bulk of jobs that can be created rapidly without much investment. Manufacturing productivity should be less sensitive to differences in labour market parameters. Besides, it is manufacturing where it is most pertinent to consider productivity as a competitive potential, because it is predominantly the ability to produce and sell

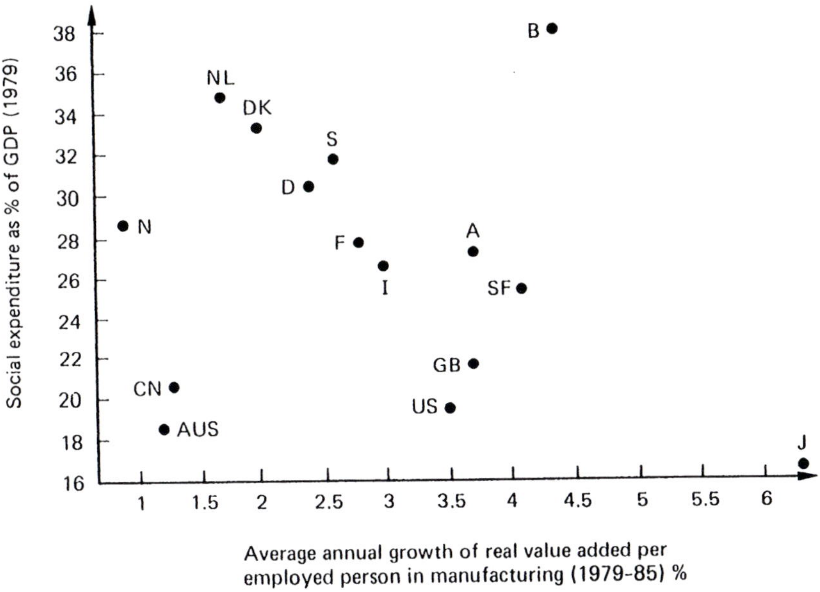

Sources: OECD, 1985a, 1987d

Figure 2.8 Social expenditure and manufacturing productivity growth in the 1980s

ever more manufactures which made for the prosperity of the rich highly industrialised countries. Figure 2.8 shows how welfare statism is associated with the growth of manufacturing productivity. The most striking difference as compared with the preceding figure is the considerably improved competitive position of the United States, Italy and to a lesser degree Britain, a shift which – together with the removal of Switzerland from the figure – produces a broad inverse relationship between our indicators of welfare statism and competitiveness. Yet the outliers Belgium, Australia, Canada and Norway keep the correlation coefficient at an insignificant −0.21. Without them it would be −0.88. If we take the sum of taxes and social security contributions as welfare state indicator (omitting Australia and Finland) the pattern remains the same, with the correlation coefficient reaching −0.59 for the whole sample.

Our synthetic index of welfare statism also produces a broad inverse relationship, even though this does not show in the correlation coefficient (−0.13). As can be seen in Figure 2.9, of the seven

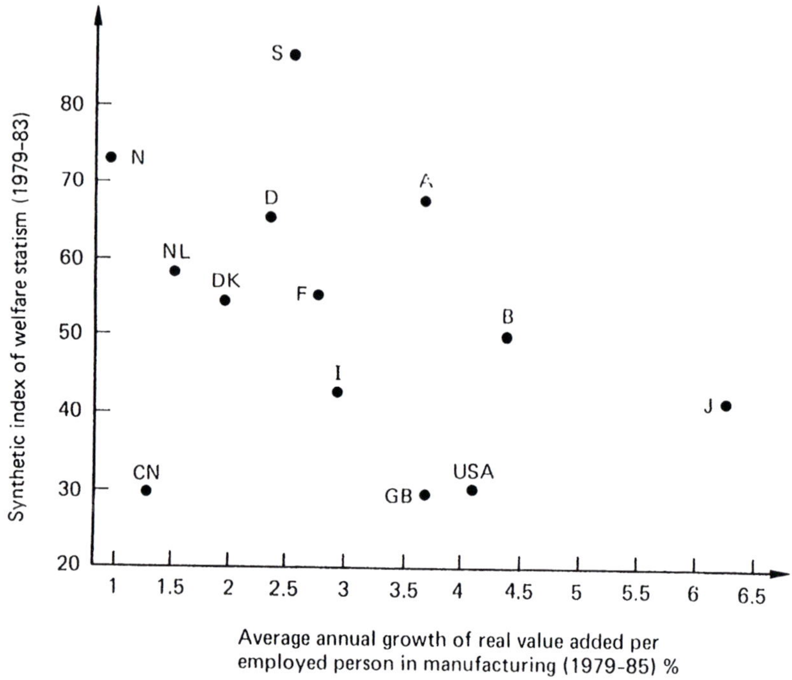

Sources: OECD, 1987d, 1988b, 1988c

Figure 2.9 Synthetic index of welfare statism and manufacturing productivity growth in the 1980s

countries with the highest score on welfare statism six are placed on the low performers' side of the productivity growth scale. In turn, all the low-scoring countries except Canada are found on the high growth side. This finding seems to lend support to the notion that freedom from market sanctions – resulting from full employment plus high social expenditures – tends to relax workers' application to their work, thus reducing productivity (cf. Weisskopf, 1987).

Focusing on tax load *changes* rather than levels renders a weak positive coefficient of 0.31, which is, however, not mirrored by the graphical impression. Both 'expansionists' and 'consolidators' seem spread fairly evenly over the productivity scale, with the 'consolidators' tending somewhat to the laggards' side. Using changes in social expenditure rather than changes in tax load as welfare state indicator gets the coefficient down to an insignificant 0.13.

Turning to the 1970s we find no association between welfare

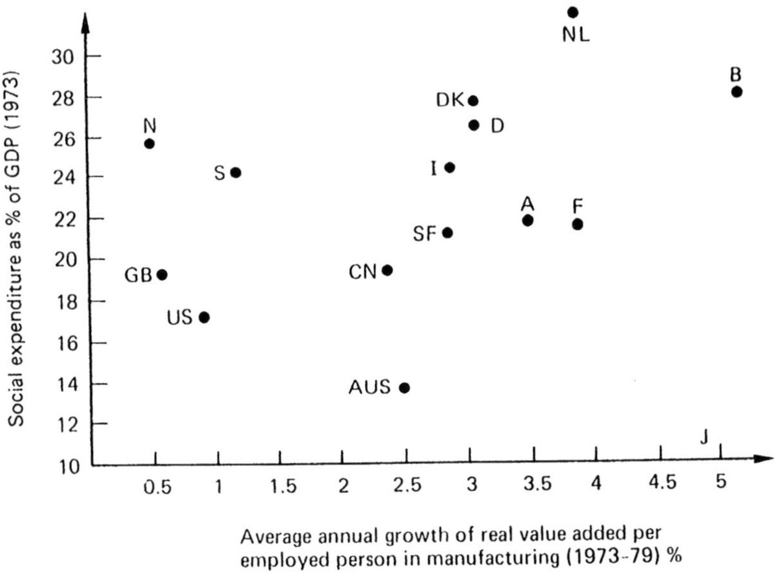

Sources: OECD, 1985a, 1987d

Figure 2.10 Social expenditure and manufacturing productivity growth in the 1970s

statism and productivity (see Figure 2.10). But we do find a significant positive correlation between the *growth* of social expenditure and of labour productivity in manufacturing (0.54). This finding, which is presented graphically in Figure 2.11, supports an alternative hypothesis that enterprises respond to rising welfare state costs with increased efforts to improve productivity, including increased substitution of capital for labour. But we might also venture the hypothesis that those countries who experienced a satisfactory growth of productivity were more inclined to extend their welfare state, while in the different ideological climate of the 1980s such ambitions had vanished. In any case, the contradictory findings for the 1970s and 1980s cast further doubt on the notion of 'iron law'-type unconditional economic mechanisms which link welfare statism to a nation's competitiveness.

By and large the productivity data might suggest that as a recent phenomenon welfare statism has come to be associated with competitive decline. But again, we should be cautious in drawing definitive conclusions. Confining our productivity measure to the manufacturing

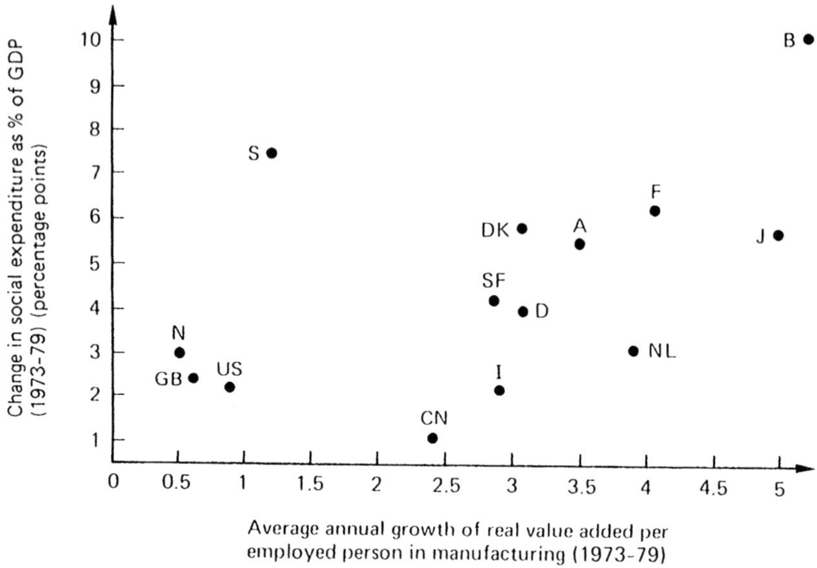

Sources: OECD, 1985a, 1987d

Figure 2.11 Changes in social expenditure and manufacturing productivity growth in the 1970s

sector does not do away with all the above-mentioned ambiguities. Even in manufacturing, value added per employed person is not only a measure of efficiency. The indicator also responds to inefficient substitution of capital for labour (for example, as a consequence of excessive labour costs) and it responds to de-industrialisation during which relative unproductive plants and firms are weeded out (cf. OECD, 1989a: pp. 35ff.). Besides, the measure of value added per employed person does not register any gains in productivity that result in increased leisure time (longer vacations, a shorter working week, and so on).

As far as the inefficient use of capital is concerned we can check this potential distortion by measuring value added not just per employed person but per unit of *all* factor inputs, that is, per unit of labour and per unit of capital. Unfortunately data on total factor productivity, as the measure is called, were available only for ten countries. Among them Sweden, Germany and Norway exhibit a considerably improved competitive position as compared with

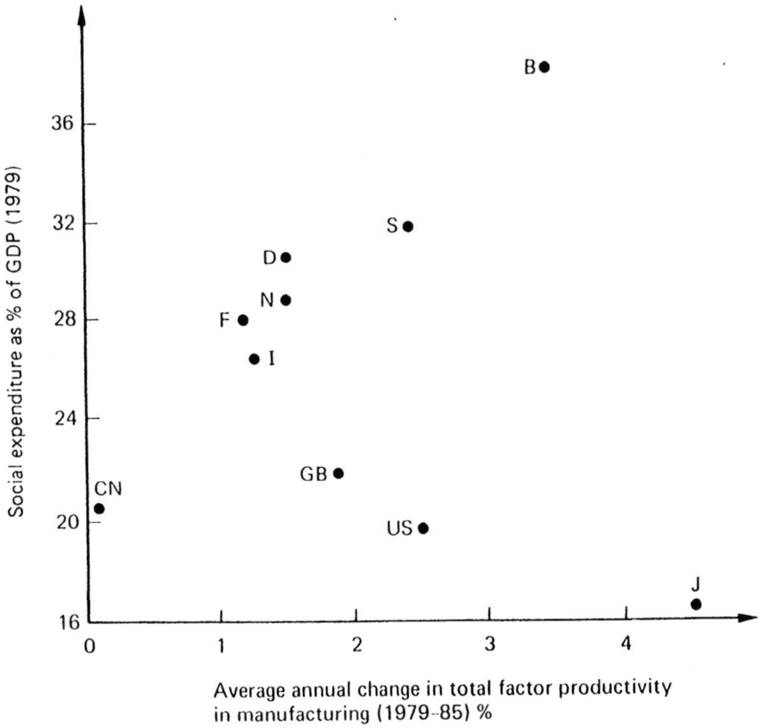

Sources: OECD, 1985a; Englander & Mittelstädt, 1988

Figure 2.12 Social expenditure and total factor productivity growth in the manufacturing sector in the 1980s

labour productivity (see Figure 2.12). Any statistical correlation disappears – *R* has a value of –0.02 (with the tax load indicator it is −0.22).

In order to catch gains in labour productivity which do not result in increased output but rather in reduced working time we can look for the same ten countries at the changes in real value added per working hour. As compared to Figure 2.10, this measure puts Germany, France, Sweden and Italy in a much better competitive position. The correlation coefficients are weaker at −0.15 for the social expenditure and −0.43 for the tax load indicator. Total factor and hourly productivity figures, thus, qualify somewhat our finding of a broadly negative association of welfare statism and productivity growth in the manufacturing sector. But the additional results are insufficient to render a fundamentally different picture of the relationship between the two variables.

ATTRACTIVENESS TO INVESTORS AND WELFARE STATISM

We have used various measures of productivity as indicators of a country's competitive potential. This is valid insofar as productivity is at the basis of the ability to earn high incomes in competition with other producers. Now productivity itself results largely from investment in machinery and other equipment, from the adoption of efficiency-improving technologies and from the efficient co-ordination of work within plants and enterprises. But in a most direct sense, it is firms and not countries who invest, innovate and co-ordinate work processes. For countries it is – with increasing internationalisation of enterprises – more and more a matter of *where* the firms do all that. Seen in this perspective, productivity is not only the basis of a country's competitiveness, it is also the result of its competitiveness in the international market of industrial locations where countries offer manpower, infrastructure, social and political structures, markets and the supply of non-tradables.[5] Being competitive in this sense means being attractive to transnational investors. For attractiveness to investors now makes for productivity gains tomorrow.

In order to catch this aspect of competitiveness we might resort to the competitiveness scoreboard the European Management Forum has constructed, taking into account a large number of factors like social stability, manpower qualification level, innovativeness, endowment with natural resources, government interventions in the economy, openness *vis-à-vis* the world market and economic growth. The resulting overall score represents an informed opinion on how well countries are presently equipped for international competition. It combines elements of existing productive capability with elements referring to the chance of enhancing this capability in the future. The latter elements are the ones which could provide for a certain correction of our previous results. To what they amount can be seen in Figure 2.13, which relates the countries' 1986 rating on the scoreboard to their tax load indicator of the same year. Again we recognise a broad inverse relation between the indicators of welfare statism and competitiveness ($R = -0.45$). The three countries with the lowest tax

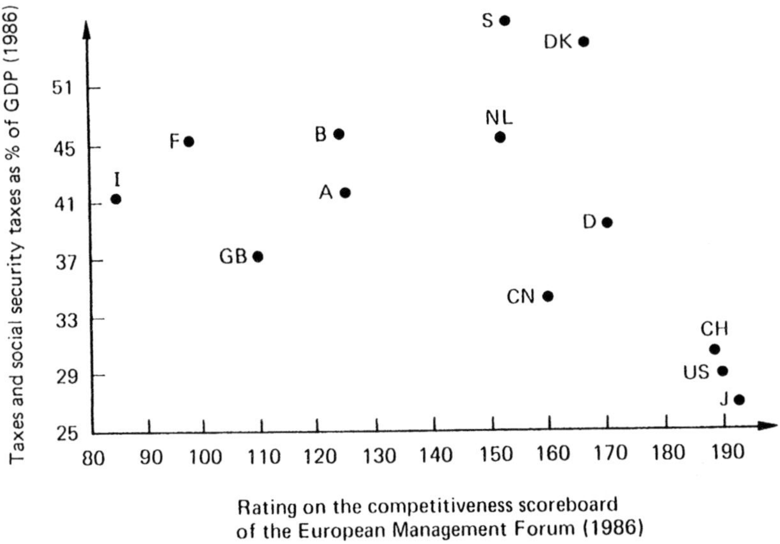

Sources: Globus Kartendienst Va-6231 and Td-6781

Figure 2.13 Tax load and competitiveness rating in 1986

load are considered most competitive. But behind them there is a group of five countries on a roughly similar medium–high level of competitiveness but with extreme tax load differences. Sweden, Denmark, Great Britain and Italy must be qualified as marked exceptions to the general pattern of inverse association.

If we use the 1979 social expenditure indicator of welfare statism the broad pattern remains the same ($R = -0.33$), with Britain, Italy, France and Austria showing an 'untypically' low competitiveness. As can be seen in Figure 2.14, the ratings on the scoreboard are also inversely related to the *growth* of taxes and social security contributions between 1979 and 1986, Denmark, Japan (growth from a very low level) and the Netherlands (contraction from an extremely high level) being the outliers this time. The coefficient amounts to -0.41. If we look at changes in social expenditure we get a more clear-cut picture: the countries with a lower rating than 130 are all, except Britain, welfare expansionists, those with a rating above 150 are all, except Canada (which expanded from a very low level), consolidators. Taken alone, the rating by the European Management Forum would not serve too well as an independent indicator of

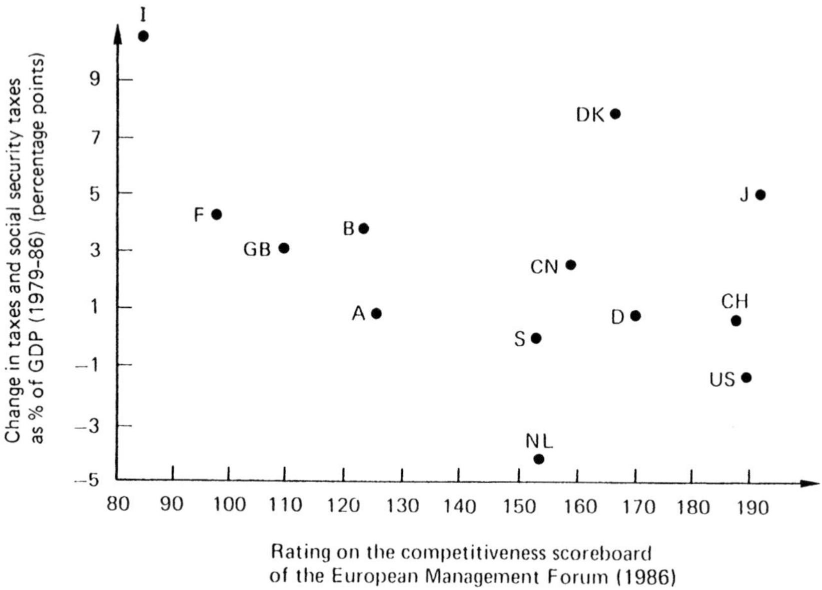

Sources: Bundesministerium der Finanzen, 1980; Globus Kartendienst Td-6781 and Va-6231

Figure 2.14 Changes in the tax load in the 1980s and competitiveness rating in 1986

competitiveness because it must be suspected that it reflects beliefs held about the economic dysfunctionality of excessive welfare statism. Nevertheless, it adds to the general impression that welfare statism has tended to become negatively associated with a country's international competitiveness in the 1980s.

ECONOMIC GROWTH AND WELFARE STATISM

A further, very important check on this hypothesis uses the ultimate performance indicator: real economic growth. We have argued that productivity, despite all corrections, may be increased at the expense of economic growth, thus distorting its meaning as indicator of a country's ability to achieve a high per capita income. On the other side, long-term economic growth achieved under exposure to international competition can be supposed to have a lot to do with this ability. Countries can, of course, grow for a while beyond their means, so to speak, expanding the production of non-tradables and running external deficits. But as we argued above in connection with over- and underpriced exports, imbalances cannot be expanded beyond certain limits. Besides, 'excessive' growth at the expense of mounting current account deficits, like the one of the United States in the 1980s, does not necessarily have to be followed by a period of relative stagnation. If the exchange rate gets adjusted and domestic consumption sufficiently restrained a phase of export-led growth can reduce the external imbalances and consolidate the previous growth gains in the international market place. In any case, sustained economic growth is not feasible without a concomitant growth in productivity. It implies the latter, but in addition it has to do with the scope of productivity. A fast growing national product means – with a constant labour force – high productivity growth for *all* workers and not just a shrinking percentage of them. To put it pointedly: growth is efficiency plus quantity.

It seems most relevant to see whether welfare statism has come to impair exactly that twin performance of national economies: efficiency cum quantity. In general it is important to use for this purpose a growth measure which covers a long time period so as to diminish the distorting effect of temporary imbalances and adjustments to them. On the other hand, we wish to keep our independent variable 'welfare statism' more or less constant so as to still get a meaningful relationship between it and the dependent variable 'growth'. To take one example, economic growth from 1973 to 1987 could not be meaningfully related to social expenditure in the base year. But in order not to let the long time period slip out of sight we may resort to the somewhat dubious procedure of using an average value of welfare statism during this long period. This is done in Figure 2.15. Its vertical scale shows the arithmetic mean of our tax load indicators for 1975 (1973 is not available), 1979 and 1986, its horizontal scale the average annual growth rates of the Gross Domestic Products. The most striking fact revealed by this figure is that nine of the 14 industrialised countries have a roughly similar average growth rate of between 2 and 2.5 per cent, even though the values of their tax load indicator are spread between 35 and 50 per cent of GDP. There are four countries with a lower tax load. Three of them have higher growth rates than the group of nine (two of them considerably higher ones), whereas the fourth of them – Switzerland – has been the absolute laggard of the whole industrialised West over the past 15 years. Oil-rich Norway appears as the odd one out.

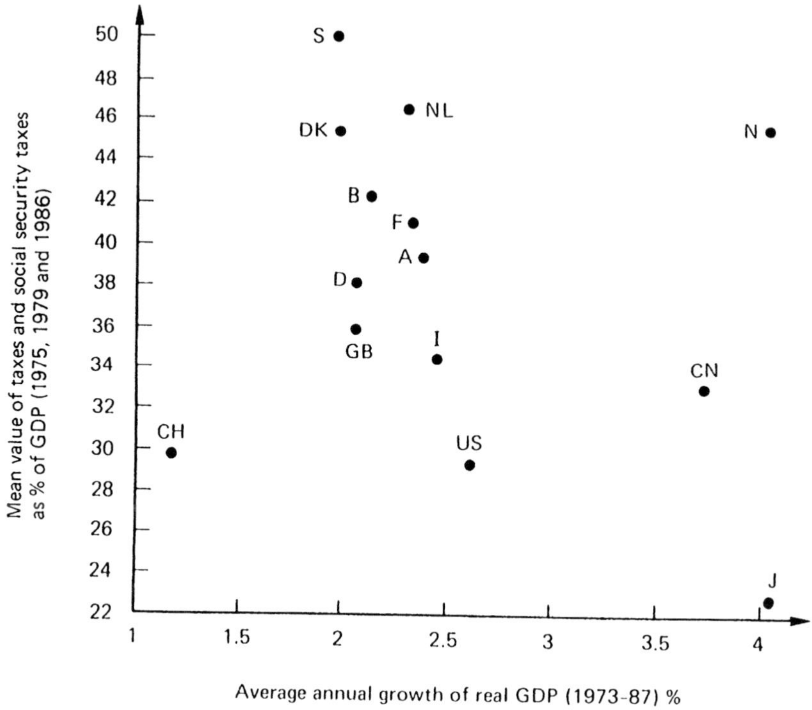

Sources: Bundesministerium der Finanzen, 1980; Globus Kartendienst Td-6781; OECD, 1988a

Figure 2.15 Tax load and economic growth in the 1970s and 1980s

The statistical measure indicates a slightly negative association (−0.26).

Altogether, one has to conclude that high-scoring welfare states have weathered the difficult time since 1973 with its recurrent crises no worse and no better than other industrialised countries. However, since we have looked at average growth rates over all the post-oil shock years the question now arises whether there have been significant changes during that period in the relationship between welfare statism and economic growth, such as those suggested by our other performance indicators. To find out we divide the time under consideration again into two periods, the 1970s and the 1980s. Figure 2.16 shows the association between the two variables (using, as in most preceding charts, the social expenditure indicator) in the 1980s. We see clearly now a broadly inverse relationship. Most remarkably,

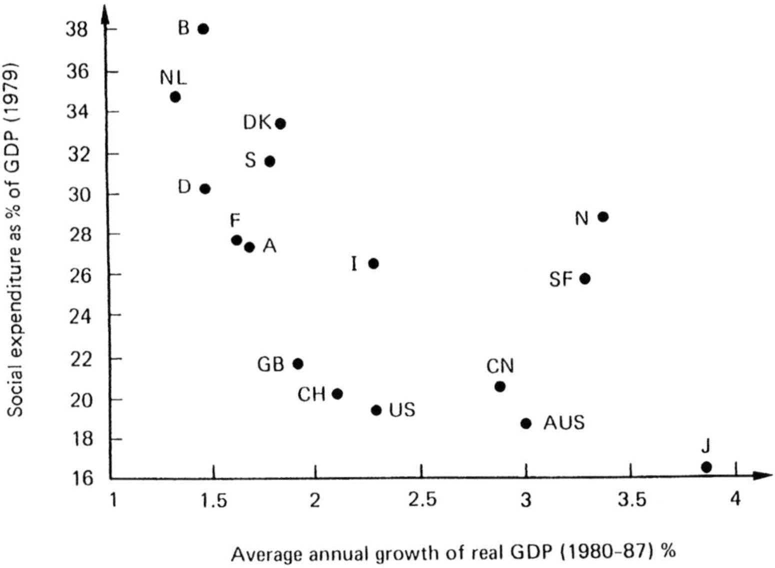

Sources: OECD, 1985a, 1988a

Figure 2.16 Social expenditure and economic growth in the 1980s

all the relatively high-scoring welfare states, except the continuous outsider Norway, have grown more slowly than any of the countries with lower welfare state scores. Also the correlation coefficient of −0.63 suggests a rather clear message. The OECD's revised social expenditure data for 1980 render even −0.67 and those for 1985 −0.7. With the tax load indicator we get −0.52, but with our synthetic index of welfare statism only −0.28. Still, in the slow growth bracket (less than 2 per cent annually) we find here six of the eight countries with above average welfare statism, but only two of the eight with below average welfare statism. The faster growing countries, in turn, do not evince any recognisable pattern.

The picture would be basically the same if we disregard the recession years 1980–82 and consider only the annual growth rates from 1983 to 1987. All the correlations would be a little bit weaker, only the one between economic growth and our synthetic indicator of welfare statism would be strengthened up to −0.33. In the 1970s, on the other hand, economic growth and welfare statism do not evince any systematic relationship at all. In Figure 2.17 we can distinguish a group of nine countries with something like a standard growth

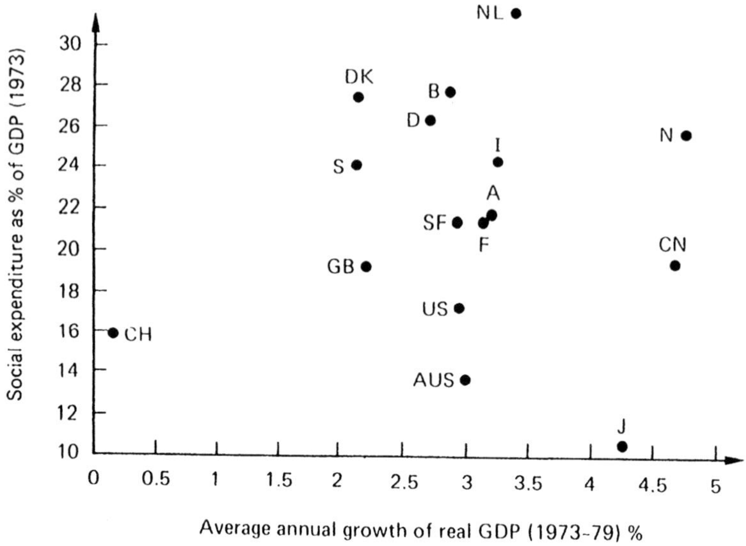

Source: see Figure 2.16

Figure 2.17 Social expenditure and economic growth in the 1970s

performance between 2.7 per cent and 3.5 per cent. These standard performers are spread practically over the whole width of the social expenditure spectrum. The four weaker performers and the three 'stars' also show considerable differences with regard to social expenditure. Statistically, we have a non-correlation (0.04).

INSTEAD OF A CONCLUSION: SOME SPECULATIVE AFTERTHOUGHTS

Our analysis cannot show in a consistent fashion that welfare states are less competitive than other industrialised capitalist countries. Nonetheless, taken together our findings add a certain support to the view that in international comparison welfare statism has come to undermine economic performance and has, thus, turned into a competitive disadvantage. If we take correlation coefficients above 0.35 as moderately significant, we have discovered nine of these and *all* of them are negative. Of these seven apply to the 1980s. If we ignore the European Management Forum index, they comprise negative associations between several measures of welfare statism and rates of economic growth, and between tax levels and export growth and productivity growth in manufacturing. There are no even modestly positive correlations between our measures of welfare statism and economic competitiveness in the 1980s. On the other hand, the significantly negative correlations amount to only seven out of many, and all the others are inconclusive. Nevertheless, there is reason to expect that international competition is putting pressure on the welfare state. Anti-efficiency charges against welfare statism nowadays cannot simply be dismissed as incompatible with the evident facts as they could be with some reason in former decades.

On the other hand, our findings do not *prove* that welfare statism is – in the economic context of the 1980s – a competitive handicap. Nor do they shed any light on the mechanisms which might link welfare statism to diminished economic performance, such as the draining of resources into unproductive uses, the demotivation of economic effort or the resistance to the flexible reallocation of resources. We have not learned anything about why welfare states have in general done worse. Even if we consider as plausible some of the arguments with regard to motivation, flexibility and resource drain, we need additional arguments to explain why these mechanisms took effect in the 1980s but not before.

It is not the place here to deal in a systematic way with the problem of how to explain our findings. But several alternative approaches to understanding the change in the association of welfare statism and competitiveness may be listed just to show the scope of uncertainty and to caution against premature conclusions.

One element which may help to explain a shift in the competitiveness of welfare states is the notion that a long time period is needed for the dysfunctional consequences of welfare statism to make themselves felt. According to this notion, the full-scale expansion of welfare statism in the 1960s and 1970s is only now having visible effects on economic performance, even though the dysfunctional forces may have been at work for quite a while (cf. Lindbeck, 1988). And indeed, our welfare-state indicators for the 1970s show various negative correlations with competitiveness indicators for the 1980s. The fact that welfare statism was most fully developed in economically rather strong countries would make it the more plausible that decline is showing only after a long erosion process.

Other approaches would emphasise changes in the economic context, which have altered the balance of the welfare state's functions and dysfunctions. One of these changes is the increasing internationalisation of production, which means that enterprises have more and more options as to where they can set up production. For a country it is then no longer enough to have competitive national enterprises. They have to compare favourably with other countries as production sites. In other words, productive competence can more easily go elsewhere and can less easily be counted upon to 'bail out' the costs of welfare statism.

Another significant contextual change is the end of the post-war syndrome of growth-conducive conditions (cf. Anell, 1987). Within this syndrome, welfare statism may be seen as having been functional because it formed an essential part of that *quid pro quo* which facilitated a relatively smooth, frictionless social process of production. The alternative was disruptive class conflict. The welfare state could, thus, be considered an investment in social consensus. It was a high-yielding investment as long as economic growth itself paid for the welfare-state guarantees and as long as no major conflicts arose between the principle of economic security and the need for adjustments. One might say in other words, that in times of high economic continuity the costs of welfare statism were outweighed by its advantages. Under this perspective, the welfare state turned into a burden when the market called for painful adjustments and welfare entitlements had to be honoured more and more in spite of the market and against the market. This explanatory paradigm does not imply that the welfare state is necessarily dysfunctional under the new economic circumstances. It leaves room for the interpretation that it is, in its concrete shape, just ill-adjusted to the changed requirements.

A variant of the foregoing paradigm focuses on the comparative costs of consensus. It stresses the fact that in the wake of the economic slow-down since the 1970s large-scale unemployment has come to provide economic discipline at lower costs than corporatist consensus formation with its heavy dose of welfare statism. Countries which are stuck with corporatist welfare statism would, therefore, pay an unnecessarily high price for discipline now and would compare unfavourably with liberal, low-welfare state countries (cf. Streeck, 1982).

But it could also be that it is misleading to focus on the economic costs of welfare statism and that the clue to explaining the welfare states' recent competitive setback lies in their simultaneous domination by interest group politics. According to this approach it would be the power of entitlement-holders throughout the economy (from unionised workers to all kinds of producer groups) which has become an increasing obstacle to swift economic adjustments as they are required by the market. The effect would be one of a cumulative economic deterioration, as is insinuated by the first account in our list. And it would be most serious in times of rapid and/or profound changes. Such 'institutional sclerosis' may have gone hand in hand with the development of welfare statism in the affluent capitalist societies (Olson 1982). And interest group politics may have got hold of much of the welfare state. But welfare statism as a generalised guarantee to a share in the nation's prosperity would definitely not be the culprit.

Our data do not permit us to say whether one of the various explanatory approaches we have mentioned is the correct one. But nor are we in a position to discard any one of them. The very existence of competing interpretations serves to circumscribe the informative content of our findings: they establish the seriousness of the challenge which international competition now poses to the welfare state, because they show that welfare statism may now be associated with inferior economic performance. But these findings do not imply that it is a challenge the welfare state cannot cope with. We hope to learn more about the chances it has in the following case studies.

3 The United States

Alfred Pfaller

THE CHALLENGE OF INTERNATIONAL COMPETITION

The US Economy since the Mid-1970s and the Issue of International Competitiveness

'Whatever one's view about the relative importance of price stability, high unemployment, and economic growth, there is general agreement that the economy did not perform well with respect to any of these goals during the 1970s.' Sawhill and Stone (1984, p. 72) thus summarise the challenge for the economic policy of the incoming Reagan administration. A quick look at some central economic indicators shows the extent of the stagflation problem, which had come to dominate the economic policy debate by the end of the 1970s. Monetary stability as well as economic growth and employment improved considerably after 1983. But the external situation of the US economy, which also had been deteriorating throughout the 1970s, became increasingly the focus of public alarm. Year after year, the trade balance showed new record deficits and the US, which had been the world's most important net exporter of capital in the 1950s and 1960s, came to be considered the world's largest debtor country by the end of the 1980s.[1]

The stagflation problem entered the American economic policy debate on the inflation side at the end of the 1960s when price rises broke out of the 3 per cent range within which they had stayed during all the post-war years (with the exception of 1957). Attempts to restitute monetary stability through general demand-dampening measures according to the prescriptions of Keynesian macroeconomics soon faced the problem of decreasing economic growth and rising unemployment. The growth–inflation trade-off deteriorated considerably in the wake of the oil crisis of 1973–1974. The economic policies of the Ford and Carter administrations first responded in a stop–go manner, trying to get both sides of the dilemma under control. However, at the end Carter saw no other way but to fight the

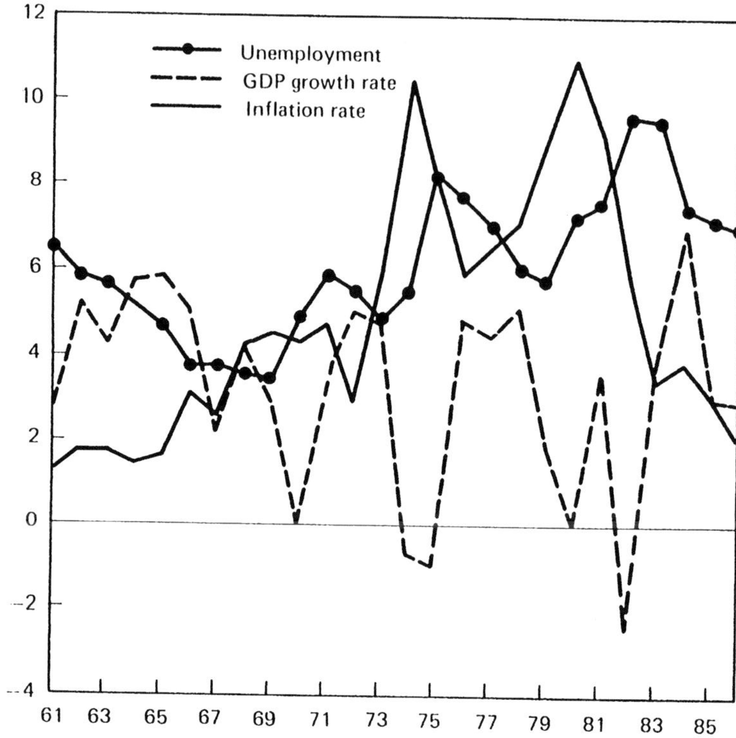

Sources: OECD, 1988a; OECD *Economic Outlook*, 44 (December 1988); AFL-CIO, 1986

Figure 3.1 Economic growth, inflation and unemployment rates in the USA, 1961–86 (%)

by then double digit inflation with highly restrictive policies which, in turn, brought economic growth to a standstill and left unemployment above 7 per cent. The obvious ineffectiveness of conventional economic policies in coming to grips with stagflation gave rise to more fundamental considerations as to what was wrong with the economy. These considerations determined economic policy from the beginning of the 1980s on.

Two basic strands can be distinguished, one focusing on the origins of inflation and the requirements of its successful eradication, the other on the weakened dynamics of economic growth. The first one, generally referred to as 'monetarism', called for a strict control of the amount of money circulating in the economy, regardless of the costs

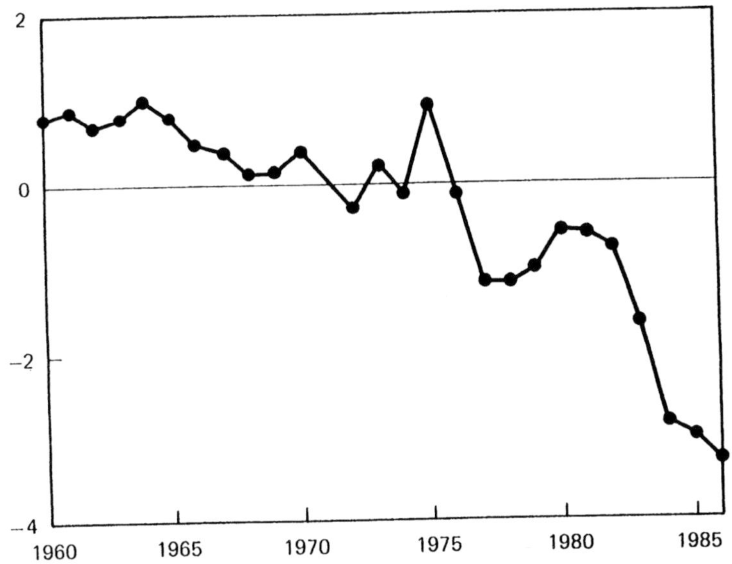

Source: OECD, 1988a

Figure 3.2 The US trade balance, 1960–86 (% of GDP)

this policy might cause in terms of economic recession, until the inflationary expectations which had been formed through years of 'accommodating' monetary policies were wiped out.[2] The monetarist cure, which the Federal Reserve Bank started to apply seriously in 1981, implied in the long run wage discipline. Otherwise unemployment would increase and public demand for credits would crowd out private investment. Thus, the monetarist approach to economic stability emphasised the limits also for welfare state expenditure.

The other economic policy strand focused on the slow-down in productivity growth, which has beset the country since the end of the 1960s. It aimed at strengthening the supply-side of the private market economy by ensuring better incentives for private entrepreneurship. One of the central targets of the supply-siders, who came to shape decisively the economic policy of both Reagan administrations, was the immobilising effect government regulations and taxes of all kinds supposedly had on private initiative. The supply-side interpretation of the stagflation malaise is of direct relevance also for the international competitiveness of the US economy; for the same deficiencies which weaken the internal dynamism of the economy also constitute a serious disadvantage when it comes to comparing US enterprises with more dynamic foreign competitors. Welfare statism, too, was directly affected. When the Reagan administration had to square the supply-side call for less taxes with the monetarist imperative of strict spending discipline and with its own unnegotiable commitment to higher defence expenditure, cuts in welfare state expenditure of all sorts were the unavoidable consequence. And as we shall show later on in more detail, severe cuts in welfare spending were indeed made. But it proved politically unfeasible to balance the budget that way. As it turned out, the impact of low taxes and high defence expenditure was far more pervasive and let the budget deficit soar to record heights.

So, contrary to its philosophy, the government of President Reagan increased *de facto* its claim on economic resources. Yet it refused to extract them out of the private sphere via higher taxes and it also took care not to expropriate private income earners indirectly via inflation. It made sure that it could borrow sufficient private funds. By offering high interest rates it outcompeted other borrowers not only in the USA, but also abroad. The massive influx of foreign savings which this induced enabled the US government to increase its spending in real terms without restricting private demand. The capacity constraint which otherwise would have been inflationary could be avoided through imports. Of course, an increasing trade deficit would be the consequence.

The Reagan government scored a victory against stagflation not by strengthening the supply capacity of the economy as it set out to do, but by combining heavy (public and private) spending with monetary discipline – at the expense of the balance of payments. Accordingly, the external situation of the US economy has become more and more the central cause of economic policy concern. But the worrying symptom has not only been the trade deficit as such and the mounting foreign debt. It has also been the advance of imports and the concomitant retreat of US producers in some important domestic markets such as steel, automobiles, consumer electronics and semiconductors. The slogan of the 'de-industrialisation of America' (Bluestone & Harrison, 1982) catches the fear which has been aroused by the inroads foreign competition has made in once American-dominated markets and by the obvious decline of the affected US industries. This aspect of the problem dates further back than the peculiar 'solution' Reaganomics provided for stagflation.

The worrying evolution of America's external economic situation has been discussed publicly under two very different perspectives. One line of reasoning says that the USA consumes and invests more than it produces, while other countries – notably Japan – produce more than they are willing to absorb. As long as these divergent patterns of economic behaviour persist there are bound to be trade deficits in the USA and export surpluses in Japan and other countries. Ultimately, this is not a matter of US competitiveness and attempts to boost American market shares at home and abroad without tackling the savings deficit would only lead to an inflationary struggle for real resources once the limits of US productive capacity are reached. If the monetary policy remains anti-inflationary, the strongest borrowers – especially the government – would, via rising interest rates, crowd out the other borrowers – especially private investors – from the capital market. Either way, real spending might eventually be brought into balance with real production. But this would be at the expense of the economy's long-term growth, because accelerating inflation undermines the basis of efficient allocation and the crowding out of real investment directly slows down the growth of productive capacity. Thus, the trade deficit in the short run is the minor evil. But in the long run, consumption as a percentage of GDP has to be reduced, with the most important step into the direction being a significant reduction of the budget deficit.[3] It is obvious from this line of reasoning that welfare expenditure is directly affected by the attempt to tackle the external deficit, even though this all has nothing to do with underlying competitiveness.

Under the second perspective, the focus is not on the trade deficit and the underlying problem of mismatched macroeconomic aggregates but on the declining competitive potential of the US economy. The point is made that foreign competitors have been increasing their productivity more rapidly than American firms and that in several branches they have managed to offer better-quality products. This means that the US could defend its market shares only at a continuously declining dollar, which, in turn, implies deteriorating terms of trade. It also means that American producers face declining shares in some of the most profitable markets regardless of the exchange rate. Connected with the diagnosis of declining competitive potential has been the fear of a general industrial decline of the country, which threatens American prosperity as well as American political and strategic interests. From this perspective, the need for devaluation is just an indicator of decreasing competitiveness and the problem with all its menacing consequences can very well co-exist even with a trade surplus if the latter is achieved through import abstinence and at the price of deteriorating terms of trade.

The theme of declining competitiveness has been present in the US economic policy debate already in the early 1970s and before. But it has gained importance in the 1980s and given rise to a number of studies by prestigious institutions and scholars – including the report of a special President's Commision.[4] In a way, it echoes the supply-side economists' concern about the weakened entrepreneurial dynamism and adds to it the comparative element: how dynamic, productive and innovative is the US compared with other countries whose companies want to sell to the same markets?[5] And how attractive is the USA as a place compared with others in which to locate high value-added production? (Cf. Mills & Lovell, 1985, pp. 450ff.) That such comparisons are increasingly unfavourable for the USA is, for those who stress this point, at the root of many of the economic difficulties which beset the country. According to them, to tackle this problem should be at the top of the economic policy agenda. As Tyson and Zysman (1983, p. 16) said: 'Our national economic well-being will rest on our capacity to accomplish the necessary ... competitive revitalisation.' And not only the economic well-being has been said to be at stake, but also the ability of the US to live up to its unique political and military commitments (cf. Scott, 1985a).

The Development of American Competitiveness

The diagnosis of a decline in competitiveness results from a specific perspective which relativises the significance of more conventional macroeconomic variables like the trade balance and the exchange rate. But it is not just a question of perspective. It is also a matter of empirical truth. In 1986 one of the main advocates of the macroeconomic approach to the balance of payments problem stated very clearly: '. . . the underlying competitive position of the US is quite strong . . .' and: '. . .the US will be extremely competitive once we stop pricing ourselves out of world markets via the exchange rate.' (Bergsten 1986, pp. 22 and 23) In contrast, the President's Commission on Industrial competitiveness stated one year before as clearly: 'Our ability to compete in world markets is eroding.' (Volume I, p. 1)

Both manufacturing market shares and real wages show a clear deterioration of the US position in comparison with other countries. But what does that mean? Market shares can be lost for different reasons. Highly developed economies come under pressure if other economies, starting from a much lower base of factor incomes, catch

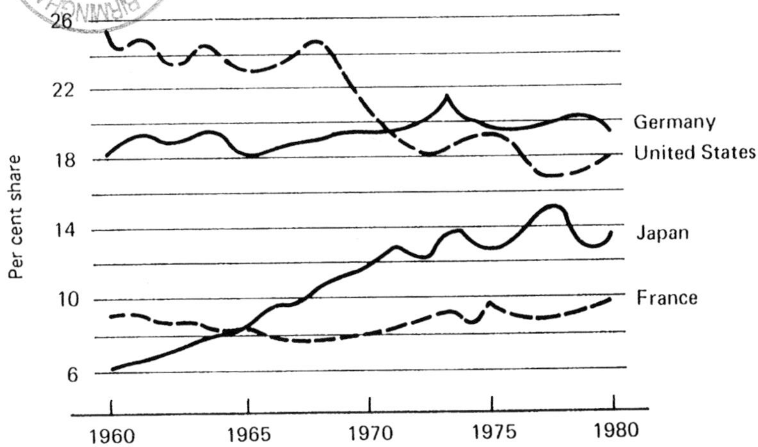

Source: Scott, 1985a, p. 27

Figure 3.3 Selected OECD countries' shares of world manufacturing exports, 1965–80

up in productivity without increasing their factor incomes proportionately. Since the USA was in the 1950s the uncontested world leader in industrial productivity and real wages, it was also most liable to become the victim of such catching up processes from the side of industrialised as well as industrialising countries.[6] From this point of view it seems quite natural that productivity and real wages should grow more slowly in the US than in most other countries. What the USA was on the way to losing here was its competitive lead over the rest of the world and hence the real basis of its wage and other income premiums. The failure to give up these premiums (for example, because of an insufficiently adjusted exchange rate) then leads necessarily to decreases in market shares on top of the ones which result anyway from the catch up. Of course, to a political and military 'superpower' it can be a cause of justifiable concern to lose the economic leadership position and become one of an increasing number of equals.[7]

The situation would be different if the USA were to lose market shares to competitors with superior productivity or superior technology. It would be particularly grave if national producers were excluded from fast-growing high-volume markets. The pertinent indicators are (a) the evolution of market shares in branches where labour costs do not play a decisive role, especially in high-technology

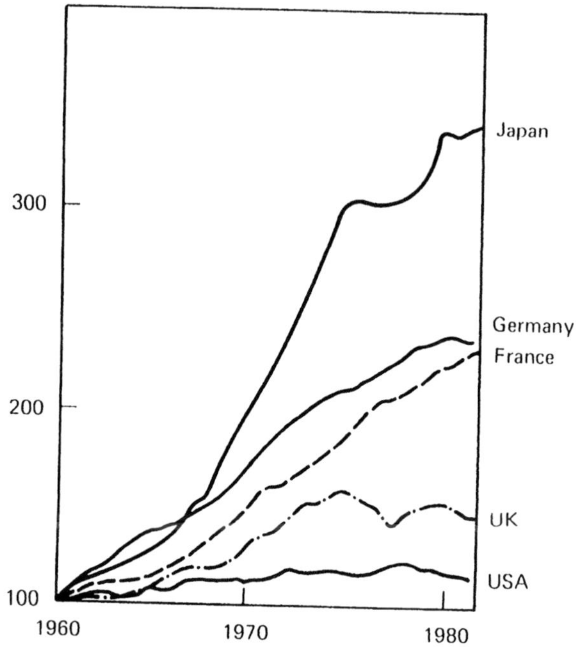

Source: Scott, 1985a, p. 41

Figure 3.4 Indices of average real hourly earnings of production workers in manufacturing, selected OECD countries, 1960–81 (1960 = 100)

branches; (b) comparative productivity values (not rates of growth!) at the level of specific industries.

In several high-technology industries we can observe the familiar pattern of the US retreating from its once overwhelmingly dominating position (cf. President's Commission, 1985, Volume I, p. 16). To this we should add that by 1986 the former huge trade surplus in high-tech goods had shrunk to zero. But the data also show a continuing strong American presence in the international markets. They do not warrant the summary conclusion that US high-tech industries have been on the decline (cf. also Aho & Rosen, 1980). In some markets, foreign competitors have not gained any ground at all. If there is anything for the USA to worry then it is the rapid advance of one single competitor, Japan.

The danger which the US begins to face is the loss of technological leadership to Japan, while maintaining a strong second place well ahead of the European countries. But this prospect appears so far

Table 3.1 Selected OECD countries' shares of exports in R&D intensive manufacturing, 1970–84 (%)

	1970	*1980*	*1984*
USA	28	24	26
Japan	12	17	25
West Germany	16	16	13
France	7	8	7
United Kingdom	10	11	8

Source: OECD, 1986a, p. 72.

only as a worst case scenario. The USA can just as well hope to keep the leading position, though with the Japanese close at its heels. Bruce Scott has developed industry profiles of comparative advantages for the major OECD countries (Scott, 1985b, pp. 77ff.) The comparison of these profiles shows the USA well equipped to meet the Japanese high-tech challenge, since it has not only been strongest in industries with a high research intensity, but has also managed to strengthen its relative position in several of these industries. In 1980 the American profile appeared much more advantageous, for instance, than the German one and at least not inferior to the Japanese one.

America's strength in high technology can give the nation some confidence that it will be present and do well in certain fast-growing markets and that its producers will receive premium prices on certain products. But this alone does not yet invalidate the widespread notion of declining US competitiveness. What matters is that national producers are competitive in enough markets, so that the whole economically active population can earn a high income. For a nation as big as the US the high-tech markets are simply not voluminous enough. Besides, the problem of the US trade deficit could hardly be solved any more through a greater surplus in high-tech goods; for, as we have seen, high-tech manufacturing competence is no longer concentrated in the United States. There are important non-high-tech markets where the chance of earning a high income per producer depends mostly on ingredients other than research and development. The key criteria which have to be met are product quality and productivity. And in some of these high-volume markets which are sometimes referred to as 'medium technology' the USA has been doing conspicuously badly. Among them are automobiles, consumer electronics, machine tools and steel. It is these sectors which account for the huge American trade deficit that emerged in the 1980s (cf. NAM, 1986, p. 6). Market success depends here on comparative production costs per unit. Therefore, as cheaper competitors catch up with US productivity, American wages would have to go down in terms of the competitors' currencies if US market shares are to be defended. The failure of doing so (an overvalued dollar!) can certainly explain much of the decline of traditional American industries in the past 20 years. Moreover, if low-wage countries in the Third World emulate American productivity standards because they get access to state-of-the-art technology there is simply no realistic way of adjusting to their cost levels.[8] A significant part of the dwindling US market shares in non-high-tech industries and of American industry's difficulties in recuperating them after 1985 with the help of the cheap dollar is accounted for by this low-wage competition.

But non-adjusted or non-adjustable factor remuneration is not the only problem the US has been facing in the medium-technology sector. In a number of important industries American producers have also become inferior to their strongest high-wage competitors in physical productivity. According to one 1985 report, the absolute level of Japanese productivity exceeded then the US level by 8 per cent in steel, by 19 per cent in electrical machinery, by 11 per cent in general machinery, by 24 per cent in the automobile sector, and by 34 per cent in precision equipment (Brooks, 1985, p. 339).[9] In addition, many US industries have been suffering from quality deficiencies which are not due to a lack of technological know-how.[10] In all these industries US producers can defend their market position only at the expense of decreasing wages and profits or of deteriorating terms of trade.

However, it could be considered as part of the catching up syndrome that some countries become more productive than the USA in *some* sectors while the US stays ahead in others. The US would have to adjust its average wages and other prices to a situation of basic equality with other highly industrialised countries as compared to its former across-the-board superiority. American companies would have to accept that there is no undisputed terrain in the internationalised markets any more, but as a group they would not have to fear the dispute, although it seems to have taken some companies and even some branches by surprise.

But there are additional observations which could indicate that the US is not heading towards a situation of basic equality with its main competitors in East Asia and Europe, and which could substantiate the fear that the country is going to fall behind in a broad range of production sectors. These observations refer to the factors on which competitive potential depends. Those countries which have caught up with American productivity and technological know-how and which have come to outperform the USA in several product markets have consistently shown certain higher measurable efforts. Most important, they have invested more in productivity-enhancing machinery. It must be expected that, as long as these differences in competitiveness-creating efforts persist, the growth of productivity and the speed of innovation will continue to be lower in the US than in competitor countries. Basic competitive equality is then for the US just a mark on the road to competitive inferiority.[11]

However, in recent years the conditions of future competitiveness have improved for the USA. While America ranked clearly behind most industrial countries in capital formation until the mid-1970s, by 1985 its gross investment ratio had got very close to that of most

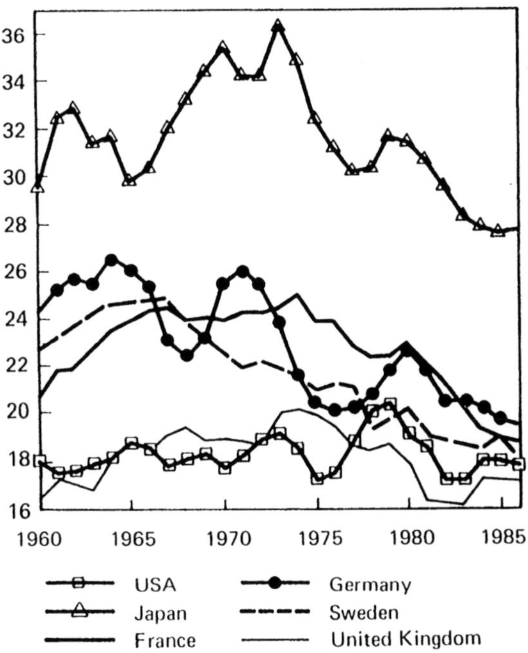

Source: OECD, 1988

Figure 3.5 Gross fixed capital formation in selected OECD industrial countries, 1960–86 (% of GDP)

Western European countries. Only Japan was still well ahead. As far as that share of GDP is concerned that goes into research and development, the US was practically equal with West Germany and Japan. But this signifies a deterioration of the clear advantage the US had until the beginning of the 1970s (President's Commission, 1985, Volume II, p. 97). Moreover, in the USA a much larger part of R&D effort than elsewhere has been reserved for military purposes which leaves the important competitors well ahead of the USA in purely civilian R&D (President's Commission, 1985, Volume II, p. 22). On the other hand, if one considers only the R&D expenditure in the private business sector, the USA is again among the frontrunners (OECD, 1986a, p. 35).

Altogether, the objectively measurable efforts during the 1980s point at improvements in American competitiveness *vis-à-vis* the European countries but not *vis-à-vis* Japan. The fear that the USA might fall back behind Germany and other European countries in average productivity and innovativeness appears less justified towards the end of the 1980s than it was a decade earlier. But as far as Japan is concerned, no such comfortable conclusion can be drawn.

SEARCHING FOR THE CAUSE OF COMPETITIVE DECLINE

The Themes of the Public Debate

The very fact that one medium-technology industry after the other fell behind in productivity and product quality had to be worrying for the future because it pointed to the existence of social processes which generate relative inefficiency and which could well continue to do so. The competitiveness debate in the USA has given much attention to such systematic deficiencies in the social fabric of the economy. Several explanatory themes have been put forward.

One is that former economic virtues became increasingly neglected as American society became complacent and more consumption and distribution orientated (cf. for example Scott & Lodge, 1985b and Scott, 1985b). As already stated, this theme is closely related to the supply-side explanation of sluggish growth. But the observation is added that the competitor countries have maintained those institutionalised virtues which have been eroding in the US. Especially, the East Asians are said not to suffer from excessive orientation towards leisure, consumption, distribution and economic security. Their economic life is production-oriented.

Another theme is that economic conditions have changed but the social organisation of the economy has not been adjusted. This refers to the declining importance of standardised mass production and the need for more flexibility to which the once successful patterns of American management and labour relations are no longer well adjusted ('the end of Fordism').

Still another theme is that other countries have come up with superior ways of organising an economy, thus challenging the conventional wisdom of American capitalism. Most important in this respect is the notion of the goal-oriented 'developmental state' which is superior to the purpose-lacking 'regulatory state' whose policies are oriented towards macroeconomic goals like full employment and price stability rather than to international competition.[12] According to this view, the US could deal with the competition of other regulatory states like those of Europe but is not equipped institutionally to match the comprehensive development and marketing strategies of Japan and its imitators.

Those who stress the increased importance and the superior strategies of foreign competitors maintain on the other hand that the US has been behaving as if the challenge did not exist. The reproach of neglect and complacency has been made about the political leadership, which would not change its traditional macroeconomic orientation, as well as about the corporate leadership, which has continued with traditional strategies, traditional management styles, and traditional products (Reich 1983, Magaziner & Reich, 1982). But attention has also been directed to objective obstacles which have made it difficult for the country to respond adequately, even if its leaders have been aware of the challenge.

Focus on Investment

What are the processes that have brought about in the US – because of neglect or of structural conduciveness – comparatively low productivity and insufficient product quality? To approach this question, we shall have a look at the economic accounts of the American productivity slow-down which have proliferated in the late 1970s and early 1980s.[13] Even though these estimates differ considerably in the weights they attribute to the various independent variables, they clearly identify insufficient investment as one major source of declining productivity growth. Another important source is what might be called inefficient use of resources. It refers to allocative efficiency as well as to x-efficiency, that is, to the performance of the production factors wherever they are allocated. This residual efficiency dimension plays an overwhelmingly important role in the estimates of Denison (1979), especially for the time period after 1973. But it cannot readily be explained. It touches upon technological know-how and innovation, the motivation of workers and managers, and the organisation of business firms. Organisation, in turn, can be the focus for explaining deficiencies in innovation as well as in motivation.[14] We shall come back to this important complex, but before that we shall deal with the other variable of high explanatory power: investment.

It is generally acknowledged that comparatively low investment ratios made the USA lag behind in the introduction of modern, productivity-increasing and quality-improving equipment into the production process. It has helped originally backward countries to catch up more rapidly with US standards than it would have been the case otherwise and it has led to an increasing backwardness of more and more US industries once foreign competitors had caught up.

The low investment ratio can be seen as reflecting the general orientation of the USA towards consumption and distribution rather than to economic performance, which has been emphasised by some critics. But what has kept American entrepreneurs from investing as much as their foreign competitors? Two basic causes have been identified: (a) insufficient incentives for private saving, (b) an inadequate business climate which has reduced entrepreneurs' willingness to invest.

Low private savings are deeply rooted in the American economic culture of the post-war period with its emphasis on consumption-led growth ('buy now – pay later'). But the tax system has also been designed to encourage borrowing and to punish saving, even though expert opinions differ as to the magnitude of the tax system's adverse impact (see for example Sawhill & Stone, 1984, pp. 95ff. and the literature cited there). The anti-saving distortions were somewhat reduced in the 1981 Economic Recovery Tax Act. But the federal budget is still considered as one of the principal mechanisms which withdraws funds from investment and channels them into consumptive use. Some regard the amount of resources the government absorbs to afford simultaneously a leading power military buildup and a welfare state as a significant drain on the nation's potential investment fund. The high costs of President Johnson's Great Society programme have been cited in this respect (for example, Bolling & Bowles, 1982, pp. 165ff. and Lodge & Crum, 1985). However, the US government's share of the national product is, like the American investment ratio, rather on the small side in international comparison. Therefore, it seems more important *how* the government finances its expenses.

Here the US scores two important minuses: firstly, the tax system is designed such that it raises the costs of capital to an extremely high level.[15] The 1986 tax reform even enhanced this adverse effect. Secondly, under the influence of its supply-side credo that taxes in general should be lower, the Reagan administration was pushed into a policy of heavy borrowing, which increased the interest rate to the general detriment of investment. The induced influx of foreign savings allowed the US temporarily to finance its budget deficit without drawing too much on its own private savings. But the ever increasing foreign indebtedness and the adverse impact of the high dollar on the vital tradables-producing sector of the economy limit the period of time this option is available. To the degree the fall in the value of the dollar, which was initiated in 1985, improves the balance of trade, fewer foreign goods will be available and the government would have to rely more on domestic savings. This, in turn, implies the crowding out of private investment if domestic savings do not grow concomitantly.

Welfare statism on credit, as it is being practised at present in the US, endangers in the long run the formation of productive capital. A taxation policy which lets the public pay for government expenditure would seem to do much less harm, unless one postulates – as the hard-line supply-siders do – that this paralyses to an even larger extent individual economic efforts. It is only this latter argument in combination with the untouchable nature of military expenses that could support the case for serious welfare state cuts on behalf of capital formation (cf. Friedman 1985).

The government's demand for private savings together with the scarce supply of such savings make, of course, easily for the high-cost-of-capital syndrome which Hatsopoulos, Brooks and others consider as a decisive cause of the comparatively low American investment ratio (cf. note 15). This view would presuppose that enterprises are generally willing to invest but cannot get the necessary funds. Yet to some degree the act of saving could be seen as following from the investment decision. In this respect, low savings indicate a lack of perceived investment opportunities. Factors like the general state of the economy, business confidence, regulative obstacles to investment, and the outlook for profits are crucial here. However, these factors could explain only the 'sluggish recovery of investment' after the 1974 recession (cf. Kendrick, 1980, p. 233). The comparatively low ratio of investment throughout most of the post-war period can hardly be attributed to a kind of permanent economic malaise in the US which would have kept potential investors in a state of caution and reluctance.

It seems that, if we take the long-term view rather than looking at the decline of the mid-1970s, an explanation is needed which combines narrowly defined economic mechanisms of the cost-of-capital type with the broader social preference for consumption. Gross private investment ratios of GNP around 15 per cent have been normal from the point of view of post-war American society. That other countries had 'abnormally' high ratios must then be attributed to certain 'extraordinary' socio-economic mechanisms which these countries possess, but not the USA. Special tax incentives for household savings as they exist, for instance, in Germany are part of such 'special features' of the high-investment countries. In Japan we have the high dependency of old-age income on personal savings, which induces the average citizen to put a sizeable part of current earnings aside as a private social security provision.

Another special feature refers to the way finance is channelled into private investment projects, an aspect to which, for example, John Zysman has directed attention with his book *Government, Markets and Growth* (1983). In the US the preferences of the public on the capital markets practically determine whether and under which conditions financial resources, including corporate profits, go into real investment, into financial speculation or back into household consumption. And the whole allocative system outside of the government sector is designed to function by responding to these decentralised preferences. In other countries, the long-term growth preferences of certain elites have much more weight, because enterprises are financially more dependent on them and less responsible to a broad public of shareholders. These institutional elites who control a significant part of the finance flow include the managers of the big banks in the German case. In Japan there is a corporatist structure consisting of the top management of the big enterprise groupings, the leadership of the ruling Liberal Democratic Party, and the government economic planning agencies. Such corporatist structures of relatively centralised economic decision-making also exist in France and in some smaller European countries, not to speak of the East Asian NICs. Whatever the concrete institutional arrangements are, they have in common that they insulate to some degree (not at all completely) the area of investment decisions from the preferences of those who supply the system with their savings. What the rest of the society wants with regard to consumption now and consumption later is simply less relevant than in the United States with its comparatively 'democratic' market system, which gives more say to those who want to consume and to speculate rather than to invest productively (cf. *Harvard Business Review*, 1987, p. 113).

This institutional explanation of the comparatively low average US investment ratio is in line with the above mentioned notions of a lack of national purpose, of consumptive and distributive rather than productive priorities, and of the superiority of the developmental *vis-à-vis* the regulatory state. But it stresses institutional set-ups rather than collective moods. It identifies an institutional deficiency of the United States which systematically puts it at a disadvantage compared with differently organised countries. This disadvantage is not naturally linked to the catching up phase. It can well persist beyond the point where competitors have reached average US productivity levels. One could speculate that the elite-supported investment drive in other countries will weaken once they find themselves in leading positions. They could turn increasingly to foreign ventures as high factor costs at home and increasing diseconomies of agglomeration (ecology) make locations abroad more interesting. But the historical fate of Britain *vis-à-vis* its competitors would rather forbid too much confidence in such levelling tendencies at the top.

Focus on Human Capital

As Denison (1979) and others have confirmed econometrically, capital formation explains only part of the long-term US productivity growth and an even smaller part of the productivity slow-down after 1973. It also explains only a minor part of the difference in productivity growth between the USA and other countries (cf. Denison, 1980, p. 221). To explain more, one can try to broaden the concept of capital itself, including in it intangible aspects like human qualification and technological expertise. Robert Eisner's Total Incomes System of Account (TISA) constitutes one of the most systematic attempts to give explicit recognition to the intangible aspects of capital formation. It attributes to them a value which is roughly twice the dollar value of conventional gross private domestic investment (cf. Eisner, 1980).

The US competitiveness debate has also laid much emphasis on the need to increase R&D funds and to train the national work force adequately.[16] However, it is not quite clear whether in these respects the USA has really substantial deficits which would weigh in the explanation of its slow productivity growth. Some point at the much larger relative number of engineers in Japan (President's Commission 1985, Volume II, p. 21). Yet the US is still well ahead of Germany and France.

Another point which has often been made is the absorption of a large part of US R&D resources by military programmes with few spin-offs for the civilian sector where competitiveness matters. To the degree the net drainage effect of military R&D on the creation of commercially usable know-how is indeed as large as many say, there is a weak spot of some importance in the organisation of the US economy.[17] It would mean that the US, in order to stay commercially competitive across a broad spectrum of R&D-intensive goods, either has to make an extra effort that would compensate for the diversion of resources into the military sphere, or has to reduce its armament effort to a level which corresponds more or less to that of its competitiors, pressing them perhaps (as they are also its military allies) to shoulder themselves a larger part of the burden.

Another weak spot, as far as intangible investment is concerned, is the lack of an institutionalised vocational training and retraining system connected with actual job work as it exists in other countries (President's Commission 1985, Volume II, pp. 148ff.). This, in turn, seems to be related to the famous flexibility of the American labour market. In the USA the incentive for firms to invest in the formation of human capital is – especially in times of relative labour abundance – weaker than in countries where workers are more firmly attached to their enterprises, where they constitute, in fact, part of their company's capital and are not just exchangeable suppliers of labour input into the production process.[18]

But while certain weaknesses can be identified with regard to the formation of intangible capital in the USA, they can hardly explain why with comparable investment efforts other countries achieved more productive effect and why the US itself achieved more effect in the 1950s and 1960s than in the past decade.

Focus on Regulation

The obvious decline in the efficiency with which productive resources have been deployed in the United States has been attributed in part to the plethora of new regulations which were imposed on American industry on behalf of the environment, consumer safety or energy conservation and which have consumed capital, labour and management attention. To the degree this argument is valid, the normal measures of productivity are inadequate because they neglect externalities. They do not distinguish, for instance, between more or less pollution resulting from the production of commercialised goods. In this respect, regulation expresses the changed preferences of the American public, which has opted for more non-commercialised 'quality of life' at the expense of additional industrial products.

As far as competitiveness is concerned, this public choice has tended to make American-produced tradables more expensive and may have required compensation in the form of wage and/or exchange-rate adjustments. But, as it is occasionally being claimed, the trade-off can be much more severe than the current costs of regulatory compliance (additional safety devices etc.) would suggest, because relatively large shares of such scarce resources as R&D effort or managerial energy are sometimes devoted to complying with and negotiating the new requirements. In addition, these requirements may have discouraged some entrepreneurial initiative.

On the other hand, one of America's principal industrial competitors, Japan, has imposed standards on behalf of externalities which are in many respects as strict as the American ones. Therefore, the regulatory wave of the 1970s may explain some of the slow-down in US productivity growth, but it can hardly be accepted as a major culprit for declining American competitiveness.

Focus on Management

Comparative inefficiency and waste of resources must be traced to other sources. In the American debate much attention has been given to the performance of management and of labour. The management-failure approach has emphasised inefficient enterprise structures and management styles on the one hand and wrong business strategies on the other. There have been reproaches of neglect of the competitive challenge, of abandonment of the national interest and of escapism into financial entrepreneurship. And there have been attempts to establish objective or typical connections between the evolution of market positions, of enterprise structures and capabilities, and of strategic dispositions. Structural disadvantages of US firms in this respect have been related to their long unchallenged position in the large domestic market. This rendered them vulnerable to competitors who were aggressively catching up. The sensitivity to the need for different strategic outlooks and for adjustments in management practices remained underdeveloped and organisational as well as cultural inertia prevented the quick adoption of superior new ways. The readiness and the ability to fight for shares in highly contested markets has also remained underdeveloped in important sectors of US industry because there were 'easy' profits secured in other markets, very important among them the Pentagon's arms procurement market (cf. McGarrah, 1987).

That rigidities in outlook and dispositions be overcome should basically be seen as a matter of time. And as far as management practices are concerned, US enterprises are certainly much more up to the challenge of international competition now than they were in the 1970s. But there are also structural disadvantages which are not so easily changed by deliberate management action. It has been shown, for example, that the dynamics of technological pioneer-follower relations assign an inherent advantage to the latter. The extremely innovative US high-tech firms had to experience this when dealing with their Japanese competitors.[19]

Even more serious is another point: in the United States, large business firms are exchangeable instruments in the hands of equity holders who expect a steady flow of dividends or who speculate with the firms' assets, thus forcing management to put heavy emphasis on short-term profitability and on the firm's rating in the stock market. Considerations of production and success in specific product markets tend to be subordinated to the owners' ultimate objective, making money. In comparison (and overdrawing the point somewhat), Japanese enterprises are committed to the task of organising national production and securing Japanese success in the international market place. Financial considerations are only instrumental. Therefore, one should expect that Japanese enterprises devote more efforts to continuous improvements in productive efficiency, whereas American enterprises are more readily inclined to shift resources to new profitable opportunities when they are confronted with difficulties in specific markets.[20]

Focus on Industrial Relations

Another serious handicap of US firms has been, according to the American debate, the system of industrial relations. It has been said to be very rigid with regard to the allocation of manpower and inefficient with regard to workers' motivation on the job. Moreover, it has deteriorated since the end of the long post-war boom, creating more friction and diminishing further workers' motivation. This theme of unsatisfactory labour relations has been treated in part as a matter of inadequate management practices which can be improved according to the principle 'learning from Japan'. But it has also been related in different ways to more comprehensive interpretations of American society, of the capitalist economy, and of the industrial mode of production.

A rather common approach focuses on the American concern with self-interest which is prone to the emergence of conflictive interest group relations and which leaves deficits in such important social virtues as loyalty, spirit of co-operation and common-goal orientation.[21] Another approach points at the technology-induced changes in industrial production to which traditional American industrial relations are ill-adjusted. In general, these changes would call for more intellectual and motivational involvement of workers and for frequent changes in the tasks to be performed by individual workers. Industrial relations in the US, in turn, have been heavily influenced by Tayloristic principles, emphasising control and a rigid job description and neglecting workers' motivational involvement.[22] As already mentioned, firms have been considering their workforces less as an asset and more as a factor in their expense calculations. To blame this discrepancy for declining American competitiveness implies that Japanese and in part European industrial relations systems have been less at odds with the new requirements to start with and that the 'second industrial divide' made their latent advantages manifest – to the disadvantage of the USA.[23]

Still another approach identifies as decisive changes not external, technological ones which created a mismatch between old structures and new functional requirements, but changes brought about by the internal dynamics of the system itself. The dominant theme here is 'the end of the post-war labour truce' (cf. Gorden *et al.*, 1982 and Bowles *et al.*, 1986). The accord between organised labour and business after the Second World War had consolidated labour's position in the bargaining over the terms of the employment contract while ensuring the autonomy of management in running the enterprise. Labour refrained from any attempts to change the nature of the free enterprise system. But it participated in the growth of output and income the system was able to generate. However, the increasing economic security which growth brought about increased the power of labour as well as citizens in general *vis-à-vis* business.[24] This power was used to further labour's own interests at the expense of profits and it was used to reduce labour's compliance with the demands of management (less work input, more resistance). This view implies, of course, that the post-war accord had always needed the disciplinary pressure of economic necessity as an essential ingredient and that it had not succeeded in endowing management authority with real, weatherproof legitimacy. With profits eroding, the system became less able to create rapid growth and to adjust to new competitive requirements. Therefore, the accord between labour and capital, which had provided the institutional basis of labour's 'nuisance potential' lost legitimacy in the eyes of business as well as of large parts of the general public (cf. Kochan and Piore 1984).

With declining growth the system's ability of providing steadily rising wages and employment security also vanished. This, in turn, eroded labour's adherence to the post-war accord because the fundamental *quid pro quo* did no longer apply. The consequence was an escalation of labour–capital antagonism with decreasing work performance (including absenteeism and even sabotage) on the one side[25] and increasing anti-union tendencies on the other. With an increasingly restive and non-compliant labour force the issue of control gained importance, leading business to step up expenses for control and supervision structures which nonetheless are only moderately effective and often blatantly inefficient in modern factories.[26]

The observation of declining labour discipline, which has been confirmed by countless complaining managers, has also been explained as a generational phenomenon. The theory is that in the general context of alienated work life on the one hand and political democracy on the other, authority patterns at the work place are no longer accepted by those generations of workers who became fully socialised into the industrial wage-dependent work life and who lack any personal or family experience with pre-industrial modes of production and the corresponding pattern of authority (cf. Tarantelli, 1984). American industrial relations with all their antagonisms and low morale would then have to be viewed as the symptom of a particularly 'advanced' industrial culture. The US (as well as the UK) would have reached the crisis of the sociologically 'mature' industrialised society which other, later industrialising countries shall still have to face.

Focus on Institutional Sclerosis

Evolutionary explanations like the last mentioned one do not put the finger on something that has gone wrong and ought to be corrected. They rather deal with inevitabilities for which there are no policy responses readily available. Another such explanation of American decline has been put forward by Mancur Olson. According to him, the allocative efficiency of the market has been increasingly impaired (like an organism that suffers from sclerosis) as interest groups and coalitions got more and more into a position to manipulate supply and prices in order to further their own distributive interests at the expense of the society at large. The increasing power of manipulation, in turn, has been the almost inevitable consequence of the long period of stability and prosperity which the United States has enjoyed. In contrast, Japan, Germany and other European countries had experienced traumatic disruptions of their normal societal evolution with the consequence that the formation of distributive coalitions had to start practically anew there and that the market could, thus, function for a longer time without disturbance. Olson even offers an explanation for the sudden slow-down of productivity growth after 1973. According to him, it is owed to the magnifying influence the distributional coalitions with their anti-adjustment stance had on the resource-absorbing effects of the 1973 oil price shock (cf. Olson, 1988). The sclerosis approach to the explanation of American decline leaves some hope for the country's relative position, as its closest competitors should be expected – after four decades of stability – to wear out rapidly their erstwhile advantage. Moreover, the US has itself some newly industrialised regions (the South) where institutional sclerosis is far less advanced than in its industrial core regions (cf. Norton, 1986).

RESPONDING TO THE CHALLENGE

The Government Level

The Report of the President's Commission on Industrial Competitiveness indicates perhaps most clearly that by the mid-1980s the

American public had become fully aware of the competitiveness problem. Such awareness should be expected to exert massive pressure to remedial action, in particular as there has emerged something like a mainstream of recommendations for concrete policy measures. Five different lines of government policies have been proposed to strengthen American competitiveness:

- dedication of more public resources, most of all in terms of institutional support structures, but also in terms of finance;
- more adequate tax incentives;
- removal of regulative barriers;
- trade policies which are more oriented towards American interests;
- macroeconomic policies which influence favourably key market parameters like the interest rate and the rate of inflation.

The overrriding theme has been 'more national purpose' as opposed to the complacency of former years. Very little of the recommended policy measures points into the direction of 'less welfare entitlements – more performance' (which dominates part of the soul-searching literature). The two fronts of action where welfare statism is potentially affected in a more than marginal way are the reduction of the government budget and the removal of regulatory barriers to production, investment and innovation.

Government action, however, was much less oriented to this technocratic approach which has been dominating the competitiveness debate than to the supply-side recipes for revitalising the American economy. Competitiveness was more an implicit concern. The explicit, more encompassing concern was the functioning of the capitalist economic system in the USA. In accordance with the supply-side diagnosis of the causes of declining economic vitality, the Reagan administration set out to restore as far as possible the freedom of action of private enterprise, to liberate it from onerous and paralysing government interference. Less government meant lower taxes, less legal and administrative restrictions, but also less protection against competition and the risks of the market.

The three main pillars of the Reagan administration's supply-side policy were the reduction of taxes, the reduction of non-military government expenditure and deregulation – at least as far as the agenda is concerned. In implementing it, the government was – albeit less so than most US administrations – forced by Congress, organised pressure groups, judicial restraints and public opinion to renounce a great deal of its initial goals. As Palmer and Sawhill (1984, p. 4) wrote: 'By 1983 ... stalemate had largely set in, and the administration had little additional success in advancing its agenda.'

Arguably, the Reagan administration was most successful in getting taxes reduced. Federal taxes went down from about 21 per cent of GNP in fiscal year 1981 to about 19 per cent in fiscal year 1985, a level they had at the end of the Eisenhower administration. The Economic Recovery Tax Act of 1981 (ERTA) reduced individual income tax rates by 23 per cent, allowed for accelerated depreciation for business, provided for upward adjustments of tax brackets so that with rising nominal income tax payers would not automatically grow into higher tax brackets, and it reduced the maximum rate for unearned income from 70 to 50 per cent. Altogether, ERTA favoured high-income earners much more than low- and middle-income earners. Some of the tax cuts of ERTA were taken back or diminished in the following year's Tax Equity and Fiscal Responsibility Act (TEFRA). Still, in 1985, corporate income taxes were only at 1.8 per cent of GNP as compared to 2.9 per cent in 1981. As a share of total taxes they had fallen from 14 to 10 per cent. The share of social security contributions, in turn, went up from 31 to 37 per cent (Mills 1984, p. 118). As to the intended supply-side effect of the 1981 tax reform, they are highly dubious. The *Financial Times* summarised: 'Empty office towers and bankrupt savings institutions are the result.' (23 May 1988)

The tax reform of 1986, which was to apply from 1988 on, brought an additional, particularly big favour to the top income earners, because it cut their tax rate by the most. On the other hand, exemptions from the corporate income tax were drastically reduced, which strongly relativised the overall tax-saving effect for business. In fact, tax rewards for investment practically disappeared from 1988 on. But many of the former resource-wasting distortions were also eliminated.

The second pillar of the Reagan policy of capitalist revitalisation was to be the reduction of non-military government spending. It turned out to be considerably weaker than projected by the government. As a sum, non-defence programme outlays (that is to say: excluding interest on outstanding debt) went down from 15.7 per cent of GNP in 1981 to 14.1 per cent in 1985. This was achieved through marked reductions in the support for education and science; in credit assistance to businesses; in federal spending for environment programmes, transport infrastructure, community and regional development programmes; in assistance to low-income and disadvantaged citizens; in unemployment insurance; in student loans; and in the government personnel. On the other hand, the expenses for medical services to those who are insured under the national Medicare system grew significantly (cf. Mills 1984).

Three quarters of the reduction in non-defence programme outlays were offset by increases in military expenditure, most of all in procurement of military hardware. Thus, what occurred on the spending side of the budget was much more a shift in priorities than the overall cut in expenditure which would have seemed to be the logical counterpart measure to a tax cut for the sake of 'less government'. In part, this can be attributed to the fact that the administration did not get its way with several of its more drastic expenditure-cutting proposals.[27]

As it turned out, the asymmetry between tax and spending cuts led to the record budget deficit which has become the paramount economic problem in the second half of the 1980s. Interest payment on accumulated debt occupied an ever-increasing share of total government expenditure and destroyed any hope the administration initially had that the growth of the supply-side-revitalised economy would increase revenues sufficiently to finance a significant part of the tax cuts. The interest payments alone made it more and more mandatory to provide additional finance either through higher tax revenues, thus undoing partially Reagan's supply-side reform, or through increased cuts in programme spending. So one could be inclined to say that ultimately there will have been but a gigantic shift in government expenditure from non-military programme outlays to interest payments. Considering only aggregate sums, this may not be too far from the truth and Regan's attempt to reduce the financial weight of government on the private economy may well, from this angle, be seen as a failure. Nevertheless, the redistribution of the tax burden in favour of the high-income strata was of a lasting nature. And this conforms to the supply-side philosophy that excessive taxation of high incomes constitutes a punishment for high economic performance.

Another lasting benefit – from the point of view of supply-side philosophy – can be discovered behind Reagan's apparent failure to reduce more than temporarily the economic weight of government: the necessity to devote large sums to current interest payments while at the same time reducing the debt makes severe restraints in programme spending unavoidable. Thus, the country might learn to live with a high level of fiscal austerity, accepting it as the norm for the time after the deficit has been brought under control.[28]

The third pillar of the Reagan supply-side reform was the loosening of administrative and legal restrictions on productive activities. In this area Reagan continued in part a policy line which had already gained momentum under Carter and had led then to the abolition of several cartel-like and other price-fixing arrangements, to which Reagan added a deregulation of buses, financial institutions and telecommunications. Besides this, he took major steps to reduce the rigour of previous anti-trust policies, making it easier for American business to concentrate efforts in the struggle for productivity, innovation and international market shares. However, Reagan's deregulatory drive was directed more than anything else at those restrictions on business which had proliferated in the two preceding decades on behalf of overrriding non-economic objectives. Here the administration scored some successes, but major breakthroughs were prevented by congressional opposition (cf. Quick, 1984, pp. 306ff.).

Reconsidering President Reagan's policy of revitalising the capitalist economy, it is only in the area of income tax rates that changes were brought about which can claim significance as part of a 'conservative revolution'. In all other respects there was much more proclamation of free-market philosophy, entrepreneurial values and pro-business attitudes than tangible policy achievements.

The second Reagan administration had to dedicate its attention increasingly to the twin problem of the budget and foreign deficits which had been created by the ill-balanced policy initiatives of the Reagan revolution's heydays. With both deficits corrective action had become indispensable for reasons of macroeconomic viability. But the government's inconsistent budget policy had also created a veritable emergency situation for US competitiveness – for two reasons: (a) increasing public claim of private savings threatened to crowd out productive investment; (b) the influx of sufficient foreign capital, which neutralised hazard (a), crowded out US tradables from domestic and foreign markets. It became more and more urgent to bring American industries back into the market in order to keep them from declining permanently. Thus, apart from all long-term supply-side policies, getting the dollar down emerged as a short-term priority task as far as competitiveness was concerned. Under the leadership of the newly appointed Secretary of the Treasury, James Baker, the Government was dramatically successful in achieving this objective. But now it faced (i) the problem of how to finance the budget deficit if an improved trade balance ends the automatic recycling of surplus dollars in the hands of foreign central banks; (ii) the disquieting fact that the external deficit did not shrink by as much as it was hoped for originally.

In fact, it turned out that despite the price advantage of the cheap dollar US industries had a hard time recuperating lost market shares. For, during the preceding period of the overvalued dollar parts of the industrial base had been eroding, supply capacity was missing, foreign competitors had consolidated their position in many markets and were able to defend them. It is in the context of this experience that from about 1986 on competitiveness became a policy focus in its own right.[29] The technocratic approach of the President's Commission on Industrial Competitiveness gained influence when the ideological approach of Reagan's early supply-side policy had become stuck in acute macroeconomic problems without fulfilling yet the implicit promise of fundamental improvements in US competitiveness. But in practice little was done. In its initiatives which were directed at the problem of competitiveness the government put by far the most emphasis on trade policy measures targeting foreign protectionism (especially in high-technology sectors, but also in services) and foreign export subsidies. Some financial support was also given to educational, training and retraining programmes. But the more hard-to-tackle, culturally and sociologically founded supply-side issues which had come up in the national competitiveness debate remained largely unattended. In *this* respect (not with regard to the stagflation problems which had plagued the country in the 1970s) the incoming Bush administration was in 1989 not much further than the Carter administration was at the end of its terms.

The Corporate Level

Meanwhile a profound cumulative change has taken place on the corporate level – a change in two directions. Firstly, companies have embarked on emulating the management practices of their seemingly more efficient foreign competitors. Secondly, business has considerably increased its bargaining power *vis-à-vis* labour. In fact, it has succeeded in reducing strongly the influence of unions as well as in cutting back on several of labour's previous bargaining conquests. On all these accounts, US enterprises can be expected to be better prepared for international competition than they had been in the early 1970s. On the other hand, the rather negative practice of financial speculation with corporate assets has become more accentuated in the past 15 years.

For the purpose of our study, the rollback of labour achievements is the most interesting tendency. Its quantitative dimension is highlighted by the decline in unionisation, which went down from 33 per cent in 1954 to 19 per cent in 1985 (cf. Harrington, 1988). It has further become manifest in many instances where labour agreed upon a cut-down of wages and fringe benefits in order to support its beleaguered companies (cf. Kassalow, 1988). To be sure, the tendency of de-unionisation cannot be attributed exclusively, not even predominantly, to the manoeuvrings of enterprises who tried to enhance their competitiveness. The weakening of organised labour must be seen, first of all, as a consequence of changes in production technology and the structure of demand. These changes led to an absolute decrease in the number of full-time blue-collar jobs, the classical base of union membership, and to an increase of white-collar jobs of all kinds as well as various less-than-full-time jobs. Both categories of workers have traditionally been much less accessible to the unions.

But labour also faced a particularly strong and effective hostility from the side of employers since the 1970s. This corresponds to the breakdown of the post-war capital–labour accord of which we spoke in the preceding section. For business, the situation was characterised (a) by an increasing squeeze on profits, due to economic stagnation and to increasing foreign competition and (b) by the chance of cutting production costs by clamping down on labour. So, business tried to relief the profit squeeze by passing it on to the workers' income. It was a way of adjusting to the decline in comparative productivity and quality (cf. Bluestone & Harrison, 1982).

But by breaking up rigid industrial relations structures, by forcing labour into more flexible working patterns business also tried to tackle what it perceived as a major cause of the decline. The defence of profits at the expense of labour blended in with attempts at forming a more committed work force for the benefit of profits and workers' incomes alike. While on the one side benefits were cut for the sake of lower production cost, on the other side new forms of company-based welfare were devised as a means to increase workers' involvement with the enterprise.[30] To the degree the second tendency came to determine corporate policy *vis-à-vis* labour it often went hand in hand with reductions in the firm's personnel. Thus, it accentuated the trend towards a two-tier labour market, consisting of privileged segments which were granted something like 'corporate citizenship' and an increasing segment which was exposed to a relatively unregulated market with cut-throat competition.

TWO CASE STUDIES

Automobiles

Increasing International Competition

Chrysler Chairman Lee Iacocca called car making the biggest single industry the world has ever seen. In 1960 half of it was American. As one observer put it, the automobile industry has 'come to represent the hinge on the door of America's economy'. (Salter *et al.*, 1985, p. 185.) Towards the end of the 1970s it employed almost 5 per cent of the work force in the manufacturing sector. But by adding those branches which one way or the other depend on the production of motor vehicles one comes to figures as high as 20 per cent (Lawrence & Dyer, 1983, p. 18). Output and employment expanded, with cyclical interruptions, until 1978. Then, in what amounted to the industry's worst crisis since the 1930s, output plunged by 38 per cent and employment by 34 per cent. In the recuperation period after 1982 neither of the two indicators reached the peak values of 1973 and 1978 any more, even though profits soared. At the end of the 1980s the US motorcar industry is facing the prospect of increasing overcapacity and an ensuing shake-out among producers (cf. *Business Week*, 7 March 1988).

The key to the mounting difficulties which have beset American automobile makers since the mid-1970s is import competition. American motor vehicle companies have always pursued a strategy of producing within important foreign markets rather than exporting to them. So the only market that has ever really mattered for American-made cars is the American market itself. And it is of this market that the US car industry has continuously been losing shares until the beginning of the 1980s, when imports caught over 28 per cent (up from 7.5 per cent in 1965 and around 15 per cent in the first half of the 1970s).

In the following years a 'voluntary' export restraint agreement with the most important competitor country, Japan, brought a certain relief. The agreement ended in 1985. But Japan maintained, this time voluntarily indeed, informal export quotas in order to help diffuse mounting tensions over trade with the US. Instead, Japanese car makers began – partly in joint ventures with American companies – to supply the American market from new production facilities within the USA. In some sense, the 'Japanisation' seems to have immunised the American car industry against foreign competition, as the world's most efficient companies chose the USA as the location where to produce, giving jobs to American workers and paying taxes to the American fiscus. But 'Japanisation' has not been an unmixed blessing because so far the foreign producers have tended to import many more components than US firms used to, and they have kept key research and development functions in Japan, thus threatening to erode American engineering skills (cf. Reich & Mankin, 1986). On the other hand, US automobile firms also have increasingly resorted to imports from their foreign subsidiaries and foreign partner firms in order to be cost-competitive. Thus, the apparent stabilisation of American-made cars' market share has been masking a further advance of foreign value-added (cf. Dunn, 1987, p. 250).

The Causes of Declining Competitiveness

For a long time low wages were considered the chief advantage of foreign car makers, whereas productivity was supposed to be the American strength. But by about 1973 the productivity advantage of the US motor vehicle industry had become eroded and then turned into a rapidly growing disadvantage. In 1983 only a quarter of the Japanese cost advantage over American-made small cars was owed to lower wages. Almost two-thirds were accounted for by better management (cf. Salter *et al.*, 1985, p. 187). As far as quality is concerned, in the 1980s imports also scored better in general than American products (cf. Abernathy *et al.*, 1983, pp. 63ff.).

Why did the US automobile industry fall back so drastically behind foreign competitors in manufacturing efficiency and quality appeal? Ultimately, it is the fault of management which did not adjust in time to the new competitive reality. The Detroit companies were caught unprepared by the changes which went on in the automobile market: shifts in consumer tastes, the rise of efficient foreign industries, the emergence of new manufacturing methods which among other things de-emphasise the importance of scale (cf. Jones, 1985), and the renewed emphasis on technological innovation in the automobiles themselves to which Abernathy *et al.* (1983) refer to as 'de-maturity'. In a way, this was the typical inertia which easily besets those who have been very well-adjusted during a long time to a very different reality. For decades, American car makers had dominated as co-operative oligopolists a booming and effectively protected sellers market which provided them with premium profits and premium wages.[31]

One important factor of competitive decline was that right decisions were not taken in time. In particular, it proved a major strategic error of the American car makers that they neglected the small car, leaving an important market segment of the future voluntarily so to speak to their foreign competitors. When they found out that it required a tremendous and long-sustained effort to gear up factories and enterprise organisations to the cost-efficient production of a sort of car which was very different from the traditional Detroit concept they backed away and settled for the formula 'the small car market for the foreigners, the rest for Detroit'. And then, after the second oil price shock, when US demand shifted dramatically towards small cars, Detroit was further away than ever from a position to compete.[32]

But apart from strategic mistakes, it also proved extremely difficult for the American car companies to adjust, once the challenge had been clearly recognised and the determination to meet it had been established. There were objective reasons which made it easier for strategic planners in the Japanese automobile industry to succeed than for their counterparts in the USA. Such objective obstacles to competitiveness had to do (a) with the dynamics of strategic competition itself, which in several respects favour the advancing challenger *vis-à-vis* once dominant firms that are forced into a defensive stance;[33] (b) with the firms' organisation on the various levels of management; (c) with labour relations.

As far as management qualities are concerned, it became increasingly obvious that less efficient ways of combining work, capital, material and expertise were rooted in mental and behaviour patterns which in turn corresponded to and were continuously reinforced by specific organisational structures.[34] Moreover, it turned out that it takes a big effort to learn new routines and that profound change as such is a major source of temporary inefficiency (cf. Lawrence & Dyer, 1983, Ch. 2 and Abernathy *et al.*, 1983, part II). Thus, the very fact that the Japanese have developed clearly superior ways of management which were rather different from American corporate traditions put the US automobile companies at a serious disadvantage.

Organisational inertia also explains in part why efficiency in Japanese-owned automobile plants in America, staffed with American personnel, started out in general on a much higher level than in American-owned plants. In fact, the high competitiveness of Japanese cars made in USA underlines that the decline of the American automobile industry is owed much more to enterprise structures and management patterns than to economic parameters.

Much of the relative inefficiency of the US motor vehicle industry has been attributed to labour relations. In fact, the automobile workers had been the pace setters in establishing the post-war American system of industrial relations. And it is the automobile industry which exhibited most clearly the typical characteristics of this system (cf. Katz, 1985, Ch. 2). Its detailed job descriptions and highly formalised rules of promotion corresponded to the distinctively Tayloristic methods of management in the American car industry. The whole system was oriented towards a rather static notion of the production process, suited to the post-war syndrome of stable demand patterns, a slow pace of technical innovation, and restricted competition. But it proved very ill-adjusted to the new reality of highly fluctuating demand and strong pressure for efficiency gains, product innovations and quality (cf. Kochan & Piore, 1984). It did not provide for sufficient flexibility in the deployment of manpower nor for the necessary broad skills nor for the commitment which is essential for quality.

In addition to rigidity by design there was a dramatic decline in motivation from the end of the 1960s onwards. Absenteeism increased 50 per cent from 1965 to 1969, labour turn-over 72 per cent and disciplinary dismissals 44 per cent.[35] The 'Lordstown Syndrome', as the expression came up in reference to a series of incidents at a new General Motors assembly plant in 1972, has been attributed to several factors we dealt with above in section II.6. They have to do with changes in the workforce and in the terms of the so-called post-war labour truce.

In a way the most obvious competitive disadvantages of the American automobile industry were the high wages and non-wage labour costs, which were no longer founded on a productivity advantage. From a macroeconomic point of view, excessive dollar wages would indicate an overvalued American currency or a loss of *comparative* American advantage in car manufacturing (that means, at US wage levels other things should be produced). But there was an additional element: automobile workers received premium wages and fringe benefits not only in international comparison but also in comparison with other American industries.[36] This reflected the market power of the oligopolistic companies as well as the particular power of labour in this highly concentrated large-plant industry.

The Response of Management[37]

Detroit responded to the challenge of international competition in a defensive and an offensive way. On the one side, the car makers tried to pass on the costs of competitive decline to the workers, the consumers and the society in general by lobbying for import protection and for relief from regulatory burdens and by demanding pay restraint from their work forces. On the other side, they undertook efforts to catch up in productivity and quality. These efforts included investment strategies and corporate re-organisation. With regard to investment, efficiency-enhancing, largely labour-saving machinery was one aspect. Others were (a) alliances with foreign, predominantly Japanese, companies as a means to get access to state-of-the-art manufacturing expertise and (b) relocation of production to Latin America and East Asia in order to get access to cheap labour. The latter aspect was of direct significance for welfare statism in the United States. It had the immediate effect of eliminating well-paid jobs and diminishing labour's bargaining power in an industry where it had been particularly high ever since the end of the Second World War. Labour-shedding in the wake of outsourcing and automatisation pushed large numbers of workers out into a labour market which by and large offered sufficient jobs but at a considerably lower average remuneration than that in the car industry. This deterioration of market chances referred to cash pay as well as fringe benefits, which always have constituted an important part of US welfare statism (see pp. 85–6 below).

The other pillar of Detroit's efforts to regain competitiveness was corporate re-organisation. It was to create the basis for more efficient future production in the USA and was largely oriented at Japanese models. Rather than a comprehensive blueprint it followed mostly a trial-and-error type of procedure. The time needed for this process of catching up with the best practice in managing manufacturing processes has been estimated to last until the early 1990s or even longer (cf. Jones 1986). Most interesting for our purposes are the attempts to reform industrial relations, which also had priority for the American automobile companies.

The Reform of Industrial Relations

From the management point of view, labour relations in the American car industry needed to be overhauled in several respects. The work process itself and the skills of the personnel had to be adjusted to meet new criteria of efficiency, providing most of all for more flexibility. The commitment of the workforce needed a tremendous lift. On the other side, labour costs had to be kept down one way or another, most of all by slimming down the workforces, but as an immediate response to the profit squeeze after 1979 also by reducing the industry's traditional pay privileges. Cost cutting, of course, conflicted with the objective of creating a high-commitment work force, favouring a strategy of doing the labour-shedding first and the commitment-building afterwards.[38] Moreover, strong unions with their adversarial orientation towards management were perceived as a major obstacle on the way to lower labour costs. Therefore, the automobile companies also tried to reduce the influence of the unions while at the same time co-opting them into more co-operative relations.

Thus, reshaping labour relations always meant both, altering the balance of power between adversaries and emphasising the communality of interests between partners. The ideal solution for management was to make success with regard to the first goal the basis for achieving the second at optimal terms. But it risked the first pursuit spoiling the second one. In the American car industry, in particular, the existing power situation made it mandatory to seek reform primarily with and not against the unions, even though they were very much part of the old rigid and costly system.[39]

In the early 1970s, triggered off by the Lordstown disturbances, General Motors started its 'Quality of Work Life' (QWL) programme, which aimed at improving the communication between workers and higher-level personnel, at introducing elements of team work, at getting the single worker involved in the larger manufacturing process to which he contributes, and, thus, at increasing his motivation to do a good job. Ford soon followed suit with a similar 'Employees Involvement Program' while the third of the three large car makers, Chrysler, came out with a somewhat more modest reform programme. All three companies restricted their reforms to part of their plants, varying between them the kind and the degree of the changes which were introduced. Some programmes were conducted as experiments and terminated after several years. In general, the changes 'remained a supplement to and not a fundamental alteration in shop-floor labour relations' (Katz, 1985, p. 77). But at General Motors' new Saturn division, for instance, a completely different labour relations system, uncontaminated so to speak by the traditional pattern, was set up. The same is true for the new Japanese-managed plants at Marysville, Ohio; Smyrna, Tennessee; and Flatrock, Michigan.

As it turned out, at the traditional American factories the results of QWL and the like were ambiguous. Some plants could report a clear success. But there was also resistance because the new work patterns threatened established privileges of craft workers and supervisors, were in a way more demanding than the old standardised jobs, and conflicted with the role and the self-understanding of the unions as negotiators on behalf of the workers' interests *vis-à-vis* the employers' demands.[40] In the view of many union militants the reforms were the means by the management of extracting more effort from the employees and get their consent for cost-cutting measures – as a way to outflank the unions.[41] Altogether, after several years of QWL programmes at General Motors no close relationship could be found between such programmes and the quality of industrial relations as measured by grievances, disciplinary actions, absenteeism, employees' attitudes etc. (Katz, 1985, Ch. 5 and Katz *et al.*, 1983).

Re-organisation of labour relations on the plant level was superseded by changes which took place on the level of collective bargaining. Here the ambiguity of power struggle and consensus-seeking became most obvious. On the other hand, the companies sought to strike a new kind of deal with the unions which would be more in line with the competitive needs of the industry. Parallel to that they tried to gain more freedom for imposing unilaterally work and pay conditions. General Motors, for instance, through outsourcing had withdrawn by 1985 more than 60 per cent of its vehicle component production from the control of the United Automobile Workers' (UAW) union.[42] Moreover, the rising newcomers in the US automobile industry, the Japanese companies, set up non-unionised plants. Even though UAW fought successfully for representation at some of them afterwards, remuneration, including fringe benefits, has so far been considerably lower than at the US-based companies. Employment levels were also lower due to more labour-saving manufacturing methods (cf. Wood, 1986, pp. 433ff.). The creation of a significant non-unionised sector within the industry provided an important bargaining chip for management: labour would now comply more readily in order to keep jobs in the unionised sector.

In the unionised mainstream plants significant transformations occurred in the early 1980s when the motor vehicle industry was confronted with a big slump in demand and a corresponding decline in profits. The unions agreed on pay and fringe benefits concessions without precedent in the post-war period. In return, labour got profit shares, some participation in management affairs as well as certain employment and income securities. Part of the deals was also more job flexibility within the plants and even within the entire enterprises as a precondition for maintaining employment levels (cf. Katz, 1985, Ch. 3). The new types of contracts were negotiated first in 1979 at the near-bankrupt Chrysler Corporation and since 1982 repeatedly at General Motors and Ford. They did not reduce the income of the employed workers very much: concessions consisted mainly in deferred wage increases and cost-of-living adjustments. Nor did they prevent massive lay-offs due to stagnating sales, productivity gains and increased outsourcing. At Ford, for example, the workforce was reduced from 190 000 in the late 1970s to 107 000 in 1987.

However, the new contracts signalled a profound change in labour's position within American capitalism – in an industry which was paradigmatic for post-war industrial relations in the USA. On the one hand, labour's bargaining power deteriorated considerably under the pressure of adverse market conditions. Besides being able to resort increasingly to non-unionised labour market segments, management could impose relatively unfavourable conditions on labour. On the other hand, the market principle itself (hiring hands at an agreed upon price) became less dominant. Employees became more 'incorporated' into their enterprises, got more 'membership' rights, but also more responsibilities. Instead of highly specified job security, the workforce had to accept more general employment security (or income security if supplementary unemployment benefits are taken into account). So far, this has been, of course, only a matter of degrees but the movement into the new direction was a significant one. And despite the unions' attempts to go back after the crisis of 1981–1982 to the old collective bargaining pattern, it went another big step further in the 1987 contract between Ford and the UAW.

Telecommunications Equipment

The production of telecommunications equipment has been one of the growth industries of the past decade, worldwide and in the United States. It is also regarded as one of the important high-technology industries of the future. According to one estimate, the world market had a size of 47 billion dollars in 1982 and will have one of 103 billion dollars in 1992 (both 1979 prices). Of this total, a good 40 per cent is and will be the US market (*Financial Times*, 6 January 1986).

US manufacturers are generally considered as leading in international competition. Their strength is based on superior product technology, which, in turn, is the result of high, timely and strategically well allocated investment in research and development. In 1983, 38 per cent of all telecommunications equipment sold was American (Mackenzie & Hesselman, 1984). In 1985 telecommunications equipment accounted for about 2 per cent of US merchandise exports. Nevertheless, the trade balance in this industry became negative in 1983, with the deficit rising steadily to 1.4 billion dollars in 1986 (Barry, 1987, pp. 5f.). Today, the US sees its position in world telecommunications challenged on various grounds.

The salient issue is foreign protectionism, which largely bars US access to the lucrative Japanese and European markets while the American home market is open to everybody. Thus, the underlying competitive strength of US producers does not lead to corresponding market shares and trade figures. The issue of market access for telecommunications equipment is embedded in the issue of national regulation of telecommunication services. The USA liberalised their market for telecommunication services from the 1970s onwards in several steps, doing away with the former *de facto* monopoly of AT&T and, thus, opening up the traditional domestic equipment market which used to be the fairly undisturbed domain of Western Electric, AT&T's manufacturing subsidiary. The newly independent regional service suppliers (the regional Bell Operating Companies) even proved especially eager to diversify their equipment purchases. On the other hand, AT&T opened up new sales outlets abroad.

At the same time, the development of electronics technology revolutionised telecommunications, changing the techniques of traditional voice transmission (digitalisation, fibre optics, satellite transmission) and creating a broad range of new ways to communicate (mobile phones, private networks, transmission of computer-readable data, video transmission). Thus, completely new markets with new types of customers – private companies outside of telecommunications – emerged and expanded rapidly. Western Electric (now AT&T Technologies) was not any better prepared for these developments than other domestic and foreign companies who could build on cheap access to the earlier technological breakthroughs of AT&T's Bell Laboratories. It was a situation which favoured companies with a high capacity for strategic market targeting. The high dollar at the time can be seen as an additional advantage for foreign producers, even though production costs matter less in this branch than the costs of product development.

Outside of the US, most industrialised countries with attractive markets kept large parts of telecommunication services under the control of public telephone companies, which use their monopsonic buying power to favour national equipment suppliers. If there were competition in the service area, so the argument goes, the service providers would be forced to shop for the most competitive equipment – to the advantage of the technologically superior US manufacturers.

But it is not only that foreign regulation prevents US companies from reaping the fruits of their competitiveness. Also American competitiveness itself is said to be put in danger. This is because the high speed of technological change has made R&D efforts mandatory which cost much more than in former times. In order to recuperate the tremendous additional outlays large sales volumes have become more and more essential. In 1986 (1 December) the *Financial Times* wrote: 'Winning orders in other peoples' backyards is a condition of survival.' From the American point of view, asymmetric deregulation has led to a situation where foreign companies with their half-way secure home market and their free access to the important US market enjoy a strategic advantage which is denied to the American firms. Again, it is the Japanese who are considered most liable to exploit this advantage, whereas the Europeans are perceived as handicapped by their relatively small, fragmented markets (cf. Mackenzie & Hesselman, 1984; and Barry, 1987).

Asymmetric market access has been the precondition of a negative American trade balance in telecommunications equipment and is maybe a long-term strategic advantage of Japanese firms. But the import surge in the wake of US deregulation also indicates that foreigners do already have some competitive advantages – even *vis-à-vis* the generally assumed technological superiority of American-made equipment. In part, this just reflects a 'normal' dispersion of strengths and weaknesses among firms in a highly diversified industry with many specialty niches. Technological advances are not just confined to the US. But there also seem to be two points of general American vulnerability. One is that which proved so decisive in the car industry: Japanese firms have a superior way of organising development, manufacturing and marketing in areas where the product technology itself would not provide for a 'leading edge'. As they have shown over and over in industries where the real technological breakthroughs have been achieved elsewhere, they also started to become formidable competitors in some telecommunications equipment markets.[43] And fears in the USA are that they use their thus established position as basis for the advance into technological leadership.

The other point of American vulnerability is low-cost production in East Asian NICs. It is not so much a challenge to US firms as to the USA as a location where equipment is being produced. Low-technology items such as ordinary telephone sets have been increasingly imported from East Asia where they are produced by or for American companies. In the beginning of the 1980s, for example AT&T transferred its telephone production from Shreveport, Louisiana, to Singapore. The Shreveport plant was closed.[44]

In industrial circles, the question how to secure the competitiveness of the American telecommunications equipment industry for the future is being cast entirely in strategic terms. The task is to manage the fast-moving product cycle so as to be ahead of the competitors in the highly profitable first phase and to achieve sufficient scale in the phases of beginning maturity. To master the basic technological innovations in time is considered as essential. This, in turn, is a function of the companies' own R&D expenditure as well as of their negotiated access to the proprietory knowledge of others. The ability to maintain a high level of investment in R&D depends on a steady flow of sufficient profits, but also on government funding.

Yet there has not been much claim on the part of the American telecommunications industry that this funding is insufficient. A minor point being made is that large-scale military R&D has a crowding-out effect on expert personnel. By far the most pressing demand on the government has been to use its trade policy in order to open up foreign markets (cf. for example the Hearing on Telecommunications Trade, US Congress, 1985b). It is also in this field that the government has mostly become active, though with limited success.

Meanwhile the companies adjusted to the new competitive 'game' by forging transnational inter-firm alliances which spread the burden of R&D, broadened the market access, the secured additional government funds (cf. Schulze, 1987). Setting new organisational fundaments for productivity and quality, as it was the case in the automobile industry, has never been part of the agenda. The same holds for the reduction of labour costs in manufacturing. Still, the firms took advantage of cost-cutting opportunities where they presented themselves. And the American labour market was an important source of such opportunities in the 1980s. Thus, in large parts of the industry the wage regime became quite restrictive because throughout the economy the price of labour had gone down and because the access to cheap foreign labour had improved. The companies used the threat of competition to oppose labour demands for higher remuneration. However, it was not the competition of foreign producers of telecommunications equipment but the one of American and foreign workers who offered their services at a lower price.

THE DEVELOPMENT OF WELFARE STATISM

Transfers[45]

The development of the welfare state in the USA began in the 1930s with the New Deal policy of President Roosevelt.[46] Its base was laid with the Social Security Act of 1935 which established an insurance system for old-age income (social security proper), an insurance for unemployment compensation and various programmes of assistance on a means-tested basis ('welfare' in the meaning of everyday language). The following New Deal years witnessed a strong expansion of the new welfare state. The second expansionary wave came in the 1960s with President Johnson's Great Society programme. It extended into the mid-1970s. During this period total federal spending for welfare statism doubled as a share of Gross National Product to about 10 per cent. Of this 10 per cent, 7 per cent went into programmes of social insurance, with social security being the most important, followed by the Medicare health insurance and by unemployment compensation. Assistance to low-income and disadvantaged population segments absorbed another 2 per cent. The remaining 1 per cent was accounted for by various social services to specific target groups. This last kind of welfare state programmes proliferated during the 'Great Society' years. They also experienced the fastest growth. Most of them were meant to help create equal opportunities for otherwise disadvantaged people. Civil rights considerations played an important role.

The Great Society project did not only bring an expansion of welfare state outlays. It also led to a certain mutation of the original idea of the social safety net. Government transfers became an important source of permanent income for increasing segments of the population, including the elderly, many of whom came to live predominantly or exclusively on social security. With an increasing liberalisation of eligibility criteria the benefits of the welfare state were more and more enjoyed by middle-income sectors as well. The idea gained ground that it is the responsibility of the society and its central agency, the state, to see to it that all its members can have some sort of a decent living.[47] However, there were always very large differences in welfare state benefits between the various states of the USA, as the system was organised along federal lines.

Under the impact of the economic crisis in general and the income squeeze on taxpayers in particular, the US Congress began to put a break on the further expansion of the welfare state under the Carter administration. Then, with President Reagan, one could say that anti-welfare statism came to power. He 'shifted the national social policy agenda from problem solving to budget cutting' (Bawden & Palmer, 1984, p. 214). Moreover, it was Reagan's explicit intention and part of his election campaign to reinforce again the principle of individual responsibility and to reduce public responsibility for people's well-being. During his first term in office he proposed welfare state cuts which would have reduced total expenditure by 17 per cent as compared with the amount required with unchanged pre-Reagan programmes. The savings would have amounted to 2 per cent of GNP. Because of congressional opposition to his saving proposals, particularly after 1982, the actual reduction achieved was just above half the proposed one.

But it was very unevenly distributed. The plethora of programmes for education, training, health, and employment, which had proliferated in the 1960s and 1970s, but which all together absorbed only about 5 per cent of the social spending budget, was cut down most drastically, that is to say by 42 per cent. Social security, which constitutes by far the largest welfare state programme, was reduced by only 4.6 per cent. The second largest item, the Medicare health insurance, also suffered with 6.8 per cent reduction less than average losses. Unemployment insurance, however, which is the third largest item, was trimmed by 17 per cent. Also the coverage quota went down from about two-thirds of the unemployed population in the mid-1970s to about one-third in 1985 (Center on Budget and Policy Priorities, 1987b). The programmes which lost most were employment and training (67 per cent), student loans (39 per cent), grants for community services (37 per cent), the work incentive programme (35 per cent) and the health services outside of the Medicare and Medicaid schemes (33 per cent).[48]

Occupational Welfare

Simultaneously with the creation and subsequent extension of state-administered income-maintenance and support schemes, welfare entitlements connected in one way or another with the employer–employee relation experienced a dramatic increase. The legal basis was the Wagner Act of 1935, which consolidated the rights of organised labour and which established among other things some protection against arbitrary dismissal. The Fair Labor Standards Act of 1938 set a minimum wage, made premium payment for over-time mandatory and limited child labour. Later on, the Great Society project gave a new impetus to the broadening of workers' legal rights *vis-à-vis* their employers: the pertinent laws are the Civil Rights Act of 1964, the Occupational Safety and Health Act of 1970 and the Employee Retirement Income Security Act of 1974.

Probably more significant for the majority of American workers were, however, the welfare arrangements which were made with the employers as a result of labour's enhanced bargaining power and which were heavily supported by federal tax policies. Supplementary social security and health insurance schemes are the most important of them. The so-called fringe benefits, which became increasingly part of a 'good' job, grew into a very significant element of the material well-being and economic security of the average permanently employed worker. Bargained benefits came to some degree to be considered an American substitute of legislated entitlements as they are known in the typical European welfare state.

In part, the rise of occupational welfare can be seen as a consequence of the stagnation of welfare state developments on a still rather rudimentary level after the Second World War (cf. Seidman, 1976). On the other hand, it probably contributed to this stagnation by providing for large parts of the population an accepted substitute.

Later on, the extension of the American welfare state proper built on the highly developed system of occupational welfare and, accordingly, acquired a strong bias towards poverty relief rather than the guarantee of basic economic 'citizen rights'.[49]

But the access to bargained benefits depends on the individual's position in the labour market. Only those who happen to have a good job enjoy them. Therefore, occupational welfare proved particularly vulnerable to changes in the structure of the labour market. The decrease of classical, union-influenced blue-collar jobs in the USA and the concomitant increase in low-quality and/or largely union-free jobs in the services sector and new industrial branches led practically to an automatic decline in occupational welfare. This decline affected an increasing part of the working population. Alone in 1982 11 million workers lost their health insurance because they lost their job (Root, 1985, p. 115). Simultaneously, a significant segment of the labour force found new well-remunerated jobs with generous fringe benefits. Thus, there has been a marked polarisation of American society since the 1970s with regard to welfare benefits.[50] Among other things this increased the part of the population which was in need of legislated welfare statism.

Much less pronounced than this indirect effect has been the direct dismantling of occupational welfare via negotiated concessions by labour. Nevertheless, the weakened bargaining position of the unions and the cost-cutting drive of business affected fringe benefits, too (cf. Kassalow, 1984, p. 60). But the whole wave of concession bargaining of the 1980s in many instances also involved an additional bit of occupational welfare: more job security and hence more income security.

Income Through Work

The high relative importance of occupational welfare is a peculiarity of the United States. But as in all highly industrialised countries, welfare statism hinges in a more general meaning on the functioning of the labour market. The effectiveness of the post-war Western welfare state has been based on the condition that, except for small marginal segments, every able-bodied head of household has a chance to earn a wage income in tune with the country's overall prosperity. In the US the segment which was by-passed by the mainstream of employment opportunities has – for various reasons – always been rather large and became in the 1960s the focus of the 'War on Poverty'. Much of today's welfare state debate in the US still centres on the merits and failures of the various policies geared towards those hard-to-employ.[51] Still, securing for them a viable access to the mainstream labout market could be considered as the core of the problem. For, it was 'decent-wage' jobs which provided the essential ingredient to the post-war American welfare society.

But since the mid-1970s an increasing part of the American labour force could no longer get a 'decent' income out of work. Economically, this resulted from a combination of sluggish growth and structural change. Due to declining demand, foreign competition and labour-saving innovations, many well-paying jobs got lost in branches like steel, automobiles and machine tools and were not recuperated in the upswing after 1982. The expanding industries in high-technology manufacturing and the services sector did not offer equally many new 'good' jobs.[52] They provided an employment chance to those left out of the better segments of the labour market and helped to bring official unemployment down to rather satisfactory levels after the recession.[53] In well over half of the eight million new jobs which emerged between 1979 and 1984, annual wages lay below the official poverty level.[54] A large part of these jobs emerged precisely because people were willing to work at low pay, that is, because wages proved flexible in the downward direction when labour supply was abundant. The most likely alternative would have been large-scale, long-term unemployment European style (cf. Thurow, 1984).

Downward wage flexibility was possible because the unions had much less control over the labour market than in most Western European countries and because lower levels of income-maintaining transfers left many American job-seekers with no alternatives but accepting the pay which was offered. Also, the officially imposed minimum wage declined by 25 per cent in the first half of the 1980s (cf. Shapiro, 1987). But it was not only that new low-wage jobs absorbed the otherwise unemployed according to the principle 'low pay is better than no pay'. The lack of organisational labour power in many of the new growth industries also had the effect that wages in these industries adjusted to the situation of relative labour abundance. Maybe, more jobs were created that way than otherwise. But many workers just received a lower income than they would have with more organisational power on their side. The beneficiaries were not only their employers but also those employed in the high-wage sectors of the economy who could take advantage of the cheap goods and services provided by the low-wage sector.

Whereas in the long growth period of the 1950s and 1960s the labour market had served as a vehicle of lifting people from poverty above a generally acceptable minimum standard of material well-being, this effect was reversed in the past decade. The labour market delegated an increasing minority of wage-dependent people actually back to poverty or close-to-poverty levels. Of 65 million households which had a member in the employable labour force in 1984 (that is, discounting the disabled or those otherwise impeded from entering the job market) 17 million received a wage income insufficient to keep a family of four above the poverty level. Of them six million were actually poor. On the other hand, almost half of the poor households had in 1983 members in the employable labour force. In 1967 only 37 per cent of poor households belonged to this group (Danziger & Gottschalk in US Congress, 1986a). In fact, the lack of sufficient adequately remunerated jobs has become a major deficiency of the overall welfare system in the United States.[55]

The Changing Effectiveness of Welfare State Arrangements

In the early 1960s more than one-fifth of the American population was officially considered as poor. In the 1970s the percentage had gone down to below 12 per cent, even though the unemployment rate was on the average somewhat higher. The strong decline in poverty can largely be accounted for by the tremendous expansion of the welfare state. Measured in constant 1972 dollars, public transfer payments in cash and kind rose from an average of 765 dollars per household in the first three years of the 1960s to 1934 dollars in the last three years of the 1970s – an increase of 150 per cent. Had it not been for the welfare state, poverty would not have declined since 1965, the first year for which comparative information is available. The official rate would have been at around 20 per cent by the end of the 1970s and slightly less at the end of the 1960s, when unemployment was exceptionally low.[56] But in 1965 welfare state arrangements lifted less than 20 per cent of those who did not have a sufficient income out of work or wealth above the poverty line. In the late 1970s, it was about 45 per cent which were saved from poverty by transfers. Under President Reagan, both the pre-transfer and the post-transfer poverty rates went up, the first one reflecting basically the worsening employment situation, the second one the lack of transfers to keep track with the increasing need. The whole development is summarised in Figure 3.6.

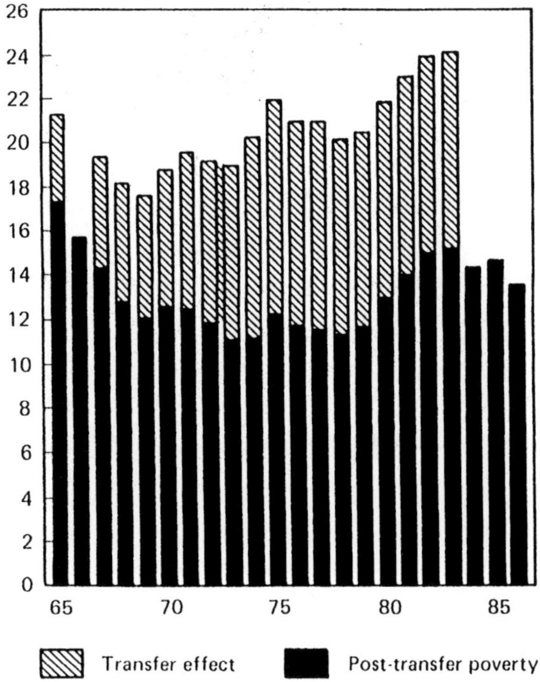

Sources: Gottschalk in US Congress, 1985a, p. 72; Center on Budget and Policy Priorities, 1987a, p. 1.

Figure 3.6 Percentage of the American population that would have been officially poor without transfers and that actually was poor, 1965–86

Until 1983, overall transfers practically stagnated in real terms at the level they had reached at the end of the 1970s, so that their effectiveness in rescuing people from poverty diminished to 38 per cent. But some of the population groups with insufficient pre-transfer income were hit considerably harder while others could improve their situation. An increasing share of public transfers was absorbed by the aged. In fact, the drastic reduction of old-age poverty, which had been so widespread in former times, probably constitutes the greatest single achievement of American welfare statism. Since the corresponding entitlements were left basically untouched by the Reagan administration's spending cuts the sum of transfers accruing to them rose with the increasing number of retirees and the mounting health-care costs covered under the Medicare insurance scheme.

With the help of the Reagan tax cuts and the slower inflation the poorest fifth of elderly families even experienced a rise in real income of 6 per cent between 1980 and 1984 (Moon & Sawhill, 1984, pp. 334ff.).

On the other hand, non-elderly families with children suffered not only from deteriorating chances in the labour market but also from the reduction of federal low-income assistance programmes. In 1979 such programmes were sufficient to diminish the poverty rate within this population segment by 37 per cent. By 1984 the figure had gone down to 18 per cent (Greenstein in US Congress 1986b, p. 36). In other words, the number of poor families with children would have increased by only about one-fifth had there been no welfare state at all.

Indeed, the twin effects of the deterioration in the lower brackets of the labour market and the lower tier of the welfare state (assistance rather than insurance) proved particularly devastating where they combined with the burden of child-rearing. The family as the primary solidarity group was strained most heavily as the broader societal ties of economic solidarity loosened. Unrelated individuals could, in general, adjust much better. If we look at the poorest 20 per cent of various population segments and disregard the elderly, who fared best on all accounts, we see that the real income of unrelated persons stayed about the same between 1980 and 1984. The 'classical' one-earner husband-wife family, however, was ten per cent worse off in 1984 than in 1980. Where there were two earners, the deterioration amounted to seven per cent. Families headed by single mothers lost 12 per cent (Moon & Sawhill, 1984, pp. 322f., cf. also Danziger & Gottschalk, 1986). The disproportionate burden of economic hardship is also reflected by the proportion of children under 18 years living in poverty. In 1986 the figure was 22 per cent (up from 14 per cent in the early 1970s) as compared with 14.4 per cent for adults.

In the 1960s, the so-called 'War on Poverty', which brought the tremendous proliferation of targeted assistance programmes, had focused on those still sizeable segments of the population which for specific reasons were separated from the earning opportunities of the booming market. The poor were basically the 'underclass' of socially handicapped, tied up in a subculture of poverty. This syndrome has not disappeared. Today, the culture of poverty is, if anything, more visible than ever.[57] But a different element has gained importance. Poverty affects – one could say: again – many Americans in the cultural mainstream, and those who want to live a traditional-style family life more than those who have individualised their life (cf. Gottschalk & Danziger in US Congress, 1986b and Gallaway & Vedder, 1986). This new phenomenon, which might be considered a natural corollary of large-scale unemployment, has not disappeared with the economic upswing of the mid-1980s. It turned out to be less the symptom of recession than of the new market structures. It also reflects a particular ineffectiveness of the American welfare state system: apart from its social insurance elements, this system was always designed to fix – within limits – the undesirable income results of the market, but not to protect in advance the essentials of people's livelihood against the potentially disastrous effects of market adversity. It left people in the first place fully exposed to the market. When market chances deteriorated considerably for a significant part of the population, the poverty effect was, therefore, rather pervasive. The victims were subjected for the fulfilment of all their material needs to the poverty relief schemes with their relatively meagre resources and their humiliating procedures (cf. Kahn & Kamerman 1983).

THE COMPETITIVENESS ISSUE AND THE DEVELOPMENT OF WELFARE STATISM

In our analysis we have traced various evolutionary processes in the American political economy:

1. Changes in economic relations with the rest of the world made the country's competitiveness a national priority issue.
2. The development of welfare statism came to a standstill and was – under increasing political pressure – eventually subjected to a certain setback.
3. There evolved an increasing lower tier of the labour market, which does not offer income chances in tune with the country's overall prosperity and which does not provide the sort of social security arrangements which had become standard for America's wage-dependent population.

As far as welfare is concerned, the last mentioned process is the more significant one. The core welfare state institutions remained intact (despite the quite severe cuts in some poverty-relief programmes), but the economic structures to which they were adjusted and on which their effectiveness was founded have changed (cf. Thurow, 1987b, p. 32f.). It is the non-adjustment of the institutions to the emerging new economic structure that is most responsible for the new spread of poverty and living conditions close to poverty. Even though the 'War on Poverty' was far from being won and significant segments of the population were still excluded from mainstream prosperity by the end of the 1970s, there was a public feeling throughout the post-war time that the underprivileged groups should and eventually would be integrated into the 'affluent American society'. The basic change that became clearly visible in the 1980s is not just the increase in the incidence of poverty but the transformation of the principal former mechanism of socio-economic integration, the labour market, into one of selective deprivation. The perspective of affluence for all, which had been an essential part of the American welfare society, has largely vanished. Sure, the long economic boom of the 1980s improved again for many the chances in the labour market. In some occupations and some locations labour became a scarce commodity again. But the life perspectives of those in the lower tier of the labour market stayed highly vulnerable to an economic down-turn. Their participation in the nation's overall prosperity is by no means secured. The threat of renewed poverty remains a very real one for many. And, in contrast with former decades, the chance to get stuck with low-paid, low-skill work is also relatively big for so-called heads of more-person households.[58]

It was changes in the economy which undermined the old structure of the labour market and its effectiveness in providing general welfare. These changes also gave rise to the new emphasis which was laid on competitiveness in the public debate, and they contributed to the rise of an economic philosophy with a strong anti-welfare state bias. Increasing foreign competition is an important element in the overall syndrome of economic changes. It put many American enterprises under pressure and induced them to emphasise cost-cutting in their relations with labour. Rapidly increasing foreign shares in some of the most important consumer-goods markets took the sense out of the old equation that high wages mean high demand and hence high turn-over, the basis of high profits. Thus, the fundament of the old accord between labour and business was shattered. As reductions in pay and fringe benefits became a priority matter for many companies they also developed an increasing interest in actively weakening labour's bargaining power.

Moreover, foreign competition was a major immediate force

behind that structural change in the US economy that led to the decline of several industries in the high-wage, highly unionised tradables sector, while low-skill, low-paying occupations, especially in the non-tradables sector, expanded. Thus, foreign competition helped to undo the economic structure on which the specific American welfare system was based. Of course, had it not been for the peculiar Reaganomics mix of monetary discipline and fiscal expansion in the context of low private savings, US tradables production would not have been crowded out by the high dollar. And demand for non-tradables would not have risen so much, because a larger share of people's purchasing power would have been absorbed by relatively expensive tradables. Thus, with a more conventional economic policy, the structural effect of temporary de-industrialisation would have been less marked. On the other hand, economic recuperation after the crisis of 1980–1982 would probably also have been slower, thus increasing the poverty toll of recession.

But economics alone cannot explain the emergence of the new 'two-tier society', if we adopt this term as an admittedly sloppy and undifferentiated short-hand characterisation of the above described trends in US welfare statism. The large-scale emergence of low-wage and no-fringe-benefits jobs was only possible because labour did not have sufficient power to bargain for 'good' jobs in the new growth branches and to prevent the employment of under-paid workers. This is primarily a consequence of the insufficient presence of unions throughout the economy. The strength of organised labour in the post-war US economy was tied to a certain distribution of production among branches and among geographic regions. The departure from this distribution under the impact of economic forces put an increasing part of business beyond the reach of the existing unions and left the workers in increasing segments of the labour market alone with their relatively low scarcity value. It was, therefore, in the context of a specific power structure that economic change pushed the US into the direction of a 'two-tier society'.

But what would have been the alternative? The flexibility of the American labour market has often been presented as a distinctively positive factor which facilitated, despite sluggish growth, the net expansion of jobs and a relatively low rate of unemployment as compared with the European average. Therefore, greater union strength might have kept a check on the development of the two-tier labour market, but that might have been very well at the expense of significantly higher unemployment. The distinction between holders and non-holders of jobs would have gained importance. To prevent either version of a two-tier society in spite of the economic changes, a more far-reaching adjustment of the whole system of welfare statism with all its dimensions would have been and would still be called for.

Organised labour was a pillar of the old system, which in its ideal form can be characterised as high-wage full employment cum supplementary welfare state security. The welfare state proper was constructed so as to rest on this pillar. Why is the system not being reconstructed now that the pillar and the structure built on it are crumbling? Why did and does the American society, which one generation before had waged a 'War on Poverty', allow that sizeable parts of the population are excluded from participation in the nation's overall prosperity? Under the perspective of this question, the labour movement is just a mechanism – abstractly speaking – for society to respond to the challenge of poverty, injustice etc. Why is there no welfare movement to respond to the challenge posed by the economic changes of the past 15 years or so?

It seems safe to speculate on the presence of some social inertia which keeps institutions from adjusting right away to changes in their environment. Taking into account the rather unlinear development of American welfare statism over several decades, one might be inclined to attribute the full weight of explanation to the inertia factor. But our observations point to more than just a naturally lagging response of welfare state adjustments to the new realities. In this context it is of importance that the dominant public perception in the past decade was not that of a deficit in welfare statism but, on the contrary, that of excessive welfare statism. In the 1980s, the main question raised in the public debate was no longer: shouldn't we do more to integrate the under-privileged into our affluent society?, as was the case in the 1960s. The dominant question was: haven't we already done more than the economy can afford?

Of course, there are those who have an interest in raising the latter question and having it answered in the affirmative. They include business as well as large parts of the middle class (the political backlash phenomenon, cf. Wilensky, 1976 and 1982). But the point here is that the performance of the economy had become very much less than satisfactory and the diagnosis had become more and more convincing that the decisive weaknesses are on the supply-side, that is having to do with the entrepreneurial response to market opportunities and challenges. The force of uncontrolled and not very well understood economic events had changed the focus of public attention.

Moreover, for all the controversial nature of the issues which were brought up, some ideas became almost generally accepted. One of them is that the overall volume of government expenditure was on the debit rather than the asset side of the country's balance sheet of supply-side conditions. This referred to the role of the government deficits in the inflation which had become endemic in the 1970s. And it referred to the disincentive effects of excessive taxation, especially if it was used to finance consumptive rather than investive expenditure. Even most of those who would not subscribe to the Laffer-curve theory considered a further programmatic expansion of the budget undesirable by the end of the 1970s. And also the supporters of the welfare state recognised that the rise of government expenditure had to be contained somehow. Later, of course, under the impact of the Reagan administration's fiscal policies, the budget deficit became eventually the central concern of US economic policy.

The erosion of certain benefits in real terms under President Carter and the drastic cuts in some assistance programmes under President Reagan were welfare state casualties in the battle for the economy. But the decisive – though not the most visible – casualty was the presence of welfare statism on the national agenda. Politically meaningful discussion on how to ensure national solidarity in face of the new economic reality was blocked by other priorities. This should also be seen as an important factor in the political weakness of those – including the labour unions – who defend the interests of the underprivileged. The economic malaise has stripped both the 1960s approach to welfare statism ('how to share the general affluence?') and the cause of labour in its traditional form of their political appeal. Neither one could attract supporters and allies in a situation in which the country's needs were generally regarded as different. In fact, the labour movement faced an increasingly unfavourable public mood – not to speak of an outrightly hostile government – because it was associated in the public perception with the economic weakness of the country.[59]

That welfare statism was pushed off the national agenda and in a subtle way discredited while at the same time the economic changes continued undermining it, this is the full effect of the factor 'economy' on the recent development of welfare statism in the USA. Again, foreign competition must be seen as an important factor. Not only that it put pressure on the US economy, declining competitiveness was also understood more and more as a central aspect of the country's problems. The priority of economic recuperation, which kept welfare statism off the agenda, meant more and more explicitly also the priority of competitiveness.

It should be noted that apart from the indirect connection between increasing concern about the country's competitiveness and the erosion of welfare statism, not much pressure can be discovered on 'uncompetitive' welfare state features. The charge that it is too costly played a certain role as part of the budget deficit issue, but not in the direct sense of making US production too expensive. In fact, the production cost issue was dominated by the exchange rate issue on the one hand and the productivity issue on the other. Competitiveness was always understood as the ability of American producers to earn a *high* income, including *high* wages and fringe benefits in the international market place. Besides, wages and non-wage labour costs did go down as a consequence of competitive pressure. In this respect, the US system did show a remarkable flexibility.

In other respects, the competitiveness debate pointed rather at deficits than excesses of welfare statism. This refers to the whole area of the formation of human capital and to the area of employee motivation. In fact, the increased urgency of international competitiveness could call for a new contract between labour and business, reconciling labour's income, security and self-fulfilment interests with business' interests in a competent, devoted and flexibly employable workforce. But, of course, in the prevailing ideological context such reforms were never considered on the more general level of labour's integration into the national system of production. Suggestions as how to reshape this system were thus far left to the radical academic scene, where they were insulated from the politically relevant debate.[60] Also the mainstream debate on welfare state reform, which reflected the experience of the 1980s' new poverty, has not picked up the fundamental theme of 'economic citizenship', but has with all its sophisticated new insights largely stuck to the traditional technocratic target group approach (cf. Center for National Policy, 1987).

However, on the level of enterprises, as we have shown, determined attempts were made to integrate labour well beyond the traditional notion of the contractual relationship between those who sell labour services and those who buy them. Whether this indicates the general direction US industrial relations will take in the future is far from certain, as an equally observable renewed emphasis on control should caution (cf. Mahon, 1987). However, even if the general trend were towards more integration of a segment of the labour force on the corporate level (towards more 'corporate citizenship' so to speak) this could well go hand in hand with a deepening rift between insiders (those who get good jobs) and outsiders. In other words, even if the requirements of competitiveness re-activated the interest in certain aspects of welfare statism, the essence of the welfare state idea – which is some sort of nation-wide 'economic citizenship' – would still be hollowed out.

Asking under which conditions 'economic citizenship' could have been safeguarded and further promoted in view of the country's economic difficulties, we have to turn again to questions of power and ideology. The system of national solidarity which had evolved since the 1930s has perhaps turned too much into a matter of economic pragmatism and convenience and stayed too little one of fundamental values and inalienable rights. This way, in times of economic adversity it was largely abandoned rather than adjusted. In a society which is shaped by the industrial mode of production the labour movement appears as the natural promoter of nation-wide economic solidarity. Therefore, the lack of firm entrenchment of this value in the country's political culture probably has to do with the history of American capital-labour relations. Maybe the decisive point is not the absence of labour unions in important sectors of the economy but the failure of the labour movement to go beyond the stage of particularistic interest organisation and to develop a strong political presence with a model idea for society as a whole.[61] The sort of social contract which would establish in a weatherproof way, so to speak, the principle of nation-wide 'economic citizenship' can only be imagined on a political level and with the backing of a powerful, ideologically committed political force.

4 The United Kingdom

Ian Gough*

'How on earth did the strong right arm of Prometheus Unbound end up with Harold Wilson, Blue Streak . . . and *Upstairs, Downstairs*?' (Nairn, 1988, p. 310)

'The 1980s will stand out as a decade of impressive improvement in economic performance, reversing a long-term trend in decline relative to other member countries' (OECD Economic Survey of the UK, 1988, p. 8).

'The Reagan and Thatcher people do not really care much about macroeconomic performance . . . (but about) the redistribution of wealth in favour of the wealthy and of power in favour of the powerful' (Professor Solow, Nobel prize-winner in economics 1987, pp. 181–2).

THE CHALLENGE OF INTERNATIONAL COMPETITIVENESS

Introduction

Awareness of, and concern over, the economic decline of Britain has been around for over a century, ever since the US and Germany overtook Britain in the production of key industrial products. The debates in the 1890s, even the book titles of that period, were harbingers of the more recent period of introspection 70 years later. Yet Britain's relative economic standing has diminished further and faster in the post-war years. In 1950 it still accounted for one quarter of world exports of manufactures (down from one-third in 1899), but by the mid-1970s this had fallen to under 10 per cent. From being the leading economy in Western Europe in 1950 Britain had declined by 1980 to become the most notorious laggard. Unlike the other nations in this study, with the partial exception of the US, it is this long-term

* I would like to thank Mike Artis, Huw Beynon, Felix Burdzhalov, Pat Devine, Bob Rowthorn and Roger Williams for helpful comments on an earlier draft.

post-war relative decline which has shaped the British political agenda in recent years. When the international crisis of the 1970s and the new conditions of international competition of the 1980s began to influence economic policy debates in Germany and elsewhere, the flow of North Sea oil dissolved these worries for a short time in Britain. At just this moment Mrs Thatcher's government of the radical Right was elected to power. That coincidence provides the setting for some of the themes and findings of this study.

At first glance the UK provides a classic example of a country where heightened competitive pressures have generated a reaction calling into question almost all aspects of post-war welfare statism. The government of Mrs Thatcher came to power with the express and overriding purpose of developing radical, long-term solutions to the British economic crisis. 'Nobody owes us a living. We must stand on our own two feet' – these are two of the most abiding slogans of the last decade. In so doing the new Conservative government has linked Britain's economic decline to the expansion of the civil activities of the British state, and notably to the British welfare state. 'Thatcherism' in other words has played an important role in shaping the discourse which has influenced our research project. It is an economic strategy for national regeneration.

But at another level this is a quite inadequate view of the present British government and cannot make sense of some significant developments and policy choices of the last decade. For the Thatcher revolution is also a political and ideological strategy, and at times these goals conflict with the economic ones. Ideologically it is an explicit 'counter-revolution' designed to reverse the tide of 'collectivism' which it saw as engulfing the nation, particularly in the crisis years of the 1970s under the governments of Heath, Wilson and Callaghan. Politically it is an attempt to fashion an electoral constituency of people with a vested interest in the newly privatised economy such that its main initiatives cannot be reversed. Together the explicit goal is to make socialism (a subset of collectivism) an unthinkable option for Britain in the future (Rowthorn, 1989). *These themes address the old agenda of national decline, not the emerging issues of the 1980s such as information technology, post-Fordism and the NICs.* These new agendas are only surfacing at the close of the 1980s. The bonanza of North Sea oil gave the government the (temporary) breathing space to tackle the old agenda whilst ignoring the new.

Of course the two are related, and the success of the Thatcher government in dealing with the first explains some of its success in halting and reversing the deteriorating competitiveness of the British economy. But the two are not identical, and this explains why some policy initiatives appear to be economically 'irrational' even to supporters of the free market strategy and why free market policies have often been rejected in favour of reforms which strengthen central state intervention. The radical reshaping of the British welfare state, now underway, cannot be seen solely as a response to new pressures of international competition, but as part of that discrediting of collectivist institutions which has become the hallmark of 'Thatcherism'. The relentless post-war decline, and the radical break with all previous post-war cures begun in 1979 – this is the historical backcloth indispensable for understanding recent developments in international competitiveness and welfare statism in Britain.

The Evolution of the Country's International Competitivensss

Income, Output and Employment

One of the most marked symptoms of Britain's national economic decline is the falling relative income of UK residents compared with other advanced countries. Figures based on purchasing power parities have undergone considerable revisions recently which have improved Britain's relative standing, but the overall pattern is one of rapid descent until the 1980s since when its relative position has stabilised (OECD, 1987d). For example compared with the EEC–12 country average the UK income per head fell from 129 per cent in 1960 to 108 per cent in 1970 to 101 per cent in 1980, since when it has begun to rise – to 104 per cent in 1985. Over time other major nations have overtaken Britain: West Germany in 1969, France in 1972 and Japan in 1980. Nevertheless it appears that the relative slide has since stopped – for the moment.

The first oil shock in 1973 resulted in 'utter dislocation of the economy' (Caves & Krause, 1980, p. 31). Stagnant output was coupled with a very high rate of price inflation (19 per cent per annum over 1973–76, double the OECD average), rising unemployment and a balance of payments deficit greater than any other Western nation. Table 4.1 charts trends in some leading indicators since then. A recovery ensued between 1976 and 1979 but unemployment did not fall and inflation moderated only slightly to 13 per cent p.a. between 1976 and 1979. There followed the worst industrial recession in

Table 4.1 UK: output, employment and productivity

	1973	*1976*	*1979*	*1981*	*1986*	*1988*
GDP f.c. (1980=100)	94.3	94.5	102.4	99.0	113.8	123.3
Manufacturing output	114.2	107.0	109.5	94.0	104.7	118.2
Manuf. employment (m)	7.7	7.1	7.1	6.1	5.1	5.1
Total employment	22.7	22.5	23.2	21.9	21.6	22.6
Total nos in work	25.1	24.8	25.4	24.3	24.6	26.2
Unemployment (m)	0.6	1.3	1.3	2.5	3.3	2.4
Output per person employed (1980=100):						
Whole economy	95.5	94.9	102.2	101.9	117.0	121.3
Manufacturing	100.0	100.9	104.1	103.5	134.6	150.9

Sources: National Income and Expenditure, *Economic Trends*

British history which between 1979 and 1981 reduced GDP, cut manufacturing output by 15 per cent and employment by one million, doubled national unemployment yet accelerated inflation (to 16 per cent in 1979–81). Since then a sustained recovery has raised national income per head by almost 3 per cent a year whilst cutting back inflation to below 5 per cent for most of the period. At the same time mass unemployment has persisted, indeed continued to rise to a plateau of over three million between 1984 and 1986. However over the three years 1986–88 the British growth rate has accelerated, employment has expanded fast and unemployment has contracted. For the economy as a whole therefore the record has been one of slow growth followed by deep slump followed by sustained expansion.

What of the manufacturing sector? A major concern in Britain over the last two decades has been the phenomenon of 'de-industrialisation' – the relative or absolute decline of output and/or employment in manufacturing and industry. Interpreted relatively, this state of affairs has existed since 1955, when the share of the workforce employed in industry in Britain reached an all-time world record of 48 per cent. Interpreted absolutely, we find de-industrialisation of employment beginning over two decades ago, following the peak of 11.5m industrial employees in 1966. Since then employment in industry has plummeted by 34 per cent and in manufacturing by 25 per cent (Rowthorn & Wells, 1987, Ch.10). The absolute numbers working in manufacturing today are back to the levels recorded at the start of the Industrial Revolution. As regards output, we find that the share of value added in manufacturing as a percentage of GDP has also declined dramatically – from 32 per cent in 1960 to 27 per cent in 1971 to 21 per cent in 1983.

Nevertheless it is possible for these trends to indicate a dynamic economy (positive de-industrialisation) as much as an unhealthy economy (negative de-industrialisation). Real output is one important indicator here, and this shows a process of absolute de-industrialisation at work in the mid-1970s and again and more virulently between 1979 and 1981, when manufacturing output fell by one-fifth. Since then and especially since 1986, manufacturing output has picked up – though by 1987 it had only regained its 1979 level. Until 1986 the labour displaced from manufacturing was not absorbed into the service sector, and unemployment therefore rose – a process of negative de-industrialisation (Rowthorn & Wells, Ch.1). The greatest success in British manufacturing in recent years has been a sustained and rapid growth in productivity. After stagnating between 1973 and 1981 output per worker in manufacturing has expanded by over 6 per cent p.a. since 1981. Over the whole of the period of the Thatcher government this amounts to a 50 per cent rise in manufacturing productivity.

Table 4.2 illustrates these developments by comparing the UK performance since 1979 with that of the three largest Western economies. Manufacturing productivity growth is second only to Japan's, but it is a strange form of growth resulting *solely* from cuts in the manufacturing workforce and resulting in no expansion of output. This is not 'jobless growth', rather a growthless leap in productivity. As a result, some argue that the 'productivity miracle' of the last decade is a statistical illusion: it is akin to a cricket team reducing the

Table 4.2 Manufacturing industry in four countries, 1979–87

	% change in			
	Output per worker	*Employment*	*Output*	*Real* earnings*
USA	29.8	−6.3	21.6	−3.9
Japan	52.2	6.7	62.4	13.4
Germany	16.5	−7.5	7.6	10.4
UK	37.8	−27.5	0.0	25.8

Source: Rowthorn, 1989, Table 1.
* Hourly earnings deflated by consumer price index.

team's size by leaving out the worst batsmen – the team's 'batting average' rises but the total 'runs scored' declines. However the continuing and even accelerating productivity growth over such a period must involve real structural improvements, which we analyse later.

Foreign Trade

If we are to relate the above trends to the question of international competitiveness, we need to take into account the external balance of payments. Since the mid-19th century Britain has run a deficit on its visible balance, relying on services and financial earnings to cover this (and to provide the funds for net capital exports at certain historical periods). Moreover, the UK has experienced an unparalleled shift in its structure of overseas trade and payments since the Second World War: a surplus on manufactured trade has turned into a deficit, a deficit on primary products, notably oil, has turned into a surplus, net interest and other income has boomed, yet the outflow of capital has mushroomed still faster (Rowthorn & Wells, 1987, Chs. 5, 6). To disentangle these and other trends Table 4.3 analyses the period since 1973 in more detail.

The current balance was in deficit from 1973 onwards until 1979 (except for a temporary surplus in 1978) to be followed by large, historically unusual surpluses between 1980 and 1985. By 1986 however these had been wiped out and the UK current account

Table 4.3 UK: balance of payments, 1973–88 (% of GDP)

Net balances	*1973*	*1976*	*1979*	*1981*	*1986*	*1988*
Manufactures	2.0	3.9	1.4	1.8	−1.5	−3.2
Oil	−1.2	−3.1	−0.4	1.2	1.1	0.6
Other visibles	−4.3	−3.9	−2.9	−1.7	−1.8	−1.9
Total visible trade	−3.5	−3.1	−1.7	1.3	−2.2	−4.5
Total services	0.9	1.8	1.9	1.5	1.3	0.8
Total invisible trade	2.2	2.4	1.4	1.2	2.0	1.3
CURRENT BALANCE	−1.3	−0.7	−0.4	2.5	−0.3	−3.2
Net overseas investment	−0.1	0.3	−1.1	−2.8	−5.4	−2.8
BASIC BALANCE	−1.5	−0.5	−1.5	−0.3	−5.7	−6.0

Source: CSO, UK Balance of Payments, 1987.

Notes: The invisible trade balance includes net flows of interest, profits, dividends and transfers as well as the services balance.

deficit has since then worsened to over 3 per cent of GDP – a greater shortfall than the US deficit at its height. All forecasts predict that this will continue into the early 1990s. This growing deficit on current account has been magnified by a strong outflow of long-term capital, which has not yet been counterbalanced by the inflow of earnings from that capital. The deficit on the basic balance has been financed by substantial short-term credits. Despite the deficit, then, Britain has built up its net foreign assets from £4.6b in 1976 to £114b in 1986, making it the world's biggest creditor after Japan and, in the words of *The Economist* (13 December 1986), 'a rentier nation once more'.

The massive and unprecedented improvement in the current balance in the first half of the 1980s was due to the exploitation of North Sea Oil coupled with domestic recession. Large deficits on the fuel account following the 1973 oil price rise were eroded by 1980 and replaced by large and expanding surpluses up to 1985. The decline in these surpluses since 1985 has reflected the levelling out of oil production coupled with a sharp fall in its price. Thus *excluding oil* the current account deteriorated from a surplus between 1975 and 1981 to record a deficit in 1983 which has widened since then. The contribution of invisibles to the current account – always important in Britain – has levelled out over the past decade due to opposing trends. Net credits on financial services and other earnings of the 'City' have expanded as has the inflow of interest, profits and dividends; however these have been offset by a deterioration in other services. Nevertheless invisibles now account for 50 per cent of UK exports and still contribute a net surplus; it is to manufacturing therefore that we must look to understand the deterioration in the non-oil account.

Figure 4.1 shows that 1983 was a watershed. For the first time since the Industrial Revolution (some say since the Roman occupation!) British trade in manufactured goods moved into deficit. Since then the deficit has continued to widen. In 1963 exports of manufactured goods were 2 times as large as imports. By 1973 most of this surplus had been eliminated, but two recoveries peaking in 1977 and 1980 helped maintain an overall surplus until 1982. Yet by 1984, when the House of Lords Select Committee on Overseas Trade was set up, manufactured imports exceeded manufactured exports by four billion pounds, or 1.2 per cent of GDP, and this has since topped £14b. In the decade up to 1983 there was no trend change in UK exports in volume terms, but the volume of imports doubled. The rising penetration of manufactured imports is more than offsetting both

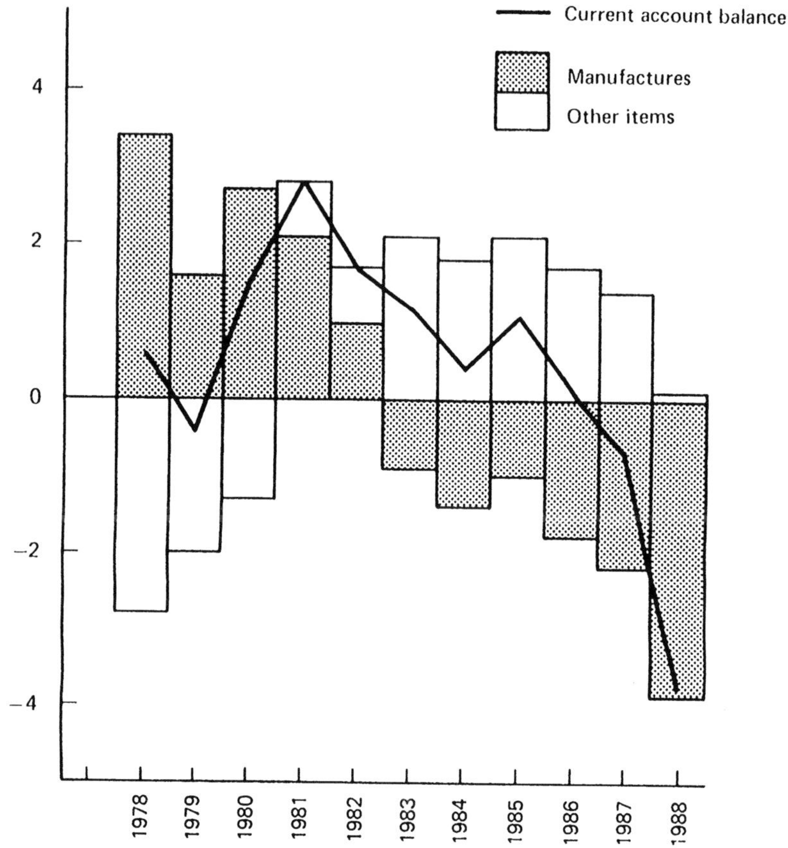

Source: Rowthorn, 1989, Figure 4.1

Figure 4.1 UK: trade balance in manufactures and other items, 1978–88 (% of GDP)

Britain's traditional strengths in invisibles and its novel – and brief – bonanza from North Sea oil. This suggests for some that the competitiveness of British manufacturing is continuing to decline.

Is this view upheld by other indicators? It is certainly confirmed by the UK share of world trade in manufactures which almost halved in the two decades from 1964 to 1983. Since then, however, it has stabilised. For more sophisticated measures for the 1970s we can turn to an OECD study (OECD, 1985b) which has produced various indices of competitiveness, distinguishing between high-, medium-

and low-technology sectors according to shares of R&D expenditure. An index of specialisation by industrial fields, showing whether Britain produces more than it consumes in particular industries, is moderately encouraging. It reveals no clear pattern of change over the decade, and no secular decline within the high-tech sector. There is in general greater specialisation in the higher technology sectors, in particular drugs, electrical machinery and instruments (and almost certainly aerospace, for which no figures are available). There is a notable shortfall only in office machinery and computers among the high-tech industries. Using export–import ratios also shows the UK to have a competitive advantage in aerospace and drugs but to perform poorly in all other high-tech sectors, with a secular deterioration in the fields of instruments and electrical machinery. Furthermore there has been a marked decline in some medium-technology industries, notably motor vehicles.

By 1984 every single branch of British manufacturing industry exhibited a balance of trade deficit, that is, imported more than they exported, with the sole exceptions of chemicals, mechanical engineering, 'other transport equipment' and two other smaller industries.

> The major contributors to the deficit other than food, drink and tobacco are motor vehicles and their parts; paper, printing and publishing; and timber and wooden furniture. But contributions of over £1b also come from electrical and electronic engineering, footwear and clothing, textiles and office machinery and data processing equipment. Thus both traditional industries and more modern sectors such as electronics are included in the deficit (House of Lords Select Committee on Overseas Trade, 1985, p. 16).

When attention is focused on the *changes* in trade balances over the six years motor vehicles remain the weakest sector, but once again the decline is manifest across high-, medium- and low-technology sectors. The same applies when import penetration is the index used. Geographically, the British deficit tends to be concentrated on trade with more developed economies, and most notably with West Germany. A notable exception to this decline in recent years has been the defence industry. UK arms exports rose to 20 per cent of the world total in 1986, making it the second arms exporter in the world after the USA.

The overall conclusion is that the deteriorating foreign trade performance of British industry has continued into the 1980s, and is not the result of spectacular individual failures, though these exist; rather it is widespread across modern and traditional industries. Nevertheless, the Treasury and others argue that the trade deficit and import penetration of the early 1980s was an inevitable result of the oil surpluses and the premium on sterling as a petro-currency, whilst that of the later 1980s follows from the strong economic expansion of the British economy compared with its major competitors. Consequently trade balances give an unnecessarily gloomy picture of the whole period. The surge in productivity, they contend, gives a more accurate and much more optimistic portrait of Britain's underlying competitiveness. Let us turn therefore to look more closely at other indicators of price and non-price competitiveness in turn.

Cost Competitiveness

Table 4.4 reveals that British unit labour costs at current exchange rates rose from the end of 1976 (relative to a weighted average of competitor nations) and this deterioration accelerated markedly in 1979 and 1980. At the start of the present decade they stood at more than double the US and Japanese levels. During the 1980s British cost competitiveness has improved considerably, especially *vis-à-vis* Japan and West Germany. However British unit costs still exceed those of most of its major competitors – in 1986 they were on a par with West Germany, but higher than Japan (by 37 per cent), France (by 52 per cent) and the USA (by 67 per cent) (Ray, 1987). The trends are much the same if we consider relative export prices or import price competitiveness. Since 1986 however all three indicators

Table 4.4 UK: indices of cost competitiveness in trade in manufactures, 1973–88

(1980=100):	*1973*	*1976*	*1979*	*1981*	*1986*	*1988*
Relative normalised unit labour costs	74.1	70.3	83.3	105.7	90.0	92.9*
Relative export prices	75.5	75.5	90.4	98.0	87.4	100.5**
Import price competitiveness	85.2	82.7	93.0	100.5	91.4	96.7
£ exchange rate index	111.8	85.6	87.3	94.9	72.9	76.1

Sources: *Economic Trends* (various issues)

Notes: * 1988, 3rd quarter
** Weighted index, 1975=100.

have registered a small deterioration; in the case of relative export prices one which took it to historically high levels in 1988. To explain these fluctuating trends we must disaggregate the measures into their three components: the exchange rate, domestic costs and productivity.

Some of the fluctuations in sterling's weighted effective exchange rate are indicated in Table 4.4. Clearly such major swings have had a considerable impact on the export prices of British goods. The appreciation of sterling harmed UK competitiveness in the first two years of the Thatcher government, and is doing so again now; but inbetween times its substantial depreciation contributed to the relative cost improvement noted above. Since the early 1970s the sterling exchange rate has been more volatile than that of any other major currency except the US dollar – a volatility which some argue has itself harmed the competitiveness of British industry. Since 1980 the depreciation of sterling has however been offset by a marked rise in domestic unit labour costs, as Table 4.2 has shown. By contrast with the modest growth in real earnings in major competitor countries, in the UK they have risen by one quarter since 1979. Until 1986 however these two trends offset one another. Moreover it should not be forgotten that in absolute terms in 1986 'Britain appears as the industrialised country with the lowest labour costs, with the sole exception of Ireland' (Ray, 1987, p. 71).

Above all therefore such improvement in British cost competitiveness as occurred in the 1980s resulted from the third factor – the dynamism of productivity. This enabled rising earnings to accompany rapidly rising profits and, until 1987, falling relative prices. However this signalled an improvement from a very low base: in absolute terms Britain remains a low productivity economy. According to one estimate, in 1980 US labour productivity in manufacturing was 2.7 times higher than in Britain, West German 2.6 times higher and French and Japanese levels 1.9 and 2.0 times higher: an extraordinary gap between otherwise similar economies, which has narrowed only slightly as a result of recent trends. OECD calculations of productivity in the whole economy show much less difference due to the higher relative efficiency of agriculture and services in the UK: in 1986 output per person employed fell short of that in North America by about one-third and of other major member countries in Europe by about one-quarter.[1] Figure 4.2 illustrates the deteriorating record up to 1980, the slight relative recovery since then and the gap that remains between all our competitors except Japan. It will require a sustained continuation of the impressive improvement in productivity

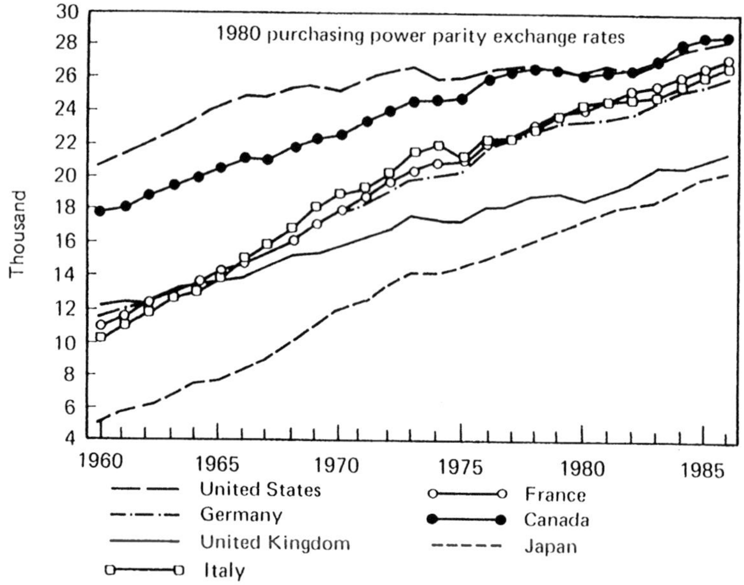

Source: OECD, 1988d, p. 52

Figure 4.2 Labour productivity levels in seven countries, 1960–86 (US$ of 1980 per employed person)

of recent years to offset such an accumulated disadvantage, especially in manufacturing.

Non-price Competitiveness: Investment and Innovation

Others argue that non-price factors are at least as important as unit costs in dictating competitiveness in a modern economy, and some believe that this is an area where Britain has for long lagged behind other advanced economies. Whether it is product quality, technological innovation, design or delivery times the view was for long common that British manufacturing is inferior to its counterparts abroad. Again supporters of the current government strategy contend that this backwardness is now being put right.

One necessary, if not sufficient, condition for non-price competitiveness is an adequate level of investment. Non-residential investment in Britain as a share of GDP has been similar to that in the Big Seven economies, with the exception of Japan, since 1971 (OECD, 1985c, p. 18). But this needs qualifying in two respects.

First, whilst fixed capital formation in the service sector remains high, manufacturing investment tells a different story. After a substantial expansion in the late 1970s manufacturing investment crashed by a third between 1979 and 1981. For the next five years recovery was so slow that it only regained its 1973 level in 1986. Since then it has been more dynamic – achieving its previous peak by 1988 – but now it is faltering again. Second, the productivity of British investment remains relatively low: a variety of measures of incremental capital-output ratios, and output per unit of net capital stock, all show that it takes twice or more investment to generate additional output in the UK than in Germany or the USA.[2] It is not clear that the obstacle of low and ineffective capital formation has yet been overcome in British industry.

Table 4.5 R&D expenditure in five countries

	UK	*US*	*FRG*	*France*	*Japan*
Total R&D/GDP, 1983	2.3	2.8	2.6	2.2	2.5
Total civil R&D/GDP	1.6	2.0	2.5	1.7	2.5
Annual growth of R&D, 1967–82 (%pa)	0.9	4.1	5.9	5.9	9.8

Source: Cable, 1986, p. 254.

This is corroborated when we turn to more direct measures of innovation. One last factor may be relevant in understanding this: the level of R&D expenditure (Table 4.5). Britain devotes about the same proportion of industrial output and GDP to R&D as other major countries, though, because her GDP is lower, the absolute level of expenditure is less. However notable differences are found when the direction of R&D is analysed. Since the 1960s about 50 per cent of the total has been devoted to just three sectors – aircraft, defence products and nuclear reactors – a pattern unlike that of any other economy except the USA. Hence the levels of R&D in all remaining sectors, including several key high-tech industries are considerably lower in Britain than in its major competitors, both relative to industrial output and even more so in absolute terms (Smith, 1984). Industry-financed R&D has been particularly sluggish, growing by just over 1 per cent p.a. in 1967–1983 – the lowest growth rate of any major Western economy. The UK share of European patenting in the US tells a similar tale: it declined steadily from 1963 up to 1985 and virtually halved as a share of the combined French and German total.[3]

In conclusion, British competitiveness suffered on almost all measures up to the end of the 1970s and worsened in the two years of deep recession up to 1981. Since then it has recorded some real successes, notably a sustained leap in manufacturing productivity and average real incomes, coupled with improved price competitiveness in the early to mid-1980s. However on several other measures – notably balance of trade and the import penetration of manufactures, non-price competitiveness and domestic labour costs – it has continued its descent. Overall it is too soon to conclude that Britain's past industrial decline has been reversed, though in some respects it has been halted.

POLICY DEBATES ON INTERNATIONAL COMPETITIVENESS

Different nations exhibit different policy discourses, which require different techniques to 'map' them. The US and Swedish case studies, for example, adopt two contrasting approaches which say much about their respective societies. The US study relies on the views and analyses of individuals – economists, intellectuals and publicists, amongst others – and of the 'think tanks' within which many of them work. The Swedish study can consult the representatives of the well-established interest groups which dominate the policy-making process. Britain combines elements of both: it has class-based interest groups and parties akin to other European countries, but during the period covered by our study many of the older corporatist institutions and processes were dissolving, and new policy positions were developing. At times like this, other opinion formers, whether individual thinkers, reporters, or the media, play a more important role than in times of stability. Hence I shall draw on a range of significant actors in reconstructing policy debates concerning welfare statism and the pressures/constraints of competitiveness.[4]

As argued earlier, the contemporary debates which impinge on the British welfare state originated from the incessant search for an understanding of the 'British disease' – the long-term economic decline evident since at least the early 1960s. This debate polarised in the 1970s following the perceived failures of the first Wilson Labour administration and the Heath Conservative administration. Identifiable 'New Right' and 'New Left' perspectives emerged. The latter played a brief and minor part in informing policy in the early days of the 1974 Wilson government, but otherwise has left no legacy in terms of policy. The New Right perspective on the other hand has come to dominate the political agenda in a remarkable way. Since it links Britain's decline to the expansion of the civil activities of the British state, it is of double importance to our study.

Too Much Government

According to Mrs Thatcher in 1968, this decline has resulted from 'too much government'. The reasons adduced are many, but can be roughly grouped into demand-side and supply-side factors. The first blames fiscal irresponsibility on the part of previous governments for the high rates of inflation in the 1970s. That a high rate of inflation is undesirable was mostly taken for granted, and when this position was defended it was rarely in terms of its effects on competitiveness. However there is no doubt that a link was assumed: inflation upsets rational economic behaviour, and forces everyone, but especially powerful unions, into destructive action (Joseph, 1986, p. 98). With the collapse of the assumed trade-off between inflation and unemployment (the Phillips curve) in the mid-1970s, 'monetarism' rapidly established itself as the leading paradigm to explain the new phenomenon of 'stagflation'. Friedman (for example, 1980a, 1980b) was important both as theorist and proselytiser, whilst bodies such as the Institute of Economic Affairs, and financial journalists Jay and Brittan were influential in spreading the ideas among opinion formers and the general public.

Monetarism, like Keynsianism, is difficult to define, but the core argument is that money supply determines the aggregate price level. For most monetarists this is linked to a more general belief in the efficacy of markets and the non-efficacy of government macro-policy intervention (Jackson, 1985a, p. 25). The rational expectations school of economics goes further in this respect, and has had some impact within economic debate. By claiming that any government-inspired reflation of demand will lead to expectations of faster price inflation, it can argue that all demand-side policies are self-defeating. Thus Britain's economic problem is perceived to have resulted from the pursuit of erroneous policy goals (full employment rather than price stability) and the use of inappropriate policy instruments (short-term fiscal policy rather than a medium-term monetary policy).

A systematic 'supply-side' analysis of the British economic predicament came later to British debates on economic policy, and has never embraced some of the nostrums (such as the Laffer curve) which emerged in the US. One strand focuses on the effect of high and unbalanced tax levels on incentives to work, save and invest – though this has been a more popular theme of business interest groups, free market research institutes and the post-1979 government than of economists. Another variation stresses the inhibiting effect of government regulations and planning controls on entrepreneurial activity.[5] But the prime focus of supply-side arguments in Britain in the 1970s was labour market rigidity supported and exacerbated by over-generous welfare measures. The British system of widely available supplementary benefit, for example, was alleged to undermine the incentive to work and also to limit the degree of wage flexibility. Wage regulation (in the form of Wages Councils and equal pay for women – there is no minimum wage in Britain) also exacerbated real wage rigidity and thus reduced the ability of the British labour market to adjust rapidly to new conditions (Minford, 1983). These ideas combined in the concept of the natural rate of unemployment, which has reappeared in the theories of non-monetarist economists and New Centrist politicians as 'NAIRU': the non-accelerating inflation rate of unemployment (Layard, 1986). Some estimates suggest that this was as high as 10 per cent in the early 1980s – due in part to the nature of social security benefits and tax measures in the UK.

Too Powerful Trades Unions

This leads on to another related explanation of Britain's poor economic performance focusing on the power, structure and beliefs of British trades unions. A concern with industrial relations in Britain has a long pedigree, and formed part of the earlier 'consensus' view of the 'British disease' in the 1950s and 1960s (Caves, 1968). In the last two decades however an influential school has developed which emphasises merely or mainly the trade union side, blaming 'too powerful unions' for the UK's declining industrial competitiveness.

According to neo-liberal economists and politicians of the New Right the British union movement has inhibited economic performance, first by contributing to real wage rigidity and, second, by blocking more efficient working practices and thus the adaptability of the economy. Examples of the real wage rigidity argument are to be found in Hayek (1984), who bemoans the unique privileges of British unions since 1906 and the disaster of 'politically determined' wages. The pay explosions of 1969–1970, 1974–1975 and 1979–1980 have been linked to subsequent periods of falling international competitiveness (House of Lords, vol. 2, 1985). Others (Joseph, 1986) argue that unions, whilst not the cause of inflation, make it harder to control and thus hamper economic recovery.

The second, supply-side, reasoning is that the organisation of British unions acts to oppose innovative work practices, flexible allocation of labour and modernisation generally. The rational expectations school of neo-classical economics assumes that all markets clear instantaneously and thus that all unemployment is voluntary (Minford, 1983). The peculiar features of the British labour market responsible for supply-side failure have been, variously: a high rate of strikes, especially disruptive, unofficial strikes; the decentralised organisational structure based on shop stewards; the craft demarcations between many small unions; and backward, class-based attitudes extolling an 'us *versus* them' mentality and hostility to the free market. The expansion of public sector workers in the 1970s created another powerful group cushioned from market forces by the non-tradable nature of their products (Keith, 1977). In all these ways British unions overstep their proper role and 'have robbed their members of . . . their own productivity'.[6]

Various versions of 'economic theories of politics' have been applied to explain the particular way that state intervention and trade union strength have mutually reinforced each other in post-war Britain (Jay, 1975; Brittan, 1977). Union pressure, the statutory links with the Labour party and party competition for votes stimulate an interventionist, Keynesian welfare state, which in turn strengthens the labour market position of workers, and popular expectations that this state of affairs will persist. In this way the circle between 'too much government' and 'too powerful unions' is self-reinforcing, and both undermine international competitiveness. Expressed in terms of a simple systems model, the effects on competitiveness of the preceding factors can be illustrated as follows:

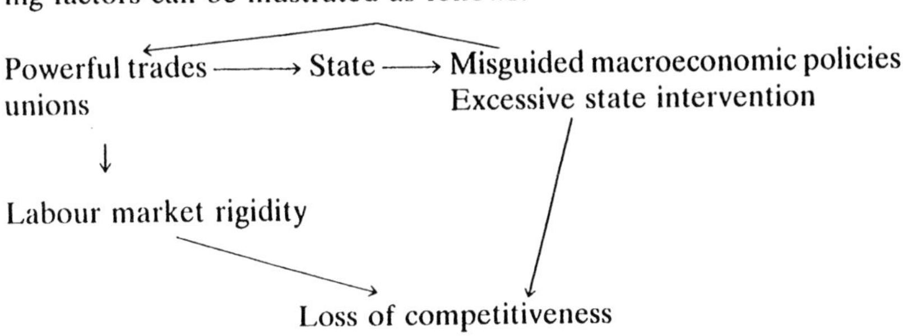

Such an analysis of the causes of declining British competitiveness will indict 'welfare statism' on several grounds:

- social security programmes and wage regulation undermine labour market flexibility;
- the high tax rates it entails diminish individual work effort, savings and entrepreneurial initiative;
- high expenditure financially 'crowds out' private expenditure and/or entails inflationary public borrowing;
- government waste, bureaucracy and regulation is an incubus on wealth creation in the private sector;
- among welfare beneficiaries a culture of dependence emerges which stifles private initiative and effort;
- 'welfare statism' embodies an arrogant and erroneous view of the powers of government, particularly as regards maintaining full employment;
- it also augments the leverage which trades unions and other corporatist-minded bodies can exert on governments to expand their intervention, thus renewing the vicious circle.

The alternative explanations of the British economic decline do not implicate 'welfare statism' in the same way. On the contrary it is inadequate and unco-ordinated state investment in human, industrial and infrastructural capital which is viewed as the root cause. It is the *lack* of state economic and social interventions which these approaches identify as the culprit. I shall consider them more briefly since they have had no influence on government policy since 1979 – indeed little since 1975.

Capital Divided

One common theme is that British manufacturing investment is too low due to the organisation and management of British capital. On the one hand British capital is highly concentrated and internationalised: a relatively large proportion of multinationals are British, and Britain has experienced a relatively large penetration of foreign multinational capital.[7] On the other hand the culprit is alleged to be the sharp division between finance capital (the City of London) and industrial capital in Britain. The City, it is argued, is both excessively foreign-oriented and excessively short-sighted and risk-averse when assessing possible investments in Britain. The rise of the Eurodollar market in London and the subsequent resumption of large scale capital exports with the relaxation of foreign exchange controls are examples where the interests of the two sections of capital conflict, such that profitable overseas investment has priority over re-industrialisation at home.[8] The Wilson Committee report on the City (1980) argued that there was no evidence of a shortage of investment funds, but in reply to this others contend that it is the absence of sustained, long-term loans at low interest rates which disadvantages British industry. The banks of competitor nations lend generously and lend long (Lever & Edwards, 1980; NEDO in House of Lords, vol. 2, 1985). By contrast British financial institutions have global interests, which make them peculiarly unable or unwilling to supply venture capital to domestic industry. Paradoxically the very strength of finance capital in Britain is disadvantageous to its indigenous manufacturers.

The Archaic State

The archaic nature of the British state is perceived to be another root cause of the British decline. The charges vary: the patrician, Oxbridge-educated liberal administrators of the war and post-war period, the Victorian 'imperial bureaucracy' that is the British civil service, Treasury indifference to the needs of industry and its commitment to the symbolic role of sterling, the absence of a modernising movement reflecting the aristocratic dominance of English society and the British state, the 'culture of containment' and the institutional sclerosis it engenders, a subservience to the interests of the United States, the illusions of the British establishment about its world role and its military over-commitment.[9] But there is a common effect: the British state is not equipped to cope with the reality of Britain's place in the post-war world, the loss of its overseas assets, empire and influence, and the consequent greater reliance on trade and industry. As a result misguided policies have been pursued which have undermined the ability of British industry to compete in world markets. These misguided economic policies have included the uncontrolled overvaluation of sterling in the early 1980s,[10] coupled with tight monetary and fiscal policies, too high interest rates and an unselective obsession with reducing government borrowing. In the late 1980s the finger has been pointed at loose monetary and credit policies coupled with a reliance on interest rates to curb the trade deficit, a widely fluctuating exchange rate and the failure of Britain fully to enter the European Monetary System.

This politico-economic structure has also been blamed for longer term absences and omissions in British governments' economic and social intervention which have a bearing on both economic competitiveness and welfare statism. The most commonly cited are, first, the insufficiency and misdirection of education and training. Numerous studies have demonstrated that the system fails all but the top quarter or so of pupils, leaving the British labour force uneducated and unskilled in comparison with its continental counterparts. Other research links this failure with poor non-price competitiveness and other attributes of industrial decline.[11] Second, there is the insufficiency and misdirection of research and development expenditure noted earlier, indicted by investigators from all parts of the political spectrum as a cause of poor economic performance. Third are the deficiencies often attributed to British management, which in turn are related to a variety of factors ranging from an anti-industrial 'culture' to the lack of proper management training.[12] Fourth, British industry policy – or rather the lack of a coherent, long-term strategy for industry – is indicted. The 1985 House of Lords Committee echoed earlier reports in its desire for more co-ordinated, medium-term public intervention in the private sector (see also Maynard, 1988).

These policy failings are not random, it is contended, but stem from the institutional links between, notably, the City of London and financial capital on the one hand and departments of government, notably the Treasury (Ingham, 1984). The themes of capital failure and the outdated British state thus come together and explain Britian's declining competitiveness as illustrated below:

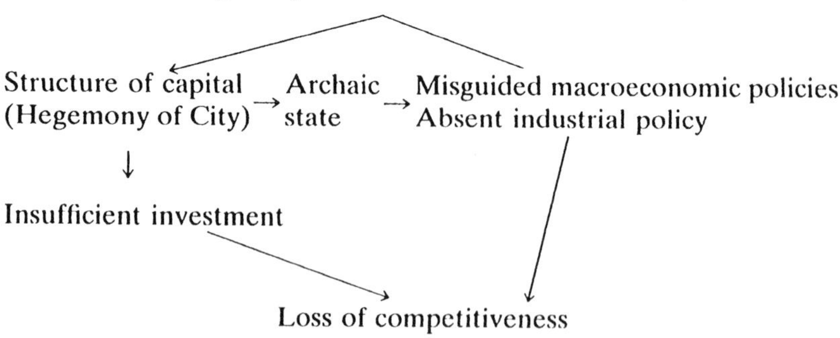

This 'New Left' paradigm of the British crisis parallels that of the New Right, but indicts the close links between capital and the British state rather than labour and the state. One result of this polarisation of perspectives is that British industry tends to be hostile to the sort of dirigiste policies supported by its counterparts in other countries because such policies have on the whole been advocated by Labour governments and thus have incorporated quasi-socialist and anti-EC goals.[13]

In the late 1980s economic debate amongst those critical of the New Right is beginning to pay more attention to the new international economy and to issues of competitiveness more narrowly conceived. Partly this reflects the very success of 'Thatcherism' both in reversing some previous trends and in changing the national agenda, and partly the imminent decline of the 'oil cushion'. This new agenda has led the Labour party to review all aspects of economic policy and to reverse some earlier policies, such as its commitment to withdraw from the EC. It has also stimulated a 'New Centrist' analysis which draws on elements of both accounts of British failure adumbrated above.[14] Thus the old agenda centred on the 'British disease' may be giving way to a newer, more specific one concerning Britain's place within a rapidly-changing global economy. In this agenda it is unlikely the welfare state will play the consistently negative role it has for the New Right. However, as we shall see, the present government believes there is still much unfinished business to be done in reigning back British 'welfare statism'.

POLICY RESPONSES

> To master inflation, proper monetary discipline is essential with publicly stated targets for the rate of growth of the money supply. At the same time a gradual reduction in the size of the government's borrowing requirement is also vital . . . The state takes too much of the nation's income: its share must be steadily reduced . . . The reduction of waste, bureaucracy and over-government will yield substantial savings. We shall cut income tax at all levels to reward hard work, responsibility and success. (Conservative Party Manifesto, 1979).

Undoubtedly the Conservative administrations under Mrs Thatcher have inaugurated a real-world experiment in applying and testing those theories of Britain's declining competitiveness which point the finger at 'welfare statism' broadly defined. The major economic policies since 1979 which have a bearing on both the role of the state and competitiveness are:

1. 'Monetarist' macroeconomic policies;
2. Policies to reduce the scale of the public sector;
3. Labour market deregulation;
4. Product and capital market deregulation.

In all these areas it is necessary to distinguish rhetoric and policy enactment, whilst recognising the importance of the former (Tomlinson, 1986). In my view the role of radical rhetoric has emerged because of the central role in the government's thinking of price stability, of expectations in generating and maintaining inflation, and hence of the government's credibility, its self-control and its refusal to contemplate U-turns in eliminating inflation from the British economy. By continually reiterating its commitment to a long-term haul, the government was binding itself against future policy changes by raising the electoral costs to the government itself should it reverse its policy stance. Thus the rhetoric *is a part of* the policy. Despite this it is true to say that the government has been characterised by remarkable caution in economic and social policy, proceeding to reform of trade unions and the welfare state, for example, only when the political cost-benefits looked most favourable. It is this combination of an unwavering commitment to certain long-term goals with short-term caution and flexibility which has characterised the Thatcher administrations.

'Monetarism'

There were four new elements in macroeconomic management introduced in 1979. First, eliminating inflation became the overriding goal of policy – it was seen as the essential pre-requisite for a *sustainable* improvement in economic performance.[15] Second and associated with this, demand management ceased to be the key goal of fiscal and monetary policy; also downgraded as policy targets was the control of interest rates, the balance of payments and the exchange rate. Third, lower government borrowing in the shape of targets for the public sector borrowing requirement (PSBR) assumed a central importance as a policy instrument. Fourth, the importance of clear, believable rules governing government behaviour was promulgated; in particular people should be certain that there would be no 'U-turn' should recession threaten (Begg, 1987; Moseley, 1984). In these ways the Thatcher government in its early years broke with the previous cross-party consensus and pioneered monetarist orthodoxy in the Western world.

Nevertheless, there was considerable disagreement about how to apply monetarism *in practice*. This was the first time that such nostrums had been implemented in an advanced Western economy, and the experiment involved much 'search behaviour' and trial and error as well as theoretical reasoning and ideological commitment (Jackson, 1985). In particular, should the government launch a 'cold turkey' treatment of drastic and sudden monetary restraint (as advocated by Hayek and Minford), or should it gradually reduce money supply growth via a set of medium-term targets (as advocated by Friedman)? The latter won the argument, but paradoxically the former actually happened!

The government initiated a novel medium-term financial strategy (MTFS) which projected falling rates of growth in the money supply £M3 and a reduction in the public sector borrowing requirement as a share of GDP. In this way fiscal and monetary policy were tied together, the former being subordinate to the latter (Fischer, 1987). Despite a rise in money supply inflation fell rapidly over 1980–1981 but at the cost of a deep recession. The OECD (1984) recognised the achievement in bringing down inflation, but argued that the policy drove up interest rates to high levels which, coupled with its newly-emerging status as a petro-currency, allowed sterling to appreciate. This combination drastically reduced investment, damaged cost competitiveness and resulted in the loss of one quarter of jobs in manufacturing. On discovering its mistake, however, the government soon adapted to and made the most of it: monetary and fiscal policy were tightened in the 1981 Budget in the teeth of the depression simply by maintaining course and eschewing any reflation. 'The government did nothing. "That", as Sherlock Holmes remarked, "was the curious incident"' (Budd, 1987, p. 190).

It was the 1981 Budget which more than any other signalled a shift in the responsibilities of government in guaranteeing the welfare of its citizens. The severe recession of 1980–1982 also had implications for Britain's industrial competitiveness by placing the burden of adjustment on those sectors most vulnerable to international competition, in particular manufacturing. However in the longer run, many argue, the tight monetarist-inspired policy played a major part in the ensuing 'productivity miracle':

> 'Although the MTFS is macroeconomic in nature, in itself it may have had an appreciable impact on the supply side of the economy... Clear non-interventionist policies, which refrained from bailing firms and individuals out of economic difficulties, may have forced both management and labour to reassess their traditional behaviour and to accept changes in order to avoid bankruptcy and unemployment.'[16]

Thus the macroeconomic strategy of the government played no small part in bringing about the most notable improvement in Britain's economic competitiveness. As Rowthorn argues, there is a certain irony in this since it is agreed that the unduly deflationary policy pursued was unintended by the government. Its success was therefore the result of a mistake! (Rowthorn, 1988; Maynard, 1988).

In some ways 1981–1982 marked a watershed. After this act of anti-Keynesian defiance, the government slowly modified its monetarist stance partly in response to its perceived deficiencies (OECD, 1984a). By 1982 the government had begun to accept the 'base drift' in money supply and chose higher targets, it evinced a new concern with interest rates and the value of the £, and the central role of £M3 was played down. In 1986 the then-Chancellor Nigel Lawson replaced money supply with exchange rate management as a key means with which to steer the economy. Indeed money supply has grown at consistently high rates since 1985, fiscal policy has turned towards tax cuts and credit has escalated in response to the strong private, mainly consumer, demand. The result in 1988–1989 was rising inflation and an overheated economy especially in the South of England. Masochistic monetarism came to be replaced by what we might call 'Home Counties hedonism'.

Cutting Back the Public Sector

'Public expenditure', according to the 1979 Public Expenditure White Paper, 'is at the heart of Britain's economic difficulties' (HMSO, 1979). For much of the last decade the government's economic strategy has involved reducing tax rates, privatising major parts of the public sector and holding public spending at a broadly constant real level. Yet, despite the uncompromising declaration, the Thatcher

Table 4.6 UK: public expenditure and taxation, 1975–87

Expenditure	*1975/6*	*1979/80*	*1982/83*	*1986/87*
£ billion, 1986–1987 prices:				
General government expenditure	149.1	149.4	158.1	165.1
– excluding privatisation	149.1	150.1	158.6	169.5
As % GDP				
General government expenditure	48.5	43.3	46.7	42.9
– excluding privatisation	48.5	43.4	46.8	44.0
Taxation	*1975*	*1979*	*1982*	*1986*
Total taxes/GDP	36.5	34.7	39.1	37.9
North Sea oil taxes/GDP	–	0.9	2.6	1.0
All other taxes/GDP	36.5	33.8	36.5	36.9
Taxes on income/total personal inc.	15.6	12.8	13.6	12.6
National insurance/employment inc.	11.0	11.3	13.1	14.3
Expenditure taxes/consumers expend.	18.8	21.9	24.4	24.2

Sources: HMSO, 1988
OECD, 1984, Table 4
CSO, National Income and Expenditure, 1987, Tables, 1.1, 3.1, 3.3, 4.1, 5.4, 7.2, 9.1.

government has utterly failed to reduce public spending, especially by contrast with the previous Labour administration. Table 4.6 shows that in real terms general government expenditure (which includes debt interest) has risen by 29 per cent since 1979–1980, an average of 4 per cent a year. Coupled with falling GDP in the first three years, this caused its share of GDP to rise by 3½ percentage points to 47 per cent in 1982–1983 – a level only exceeded in 1975–1976.[17] Since 1982 faster growth has reduced its share to 44 per cent (excluding privatisation proceeds dealt with below), though this remains higher than the level it inherited from Labour. The 1988 White Paper plans a slower growth of 1.25 per cent p.a. up to 1990–1991, and a further decline to 41.25 per cent of GDP.

On the revenue side the government has notably failed to cut overall taxation, but has succeeded in restructuring the tax burden in significant ways. Partly due to falling GDP, total taxation rose by five percentage points in four years to reach a post-war high of 39 per cent of GDP in 1982. Since then, and notably since 1986, the share of taxes has begun to decline, though they remain higher than at the previous peak of 1975. Despite the greater than expected contribution from taxes on North Sea oil, other taxes have recently outstripped 1975 levels as a share of GDP. The restructuring of the tax burden away from direct taxation has however proceeded apace. The standard rate of income tax has been cut over nine years from 33 per cent to 25 per cent, whilst the top rate of personal tax has been halved – from 83 per cent to 40 per cent; rising real tax allowances have also removed one million people from the tax net. The standard corporation tax rate has been cut from 40 per cent in 1981 to 27 per cent in 1987. At the same time, VAT (Value Added Tax), National Insurance contributions and the petroleum revenue tax have yielded a greater share of revenue. Thus in the years since the early monetarist experiment (when all taxes rose), the government has systematically switched the tax burden from direct taxes on income to other sources, a policy which has reduced income redistribution via the welfare state.

Labour Market Deregulation

A major element here has been legislation to curb the power and reduce the legal immunities of trade unions, which is sufficiently explicit and extensive to warrant treating it separately from other labour market policies. Legislation has removed union legal immunities for most picketing and secondary industrial action, strengthened the rights of individuals not wishing to join closed shops, instituted secret ballots for certain key union policy decisions, removed union immunities from civil action and restricted the unfair dismissals procedure (OECD, 1985c, p. 26). At the same time mass unemployment has seriously eroded union membership – since 1979 the affiliated membership of the Trades Unions Congress has declined from 12.2m to 9.2m – and altered employment practices to an unprecedented degree, via such arrangements as the growth of part-time work, unstandardised shift patterns, self-employment, temporary employment, and the decline in apprenticeships (Metcalf & Richardson, 1986). Lastly, the government has adopted an uncompromising stand over strikes in the public sector (OECD, 1985c), culminating in its victory over the miners in the year-long strike from 1984–1985. These measures have weakened British trade unions nationally and industrially, and have also pushed the UK towards a dual and less solidaristic labour market, with implications for the effectiveness of the inherited welfare state.

Other policies to deregulate the labour market include de-linking the rise of social security benefits to earnings, taxing some benefits and restricting entitlement to others. Together they have brought about a sharp fall in replacement ratios, in a country which already had low relative levels of social security benefit (OECD, 1986b). As such the government intends and believes that they enhance the incentive effect of the combined tax-benefit system (Matthews & Minford, 1987). Alongside these have been measures directly to deregulate the labour market, such as the Young Workers' Scheme (which from 1982 to 1986 offered employers a subsidy for every young worker they took on, provided they paid them less than a certain amount), cuts in the scope and powers of Wages Councils and in the protection offered employees against unfair dismissal. These last measures required the government to de-ratify ILO Convention 26. In all these ways then the Thatcher administration has sought to undermine constraints on labour market flexibility, with significant implications for income security.

Product and Capital Market Deregulation

The Thatcher administration has pursued a deregulatory policy of 'rolling back the state' here by: ending exchange controls, privatisation, competition policy and business tax reform. Elsewhere industrial policy has continued past practice, precisely by eschewing any coherent policy. The greater institutional continuity (Devine, 1986) of industrial policy under Thatcher signals that there was no coherent system of intervention to dismantle, unlike other domains of economic and social policy. However we shall focus on the four areas where an undoubted shift has taken place.

First, in 1979 all exchange controls for UK residents were abolished (non-resident sterling holders had been free of controls since convertibility in 1958). This was followed by the removal of controls over bank lending and credit in 1980 and consumer credit in 1982. In 1986 the Financial Services Act reorganised the London Stock Exchange and paved the way for the 'Big Bang' in October 1987 – the launch of deregulated-cum-self-regulated City markets. Second was the deregulation – 'the removal of statutory restrictions on market entry' (Kay & Thompson, 1987) – of many businesses, including long-distance coaches, bus services, gas production, electricity supply, opticians, house conveyancing, domestic airlines and the Post Office monopoly in carrying mail (Cable, 1986). Tendering has also been introduced for various local authority services, such as refuse collection, and in the National Health Service. Third, the government has established a less directive and discriminatory system of company taxation, cutting the standard rate of corporation tax whilst abolishing initial investment allowances and stock relief (OECD, 1985c).

Privatisation is the fourth, and perhaps the most revolutionary, area of state disengagement in economic policy. Its original rationale was a supply-side one: to increase efficiency via the exposure of enterprises to capital market sanctions and product market competition. The list of enterprises partly or wholly privatised is extensive and includes Britoil, British Aerospace, the National Freight Corporation, the National Bus Company, Cable & Wireless, British Telecom, British Gas, British Airways, the British Airports Authority and the Rover car group. These will shortly be followed by electricity supply and distribution and the regional water authorities. However during this period another rationale was adumbrated – that privatisation permits reductions in state borrowing without raising taxes – and this has now displaced the original competitive arguments. Since 1985 the Exchequer has raised about five billion pounds a year in this way. Many claim that in consequence competition policy has been sacrificed to the revenue raising potential of asset sales.[18]

The remaining parts of industrial policy have been marked by broad institutional continuity, albeit with shifts of emphasis. To begin with, under Sir Keith Joseph at the Department of Trade and Industry, policy was marked by substantial planned cuts in expenditure and a ferocious free market rhetoric. In practice public expenditure on industry, trade and energy has fallen sharply from 5.1 per cent in 1978–1979 to 2.4 per cent in 1986–1987. Subsidies to British Leyland and Rolls Royce were continued and British Steel was given a huge write-off, but no new rescues of firms were undertaken. Some new initiatives, such as the 'Alvey' initiative to develop 'fifth generation' computers, marked a move towards 'state-led inter-firm collaboration on the Japanese model' (Wilks, 1985; Devine, 1986). On the other hand, total government spending on science and technology has fallen as a share from 1.3 per cent in 1982–1983 to 1.2 per cent in 1987–1988, and retained its bias towards defence-related projects, whilst civilian spending also fell from 0.7 per cent to 0.6 per cent over the same period (HMSO, 1988, Table 2.12). Britain has also opposed several European Community initiatives, such as enhanced regional policy and several collaborative scientific projects including the European Space Agency's pure space science budget and CERN.

Overall, the Thatcher government's policy on capital and product markets has reversed the post-war consensus: 'Current policy is motivated primarily by concern for regulatory failure even at the expense of ignoring market failure' (Kay & Thompson, 1987, p. 181). The effect of these policies on Britain's manufacturing competitiveness is much disputed. According to the OECD, the effects of trade union reform has been mixed: 'the weakening of the unions has certainly contributed to greater flexibility in the labour market in changing working practices but has still not succeeded in imparting any downward flexibility in real wages'.[19] Many commentators question whether privatisation necessarily enhances competition. In some industries such as cars, shipbuilding and international airlines, world competition is fierce and will act on public as well as private companies; other industries, such as water, electricity distribution, posts and telecommunications, are close to natural monopolies, such that privatisation replaces a public with a private monopoly (Cable, 1986). About 40 per cent of all privatisation receipts thus far have come from the sale of natural monopolies (OECD, 1988d, p. 69).

Thus the rapid disposal of state assets and state responsibilities may undermine rather than enhance industrial performance (see Kay & Thompson, 1987). Paradoxically, the wish to reverse the tide of statism may interfere with other attempts to improve competitiveness.

TWO CASE STUDIES

To focus on cars and telecommunications as case studies in economic competitiveness is automatically to present the UK in a poor light, for these have been among the least competitive sectors of British industry over at least the past decade. If aerospace or pharmaceuticals, let alone financial services, had been chosen the British performance would have better withstood international comparison. We analyse here the competitiveness in, so to speak, two of Britain's many Achilles heels.

The Car Industry

The British car industry is an example of, and a major contributor to, the decline in manufacturing which we have charted. On almost every indicator its performance has been bad and, though there are now many who are optimistic, there is no sign yet of the long-awaited

Table 4.7 UK car industry: selected statistics

	1973–6	*1977–80*	*1981–4*
Revealed comparative advantage	1.12	0.87	0.72
	1978	*1986*	*1978–86*
Exports/home demand (%)	39	25	−14
Imports/home demand (%)	35	51	+16

Source: Patel and Pavitt, 1987, Table 7; Mayes, 1987, Table 8.

Notes: See text for definition of RCA
Home demand = manufacturers' sales + imports − exports.

turn-around. Table 4.7 shows the widening trade gap in the late-1970s to early 1980s as exports plumeted whilst import shares soared. The balance of trade in cars had deteriorated from large surpluses of three to four billion pounds up to 1976 to a rough balance in 1977–1980 to worsening deficits thereafter – six billion pounds by 1988. An index of 'revealed comparative advantage' has also declined steadily since the 1960s: it measures the ratio of Britain's share of world exports in motor vehicles to its share in all sectors, a ratio below unity therefore denotes relative weakness.

Until the mid-1980s all indicators told the same story. Domestic production fell from 1.9m vehicles in 1972 to around the 1m level in just seven years, and, though it stabilised thereafter, the rising import of components meant that the output of 'car equivalents' continued to decline to 0.7m in 1984. Car workers earnings, which were 17 per cent higher than those of average male manual wages in 1972 reached rough parity by the mid-1980s. Apart from Ford, all UK producers reported losses after 1979, including a cumulative one billion pound loss at Austin–Rover between 1979 and 1983 (Marsden *et al.*, 1985). R&D expenditure as a share of value added in motor vehicles was low relative to its major competitors in the 1970s (Jones, 1983, Table 1), though it was increasing as a share of output. A measure of 'revealed technology advantage' (RTA), (calculated as Britain's share of all patenting in the US in a sector divided by Britain's share of all US patenting) shows a declining value for UK road vehicles between 1969–1972 and 1981–1984. On every measure therefore the competitiveness of the British car industry plumeted in the 1970s and up to the mid-1980s.

However some claim that present portents are more optimistic. Profits are rising sharply in all UK based car firms, and productivity is now much higher as a result of the rationalisation of the early 1980s. Above all there is substantial inward investment by Japanese firms for whom the UK is emerging as a favoured location. Nissan is already producing in the North East of England, and Toyota will shortly follow with a large factory in Derbyshire. Peugeot too is increasing investment in its Talbot plant. One estimate suggests that by 1992 car output in Britain will have recovered to two million a year. This, however, is an equivocal verdict on British competitiveness. On the one hand, it signals a sea-change in British industrial relations. Though union membership in the industry remains high and organisation at plant level has changed little, there is greater co-operation and a 'new realism' on the union side coupled with greater consultation, more briefings and involvement on the management side. This has all contributed to the long-run improvement in productivity. On the other hand, one reason car firms favour Britain is its low labour costs and an untrained workforce less critical of unskilled, repetitive tasks (*The Economist*, 1989).

There are currently three major firms in the British car industry: Ford and Vauxhall, both US subsidiaries, and Rover, the once-nationalised and now privatised remnant of the British Motor Corporation. In 1984 they accounted for 18 per cent, 28 per cent and 16 per cent respectively of the UK car market. It is apparent that Rover is extremely small: its output of about 0.4m cars a year is about a quarter that of major European competitors such as Volkswagen, Renault, Peugeot and Fiat, let alone the US and Japanese giants. Its present size is the result of a drastic loss of market shares in the 1970s which continued right through the 1980s. As such it has been symptomatic of the decline described above, and we shall concentrate on its fortunes here.

Government policy towards Rover entered a new phase in 1975 when the company was reluctantly nationalised. In 1978 Sir Michael Edwardes was appointed chairman and began a government-funded programme of rationalisation, adaptation, new model development and confrontation with the trades unions. The funding and general government support continued after the change of government, even with Sir Keith Joseph as Secretary of State. In 1980 the first of the BL contracts with Honda of Japan was signed – a pioneering form of international collaboration which has most probably saved the firm from further falls in output and market share. In 1984 a switch in policy began: Jaguar was hived off and sold in a public flotation, and the government indicated it wished the rest of the corporation to be privatised. However an attempt by General Motors to purchase the Land Rover section was forestalled in 1986 by a nationalist political reaction in all political parties. With an election due the government backed down, although it authorised the sale of Leyland Trucks to DAF in 1987. In March 1988 it was announced that British Aerospace had an option to purchase the whole company, now named the Rover Group. To this end it was revealed that the £2.7b past losses were to be written off (the EC Commission permitting) in order to make the sale more attractive.

Thus during the last three years the privatisation and disengagement aims of the administration have begun to win out over the inherited policy stance. Despite the recent improvements noted above, Rover remains a vulnerable small producer of volume cars. The proposed sale to British Aerospace caused much surprise (see for example *The Economist*, 5 March 1988), and may risk future output and employment whilst offering little to combat the structural problems the group faces. In cars too the government has finally broken with bipartisan policy and prioritised privatisation over a longer term industrial strategy (Jones, 1983, 1986; *The Economist*, 1985, 1988).

Telecommunications

> 'Under the Thatcher government after 1979 Britain's experience in telecommunications is without precedent in Western Europe' (Morgan & Webber, 1986, p. 5).

Telecommunications is a sector which has been a flagship for the Thatcher government's liberalisation and privatisation policies since 1981. Before that it was organised in the traditional European way with a dominant public provider of telephone and allied services (British Telecom after 1981) linked to a small, closed ring of private suppliers of telecommunications equipment (GEC, Plessey, STC). In many respects, despite the very different nature of the industry, trends in competitiveness have mirrored those in the car industry: declining competitiveness in the 1970s, followed by restructuring in the 1980s which has yet to produce any clear improvement. Although it is difficult to assemble comprehensive data on the competitiveness of the telecommunications industry (it does not correspond to any one of the ISTC categories) Table 4.8 indicates recent trends.

Table 4.8 UK telecommunications industry: selected statistics

Output (1980=100):	1978	1981	1985
Electrical & instrument engineering	102	93	131
Telephone/telegraphic equipment	85	100	115
UK Exports of telecom equipment (£m)	98	131	242
UK Imports	54	96	317
Balance of trade	44	35	−75

Investment per capita, $US, 1980 exchange rates	*UK*	*US*	*FRG*	*FR*	*SW*
1975–77	53	71	59	85	37
1983–85	49	67	104	83	93

Sources: Top: Foreman-Peck & Manning, 1986, Tables 2, 3.
Middle: Patel & Pavitt, 1987, Table 7.
Bottom: Ypsilanti & Mansell, 1987, Table 2.

Resolute action by the Conservative administration has wrought two revolutions in UK telecommunications: liberalisation in 1981 was followed by privatisation in 1984. In the 1981 Telecommunications Act the telecommunications function of the Post Office was hived off and invested in the newly formed British Telecom (BT). The formerly rigid rules governing equipment sales and value added network services (VANS) were liberalised; and subsequently another company (Mercury, a subsidiary of Cable & Wireless) was licensed to operate a digital network with public access. Thus an unequal duopoly was substituted for a traditional monopoly, though BT were freed to buy wherever they chose. The pioneering privatisation of BT occurred under the 1984 Act when 51 per cent of government shares were sold. At the same time a new regulatory body – the Office of Telecommunications (OFTEL) – was set up. By these measures Britain, alongside the USA and Japan, has liberalised its telecommunications market – but in the absence of similar arrangements in Europe.

The traditional suppliers of equipment (GEC, Plessey and STC) have suffered as BT has sought overseas sourcing, for example from Thorn–Ericsson. Output and exports have risen in a dynamic market, but the trade balance in telecom equipment has deteriorated sharply as imports from the US, Japan and Sweden have mushroomed. This would seem to be an inevitable short-term consequence of 'a strategy which puts market-led demand before indigenous supply capacity' (Morgan & Webber, 1986, p. 81). Second, the longer term consequences are less clear. On the positive side, foreign multinationals are choosing Britain as their chief location in Europe as a result of its liberal market and productivity is rising fast with falling payrolls in both BT and the suppliers. All these trends may be expected to enhance productivity and thus longer run competitiveness. UK business in general has also benefited as the tariff structure is shifted (in response to competition from Mercury) to favour business users and penalise domestic users: the UK now has the lowest business tariffs in Europe.

On the other hand, the government's policy of 'asymmetric deregulation' (introducing a competitive environment for UK suppliers in the absence of a *quid pro quo* in Europe) is certainly harming the domestic telecommunications suppliers.[20] Furthermore BT's continuing domination as telecommunications carrier may inhibit its dynamism – its interest in product development has already waned – with spillover effects on the non-price competitiveness of UK suppliers. In order to maximise its revenue from the sale of BT the government sold it as a single concern, rather than breaking it up along the lines of the AT&T divestiture in the USA. Thus 'privatisation tempered the government's "animal spirits" with respect to liberalisation' (Morgan & Webber, 1986, p. 131). In telecommunications, the government's wish to diminish public borrowing and the role of the state may yet clash with its drive to resurrect a key British high-tech industry.

TRENDS IN WELFARE STATISM

The modern British welfare state, despite Edwardian foundations, is a product of the Second World War (Parry, 1986). In 1942 the Beveridge Report recommended a unified and universal system of flat-rate national insurance; in 1944 the Coalition government under Churchill committed itself to full employment and passed Butler's Education Act providing universal, free primary and secondary education; and on 5 July 1948 the Attlee Labour government inaugurated the free and universal National Health Service (NHS), put into operation the new National Insurance Scheme covering retirement, widowhood, sickness and unemployment (among other contingencies), and in a final *coup de grâce* abolished the remnants of the Poor Law from the statute books. Thus in the space of four years Britain acquired a 'mature' welfare state which served as a pioneering model for other countries. Over the next three decades many changes occured, yet, apart from the Social Security Act 1975 which introduced a state earnings-related pension scheme (SERPS), none involved fundamental reform: they were incremental encrustations on the basic Beveridge/Butler/Bevan edifice.

All this is now changing. In 1975–1976, the Labour government successfully implemented the first plans to cut back some items of social spending. The public commitment to maintain full employment has disappeared and mass unemployment has persisted throughout the 1980s. The election of 1979 brought to power a government committed to rolling back the state and especially the welfare state. In its first two periods of office it acted to cut and retrench state housing, some social benefits, taxation and the powers of local government; but it steered clear of the central institutions of the welfare state. Now, in its third term of office it has begun fundamentally to reform the social security, taxation, health and education systems. In retrospect, 1988 may mark the year when British 'welfare statism' was finally and radically restructured.

Unemployment and Employment Policy

I begin with unemployment and employment policy for two reasons: first, it is impossible to analyse trends in British social policy over the last decade without taking into account the emergence of mass unemployment. Second, the goal of full employment was a crucial component of the British post-war settlement and is thus an integral aspect of British 'welfare statism'.

Britain was one of the first countries to experience mass unemployment in the 1980s. After edging beyond the half million mark (about 2 per cent) in the 1960s, unemployment exceeded one million in 1975 and remained at around 1.4m or 5½ per cent from 1976–1979. In the deep two-year depression from 1979–1981 it then doubled to three million people or 12 per cent of the employed population. From 1981 to 1986 the numbers unemployed continued to grow albeit more slowly to a peak of 3.3m, 13.6 per cent, according to the official figures. However numerous changes to the offical definition make comparisons over time hazardous: one measure of the unadjusted figure (that is, using the same count as in 1981) puts the numbers out of work in 1986 at 3.8m or one in six of the employed population (Unemployment Unit, August, 1987). Since late 1986 the official count shows a rapid decline in the unemployed to under two million or 9.2 per cent in January 1988; the unadjusted numbers shadow this decline but at higher absolute numbers. Within this total, long-term unemployment has grown the fastest and is declining more slowly: still almost one million people have been out of work for more than one year. It is long-term unemployment which has the most serious consequences for both income and health, especially mental health, according to numerous studies.

Table 4.9 UK: employment and unemployment, 1979, 1983 and 1987

	1979	*1983*	*1987*	*Δ79–87*
Working population	25.9	25.8	27.3	+1.4
Manufacturing employees	7.1	5.5	5.1	−2.1
+ Other employees	15.4	15.0	16.2	+0.8
= All employees	22.5	20.5	21.3	−1.3
+ Self-employed	1.8	2.1	2.6	+0.8
= All in work (incl. HM Forces)	24.7	23.0	24.2	−0.5
∴ Unemployed	1.2	2.8	3.1	+1.9
% unemployed	5.1	12.1	12.8	
of which: nos long-term	0.3	1.1	1.2	+0.9
% long-term	25	36	42	
Nos on Special Employment Measures	0.26	0.44	0.78	+0.52
– register effect	n/a	0.31	0.59	+0.28
– register effect less YTS		0.17	0.30	+0.13

Sources: Lloyds Bank Economic Bulletin, 105, September 1987, Table 4. Unemployment Unit Bulletin, August 1987.

Table 4.9 explains this development by comparing trends in employment and the working population. We have already referred to the haemorrhage of jobs between 1979 and 1983 when a million and a half manufacturing jobs alone were lost. Since then manufacturing employment has continued its decline, but service employment has staged a recovery. Between 1983 and 1987 the numbers in work continued to grow alongside rising unemployment. However the jobs were almost all female and part-time: part-time working increased by 0.7 million from 21 per cent to 24 per cent of total employment between 1981 and 1987, and Britain now has the highest proportion of part-time work in the OECD after the Nordic countries and

Holland. Despite this, the numbers at work have not recovered 1979 levels. Self-employment has boomed since 1979, encouraged in recent years by the Enterprise Allowance Scheme: by 1987 over three-quarters of a million people were attached to this or one of the many other special employment schemes developed in the 1980s. Together these deflated the unemployment total by one-third of a million (if the YTS trainees are excluded – see below). These special employment schemes have come to replace the previous government commitment to maintain full employment, so we should briefly review them here.

Since 1983 the Youth Training Scheme (YTS) has provided training-cum-work experience for every school leaver who wishes to take it up; in 1986 this was extended to two years. Places are provided by paid private employers (a minority), local authorities, voluntary bodies and other 'managing agents'. Trainees are paid £27 per week and £35 in their second year. The YTS was the first systematic state training programme to be provided in the UK; it is also claimed to be cost-efficient and have around a 50 per cent success rate in leading to subsequent employment. However critics claim that it offers poor quality training by comparison with Britain's competitors, and is more akin to a low-quality work experience scheme. Another big scheme, the Community Programme (CP), provided work programmes targeted on the long-term unemployed – mainly environmental improvement and services for disadvantaged groups. The programme has been criticised for the low rate of pay, the consequent low take-up by older men, its discrimination against women, and its poor success rate in placing people in permanent work. The major claim made on its behalf is that it was targeted on the most vulnerable group: the long-term unemployed.

In November 1987 the government proposed a new 'unified training programme' targeted on the long-term unemployed which represents a shift in direction. It will link social security and work experience/training by paying participants 'benefits-plus', which means they continue to receive income-related supplementary benefit with an extra £5–£10 per week. It is not clear as yet whether this will amount to a new form of training grant, or semi-compulsory work for claimants. Since no extra resources are provided for the scheme it seems unlikely that it will develop into an element of a new unified training programme. The legislation enacts that anybody refusing to take a place on a designated training scheme will have their benefit cut. This combination of measures has been interpreted by some as the first step towards a form of American-style 'workfare' (*The Economist*, 'Forward to the workfare state', 28 November 1987, pp. 25–7). If this is so it marks a break with previous policies and a significant integration of social security and employment programmes. An important element of welfare statism is being modified in the pursuit of labour market flexibility (and, to a minor extent, of labour force quality) according to the supply-side theory of neo-liberal economists.[21]

Expenditure on the Welfare State

Turning to the social benefits and services which form the traditional core of the welfare state, Table 4.10 summarises developments over the last decade and a half. In the first year of the 1974 Labour government spending and public sector employment all soared in the British welfare state's last and finest boom (Parry, 1986; Levitt & Joyce, 1987). Then came the cuts of 1975 and the further retrenchment ordered by the IMF in 1976. In real terms spending on all social programmes slowed down markedly and the share of social expenditure in GDP fell. The major cut was in capital expenditure programmes, economically and politically the easiest to reduce in a short space of time. Nevertheless the net result of the Labour administrations of 1974–1979 was a substantial increase in resources devoted to social security and the health and personal social services (but a decline in education spending and a levelling out of housing spending), and a rise in the relative claims of the welfare state on national resources.

Despite the intention of the Thatcher government to reduce state spending, especially on social and economic services, in its first term it presided over a sizeable increase in social expenditure. This was so in absolute terms and, because of the recession, relative to GDP – indeed the share of spending on the welfare state recaptured the heights it had reached in 1975. Transfer spending soared, notably on the social security programmes, whilst capital spending was cut back still further – notably local authority house building. In the government's second term the rate of absolute increase slowed down, though it was by no means reversed, and a faster rate of economic growth meant that its share of GDP began once again to fall. The switch of priorities was generally continued with a fast increase in social security spending, slower growth in health, personal social services and education, and further cuts in housing. Thus within a

Table 4.10 UK: social expenditure, 1973–87

	1973/4	*75/6*	*78/9*	*83/4*	*86/7*	*Δ78/9–86/7*
Volume terms: £b 1986/7 prices						
Social security	25.4	30.2	34.2	41.8	46.5	+36%
Health	12.5	15.1	15.1	17.6	18.8	+24%
PSS	2.1	2.7	2.8	3.2	3.5	+28%
Education	18.1	17.7	17.6	18.0	18.7	+6%
Housing	8.5	9.9	8.8	5.0	4.0	−55%
Total social expenditure	66.6	75.6	78.5	85.6	91.5	+17%
Per cent GDP						
Social security	8.1	9.8	10.2	12.0	12.2	
Health	4.0	4.9	4.5	5.1	4.9	
PSS	0.7	0.9	0.8	0.9	0.9	
Education	5.8	5.8	5.3	5.2	4.9	
Housing	2.7	3.2	2.6	1.4	1.1	
Total social expenditure	21.3	24.6	23.4	24.6	24.0	

Sources: Atkinson *et al.* (1987), Table 7.1; Hills (1987), Table 1

Notes: The figures in brackets are reweighted by myself.
The figures are adjusted to take into account changes in the balance of tax and direct expenditures (for example, in child benefits before 1978–1979, and the transfer of part of sickness benefits to employers in 1983–1984), in the taxation of benefits, and in the transfer of benefits between programmes (for example, Supplementary Benefit rent payments in the first two years are shown under housing expenditures).
Deflators: Social security – mainly by RPI
Health – implicit NHS deflator in Nat Inc & Expend Accounts
PSS – GDP deflator
Education – implicit education deflator in NIE Accounts
Housing – mixed GDP and RPI deflators

rising aggregate expenditure on the welfare state the Thatcher government has effected a sustained shift in priorities away from housing towards income maintenance.

The years since 1979 have also witnessed a surge in the 'alternative welfare states'. For example 'tax expenditures' have grown – that on mortgage interest relief claimed by house buyers has more than doubled in real terms from £2.1b in 1978–1979 to £4.5b in 1986–1987 (Hills, 1987, p. 99). After a slow growth the extent of occupationally-based welfare has also increased – occupational pensions surged from £3.7b in 1978–1979 to £5.6b in 1983–1984 (Atkinson *et al.*, 1987, p. 226). Hence since 1979 there has been a swing of emphasis away from social welfare towards what Titmuss has called fiscal and occupational welfare.

The 'Output' of Social Programmes

To understand what these figures mean in terms of real benefits and services, we must analyse trends in needs, demand and clienteles.[22] As regards the income maintenance system, it is the growing number of claimants, especially the unemployed, which accounts for two-thirds of the real growth in spending since 1978–1979 noted above (Hills, 1987, p. 94). Despite this the numbers receiving insurance-based unemployment benefit *per se* rose by only 63 per cent up to 1986: it remains conditional on past employment record and is limited in duration. As a result it has been the income-related Supplementary Benefit (SB) system which has borne the brunt of the rising demand: the numbers of non-pensioner claimants have risen 150 per cent. The final income guaranteed to SB claimants has risen by 5 per cent in real terms since 1979 – well below the 14 per cent rise in the average disposable incomes of those in work over the same period. Pensions and child benefit have risen by a similar proportion in real terms, but have also declined as a share of net earnings. Up to 1988 no basic benefit has been reduced in real terms, but the welfare state safety net is now about 12 per cent lower relative to average living standards.

Trends in standards in the direct service areas of the welfare state – particularly the National Health Service (NHS) – have been the subject of bitter debate for several years now. The Conservative government increased public spending on health considerably in its first five years, albeit at a slower rate than under its predecessor. However the relative price effect (the tendency for costs to rise faster in the public sector) continued to be positive and quite large due to pay increases: it halved the rate of growth in volume terms. Although the post-war rise in the size of the dependent population came to an end in this period, the numbers of very elderly continued to grow and this has also exerted an upward pressure on costs (the over-75s cost, on average, six times as much as those of working age in health and personal services) (Levitt & Joyce, 1987). When this is taken into account spending on health services in relation to need grew by about 0.8 per cent p.a. between 1979–1980 and 1984–1985, and spending on hospitals by only 0.3 per cent p.a. (Robinson, 1986). Furthermore, the DHSS estimates that medical advances in medicine absorb half a percent p.a. extra resources, assuming as all these estimates do that productivity does not improve. Thus the contradictory positions of the different parties can be resolved: spending has increased but it has not called forth any improvement in standards. In the more recent period since 1984 spending in relation to need has almost certainly declined (*The Economist*, 23 January 1988, p. 27).

In primary and secondary education the situation is very different: real reductions in volume expenditure have been achieved, but the number of primary and secondary pupils has fallen faster, resulting in a rising per capita expenditure (Robinson, 1986). However in further and higher education quite marked reductions in unit costs have been achieved as tightened budgets have been stretched over more students. Housing has been hit harder than any other area of welfare state spending since 1979. The decline in public house building continued the cuts begun in 1976: housing starts fell from 180 000 in 1975 and 1976 to 84 000 in 1979 to 36 000 in 1985. In general, following the resumption of economic growth after 1981, the goal of reducing spending on the welfare state has been quietly replaced by the target to reduce its share of GDP. Yet the resources for some services have been squeezed as a result of deliberate restructuring and inadequate recompense for cost and demand growth. If the retrenchment of spending on the British welfare state does not match the government's rhetoric, this should not obscure the fact that parts of the welfare state have been reduced in scale.

Outcomes: Poverty, Inequality and Redistribution

The New Right policies pursued since 1979 have generated wider inequalities in British society: directly, via such measures as tax cuts and the de-indexation of benefits; and indirectly, via unemployment and a more 'dualised' labour market. Between 1979 and 1986 average gross household income increased by 12 per cent, but this disguised a widening disparity in living standards. For the top 10 per cent of households the rise was 31 per cent and for the top 1 per cent it was 55 per cent; the poorest 40 per cent suffered a drop in real income – for the bottom 10 per cent this loss amounted to 8 per cent of their 1979 income (Stark, 1988). The following attempts to explain these trends.

Table 4.11 presents different data showing the income shares of different income groups. Market incomes have become markedly

Table 4.11 UK: income distribution and redistribution, 1976, 1979 and 1984

Share of income (%)		*1976*	*1979*	*1984*
Market income:	top 5%	16.0	15.8	17.5
	top quintile	44.4	44.9	48.6
	4th quintile	9.4	8.7	6.1
	lowest quintile	0.8	0.5	0.3
Net income:	top 5%	13.2	13.0	13.8
	top quintile	37.6	38.2	39.2
	4th quintile	12.8	12.3	11.4
	lowest quintile	7.8	7.2	8.1

Source: O'Higgins, 1987, Tables 4.1, 4.2, 4.4

Notes: Quintiles ranked by market income throughout table.
Market income = earned income, investment income, self-employment income and occupational pensions
Net income = market income + cash transfers – income tax and employees national insurance contributions

more unequal since 1979 partly due to a decline in the share of aggregate household incomes derived from wages and salaries as a result of unemployment – it shrank from 69 per cent in 1976 to 60 per cent in 1985 – whilst the shares accruing from property income, occupational welfare and state benefits have increased. At the same time income from both labour and property is distributed more unequally than a decade ago. Earnings have become more dispersed since 1976. The spread of male earnings widened greatly: the top decile increasing their earnings from 160 per cent to 173 per cent of the average between 1976 and 1986, whilst the lowest decile's fell from 68 per cent to 60 per cent of the average (Stark, 1987, Table b). Since 1979 another trend has been superimposed on this: the tendency for investment and private pension income to become concentrated among the upper income groups (O'Higgins, 1987, Table 4.2). The recession and associated changes has thus widened inequality in factor incomes.

Has the growing expenditure on state welfare benefits offset this? Table 4.11 compares the distribution of market and net incomes using O'Higgins' careful study (1985, 1987). Taxation and state benefits are clearly critical in redistributing income vertically at any moment in time, but access to factor incomes has been the predominant influence over time. The fourth (second from bottom) quintile has lost access to market incomes over the period and, like the bottom group, is becoming more dependent on transfers. Since 1979, the income share of the bottom quintile after state benefits and direct taxes has increased by one percentage point, but this is due to a change in household composition.[23] When the figures are adjusted to take account of these compositional shifts, the share of the bottom 20 per cent in net income registers almost no change (O'Higgins, 1987, Table 4.1). Since 1979, the (adjusted and unadjusted) share of the top income groups in net income has grown, but by less than their share of market income. Thus the tax and transfer system has moderated but not negated the trend towards greater inequality since 1979.

One result is that the numbers in poverty have mushroomed over the last decade. The numbers on and below the state Supplementary Benefit level – the conventional measure – rose from 6.1m to 1979 to nine million people or one in six of the population by 1985, a higher proportion than at any time since the war. Whilst the number of poor elderly people has remained stable, the numbers of both the working and the unemployed poor – and of poor children – has risen sharply.[24]

Thus, since 1979 Britain has become an economically more unequal society on every count. But it is economic policy and mass unemployment which has brought about the move towards a dual society, not (as yet) the government's social policies for the welfare state. O'Higgins concludes: 'Recession, rather than (political) reaction, has been the main pressure resulting in a rise in poverty and inequality' (1985, p. 303). 'When access to market income is truncated, social spending has a demand-driven, reactive role in limiting the rise in inequality' (1987, p. 65). The social welfare system must run hard simply to stand still: in the event it has not run hard enough. It is the combination of high unemployment and neo-liberal economic policies with relatively unchanged social policies which explains the inegalitarian outcome of the Thatcher experiment. If equality and an end to want are key goals of the welfare state, then welfare statist outcomes have deteriorated in contemporary Britain.

Social Policies: Restructuring the Welfare State?

Thus far I have evaluated developments in British 'welfare statism' via broad measures of inputs (expenditure levels), outputs (service and benefit levels) and outcomes (unemployment, inequality and poverty). Apart from employment policy changes in social programmes have been ignored. Since the election of June 1987 however the Thatcher government has produced a series of bills to restructure the education, housing, health and taxation systems – presaging a more direct focus on the core areas of the welfare state which it is impossible for us to disregard.

Housing is one area of social policy where the Thatcher administration within a short time achieved and even exceeded its manifesto commitments. In a series of measures the Conservative administration has transformed the British housing market and the role of the state within it. They include the sale of local authority homes to sitting tenants at a large price discount (by the end of 1985 860 000 council dwellings had been sold out of a stock of six and a half million – mostly houses rather than flats (CSO, 1987)), cuts in state subsidies, and higher rents for local authority housing, cuts in public sector housing investment, and (in the 1988 Housing Act) the removal of statutory restrictions on the rented sector and the promised demise of local authorities as developers and managers of rented housing. The upshot of these measures is to increase owner occupation and favour the private sector, to eliminate council house subsidies and to deregulate the housing market. However tax expenditures on house purchase have not been cut back and in the aggregate have expanded very rapidly (see above). One effect of this is a remarkable widening of house prices between the South and North of Britain which may impair labour mobility and hence some aspects of competitiveness. At the same time tenure differences have widened as local authority housing assumes more the status of a residual service for the poor and disadvantaged groups and homelessness is climbing despite a surplus of dwellings (Atkinson *et al.*, 1987; *The Economist*, 26 December 1987, p. 25).

The 1979 Conservative Manifesto described the social security goals of the future government as: to simplify the system and cut bureaucracy, to improve incentives to work, and to concentrate benefits on those in 'real need' (MacGregor, 1985). To reduce administrative costs in practice it has devolved the payment of initial sickness insurance benefit to employers, and all income-related housing benefit to local authorities. The latter especially is an example of the technique which Tarschys (1985) refers to as 'decentralising hard choices'. It also abolished the Supplementary Benefits Commission, an example of removing awkward, corporatist bodies which exert upward pressures on state spending. To improve work incentives it abolished earnings-related sickness and unemployment insurance benefits, made them liable to tax, de-indexed pensions and long-term benefits from their link with earnings, and abolished the statutory indexation of short-term benefits. The overall effect of these initial measures was to maintain the absolute value of 'safety-net' benefits, but to enhance the stigma associated with claiming them, according to MacGregor (1985).

This was followed by the Social Security Act of 1986 which has been implemented in stages up to April 1988. Its goals are to direct benefit to those in genuine need, to facilitate the government's overall economic strategy (with regard to costs, incentives and labour market flexibility) and to reduce the existing complexity and administrative costs: aims remarkably similar to those adumbrated in 1979. Its strategy is to shrink, privatise and de-regulate the post-Beveridge structures of income maintenance. The SERPS pension benefits will be cut for those retiring after 1998, a measure which will mainly affect the entitlements of the intermittently employed – chiefly women. Contracting out from occupational pensions or SERPS into private pension plans will also be encouraged. It is intended to halve the burden on the Exchequer by the year 2033. Britain's burgeoning means-tested or income-related benefit system is also to be restructured, though it is as yet difficult to predict the distributive and economic impacts of these changes. Critics argue that a majority of the poverty population will lose income, especially when other policy reforms are taken into account (notably the new flat rate poll tax levied on all adults 18 years and over and the new employment policy) (Social Security Consortium, 1987). It would appear that long-term reform along negative income tax lines has been ruled out, but that further moves towards US-style 'workfare', coupled with the phasing out of universal child benefit, are possible.

Following the 1987 election the government has also inaugurated the first major Education Act since 1944. It removes much of local authorities' power over schools, by increasing parental choice of school and enhancing the power of head teachers. For the first time in Britain a national curriculum will be imposed and all children will be uniformally tested at seven, eleven, 14 and 16 years. Schools will be allowed, if parents and governors want and the education department agrees, to opt out entirely from local authority control. The financing of higher and further education is also to become more centralised in order to gear its output more closely to the requirements of the economy. The Act embraces two philosophies: on the one hand to extend parental choice and encourage middle class 'exit' from the state system and on the other to enhance the control exercised by the central state over the education service.

The National Heath Service escaped significant reform in the first two Conservative administrations despite the commitments in Conservative party manifestos to cut bureaucracy and waste and encourage private health provision and insurance. Early measures included abolishing the Health Services Board, which regulated the activities of private providers, reversing the previous pay-beds policy, changing consultants' contracts, and restoring tax exemption of employer-provided medical insurance for lower paid employees (Atkinson *et al.*, 1987). Initially this boosted coverage of private medical insurance from over two million persons in 1978 to over four million by 1981. Since then however the rate of increase has tailed off (CSO, 1987, Table 7.32). The number of commercial, mainly American, hospitals and nursing homes has risen, whilst the supply of private old peoples' homes has boomed. Charges for drugs have risen 1000 per cent since 1979, although because of exemptions their share of NHS funding has not fundamentally changed. In 1989 the government's review of the NHS proposed to develop 'internal markets' within the health service and diminish the role of centralised planned budgets. The expressed goals combine responsiveness 'downwards' to consumers with 'upward' accountability to top management.

The above shifts mark a fundamental questioning of the post-war British welfare state consensus, especially when read in conjunction with the changes in taxation and employment policy detailed earlier. Some common themes can be discerned:

- the encouragement of market choice and options for 'exit';
- a broader role for private and occupational provision;
- de-regulation and less government planning; yet
- the removal of local government powers with *more extensive* centralised intervention in some social policy domains;
- a sustained redistribution of income and wealth towards the upper income groups.

Middlemas (1986) and others have dwelt on the 'moment of 1944' when the 'post-war settlement' began to be constructed, a major component of which was the Beveridge/Butler/Bevan welfare state. The recent Budget and series of welfare reforms may mark the end of that welfare state and its replacement by something very different. History may discern another dividing line: the moment of 1988.

The erosion of traditional 'welfare statism' in Britain bears an ambivalent relationship to the debates and policies for arresting national decline and enhancing competitiveness addressed in the second and third sections of this chapter. Many of the trends and policy shifts listed above flow directly from the perspectives, analyses and proposals of the New Right, and can be connected to their economic diagnoses of the causes of and cures for the 'British disease'. Insofar as the latter are correct, they can be argued to be economically 'rational'. Others however contradict and may interfere with the goal of improving competitiveness: they are directed to ending 'collectivism' in British life along with the power of those groups which espouse it irrespective of the economic effects. In part British 'welfare statism' has been eroded *despite* the pressures of international competition. Some of these conflicts are addressed in the conclusion.

CONCLUSION: THE INTERRELATION OF WELFARE STATISM AND INTERNATIONAL COMPETITIVENESS

Welfare statism in Britain has been rolled back over the past decade and a half in respect of inputs, outputs and outcomes. Though profound upward pressures stemming from the sharp recession of 1979–81 confounded the government's plans to reduce absolute expenditure and tax levels, some social programmes have been cut back whilst others failed to match the rising demands on them. Social programmes are being radically overhauled in the government's third term of office to encourage occupational and private provision and 'exit' from state schemes, to deregulate those that remain and to diminish the role of local authorities within the social policy field. Welfare outcomes are deteriorating as those in relative poverty become more numerous and inequality mounts throughout British society. Despite recent reductions in unemployment, regional, class, gender and race divisions in job opportunities remain deep.

The collective guarantee of living standards has receded in Britain as a result of both 'automatic' and 'political' factors. On the one hand, a welfare state designed for a period of full employment and diminishing inequalities in factor incomes has had to cope with a society of mass unemployment, dualisation and widening inequality (partly as a result of government policy). On the other hand, the successful mobilisation of a New Right political programme under the government of Mrs Thatcher has targeted the collectivist ethos of the welfare state and many state programmes on which it rests. It is the combination of these two trends which makes the British (and American) experience of the last decade quite different from that of Germany and France, let alone Sweden.

Are these shifts a result of new forms of international competition impinging on the British economy? As argued throughout this chapter I do not think so. Whilst the depressed state of the world economy contributed to the British recession at the turn of the decade, Britain has been protected by its oil until recently from some of the new competitive pressures of the 1980s. Of course the British economy faced dire problems in the 1970s and 1980s, but all agreed they were precisely of a long-run nature (even though there was sharp disagreement on their causes). Hence government policies, notably since 1979, have reflected a concern to overcome the deep-seated impasse of the British economy. 'Thatcherism' and the attempt to roll back the state stemmed from this central political concern. Social policies have in part been redesigned to make them more congruent with the deregulatory thrust of economic strategy. However they have in part served complementary or contrasting policy goals: to maintain social order when society is perceived to be increasingly unfair, and to remove collectivist goals and solutions from the political agenda.

What then has been the reverse impact of this erosion of welfare statism on the competitiveness of the British economy? The sharp divide between economic and social policy in Britain, institutionalised after the Second World War, bears part of the blame for its post-war economic failure (Marquand, 1988). An initially generous and redistributive welfare system was combined with a weak form of economic steering oriented towards the interests of a powerful, internationally-minded financial sector. This structural impasse seemed to rule out either a Swedish-style 'integrated welfare state' or a US-style 'residual welfare state', both of which, comparative evidence suggests, may enhance labour market performance (Åberg, 1984; Calmfors & Driffill, 1988). The inability of prior Labour and conservative governments to develop an economic programme compatible with welfare goals, and the corporatist/consensus structures to implement it, helps us understand why since 1979 the opposite option has been so resolutely pursued.

Since 1979 trends in the competitiveness of the British economy have been mixed: a strong upswing in productivity, inward investment by multinationals and higher profits indicate a flourishing and more competitive economy; an unprecedented trade deficit, high interest rates and renewed inflation and wage pressures suggest that it is not sustainable. But what is the contribution of recent government policies on the *welfare state* to these successes and failures? Whilst the shake-out, fear and greater co-operation which followed the rise in unemployment is identified by many as a significant cause of the economic renaissance (such as it is), few seem to regard the weakening of welfare statism *per se* as playing a positive role.[25]

On the contrary, there are now several domains where the neglect of the welfare state may threaten future competitiveness. First, there is the growing evidence of insufficient investment in human capital. The achievement of the lower half of English children in mathematics falls short of their German counterparts, and this pattern is repeated in science. A majority of pupils then leave full-time education or training at the age of sixteen, a higher drop-out rate than the average for the whole OECD. On top of this employer-based training is poorer in quality and quantity than on the Continent, and is now declining from a low level. Apart from the elite group, then, the British labour force is significantly poorer in skills and training than its competitors.[26] Of course this is the result of many decades of neglect; moreover the present government has begun to act by introducing the Youth Training Scheme and its offshoots and undertaking the first serious reform of education since the war. But evidence on the standards of the former is patchy and discouraging, whilst the effect of the latter is still open.

This neglect of investment in human capital is harming British economic performance. The expansion of several growth sectors is presently hindered by skill shortages; they include engineering, information technology and maths teaching. The mismatch of skills also contributes to a high rate of wage inflation in Britain despite a still high level of unemployment. In the longer run the lack of skills may well inhibit the further growth in productivity necessary if Britain is to close the productivity deficit with its competitor nations.[27]

A second way in which public sector neglect may harm economic competitiveness is through the rundown of physical infrastructure. In the South of England especially the public transport network is heavily overloaded whilst the government boasts of its lack of a co-ordinated transport policy. The contrast between the forward planning in France and the UK for the Channel Tunnel links is illuminating.

More generally, the last decade has witnessed a rundown of public sector assets in housing, social infrastructure and public utilities. Since 1981 public investment has only just kept ahead of depreciation, so that net investment has been negligible (Hills, 1987). Here too 'public squalor' may in the end impeded 'private affluence'.

If these arguments for a substantial public sector emphasise its 'accumulation' role, the third reiterates the 'legitimacy' role of welfare statism (Gough, 1979). Until now the 'productivity miracle' has stemmed predominantly from fear – notably the fear of redundancy and poverty among workers. Now that the economy is growing strongly and unemployment is declining, it is becoming apparent that this cannot provide a long-term source of motivation in the labour force, unless British trades unions are weakened much further than the government has so far managed. Writers from very different perspectives note that, whilst trade unions have been forced to adopt new working practices, they have not relinquished their power to determine wages (Matthews & Minford, 1987; Rowthorn, 1989). Consequently real wage rises have outstripped those in other countries and profits in British manufacturing, though recovering, remain below what is achieved abroad.

More worrying in the longer term, the old confrontational style of British industrial relations may return unless fear is replaced by greater participation and involvement in industry, along the lines suggested in the Delors plan for a 'Social Europe'. However, though there has been a shift in this direction among individual managements, it contradicts the main thrust of government policy which is still to discipline trades unions and exorcise the memory of 'corporatism'. Furthermore, a more consensual pattern of industrial relations depends crucially for its success on the belief by workers that the economic and social arrangements of society are not grossly 'unfair'. By its attacks on the welfare state, the present government has already been accused of creating a more unjust society. If this inhibits co-operation in improving labour allocation and flexibility, it may jeopardise the economic recovery.

It is this recognition that a restructured welfare statism can *advance* economic competitiveness which motivates those arguing for a new policy mix in Britain, one which combines some of the supply-side shifts introduced by the Thatcher government with a developed and productive welfare state. However, it may be that the government of Mrs Thatcher cannot undertake the policy switch. If the other thesis argued here is correct, present government policy is primarily guided, not by an economic programme to renew Britain's competitiveness, but precisely by a desire to erode British welfare statism for its own sake.

5 France

Xavier Greffe

The French economy is in real difficulty. This French 'decline' much debated by the end of the 1980s, is characterised by a persistent disequilibrium in certain fields. Even if this situation is not as serious as it seems, nevertheless the debate is all the more important since the country, for the first time in more than 25 years, has experienced a political change (Greffe, 1987c, and 1989).

As in other countries, many people think that the main cause of rising labour costs is to be found in the numerous social benefits provided by the welfare state. Consequently bringing the welfare state into question would be the only way to re-stimulate the French economy.

Of course, things are not so simple. The competitiveness of French products can be explained by cost factors as much as by non-cost factors inherited from the past. Another question should be asked. Is it necessary to see the relation between competitiveness and the welfare state as one of opposition? The only solution for France as for other European countries consists in turning towards very high value added products. Very high scientific potential, efficient substructures and a qualified manpower become the imperative priorities. A modernised welfare state will contribute more to the achievement of these priorities than a welfare state constantly under criticism.

THE CHALLENGE OF INTERNATIONAL COMPETITIVENESS

Let us first consider the evolution of various significant indicators (Table 5.1).

At first sight, the results are not bad: that is referring to the last few years. The trade balance improved – except for a sudden deterioration in 1985 which reappeared more severely in 1987 – and the French government has been able to begin repaying a part (FFs 0.6 billion) of the foreign public debt accumulated during the preceding four years.

But a more detailed examination reveals that the evolution is in

Table 5.1 France: external and domestic competitiveness: main indicators, 1979–86 (1979=100)

Indicators/Years	*1979*	*1980*	*1981*	*1982*	*1983*	*1984*	*1985*	*1986*
With the seven main partners*:								
Export price index	100	100.1	104.3	105.8	105.5	103.3	100.6	99.3
Unit wage cost index	100	96.9	98.2	100.8	101.9	102	100.6	99.6
Consumption price index	100	97.2	100.1	104.5	109.1	110	107.4	104.7
With the four main countries from the E.M.S.**								
Export price index	100	99.7	99.1	99.9	90.9	95	93	95.2
Unit wage cost index	100	94.9	91.5	93.5	94.9	93.6	91.5	93
Consumption price index	100	95.2	93.1	96.7	101	100.3	97.1	98.9
French industrial export/world demand ratio variations	100	97.6	100.1	98	99.3	97.9	95	91.9

* USA, Japan, UK, FRG, Italy, Netherlands, Belgium
** FRG, Italy, Netherlands, Belgium

Source: OECD, 1987c

Notes: Export price index: French export price/partner's average export price index
Unit wage cost index: French unit wage cost/partner's wage cost index
Consumption price index: French consumption price/partner's consumption price index

fact less satisfactory than it seems. During the early 1980s, the French recovery was due to the growth of industrial surplus and to good results in agrobusiness. However, the more recent recovery is due to the reduction in energy expenses. Obviously, the traditional industrial surplus is vanishing, falling from FFs 97.3 billion in 1984 to FFs 32.7 billion in 1986. Even worse, the last available data show that in 1987 the results were unsatisfactory. There was a deficit in the external balance of the manufacturing sector for the first time since 1959: France could not even benefit from the large reduction in its energy expenses (Table 5.2), (INSEE, 1987).

Table 5.2 France: main results of foreign exchange, 1980–86 (billion French francs)

	1980	*1981*	*1982*	*1983*	*1984*	*1985*	*1986*
Products	−87.6	−87.1	−136.4	−88.4	−69.3	−69.4	−33.1
(industry)	35.1	55.4	29.7	60.2	97.1	83	32.7
(oil)	−133.5	−162.6	−179.6	−168.9	−190.5	−181.9	−91.4
Services	53.2	56.6	67.2	81.7	97.9	97.4	85.7
(tourism)	9.2	7.7	11.7	21.8	28.6	30.1	21.8
Products & Services	−34.4	−30.5	−69.2	−6.7	28.6	28	52.6
Transfers	15.7	2.7	−10.7	−28.3	−32.5	−26.7	−23.7
Net financial position	−18.7	−27.8	−79.9	−35	−3.9	1.3	28.9
% G.N.P.	−0.7	−0.9	−2.2	−0.9	−0.1	0.03	0.6

Source: INSEE, 1987

When we look at the total export of the eight most developed countries, we see that the French share of this total has remained fairly stable for ten years in spite of constant efforts by the French government to increase it. In 1977, it reached 10.8 per cent and after a slight drop to 9.5 per cent in 1984, it rose again to 10 per cent. Even if this evolution is quite comparable to that of the United States or of the United Kingdom, it is well below that of Japan, Italy or West Germany for the same period (OECD, 1987c).

If we now consider the respective share of French exports in every international market, we can more easily specify the trend of competitiveness. Once more disappointment is the prevailing feeling that market shares have not increased except in the OPEC countries (from 9.4 to 12.6 per cent); in every other market, the situation is at best stable (OECD without EEC countries) but in decline generally (EEC, developing countries, Comecon countries).

If we consider the sectoral aspects, 20 per cent of French exports come from high-technology industries whose growth has been quicker than all other industries since 1980. But those results are far from being satisfactory if compared to that of competing countries. We first notice that these industries' export ratio is slightly inferior to that of our main competitors (the average is 22 per cent in the OECD countries). For that reason, French high-technology industries only have a 6.3 per cent share of the world market, against 22 per cent in Japan or 12 per cent in West Germany. Besides, this share has been reduced by 0.5 per cent percentage points between 1981 and 1985.

If we differentiate products according to their technological intensity (high, medium, low) in OECD countries (OECD, 1987c, pp. 19–23), we see that French and Italian market shares decrease when technological intensity increases whereas in the United States, Japan and even the United Kingdom, the two elements evolve together, West Germany and Canada being in a medium position. Though France excels in certain high technologies (such as telecommunications, transport, nuclear industries), these technological achievements have not been followed by commercial success. A good example is that of the High Speed Train which, surprisingly, France has not really succeeded in exporting.

On the other hand, France exports more to developing countries (one-third of its high-technology products) than to its competitors. This leads to insoluble debt problems.

Finally, French high-technology industries are very badly positioned on the domestic market. This, too, is prejudicial to the trade balance since this market grows more quickly than others; therefore, stimulating investments inevitably leads to stimulating imports. The penetration rate for high-technology products is 37 per cent (it is only 22 per cent for low-technology products). Moreover, the export/import ratio has been decreasing for two years and is lower for invisible items (patents, licences, technical aid) than for visible ones.

Though there has been considerable public financing, two overriding elements account for this situation: (a) a lack of dynamic trade strategies backed by international partnership and (b) extensive subcontracting networks which, far from securing the expected flexibility, lead rather to archaism and to an extensive dilution of resources.

In fact, in order to understand the situation of French industrial exports, we must refer again to French data. In Table 5.3, we find the

Table 5.3 France: export/import ratios, 1977–86

	Agriculture	*Food industry*	*Energy*	*Manufactured goods*	*Services*
1977	89	102	14	120	175
1979	98	106	16	116	193
1981	127	123	15	114	169
1983	133	108	15	111	183
1985	146	106	17	113	177
1986	144	106	21	104	164

Source: OECD, 1987c

evolution of export/import ratios by categories of products. During the last ten years, progress has been seen in every category, often in a limited way; only manufactures, and to a lesser extent services, have regressed.

To sum up, as the *Commissariat Général du Plan* recently showed, the deterioration of French price competitiveness slowed in 1985–1986 and monetary readjustments have continued to offset the difference between the French rate of inflation and that of West Germany, France's main partner. But price competitiveness does not explain everything: we must also consider the structure of French export supply. We can venture a conclusion which will be confirmed later on: the French government should not only try to control production costs, it should also restructure the French productive system.

THE INPUTS OF THE DEBATE

The disappointing results of French foreign trade are traditionally explained by comparatively high real labour costs.

The first important point here has been the slowing down of the increase in labour costs for about ten years: the annual rate of growth was 11.8 per cent for the 1977–1981 period but only 2.3 per cent in 1986 and 1.7 per cent in 1987 (INSEE, 1986), (OECD, 1987c, p. 13). The decrease in labour unit cost was less marked in manufacturing industries than in other sectors since in France, the larger the firms the higher the wages.

This tendency is confirmed by the distribution of income over the last ten years. The share of value added accruing to wage earners decreased by two points (from 66.6 to 64.2 per cent) while that accruing to profits increased by two points (from 26.4 to 28.1) (OECD, 1987, p. 13). This result is still more striking if we distinguish between the evolution of wages and that of welfare benefits. The decline in real wages is nearly four points which is partly offset by the increase in welfare benefits.

This growing control over unit labour costs is to be found everywhere internationally. France has not yet regained its place among the more competitive nations. Its unit labour costs are still relatively high but its position has improved since the beginning of the 1980s and can now be regarded as 'average'. If we compare France to West Germany and to its main European partners, we notice that from the early 1980s the difference in labour costs has slowed down and even decreased since 1986. If we compare France to the average of OECD countries, French unit labour cost is relatively high but it is now comparable and even sometimes lower than the American or West German ones (OECD, 1987c, p. 11).

To analyse unit labour costs thoroughly it is necessary to study the evolution of its two components: wages and productivity per capita. French national accounts data can then explain the traditional unit labour cost gap that exists between France and its main competitors, as well as the reduction of this gap (INSEE, 1987).

The conclusion is quite different if we only consider European countries or if we take also the United States and Japan into account.

In comparison with European countries, the evolution of French productivity has been quite satisfactory. Increases in wages explain unfavourable unit costs. Good productivity results therefore offset wage increases to a considerable but still insufficient extent. The decrease in labour costs is therefore due to a faster decrease in real wages while the effect of improvements in productivity remains marginal.

In comparison with the United States and Japan, productivity performance is disappointing and a wage squeeze is not sufficient to curb the evolution of unit costs.

To sum up, the French competitiveness problems should be related either to wages that may be too high in comparison with other European countries or to a productivity that remains still too low in comparison with the rest of the world.

The productivity improvement which was already noticed appears here again. It seems that it can be explained in two ways: first owing to the work reorganisation that followed the reduction of working time and then by the important capital for labour substitution which clearly appears in financial services. We cannot conclude then that in France the efforts made from 1981 onwards to improve welfare protection led to a decrease in productivity. It seems that it was an incentive for firms to reorganise their productive structures.

This last point is very important and we probably have to study this question over a much longer period of time if we want to appreciate correctly the relations between the welfare state, productivity and competitiveness. To do so, we shall refer to Maddison's recent work on growth and its decline (Maddison, 1987).

Maddison first showed that as regards labour productivity, France lagged far behind others a century ago and even after the Second World War but that since then it has succeeded in catching up (Table 5.4). This fact is quite clear in the export development (Maddison, 1987, p. 694). Only Japan progresses faster than France. French difficulties with the balance of trade mainly result from an unsatisfactory import control and from an insufficient qualitative structure of exports.

Table 5.4 Comparative levels of productivity, 1950, 1973 and 1984

	1950	*1973*	*1984*
France	41.5	74.7	97.7
Germany	33.6	72.8	90.5
Japan	13.9	43.8	55.6
United Kingdom	58.6	68.8	80.6

GDP per hour worked (US GDP per hours worked=100)
Source: Maddison, 1987, p. 694

Sectoral data enable us to improve this first diagnosis (Table 5.5). In every sector labour productivity increases more quickly than the international average. French industrial performance has only been surpassed by Japan in recent years. The situation of agriculture seems better, that of services less satisfactory because new methods in the tertiary sectors are lagging.

If we now consider the growth of capital productivity, the results are not so clear but they reveal once more a narrowing gap (Maddison, 1987, p. 685). As in other countries, French capital productivity has decreased strongly in recent years. This decrease was caused by the strong slow-down of investment and by the resulting obsolescence of

Table 5.5 Sectoral labour productivity growth in selected OECD countries

	1950–73			*1973–84*		
	Agriculture	*Industry*	*Services*	*Agriculture*	*Industry*	*Services*
Average	5.9	5.2	2.5	4	2.6	1
France	5.9	5.2	3	4.8	3.1	1.1
Germany	6.3	5.6	2.8	4.5	2.7	1.7
Japan	7.3	9.5	4	2.1	3.7	1.9
United Kingdom	4.6	2.9	2	4.2	2.9	0.6
United States	5.4	2.2	1.4	2.5	0.8	0.4

Value added per person employed: annual average compound growth rate
Source: Maddison, 1987, p. 694

the productive system, new technologies being introduced at a slow pace. On the other hand, capital productivity strongly increased in France during the 1950–1973 period whereas it decreased in other countries. Consequently, over a long period French performance in this sphere remained superior to the international average and reveal, as we have already seen, that France did succeed in bridging the gap.

If we now consider productive investment, excluding inventory changes, we find ambiguous results for France here, too. We notice a slight investment upturn at the end of the period but it neither enabled the country to recover the average investment ratio of the 1970s, nor even of the early 1980s (INSEE, 1987). Besides, we must point out that the relative decrease in investment expenditures would have been even stronger if investment in nationalised industries had not been so active.

So France was outpaced here by West Germany, even if it is still ahead of the United States and the United Kingdom. Its inferiority to Japan is obvious but, as with other indicators, it is less marked now than in the past (INSEE, 1987).

How can we explain this decrease in investment in comparison with other countries? Conservative parties argue that the left wing policy reversed a favourable trend. Is this argument relevant? If we analyse the problem more carefully, we must admit that there is indeed a decline in France in investment which started approximately ten years ago. Undoubtedly the national income distribution which was unfavourable to firms during the 1970s can account for most of this situation but we must admit that the new income distribution did not bring the expected changes.

In France, after three decades of fast growth, the behaviour of economic agents did not favour investment. Rentiers intensified their traditional behaviour since they enjoyed high inflationary windfall gains in real estate. Entrepreneurs underestimated the effort of modernisation required for a broader economic growth. This attempted policy of modernisation started in 1984, that is, when inflation was curbed and modernisation became an obvious necessity.

The evolution of the respective share of R&D expenditures in Gross Domestic Product is also a source of concern although it has been increasing since the early 1980s (INSEE, 1987). There are two serious problems:

- The share of R&D expenditures remains substantially lower in France in comparison with other countries that are both France's main competitors and the leaders in this field. The United States, West Germany and Japan have already gone beyond the 2.5 per cent figure;
- The share of R&D expenditures financed by French private firms has sharply decreased since 1980 after remaining nearly stable from 1976 to 1980.

If we extend the notion of R&D investment to include non-material investment, which is a fairly delicate extension from a statistical point of view, the result is hardly improved.

THE DEBATE ON COMPETITIVENESS

The competitiveness of the French economy appears relatively low, even though some encouraging elements can be found today.

These elements are difficult to appreciate because the economic policy has changed several times during recent years. In any case, the basic indicator in this field, the export/import ratio for industrial trade, did not evolve in a favourable way and satisfactory elements in French trade are due more to the fall in the energy bill than to a positive restructuring of the trade in manufactured goods. Several explanations have been put forward: they refer to different periods of time or to different levels of analysis but they all go against the theory which considers unit labour costs as the only cause of French difficulties.

First, changes in demand proved unfavourable to France. Domestic demand remained high until 1983, which led to price increases and restrained the country's export capacity. The demand from developing countries is traditionally important for France because it mainly concerns current consumption goods and is thus adapted to the traditional structure of the country's productive system. Unfortunately, this demand decreased significantly during the last years, as these countries were experiencing financial crises and as the real price of energy was falling. Although reduced, the difference in the rates of inflation did not enable France to take advantage of the growth of world demand as did French partners in 1985–1986. The world demand for French products only increased 3.2 per cent whereas the average for OECD was 4.3 per cent (and even 4.8 per cent for West Germany) (*Commissariat Général du Plan*, 1985, and Cuneo & Zakia, 1987).

Unquestionably, these elements can account for many things but not for everything and we are obliged to consider production costs.

The Labour Cost Hypothesis

The evolution of unit labour costs has been unfavourable to France: their rise could not be wholly offset by higher productivity gains during recent years. This accounts for the regular drift of the French franc away from the German mark and it can explain why 'manpower' is considered in France as one of the main causes of its lagging behind other countries and why all the protections provided to wage earners by the welfare state are called into question. Then the policy to implement in order to restore competitiveness is clear: wage increases must be controlled, work must be more flexible and anything which hinders a more economical and less social management of work must be suppressed. The arguments concerning demand are very quickly forgotten in such a context (Debonneuil & Delattre, 1987 and Mathis & Mazier, 1987).

But some people consider that this argument of excessive labour costs is being overemphasised. It is the opinion of the Institute for Economic and Social Research (IRES), which, at the end of a fairly long study, concludes:

– Unit labour costs are higher than or nearly as high as those of French competitors. In only two other European countries are they comparable. But if we take into account the differences between

taxes and welfare contributions, the gap between these unit labour costs would probably disappear since the relative share of welfare contributions is much higher in France.
– The considerable difference with the United States was caused mainly by the exchange value of the dollar.
– As to Japan, practically nothing new can be said, except that the situation is slightly less unfavourable than it was in the past (Mathis & Mazier, 1987).

Why then the emphasis on the wage argument as an explanation for France's exports difficulties? Employers' federations consider that the entrepreneurs have to pay very high welfare contributions to finance welfare programmes which are paid by general taxation in other countries. France is therefore in a difficult position in comparison with its foreign competitors. This point is obvious at the outset since on the average welfare contributions represent in France more than 60 per cent of the basic wage cost. But does this difference tend to increase or decrease?

In fact, we do notice that welfare contributions increased more quickly than taxes from 1975 to 1980 but that the situation was reversed from 1980 to 1985 (INSEE, 1986). During both periods, the effort required from the employers was weaker than that required from workers.

The Structural Hypothesis

Nevertheless it is not sufficient to look at the relation between labour costs and economic competitiveness.

The aforementioned IRES study shows that by pursuing this analysis and by thinking in terms of 'total unit costs' instead of 'unit labour costs', the conclusions are quite different. This study reveals some important points (Mathis & Mazier, 1987).

When compared to its main competitors, France is in a better position when total unit costs rather than unit labour costs are considered. In a more general way, the gap narrows because of the moderating influence of its intermediate production. For instance, if we consider Japan, the low level of its labour costs is mainly due to the importance of subcontracting which increases the cost of its intermediate consumption. For this reason, France is in an intermediate position when we consider total unit costs. The relative share of intermediate consumption is lower in France than in its competitor countries because activities are more integrated inside every sector. The relatively low price of energy enhanced this effect.

A diagnosis concerning only labour costs is not fully relevant. We have to consider non-cost advantages and not only cost advantages. Thus, some countries enjoy both cost advantages and non-cost advantages. This is the case for Japan which has probably organised its poles of competitiveness well.

In other countries, cost disadvantages are offset by non-cost advantages. It is the case of West Germany which specialises in high quality goods.

In a third category of countries, non-cost disadvantages are offset by cost advantages. This is the case of Italy and, at quite a lower degree, of the United Kingdom if we take its trade results in consideration.

But, as far as France is concerned, we find both non-cost disadvantages and cost disadvantages. Cost disadvantages cannot then be considered as the unique reason for the whole French deficit.

A comprehensive explanation is to be found in the prevailing pattern of industrial and trade specialisation. This specialisation is unfavourable in the French case and favourable in the German case. We are then led to quite a different analysis which takes into consideration the fact that established past choices made by firms and by the state in favour of some traditional products and customers are responsible for the inadequate competitiveness of France.

We can then test the two possible explanations of these deficits. Let us consider the French specialisation product by product. We then build a specialisation matrix coupling comparative costs (in rows) with comparative export/import ratios (in columns). If specialisation, and thus international competitiveness, depended on comparative costs, the matrix would be diagonal (Table 5.6). This is not the case in France: non-cost advantages and disadvantages appear as fundamental in our analysis.

It is especially remarkable to see that high export/import ratios in iron, agrobusiness and textiles are not due to the cost advantages. The reason is to be found in choices for high quality products or high technology (textile and transports) or by the persistence of a solid trade specialisation in traditional and relatively protected markets (agrobusiness). On the other hand, export/import ratios are disappointing for chemicals, industrial machinery, electrical equipment and computers which are basic industries for economic development and whose costs are not unfavourable.

Table 5.6 France: ranking of the products according to the relative export/import ratio and to relative costs

Ratio of domestic costs/foreign costs	*Export/import ratio*		
	> 1	*1*	*< 1*
< 1	4	2	2
1	1 food, etc.		2 chemistry, etc.
> 1	1 textiles	1	3 office equipment

1: non-cost advantages > cost disadvantages
2: non-cost disadvantages > cost advantages
3: cost disadvantages not offset by non-cost advantages
4: cost advantages not offset by non-cost disadvantages

Source: Mathis & Mazier, 1987.

We are then led to refer to a final hypothesis developed in France: economic competitiveness would depend as much on the social and economic 'matrix' as on costs. Qualitative elements, mostly inherited from the past, reveal that the French productive system is not adapted to world demand and some elements are prioritised in the debate: the bias of the productive system towards captive and not very dynamic markets, too loose a specialisation, an insufficiently active trade policy... This does not mean that there are no problems connected to labour costs but these must not be overemphasised.

Several recent studies by INSEE, the National Institute of Statistics and Economic Studies, (Cuneo & Zakia, 1987 and Debonneuil & Delattre, 1987) have justified this broadening of the analysis of competitiveness. The INSEE procedure is here a little different from previous studies. Since it is based on a price analysis, it does not consider non-cost advantages or disadvantages *a priori* but its conclusions are quite similar.

The origin of the study is quite identical: the French relative share in the volume of world production was much reduced from 1979 (5.5 per cent) to 1985 (4.9 per cent). Before 1979, even if France was losing ground on its domestic market, it progressed on the world market. But today, the situation is quite different. French industrial activity has decreased by 14 per cent on the domestic market and French industrial exports have decreased by 7 per cent. But a simple analysis of price effects is not very informative and in fact we must separate two effects of price competitiveness.

Traditionally, in order to appreciate competitiveness and its evolution, one used to compare export and import terms of trade. But this indicator is difficult to interpret even if its underlying tendency is unquestionably negative.

The evolution can be explained in two ways:

– Either it is due to an unfavourable evolution of export and import basic prices for a basket of goods which would be specified at the beginning of the period. We shall call this the *basic price effect*;
– or it is due to a change in the original basket or to a structural effect where the country is becoming specialised in the production of expensive goods and not in cheap goods. We shall call this the *structural effect*.

What do we see? The basic price effect does not seem to have been important for ten years: one main reason is the introduction of the European Monetary System which strongly limited the fluctuating margins of the French currency and thus of export and import prices. On the other hand, the structural change of export and import has been very important. So, since 1979, France has become more specialised than other countries in the production of goods whose prices increased less than the average. We thus notice a strong increase of export/import ratios concerning intermediate goods whose price increases are moderate: organic chemistry, unprocessed plastic materials, unprocessed steel and electrical equipment.

It is difficult not to link this deterioration to the weakness of French productive investments whether they concern products or processes. What we have said before puts the emphasis on two problems: the decreasing investment/GDP ratio and the insufficient shares of R&D expenditures in GDP. Both trends would be still more unfavourable if we did not take public intervention into account. And we cannot impute the deterioration of investment and competitiveness only to the distribution of national income. This element probably weighed heavily during the 1970s on financial capacity but the evolution has been reversed since 1983.

To sum up, the loss of competitiveness of the French economy must be explained by several factors:

– The distribution of national income was for a long time unfavourable to investment. Its upturn has only been felt after 1985. Unfortunately then the dollar drift made the problem more complex for French industry.
– The behaviour of firms is traditionally motivated more by the protection of real estate or a preference for purely financial investment than for innovation.
– Unfavourable trends in the components of demand were noticed.
– More generally, French leaders, whether private or public, have traditionally underestimated the costs of modernisation.

THE POLICY OF COMPETITIVENESS

Since 1981, French governments have pursued quite different policies.

The left wing government formed in June 1981 analysed the French economic situation in the following way: the distribution of national income was unfavourable to profits and thus to investments: but this did not mean that cutting down labour costs was enough to stimulate investment and restore French competitiveness.

This can explain why the left wing government at first did not take any measures to improve the financial situation of firms. It considered that the country's poor performance was not due to excessive labour costs but to more structural defects: the irrelevant specialisation of the French productive system, the traditional weakness of private investment and the insufficient level of demand. This diagnosis determined economic policy: supply should be reorganised by increasing considerably its coherence and by strengthening the country's productive potential; demand should be stimulated in order to provide outlets for current investment (Bauchet, 1986, Greffe 1987a).

The nationalisation of several industrial groups and of all private banks with deposits over FF one billion took place in 1982 and was the main measure for positive reinsertion of France into the world economy. At that time, some of the nationalised firms were in financial difficulties, which led the state to come to their relief (Rhône-Poulenc) but others were in good economic health (CGE). This means that even if part of those nationalisations was aimed at protecting firms which were on the brink of bankruptcy, the ambition was wider: the restructuring aimed at clarifying development strategies and giving birth to much more solid organisational structures.

Several sectors soon benefited from this restructuring: chemistry, popular electronics and even computers (Lipietz, 1984b).

The state did not merely restructure but initiated a very important policy of capital endowments which should last several years: in 1982, the nationalised industrial groups received endowments amounting to FF eight billion and participating loans amounting to FF three billion.

Aids to firms were granted in order to boost investment and thus to enable the domestic productive system to react positively to the increasing purchasing power. Investing firms benefited from higher tax reductions and fiscal benefits except if their manpower decreased (these conditions made things much more difficult). On the other hand, special or preferential loans were considerably increased. This last measure was to be questioned three years later when financial flows were deregulated.

Another measure reinforced this policy for more competitiveness: the progressive dismantling of price and profit margin regulation. As early as 1978, the government of M. Barre started to abandon this traditional policy and initiated a policy of price liberalisation which could not progress very quickly.

When the freeze was suppressed, the government put into practice contractual policies which proved efficient: professional groups had to negotiate with the Minister. This way, the free formation of prices and margins was reconciled with certain national objectives. The administration could break the resulting agreement if professional groups did not respect it.

The positive results of this policy were seen as soon as 1983. Simultaneously, the financial situation of the firms started to recover and inflation decelerated. Price increases eased from 11 per cent in 1982 to 8 per cent in 1983. But the policy was accompanied by a strong stimulation of demand: lower wages increased, jobs were created in the public sector, the length of the working week decreased though salaries did not. Nevertheless supply did not increase enough to satisfy the growing demand. Consequently, an external deficit and a growing indebtedness appeared. Besides the difference in the rates of inflation remained too high, although it lessened.

1983 was then an austerity year. A policy of price and wage restraint was implemented in March 1983 simultaneously with the European monetary readjustment and the major devaluation of the French franc. A greater competitiveness was then sought in two directions: the role of the extended public sector was tempered but not abandoned; competitiveness was to result from a general improvement of economic life as well as from the efforts made by the new state corporations.

Two types of measures were adopted:

– State enterprises again received capital endowments (they rose from FF nine billion to 14); regional diversification schemes helped traditional regions (such as Lorraine) to adapt; procedures to finance investments were diversified;
– Public expenditures and prices were strictly controlled. The procedure for wage increases was changed in order to suppress indexation. De-indexation and unemployment reduced the inflation rate from 8 per cent to 5 per cent, which was below the increase in productivity.

The effects of this policy of price and wage restraint materialised in 1985. The probability of suppressing the main disequilibria was now actually high, and no major change to macroeconomic policy was adopted later on.

More structural reforms were added to those conjunctural measures.
– As far as R&D was concerned, 2.5 per cent of GDP should be devoted to it instead of 1.5 per cent within a period of five years.
– As far as education was concerned, the objective proclaimed in 1984 was that 80 per cent of pupils should get the *baccalauréat*. This required high expenditure.
– As far as workers' rights were concerned, the Auroux Laws gave birth to new information, discussion and negotiation opportunities (see below). The double objective of the laws, economic and social, consisted in associating workers with the efforts to modernise firms in order to make restructuring easier.
– As far as working time was concerned, the evolution was slow and complex as we shall see later on. At the beginning, the government intended to reduce working time in a fairly uniform way. As the results were very disappointing the attempt was made to give more flexibility to employers without penalising workers.

In 1986, there should have been a major change in economic policy after the constitution of the new Chirac government. Privatisation, deregulation, liberalisation, supply-side economics, all these policies seemed to contradict the traditional measures of a left government. But if this opposition was obvious as far as privatisation was concerned, it was not true for the other policies mentioned. The real change in French economic policy happened in 1983 and if we except privatisations and reductions in income inequalities, the differences between the post-1983 left wing and conservative governments are more a matter of degree than of structure.

In particular, two important measures were made possible because past governments had prepared them: the suppression on 1 January 1987 of the famous law established in 1945 which instituted price control; and the suppression of selective credit control established in 1972. A mere control of bank liquidity through interest rates survived.

On the other hand, the suppression of foreign exchange controls established in 1968 was an innovation and the left wing government would probably not have acted so quickly in this field.

Despite all this, we could find in the policy adopted a supply-side aspect to which the preceding left wing government did not adhere even if it had rehabilitated the role of firms and profits in French society. By freeing firms from any regulation concerning the dismissal of employees, the conservative government thought it would enable them to invest and create employment. It was also hoped that deregulation in certain sectors would result in increased competition and competitiveness. The right wing government intended to ease other sectors as well: transport, energy and telecommunications, but at the end of 1987 many important measures that had been announced had not yet been adopted.

Privatisations gave rise to the same hope: they were to foster productivity and competitiveness. But it is doubtful whether these targets were reached. The privatisation plan was progressively delayed, and the October 1987 financial crisis stopped it just when it should have been accelerated. Funds collected when privatisation took place were not to reinforce investment but to repay public debt.

Workers' trade unions remained fairly passive when wage increases were strictly controlled. This could be understood at the beginning: the wage policy was part of the left wing policy which aimed at reducing inequalities, but such a mild opposition was more surprising when the wage policy was managed by the right wing government which moreover suppressed the wealth taxes. Undoubtedly, the popular classes realised that France would only maintain its standard of living and its industrial power if its inflation rate was comparable to those of other countries. The difference in the rates of inflation became an accepted indicator in the politico-economic debate.

Employers' federations should have reacted positively to this policy of competitiveness. Yet, their reaction was quite moderate under the left government due to nationalisations. It became positive when the conservative government came to power. Of course, the employers' federations sided with the Chirac government even if their rank and file did not always agree: the rank and file preferred not to enter the political debate. They did not want to choose between a left wing representative more and more favourable to firms and a conservative lobby that was far from granting them the expected guarantees even though privatisation and deregulation were being implemented.

As opinions within the employers' federations were split with regard to the policies of competitiveness of the government, they took no new initiative in this matter other than the traditional responses.

Employers' federations spoke in favour of open and participative management of firms, and they stressed the advantages which small and medium-sized firms could draw from it. At the same time, they explained that the entrepreneur's responsibility was not at all to be questioned.

Employers federations' also asked for the creation of new firms. They supported all the measures enabling unemployed people to create new activities. But once more, this was merely a verbal response.

THE CASE OF THE CAR INDUSTRY

An analysis of the French car industry gives a good idea of the problems facing France. Seven per cent of active workers are employed in this sector and car exports represent 11 per cent of all French exports. Besides, this activity expanded very quickly during the three decades that followed the Second World War. Technical success often outpaced trade success, as is so often the case in France.

There are only two car producers in France: one is private (Peugeot SA), the other public (Renault). Renault has always been used as one of the main 'guinea pigs' for public intervention for two reasons: it has the traditional characteristics of public corporations, and it was meant to be a leader for social innovation. Many social reforms were first introduced at Renault and were then generalised to other public and private firms.

In 1984, the situation in the automobile sector was rather alarming: trade positions, productivity and profitability had degraded. Worse was to be feared for this quasi-public industry, but those dark years were probably at the origin of a recovery in which the role of the welfare state was quite subtle.

In the mid-1980s, the car industry obviously went through a crisis. The two main performance indicators evolved unfavourably: the import penetration rate, which had remained stable (around 21–22 per cent), rose to 23 per cent in 1980, 28 per cent in 1981, 30 per cent in 1982, 33 per cent in 1983, and 35 per cent in 1984. It even reached the record level of 36.9 per cent in 1986. The French relative share of the European market decreased from 30.1 per cent in 1979 to 27 per cent in 1981 and to 24.3 per cent in 1983 (Cuneo & Zakia, 1987, OECD, 1987c).

This deterioration of trade performance reveals a productivity decrease. Between 1979 and 1984, French productivity indicators stagnated whereas they regularly progressed in competing countries. The most disastrous comparison is with Japan: French firms need about 8000 workers to build 1200 cars a day. Japanese firms only need 4000 workers!

The decline in competitiveness was followed by that of profitability. Whereas in 1979, profits were quite substantial, Peugeot and Renault were both confronted with losses from 1982 onwards: Peugeot's losses amounted to FF 2.2 billion; those of Renault to FF 1.3 billion. The consequences of this situation were quite predictable: debts increased (especially in the Renault case since the public firm could rely on permanent public subsidies) and the investment capacities declined.

Many causes can be found for such a downturn.

– Price control was considered as a cause of delay;
– Industrial relations were difficult in the French car industry. An unquestionable characteristic is the importance of an insufficiently skilled manpower, generally recruited among immigrants for whom no training or adaptation effort was actually made, at least until the early 1980s. Overemployment being considerable, the only solution consisted in brutal dismissals which were often expensive and gave rise to hopeless labour conflicts;
– Another cause must be considered here: the deficiencies in the distribution network. It was very scattered, producers did not control it well enough and paid according to the number and not to the value of sold cars!

When the crisis of the French car industry broke out openly some recovery elements appeared at the same time. Those elements materialised as early as 1987.

Peugeot led the way by creating a new 'enterprise culture'. Having succeeded in strongly reducing its manpower (from 41 000 in 1979 to 25 000 in 1986), Peugeot decided to invest thoroughly in new technologies (the corresponding annual budget amounted to FF one billion for seven years). Equally – and this breaks with tradition – Peugeot decided to systematically qualify its manpower. Consequently, training expenditures rose to 3.5 per cent of the wage bill, which is quite superior to the legal requirement (1.1 per cent).

Renault tried to adopt a similar policy, but the decrease in manpower was slower as trade unions are well-entrenched in that firm. The situation of the firm should improve anyway, however, since public claims were cancelled and financial results now look much better than two years ago.

As early as 1987, the result of these strategies of renewal became noticeable: output reached an unprecedented level and import penetration ratio began to decrease after a ten years' increase. It fell from 36.9 per cent in 1986 to 36.1 per cent in 1987. Overemployment being drastically reduced, firms put in practice a manpower training policy which went beyond what the welfare state laws recommended.

THE CASE OF THE TELECOMMUNICATIONS INDUSTRY

There exist no reliable data on competitiveness in the telecommunications sector, except in the electronic sector, which is broader. Besides, this sector has been transformed since 1981 by important internal restructurings: Thomson and CGE were first nationalised and reorganised, and then the privatisation of CGE took place (Greffe 1987a).

At first sight, the achievements of this sector have been significant even if the growth of its activity was slower between 1983 and 1988 than between 1979 and 1983. The average annual rate of growth decreased from 7.1 per cent to 5.3 per cent. Exports grew quickly during the whole period at the annual rate of 14.3 per cent. During the same period productivity grew by 7 per cent and relative prices decreased by 2 per cent a year. Now French production represents 48 per cent of the sales on the domestic market.

Nevertheless, a few reservations must be expressed on this fairly satisfactory diagnosis.

Nearly 7 per cent of French exports go to developing countries. At the same time, France needs to change its strategies with respect to developed markets. It must penetrate there with the help of local distribution networks; and it must pay more attention to the public regulations in the targeted markets and embark on active marketing.

A product disequilibrium exists alongside this market disequilibrium: non-cabled production is dramatically lagging within the French supply, which is counterbalanced by cabled and telematic products. If this situation is acceptable on the domestic market, it is unacceptable in the view of growing world market integration. Non-cabled products can be exported fairly easily but not cabled products or networks. One of today's difficulties consists in exporting networks to developing countries: neither their economic structures nor their legal structures are adapted to those networks.

If we compare this industry with the car industry, we find a common feature. All firms realise today that competitiveness cannot improve if manpower is not more qualified. Between 1975 and 1988, the percentage of unskilled workers decreased from 63.8 per cent to 37.7 per cent, that of engineers rose from 4.9 per cent to 7.5 per cent, and that of managers and technicians rose from 4.5 per cent to 13.3 per cent. Once more the crisis can only be overcome by an intensified training of personnel, which tallies with welfare state ideas. But this kind of change is easier for large, expanding firms.

TRENDS IN THE WELFARE STATE

The modern French welfare state is a product of the post-war period. During the war, the National Committee for Resistance decided upon an extension of the system which began some years before with the 'Front Populaire' policy: extension of the insurance system, nationalisation of the main industries, new social regulations. Between 1945 and 1948, these main programmes were initiated. But unlike other countries, France was still fundamentally an agricultural country.

Over the next three decades, we then saw a progressive extension of the welfare state to people who were outside the industrial and service sectors. This was related to a strong social demand for equality and solidarity and the necessity to fill some gaps in social protection. The new policy which began in 1983 did not change this trend. But in 1986 the new conservative majority was openly hostile to the welfare state and we were then confronted by an upheaval in many social policies (Euvrard, 1987, Greffe, 1987b and Ray, Dupuis & Gazier, 1989).

Transfers and Income Distribution

There was a 2.5 fold increase in the real incomes of households between 1960 and 1985 and the corresponding inequalities were strongly reduced. This real income growth slowed down between 1974 and 1979, and came to an end in 1983–1984 with the policy of price and wage restraint. The respective share of social transfers in real income increased from 19 per cent to 36 per cent during the same period. This increase was partly related to the rise in unemployment and implied a strong increase of social contributions (from 16 per cent to 36 per cent of national income) and taxes.

Reduction of Real Income Inequalities

Average real income has strongly increased for the last 25 years. But in the recent period this increase first slowed down and then since 1984 stopped. The pattern of growth may be explained both by fast economic growth and the increasing share of the wage earners in the working population. Besides, when the growth of primary incomes slowed down, the growth of social contributions still continued.

This increase then induced a reduction in income inequalities. The multiplier between the average incomes of the upper and the lower deciles which was about 5.3 in 1960 became only 4.3 in 1979 and 2.8 in 1987. Low-wage categories were the main beneficiaries of this reduction. The increase in income tax rates and social contributions were the main factors in this new trend (Chassard & Concialdi, 1989, and Ray, Dupuis & Gazier, 1989).

Let us first consider the increase in the tax burden. In France it is quite difficult to make automatic deductions from the existence of high marginal taxes since the share of indirect taxes is very high. But the income tax burden has actually increased since the 1970s for the highest incomes: the average real income tax was 5.8 per cent in 1974, 7.5 per cent in 1979 and 9.1 per cent in 1985. This was due to a limited revision of income brackets in relationship to inflation rates, the existence of exceptional contributions and the creation of a new marginal tax rate for higher incomes (65 per cent).

Social contributions were increased, too, in a more redistributive direction. But we are confronted here with a traditional failure of the French system: these contributions are not progressive and are only applied on the lower parts of the income. There have been only few changes here.

Turning to a study of welfare benefits, family income allowances have fallen relatively since the number of children per family has also been reduced.

Pensions considerably reduced income inequalities. Since the beginning of the 1970s, both a generalisation and an upgrading of these benefits have taken place. Whereas these benefits were 40 per cent of the legal minimum wage in 1963, they now represent approximately 65 per cent of this minimum wage.

Health-related benefits have strongly increased. Yet their redistributive effects are not obvious, even if low-income families have mainly benefited from this extension. Unemployment benefits have been increased, but in real terms we have noticed their stagnation since 1979.

Development of Welfare Assistance

In France, welfare assistance is usually targeted toward people who do not benefit from any insurance service. Assistance has developed during the last years since many people have lost their entitlement to insurance systems. Welfare assistance includes five important programmes:

- Medical aid which is now increasing with the development of the new poverty;
- welfare assistance for children, revalued in 1975, whose amount has been increasing in real terms;
- welfare assistance for old people which has not progressed rapidly;
- welfare aid for socially non-adapted people, which is increasing.

Towards a Policy of Supplementary Benefits

The increase in welfare assistance benefits did not prevent the development of poverty (Euvrard, 1987; and Murard, 1989).

Local authorities were then obliged first to find new financial measures to counteract the lack of resources of an increasing number of people. The central authorities are now compelled to devise new systems of 'supplementary benefits' or 'negative income taxes' (Euvrard, 1987). The basic idea was already brought up twenty years ago, when old people could benefit from an additional income if their own resources were below a minimum level. But in order to be eligible, people had to be already receiving one of the existing old-age benefits, which drastically reduced the number of beneficiaries.

Therefore, many local authorities have recently initiated new programmes to fight poverty. Thanks to these initiatives, central authorities take a more positive stance towards these systems of supplementary benefits. In 1986, they decided to support local initiatives by specific financial agreements. In May 1988, the new Rocard government decided to organise a national negative income tax system. The average amount of supplementary benefits for a two-children family is approximatively FF 3600 and this aid is associated with 'social insertion' goals. The new system is centrally financed but locally managed.

Development of Collective Facilities

Instead of withdrawing collective goods and services as soon as the economic crisis appeared, the French welfare state tried to enlarge their scope.

Education is still the main collective service. But the respective share of education expenditures has reached a ceiling: from 3.3 per cent of the GDP in 1970, it increased to 3.5 per cent between 1982 and 1985 before declining to 3.3 per cent in 1986. In terms of public expenditures, the share of education is now 15 per cent which represents the same amount as 25 years ago.

This relative stability of the public education expenditure may be partially explained by the slowing down of the demographic trend. At the level of primary schools the number of pupils is now decreasing. At the level of the secondary schools the trend is still growing. As a matter of fact, educational expenditures could have increased since the average costs of a secondary school are much higher than the costs of a primary school, and everybody agrees today on the necessity of increasing the corresponding budget. But reality is quite different: expenditures have actually increased in some sectors (pedagogical expenditures) but in other sectors drastic reductions have been decided (staff and technical expenditures). Moreover central authorities expect local authorites to take on more responsibilities in the financing of schools and colleges according to the decentralisation laws.

Health expenditure trends are more difficult to analyse since private financing is more significant (more than 20 per cent of the aggregate health expenditures). These expenditures have been relatively reduced: their rate of growth is now 9 per cent instead of 18 per cent ten years ago.

But this slowing down has not been considered as a loss of quality and social indicators reveal a better situation than before. This result may be explained by the following facts:

- An increase in pre-natal health care;
- a strict control over the number of doctors, which allows the state to keep expenditures under control without diminishing incomes: the annual rate of growth of physicians which was plus 6 per cent between 1976 and 1981 is now only 4 per cent;
- a reduction in the number of the nurses and technical staff in hospitals;
- a transformation of the financing rules for hospitals. The system of 'day rate' which induced high expenditures was suppressed in favour of the 'annual budget' system which places these expenditures under *a priori* control;
- the payment of a lump sum per day for those who belong to an upper income category.

From a more general point of view we can see that collective equipment and consumption has not declined as some observers would have expected. The traditional demand for social collective goods has counterbalanced the accusations of bureaucratic management. The main attitude of successive governments has been to maintain them. But some adjustments have been effected: a lower quality of some services, the postponement of new programmes, the decentralisation of the financial pressure. In that sense, the results of these new policies are under debate.

The Issue of Employment

The first programme relative to unemployment was to create new public activities and employment. In 1981, this programme dealt with

56 000 people; in 1982 with 79 500 and in 1983 with 38 000. But in 1984 everything was stopped. Only one programme, called *Travaux d'Utilité Collective*, continued. It consisted of temporary jobs for young people employed at a low wage in fields related to social or environmental services. Instead, the *Entreprises Intermédiaires* programme was created. It consisted in the financial support of regular economic activities which hired young people who had never worked before. The enterprise could then be considered as a multiproduct firm: one product was the delivery of a good or a service; another product was the 'ability to work' of a previously unemployed person. The market price was paid for the first product, the public financial aid was paid for the second one. This last programme was the real beginning of what has been called: 'social treatment for unemployment' (Greffe 1987a and 1987b).

With the arrival of the conservative government of Prime Minister Chirac in 1986 the programmes continued. But some differences progressively appeared: instead of using the *travaux d'utilité collectives* and the intermediary activities, public authorities preferred to maintain young people in post-educational activity.

As to the organisation of working time, important measures were adopted in the early 1980s but some of them, which were however to be enforced later, were dropped. At the beginning of this period, a decrease in working hours was considered both as a way to increase employment and as an answer to a new social demand: but only the last aspect now persists. On 1 January 1982 the legal working week was reduced from 40 to 39 hours and a five week vacation period was generalised. On 1 January 1983, the age of retirement was reduced from 65 years to 60.

The real impact of these measures was very low. According to the INSEE experts, they created only 17 000 new jobs instead of the 400 000 expected! (INSEE, 1986). Since the employers had to maintain the 40 hours' remuneration, they increased their search for productivity gains which could save labour and they resorted more to the use of temporary workers.

In 1984, an important law was adopted in order to organise a more flexible management of working hours. The reduction of working time would not be uniform any more but could vary according to the sectors, the enterprises, the qualifications and so on. The agreements were then decentralised but one control remained: a local agreement could be signed only if a sector agreement existed previously or if a retrospective administrative agreement could be secured. But in 1986, the conservative government suppressed these conditions in favour of a purely local agreement.

During this period, a large number of part-time, temporary, 'unofficial' and generally poorly paid jobs appeared.

As to unemployment benefits, the period shows a substantial transformation of welfare statism. Because of financial restrictions the logic of insurance induces a sensible restriction of both the main unemployment benefit and the so-called 'end-of-rights benefit' which is given to unemployed people when they are no longer eligible for the main benefit. For the same reasons, the rate of compensation (the ratio between the amount of benefits and the amount of average wage) was reduced: from 80 per cent of the normal wage in 1978 to 58 per cent in 1985.

Also for financial reasons social assistance was reduced although the demand for it increased strongly. In 1986, 40 per cent of unemployed people had no benefit and this proportion covered an important inequality between male and female workers: 32.3 per cent of male and 45 per cent of female unemployed were left unprotected.

With respect to training, the important programmes which were adopted in favour of some specific groups never were cancelled or even restricted. But their quality is highly questionable.

Youth programmes have developed continuously since 1977. In 1981, a new programme reiterated the previous formula both quantitatively and qualitatively. In 1982, the idea was accepted that the problems of young people were not only economic but social. Public authorities had to organise new procedures in order to consider jointly housing, social and training problems. New programmes were therefore organised:

- The creation of specific information centres which took in consideration all these problems;
- the specification of training programmes according to the real level of qualifications.

Social Rights at the Workplace

As to working conditions and industrial relations, an important reform was adopted in 1982 (*Auroux Laws*). Four acts were then adopted based on the following premise: the modernisation of the productive structure would only succeed with the active participation of every worker. Without this participation, any modernisation policy would fail.

As to industrial relations inside the public sector, the regulation was even more severe. An Act adopted in 1983 reinforced the conditions for representation and negotiation inside these enterprises.

This substantial extension of social rights was not reversed by the conservative government in 1986. But it must be pointed out that many of these powers were not really applied: the increasing weakness of the French trade unions and the pressure of competitiveness led to a failure to implement these regulations.

INTERNATIONAL COMPETITIVENESS AND THE WELFARE STATE: A SUGGESTED INTERPRETATION

The Configuration of the Debate

Having studied the main trends of international competitiveness and the progress of the welfare state, we have to deal with their relationship. Here we are confronted by an important hypothesis. By exaggeratedly protecting employment income and collective consumption, does not the welfare state lessen the competitiveness of the economy? In face of strong international pressure, is it not necessary to dismantle some important components of the welfare state?

This policy discourse relies on some 'traditional' arguments that can be listed in the following way:

- Too much government is bad for the economy since it diminishes the size of the productive sectors and encourages a political bias against the market;
- too precise economic regulation may induce inadequacies in the allocation of resources and investment;
- too excessive social regulations allow trade unions to paralyse the restructuring justified by economic competition;
- high collective consumption induces a pressure on production costs, which weakens international competitiveness.

France is not outside this debate, but we have to stress two distinctive features. Firstly, the weakness of its international competitiveness is not only related to high unit wage costs but also to inadequacies of the industrial structure which existed long before the development of the welfare state. Secondly, the development of the welfare state is quite recent relative to other countries, and during the early 1980s, many measures have been adopted in order to suppress important poverty problems.

These last two elements are interconnected and as a matter of fact it seems that we are confronted in France not by one but by two hypotheses.

Consistent with the previous traditional hypothesis, the need for greater international competitiveness seems to require important corrections to the welfare state system. This adaptation may have different contents, beginning with the suppression of some policies and ending with the revision of some needs.

But the welfare state is not only a levy on international competitiveness: it can enforce the required adjustments which will strengthen international competitiveness. The French debate on both the specific role of public enterprises for industrial policy and the contribution of the national education system to manpower policy is illustrative here.

The Questioning of Welfare Statism due to the Concern for International Competitiveness

Since the beginning of the 1980s we have witnessed a strong questioning of the institutions of the welfare state.

A first illustration is to be found in 1984 with the rise of the policy of price and wage restraint. The share of taxes and social contributions on national income had by then bypassed the level of 45 per cent, and this was considered too dangerous for unit wage cost pressure. A surprising decision came then from the Presidency of the Republic which had not acted before on this specific point: it was decided not only to stop this rise but to organise a decrease. Something which was not even thought of one year before became a reality: the reduction was not exactly what was expected (a return to the level of 44 per cent), but the new trend was initiated and for the first time since the Second World War this charge was actually reduced (by approximately 0.3 point).

A second illustration of the effects of international competitiveness on the welfare state deals with the changing of the ratio between employers' and employees' contributions. The income elasticity of social contributions has always been superior to the income elasticity of taxes since 1975. But in order to keep unit wage cost under control, the main contribution was requested from employees and not from employers.

This trend is increasing now, despite strong opposition. The conservative government decided on a new policy for financing retirement. The financial burden is continuously increasing but it is impossible always to ask for more contributions and consequently higher unit wage costs. The solution found was to open opportunities for voluntary retirement programmes which enjoy very important fiscal exemptions. As a result, it is then expected that the pressure for extending the socialised retirement programme will not be so high.

A third illustration is to be found in labour law. Instead of defining new rights at the national level, public authorities decided to give more importance to contractual agreements at the local level and to strictly limit state intervention in the labour market. This was the case first with the new legislation on working time, but the more significant one was the suppression of the administrative authorisation of dismissals (1987).

A fourth example is the redistribution of the social efforts inside the public sectors. As in many other countries, the central state reduced some of its liabilities in the social fields, expecting the local authorities to offset the resultant gaps. At first, this change was suggested more than formally organised, as was the case for the supplementary benefits programmes. But with the decentralisation laws in 1982–1983, the transfer of the financial burden of social programmes has been formally achieved. This appeared mainly with some specific social aid programmes for vulnerable sectors of society and it deals now with redistributive measures in fields like education and housing.

Fifth is the call for private charity in order to compensate for public financial constraints. In France important voluntary organisations as strong as in other countries do not exist and private charity is largely disseminated through the whole country. The first efforts came from private initiatives, mainly the one organising the distribution of free meals for poor people at the national level: it was called 'Restaurants of the Heart' (1985). But the state progressively supported these kinds of interventions, and new fiscal credits were decided in 1986–1987 in order to reduce the financial costs of these private initiatives.

A sixth example lies in the moving of the references. The welfare state is now confronted with a dualism between one part of the society which enjoys employment and incomes and another part which is more and more excluded from income and employment. Management of a dual society has nothing to do with the management of the dividends of growth and the French welfare state does not actually know how to deal with this new reality. The debates on the adequacy of the struggle against the new poverty or against educational failures show this very clearly.

The new poverty requires tools and instruments that traditional social work does not have. The grass root organisations could experiment with these tools and instruments and inspire some relevant reforms: but in France these kinds of organisations have always been weak. One counter-example exists: the association *Aide à toute détresse* which showed to the entire country the importance of newly perceived handicaps (illiteracy), and the necessity to define completely new social treatments for deprived people.

Persistent educational failure has opened an interesting debate on the necessity for the inequality of social treatment. The French system was organised on the principle of equality, understood as a principle of uniformity of treatment. But in face of situations where differences are very important, this principle of uniformity does not really contribute to reducing inequalities. It appeared then necessary to some policy-makers to change the references and to organise in a different way the existing resources. For example, some schools located in deprived areas have enjoyed many more resources than schools localised in less deprived areas. But this policy is still under debate, and the good results obtained do not compensate for the hostility of some pressure groups.

Could the Welfare State be a Positive Factor for Higher International Competitiveness?

The effects of international competition on the welfare state are easy to foresee. On the contrary, the effects of the welfare state on international competitiveness are very debatable.

But the most current ideas are not so evident here. It is very true that several institutions of the welfare state undermined the international competitiveness of the French economy, namely the different financing instruments which more rapidly than in any other country contributed to an increase in unit labour costs. This may be easily explained by the social structures: French industrialisation has been very slow and the organisation of social protection relied mainly on wage contributions. The taxation system was never used for that purpose since other social groups were not ready to pay for the wage earners. And this naturally explains why the pressure of international competition induced revisions in the definitions of social benefits and contributions.

But the study of positive and negative factors for international competitiveness shows that things are not that simple. Contrary to the traditional hypothesis, one argument has to be considered: does not the welfare state strengthen international competitiveness by creating conditions for modernisation? (Greffe, 1987c).

This idea is not new for France. The economic side of the welfare state – public enterprises and financial aids – has always been legitimised by the necessity to build and modernise the French economy. This idea is constant throughout French history. It began with Colbert, appeared again many times during the 19th century and was institutionalised after the Second World War. But this specific argument is out of date today, and many people consider that the same results could be obtained without organising an institutionalised interventionism.

Disappearing from the economic field, this argument now appears again in the social field. The debate on the necessity for a highly skilled active population informs arguments for high-quality public education. In 1985 it was said that in order to get modernised, France had to have 80 per cent of its school leavers at the level of the *baccalauréat* instead of 45 per cent then. This implied a tremendous endeavour in extending and modernising equipment mainly in the sector of technical and professional education. Decisions have been taken in that direction and the political consensus is here very important.

Another debate is now underway in order to know whether public authorities should change their attitude towards welfare statism. The costs of traditional welfare are recognised, but many people feel that it is important to create today another kind of welfare state, since private initiative cannot do everything. In their opinion public authorities do not have to take productive and allocative decisions but to organise an environment favourable to private decisions. The public goods are not only the traditional social ones but also those that provide services for enterprises: technical information, access to venture capital, human resource management services and so on. With this perspective, the content of the debate on welfare statism has changed greatly: the problem is not only to keep social and economic costs under control, it is also to change the profile and the content of many traditional policy instruments.

In that sense, the traditional debate between efficiency and equity takes new forms. Efficiency could not progress without solidarity, and it would be impossible to back solidarity if we do not care about efficiency. After a long dissent on this point, it seems that a new kind of equilibrium could be attained between social partners and political parties. But it still remains to organise this 'New Deal', and many professional interests are not moving in this direction. The main problem is not to know what to do with the welfare state, it is to deal with these interest groups, which are located either outside (some groups of enterprises) or inside the state (some groups of officials) and which enjoy and support the old forms of public interventionism.

This is the real agenda for French welfare state reform.

6 The Federal Republic of Germany

Michael Krüger and Alfred Pfaller

THE CHALLENGE OF INTERNATIONAL COMPETITION

International Competitiveness and the Basic Orientation of Economic Policy in West Germany

Throughout its history, the trading position in international markets has been a central economic parameter for the Federal Republic of Germany. From the very beginning, West German economic policy has been internationally orientated. One of the guiding ideas was that the country is poorly endowed with raw materials and has to earn the foreign exchange which is needed to buy them abroad with the export of manufactures. This orientation actually can be traced back to the early years of the German Reich in the 19th century. The other guiding idea behind West Germany's determined world-market orientation was the neo-liberal conviction that a free, unrestricted market renders the best results in terms of national prosperity.

Still, the government has always considered it its responsibility to support German export activities. As early as the beginning of the 1950s a heavily subsidised export credit insurance (Hermes) was established. Several institutions were added which supply market information and other export-related services, especially to the smaller enterprises. Macroeconomic policy also paid much attention to the country's export interests. The same is true for collective bargaining between labour and employers. Not to endanger the price competitiveness of German manufacturers was an overriding concern for the government and the bargaining partners. Wage discipline and price discipline which were both outstanding in international comparison and an exchange rate firmly tied to the dollar created a permanent slight undervaluation of the D-mark, which was, of course, conducive to export success and a positive trade balance (see also below, p. 204).

One result of the country's economic policy orientation, which is

Table 6.1 Ratio of exports/GDP in West Germany, 1970–85

Year	%
1960	20.0
1970	22.6
1971–4	24.2
1975	26.3
1976–9	27.1
1980	28.4
1981–4	32.0
1985	35.0
1986–8	32.2

Source: *Monatsberichte der Deutschen Bundesbank*, various issues

mirrored in the export orientation of German enterprises, was an extremely high degree of integration of the German economy into the world market. The ratio of exports (as well as of imports) to Gross Domestic Product rose steadily from 1949 to 1985. Since the beginning of the 1970s, when West Germany had already long been established in the world as an export giant, world-market exposure still grew by about 50 per cent until 1985 (see Table 6.1).

The Evolution of the Country's International Competitiveness

Already in 1960 the Federal Republic was the second largest exporter of manufactures in the world. But its 18 per cent share stood at that time still well in the shadow of the USA who had 26 per cent (see Figure 3.3 in the chapter on the United States). In the following 20 years the German share of world exports grew only slightly with some ups and downs to about 20 per cent. But the same period witnesses a dramatic decline in the position of the US and also a dramatic rise of Japan. In the early 1970s West Germany became number one in manufacturing exports, a position it kept until today – by all means remarkable for a medium-size country. Of course, Germany's world market share does not only reflect sheer competitiveness, but also that high degree of openness which resulted from its internationalist economic policy orientation.

During most of the period of the country's rise to first place in world manufacturing exports, German real wages grew more rapidly than the ones in the other large OECD countries, with the exception

Table 6.2 Development of unit labour costs in selected OECD countries, 1970–88

	Germany (%)	*France (%)*	*UK (%)*	*USA (%)*
1970–5	+ 47.0	+ 68.6	+101.1	+ 35.5
1975–80	+ 22.1	+ 66.1	+ 84.8	+ 45.6
1980–5	+ 10.8	+ 49.2	+ 15.9	+ 9.0
1985–8	+ 4.6	+ 4.4	+ 14.9	+ 9.9
1970–88	+108.0	+336.2	+394.9	+136.3

Source: Sachverständigenrat 1986, Statistischer Anhang, 198; Sachverständigenrat 1989, p. 114; DIW-Wochenbericht, various issues

of Japan (see Figure 3.4 in Chapter 3). Yet unit labour costs grew in general more slowly, as can be seen in Table 6.2.

The relative improvement of real wages indicates that market shares have not been conquered at the expense of factor remuneration but that they reflect indeed the underlying strength of the West German economy in comparison with the other three countries. On the other hand, the slow rise of German unit labour costs is an indicator of wage and price discipline, which favours performing competitiveness. It means that increases in nominal labour remuneration have been more in line with productivity growth than in the other countries. The conclusion which is drawn from the improvement of real wages until 1980 is corroborated by the comparative data on productivity which are presented in Chapter 2, Figure 2.8, and which show the Federal Republic relatively well placed among its competitor countries.

However, in the 1980s the country fell back considerably in manufacturing productivity growth (see Figures 2.7 and 2.9). This links in with the comparative data on economic growth, which show Germany at the end of the OECD rank order during that period (see Figure 2.13). Thus, in contrast with the preceding decades, after the second oil crisis the favourable development of West German unit labour costs was achieved entirely through wage discipline and a cheap D-mark. Export success was 'bought' at the price of renouncing claims on the domestic economy's and on foreign economies' product. Paradoxically, this is also the meaning of the high surplus on the country's current account, which emerged during the 1980s. 'Normally' Germany would have had an internationally more expensive currency, exported less and imported more (see also below pp. 200–1). Performing competitiveness was clearly above underlying competitiveness in this latest period.

Underlying competitiveness refers to the ability of national producers to earn a high income in the international market place. This ability derives from superior productivity and superior product quality. We have seen that, as far as productivity is concerned, West German manufacturing industry has lost some ground *vis-à-vis* its competitors during the 1980s. In this respect, the basis for wage and other income premiums has become narrower. Or put differently, most competitor countries had more leeway for raising real wages, fringe benefits, taxes, environmental standards, etc. in the tradables sector. But premiums are also earned with products for which there is much demand but little competitive supply. These are products of an exceptionally high quality and products which incorporate a know-how that few competitors possess, that is, so-called high-technology goods. Of those goods which require for their production a particularly high investment in the creation of expertise (R&D-intensive goods) Germany held in 1980 a 16 per cent share of world exports. In 1984 this share had gone down to 13 per cent, whereas the Japanese share has increased from 17 to 25 per cent and the US share stayed more or less the same around 25 per cent (OECD, 1986, p. 72). So, high technology does not seem to have been the particular strength of West German industry either. Into this direction points also the observation that the share of high-technology goods in the total output of German manufacturing industries has been stagnating at the 12 per cent level throughout the 1970s (OECD, 1985b, pp. 40ff.). Referring to the country's far from brilliant high-tech performance it has been said sarcastically that Germany is excellent at making yesterday's goods.

On the other hand, by the end of the 1980s Germany's industrial structure was still very much orientated to today's profitable markets, as an investigation of the Munich-based ifo-Institute for Economic Research shows (cf. Gerstenberger, 1988a and 1988b). While German enterprises did not participate very much in the more spectacular product innovations in the information and communications industry they showed a remarkable strength in incorporating these innovations into more conventional types of products, such as machine tools and automobiles, and transforming them, thus, into high-technology hybrids. To do this, traditional manufacturing virtues like craftsmanship and manpower training were combined with continuous high

Table 6.3 R&D expenditure as percentage of GDP in selected OECD countries, 1986

USA	2.9
West Germany	2.8
Japan	2.7
France	2.3
United Kingdom	2.2
Sweden (1984)	2.6

Source: Globus Kartendienst 1988, IC-7160

investment in research and development. And in fact, the Federal Republic compares favourably with other countries in R&D effort, as Table 6.3 shows.

Considering the information we have on the structure of the German industry with regard to international market chances and on the efforts which are taken to create productive skills and human capital, we should rather be confident that despite a certain setback in the 1980s the underlying competitiveness of the West German economy will not deteriorate very much in the future. On the other hand, the country has shown precisely during the 1980s that it is capable of getting a maximum of performing competitiveness out of its underlying potential.

THE NATIONAL COMPETITIVENESS DEBATE

Renewed Emphasis on Export Performance

Even a hundred years ago, Emperor Wilhelm II had already referred to 'the necessity to maintain the competitiveness of the German industry in the world market' as an important restriction to be taken into account when introducing new elements of social security for the workers (cf. Erdmann 1957, p. 11). Concern about the country's ability to compete in international markets has tradition in Germany. Exaggerating somewhat, one could say that the tradition became an obsession in the Federal Republic with its extreme and ever-increasing dependency on exports. But of course, in times of stable economic growth, with a rising share of West German exports in world imports and a positive trade balance year after year there was no reason to be worried about a competitive decline. It was sufficient to be aware of potential dangers.

The awareness was heightened by the abrupt changes in external parameters as they appeared with the break-down of the post-war international economic order in the 1970s. The country's export strength was then widely considered a kind of insurance protecting German prosperity, employment and so on in the rougher international economic environment. In particular, it was supposed to secure the supply of vital raw materials for import-dependent Germany in view of rising world market prices. Therefore, the nation was truly alarmed when in 1979, under the impact of the second oil shock, the country's current account suddenly showed a large deficit.[1] Fears came up that the economic lifelines of the Federal Republic might be endangered. And the country's international competitiveness became the subject of extensive discussion and investigation.[2]

The national debate in the wake of the balance of payments shock focused largely on the macroeconomic conditions which would enable the Federal Republic to cope with the oil price increase while facing ever tougher international competition (Japan, NICs). Emphasis was laid (a) on the reduction of imports, not only by substituting oil and cutting energy consumption, but also by restricting overall demand; (b) on the need to invest in the improvement of the country's export capacity and to divert the necessary resources from competing uses, most of all consumption. Price competitiveness based on wage restraint and monetary stability was also stressed. In short, external performance was re-emphasised as the primary criterion at which to orientate economic policy (cf. Wolff von Amerongen 1981). This meant that the stronger orientation towards domestic priorities, which the Social Democratic governments had brought about since the end of the 1960s, was to be corrected.

Renewed emphasis on export performance did not necessarily imply specific fears of competitive decline. And in general confidence prevailed that the balance of payments difficulties could be mastered. But the debate also focused on two issues which were in fact reasons for concern about future German competitiveness.

The Issue of High-tech Competency

Long before the dramatic deterioration of the German balance of trade there had already been worries about a technology gap between the world's leading industrial powers and the Federal Republic. Both the long-standing American supremacy in the area of high technology and the rapid advance of Japan were considered a serious challenge. At the beginning of the 1980s it had become obvious that German industry was well behind its competitors in the new key technology of electronic data processing. Catching up with the USA and Japan then took on the quality of a national goal enhanced by a European dimension. Foreign Minister Dietrich Genscher expressed the prevailing mood when he wrote in 1984: 'The Federal Republic of Germany and Western Europe can maintain their prosperity only if they manage to catch up with the third industrial revolution which has its origin in America and Japan.'[3] Many attributed Germany's (and Europe's) lagging behind in the international technology race predominantly to a certain neglect of the new technological developments on the side of enterprises and governments alike. Consequently, catching up was seen as a matter of increasing effort and of mobilising additional resources, especially for research and development. At government level, the pertinent agenda included the promotion of targeted R&D programmes and the national or European orchestration of the various decentralised efforts.[4]

'We have slept in the 1960s and 1970s and therefore we have to run the faster now', this rather optimistic interpretation of the technology issue characterises, however, only part of the national debate. There was also a much gloomier assessment of the situation. More than just the perceived weakness of certain key high-tech industries, it reflected the general economic malaise which had evolved in the wake of the energy crisis of 1973. While the technology worries themselves subsided towards the end of the 1980s and some specific high-tech strengths of German industry (for example, the application of micro-electronics in machine tools) relativised their weaknesses in the information and communication field (cf. Gerstenberger 1988a), the more fundamental gloom about West Germany's economic health persisted.

The Issue of the Country's Weakened Economic Vitality

The traumatic stagflation experience of the 1970s had given rise – in Germany as throughout the Western world – to a growing criticism of society's interference with the market mechanism. The charge was made that this interference on behalf of all sorts of particularistic interests had become so massive that the vitality of the economy's supply-side finally became more and more paralysed. The political agenda derived from this diagnosis had as its central objective the creation of conditions which would make sustained economic growth again feasible. It was basically a domestic agenda. But in competitiveness-minded Germany, conditions which weakened economic vitality soon had to be seen also as a disadvantage *vis-à-vis* other, less sclerotic countries. Thus, the radical supply-side diagnosis entailed a profound warning about Germany's competitiveness as well. The main topics addressed were:

- the many regulatory restrictions of entrepreneurial freedom;
- the high taxes, especially taxes on enterprises;
- the heavy subsidising of some sectors of the economy and the tremendous waste of resources this implied;
- the high and ever-rising non-wage labour costs, consisting of employers' social security contributions and paid non-working time;
- the rigidities of the labour market which had evolved in the past 15 to 20 years;
- the erosion of the former achievement and work ethic and the rise of a general entitlement mentality.

In sum, the supply-side diagnosis of creeping competitive decline had one major institutional culprit: excessive welfare statism.

Partially because the dominant theme of the competitiveness debate was still the high-technology deficit, partially because the current account improved dramatically after 1981, and partially because other industrialised countries (with the exception of Japan) did not show much more economic vitality than the Federal Republic, the sclerosis theme had more impact within the domestically oriented economic policy discourse than in the competitiveness debate during the early 1980s. By and large, there was still widespread confidence in the country's international competitiveness. Confirmed again by the obvious export strength of German industry, the opinion prevailed that the high level of qualifications of the German workforce and co-operative labour relations (the so-called 'productivity coalition' between industry and labour) (cf. Dauderstädt 1983) provided a solid fundament for the high wages and social benefits in the Federal Republic. And the well functioning welfare state was generally considered an essential part of that high-efficiency syndrome which has made for Germany's economic strength in the post-war period.

But in the mid-1980s, when it became obvious that Germany's economy showed conspicuously less dynamism than several other industrialised countries (most of all the UK and the USA), the concern about German international competitiveness re-emerged in public debate. The themes were familiar. The issue was, however, cast in different conceptual terms.

The Issue of the Country's Attractiveness as an Industrial Location

It was said that Germany was becoming less and less attractive to domestic and foreign investors as a place to set up production. Thus, regardless of current export performance, the industrial base of German prosperity would little by little be thinned out. Economic growth would emigrate to other countries. The case for declining '*Standort*' (i.e locational) attractiveness was strongly pushed by the manufacturers' association and has been coloured by the distributive interests of business. Hard-pressed industrial branches used the 'Standort' issue to portray their specific difficulties as a matter of national concern. Accordingly, much of the debate was carried on with emotions running high and labour dismissing the whole idea as just a pretext for an unwarranted attack on welfare statist achievements (cf. Hans-Böckler-Stiftung & DGB, 1988). There was much exchange of one-sided arguments.

But the manufacturers' initiative also revived soul-searching of a sincere kind for the country's competitive position. Mostly, the search was conducted in form of a comparison of Germany's competitive advantages and disadvantages, with the objective of weighing them against each other. However, simple and clear as such a procedure may appear, it departed from a blurred notion of competitiveness. And this deficiency has been haunting the German 'Standort' debate. Business has basically been interested in what above was called performing competitiveness,[5] the central worry being that profits get squeezed between rising domestic costs and tough international price competition. Others, mostly academics and journalistic observers, have also voiced concern that Germany's underlying competitiveness is at stake, that is, that the economic basis for high wages, long vacations and generous welfare state benefits is eroding. But it has not always been quite clear whether this is the reason *why* the industrial location West Germany loses attractiveness or whether it would occur *because* investors shy away from that location. An adequate understanding of the issue requires two dimensions to be taken into account: (a) the development of production costs, productivity and product quality in the Federal Republic of Germany; (b) the way the elements of dimension (a) are transformed into international prices. As we shall see, a general shortcoming of the German debate has been that it focused too much on the first dimension and implied a too simplistic notion of the second one.

Production Costs and Productivity

Published opinions on the competitive advantages and disadvantages of the industrial location West Germany towards the end of the 1980s rendered a fairly consistent pattern: in international comparison it is expensive to produce in Germany, but the country also offers exceptionally good conditions (human capital, social discipline, infrastructure, inter-firm supply networks) as far as productivity and product quality are concerned. This has been so for many years, but – so runs the general feeling – the balance has been deteriorating. Productive performance has come to support less and less well all the claims which are made by labour and government to the yield of productive activity.[6] As to the point up to which this deterioration has already reached, most observers would subscribe to a cautious assessment, considering the overall balance still as positive but in danger of turning negative if the trend were to continue.

In line with business' long-standing concerns, most emphasis has been laid on the disproportionate rise of non-wage labour costs (including the decrease in annual working time) and on the country's lagging behind in the international tax-cutting race which supposedly left the taxation of enterprises in West Germany on a particularly high level.[7] Ever tougher environmental regulations have also been considered a cost-raising factor of some importance.

In addition, the argument has been gaining weight that Germany's former productivity and quality advantage is eroding. This means, on the one hand, that other countries have improved. In part they have cut out some of their former handicaps, as has the United Kingdom in the wake of the Thatcher revolution. In part they are benefiting from the increasing international mobility of enterprises, which transfer technology and productivity to other locations. On the other hand, the argument implies that the retarding elements in Germany itself have been developing unchecked: that excessive regulatory and union-imposed restrictions have come to impede entrepreneurial initiative and to keep the productivity of machinery and equipment lower than necessary. The generalising charge of societal sclerosis, that is, of West Germany's excessive preoccupation with stability, entitlements, leisure and the enjoyment of the good life has kept providing the ideological umbrella to all these critical observations (cf. Giersch, 1984; and Donges *et al.*, 1988).

Societal sclerosis, of course, would imply a high level of aversion to risks, a high degree of immobility and a tendency to stick to existing economic structures, outdated and costly as they may be. It would make it difficult on enterprises to improve efficiency, to innovate and to seize new market opportunities, when located in West Germany. And high labour costs and taxes would, thus, be warranted all the less. Increasingly they would squeeze profits which can be achieved with the production of tradables in West Germany.

Do the charges conform to the observable reality? Apart from the possibility of compensating exchange-rate adjustments, a point to which we shall turn in the next section, there are three observations which weaken the case for a deteriorating balance of competitive advantages and disadvantages. First of all, we have the fact that in 1986 the Federal Republic had become the biggest exporter in the world, while profits improved steadily after the recession years' low of 1981 and 1982. So, the overall price competitiveness of German tradables cannot have deteriorated during the years which witnessed and preceded the 'Standort' debate. But in comparison with the 1960s and 1970s there certainly has been a deterioration of profits.[8] Second, in the 1980s, as previously in the 1970s, unit labour costs, which are the result of labour costs and labour productivity, have increased less in Germany than in most other industrialised countries (as measured in local currencies). Thus, labour costs cannot be considered a factor so far which contributed to the competitive decline of German industry. However, this may well have been the case for certain industrial activities which are not carried out more efficiently in Germany than elsewhere. Thirdly, the emphasis placed on high non-wage labour costs throughout the 'Standort' debate appears exaggerated when it is taken into consideration that all non-wage labour costs together (obligatory social security contributions, remunerated non-working time, fringe benefits negotiated with organised labour) constitute but about 11 per cent of total production costs in West German mining and manufacturing industries (cf. Uhlmann, 1986; and Welzmüller, 1988). Efficiency in the use of raw materials, for instance, would seem to be a much more relevant factor when it comes to the cutting of costs.

So, aggregate empirical data on West German price competitiveness seem to take quite a bit of substance away from the position that the attractiveness to investors of the industrial location West Germany has been decreasing. Products made in Germany kept selling extremely well in the international marketplace and companies made handsome profits with them. Additionally, in 1989 a study commissioned by the Federal Minister of the Economy showed that the Federal Republic does not tax enterprises any more than most other countries if depreciation allowances are duly taken into account (*Süddeutsche Zeitung*, 18 May 1989). This finding made another important pillar of the disadvantaged-industrial-location thesis tumble. Yet, since the beginning of the 1980s the net outflow of capital from the Federal Republic has increased considerably. German direct investments abroad soared, while foreign direct investment in Germany stayed more or less on the level of the late 1970s. Germany attracted less foreign investment than most other OECD countries, with the notable exception of Japan. Low investment in new productive capacity has in fact been the weak flank of the West German economy in the 1980s.

This points to the possibility that the obvious competitiveness of German-made products has been much more the merit of German entrepreneurs than the natural consequence of productivity-prone locational conditions such as qualified manpower for example, and that German entrepreneurial efficiency could bring about excellent results in foreign locations as well. Transferring production abroad could then be an attractive option to German enterprises even though their activities at home are still profitable. The decisive question would then be: is production elsewhere *more* profitable? It would not only be a matter of observable facts. It would very much be also a matter of expectations concerning future developments. Transferable enterprise-specific efficiency plus a loss of confidence in the future profitability of German-located ventures could indeed add up to a threat of creeping de-industrialisation.

However, surveys show that German companies invested in real capital abroad overwhelmingly for the purpose of consolidating and extending their position in foreign markets. A large part of these investments was in fact done in support of the companies' exports from Germany. Only a very small part transferred productive capacity from Germany abroad or constituted a choice in favour of a foreign location.[9] So, as far as German enterprises are concerned, we do have a lack of investment, but not a significantly growing preference for non-German locations. In order to use this phenomenon in support of the hypothesis of declining 'Standort' attractiveness we would have to argue that German companies had logistic difficulties with transferring production abroad, even though they would have liked to do this and that, as a consequence, they just abstained from expanding productive capacity, going instead into purely financial investments. But, as we shall see, there are alternative explanations which are at least as plausible.

There remains the obvious reluctance of foreign companies to set up production in the Federal Republic. The president of the West German federation of employers' associations suspected that foreigners unacquainted with the German reality are just afraid of the very visible high costs and of the degree to which managerial prerogatives are restricted by workers' rights, while local businessmen have learned as well to appreciate the advantages of producing in Germany.[10] He added that the protracted national debate on the competitiveness of the industrial location West Germany has done nothing to increase foreign confidence.[11]

But it may be that foreign companies' anti-German bias when it comes to direct investment also serves to highlight the specific competitive conditions of the Federal Republic. In a nutshell, German products are highly competitive in international markets *despite* high factor costs, high taxes, regulative burdens and so on. A large part of this competitiveness is embodied in the local enterprises, their internal and external organisation, their expertise and their fund of motivational forces. German enterprises have developed their firm-specific efficiency in interaction with the specific locational factors, which they have learned to use as advantages. Therefore, to some degree it may be that German firms perform best in Germany whereas foreign companies lack this affinity to the particular German location. They have their own firm-specific strengths, which have been developed in different business and work cultures.[12] When they set up production abroad they must have consolidated their firm-specific efficiency thus far that it can be maintained also in alien social and cultural environments. It should be expected that in this case they place emphasis (a) on the direct costs of foreign inputs (b) on the chance of shaping them in accordance with the firm's native corporate culture and its organisational standards. Both criteria would speak against selecting high-cost locations with very pronounced idiosyncracies such as West Germany, Sweden or Japan.

This still leaves us with the West German companies' reluctance to expand production at home, their (as we have just argued) favourite location. A ready macroeconomic explanation is the high real interest rate which has prevailed in the international financial markets and raised the profitability threshold for real investment to become worthwhile (cf. Scharpf, 1987). However, this crowding-out hypothesis does not explain why German enterprises have expanded productive capacity less than British or American enterprises, who also faced a high interest rate. To come to grips with this problem we have to consider the way German competitiveness is related to global macroeconomics.

German Competitiveness and Global Macroeconomics

German goods were selling well in international markets because two conditions were met: (a) goods were offered for which there was plenty of demand; (b) the exchange rate enabled the producers to price them competitively. Whatever the level of unit costs was in terms of D-marks, the exchange rate related it to foreign unit costs in such a way (allowing for quality differentials) that a tremendous German export surplus became possible throughout the 1980s. But why did the international currency markets value the D-mark so low that trade with the rest of the world got more and more out of balance? The answer is that German savings went during all these years abroad rather than into real investment at home. Germans earned more money than they were willing to spend and lent it to those who wanted to spend more than they earned (most important among them: the Americans). They supplied the currency markets with D-marks (depressing their international value) in order to buy foreign securities and financial titles. Thus, the rest of the world got sufficient D-marks to buy German goods without having to earn them all by exporting to Germany.[13]

As long as this situation of German oversaving prevails the performing competitiveness of German enterprises is practically secured. If unit costs should rise faster than abroad – as it has been the predominant concern in the 'Standort' debate – currency adjustments will keep the international prices of German-made products at a level which maintains that trade surplus which necessarily goes along with continuing capital export. Of course, devaluation would mean a reduction of real incomes – which is the price to be paid for a decline in underlying competitiveness. But German products would not be pushed out of the market, German enterprises would go on selling and making profits. In any case, they keep benefiting from increasing demand for German exports which is alimented by foreign economic growth.

On the other hand, Germany's one-sided success in foreign markets has pushed her into a rather precarious position *vis-à-vis* the rest of the world. If anything, then an appreciation of the D-mark, making German tradables less competitive, has been indicated since the mid-1980s. Lower production costs and higher productivity would just have intensified this need for currency appreciation. What does this imply for the country's attractiveness as an industrial location? First, as long as investors lack confidence the balance cannot be restored because the D-mark is kept undervalued, thus boosting the price competitiveness of the products which are made at the distrusted location. Inversely, more investment by German or foreign enterprises has the consequence of reducing in the short run German export chances because it reduces the supply of (or increases the demand for) D-marks on the currency markets. In other words, any return to a more 'normal' relationship between national earnings and national spending implies a correction of Germany's excessive export strength. Therefore, it has to lead to a squeeze on the profits of enterprises which produce tradables in Germany – no matter how production costs as measured in D-marks develop. Wage concessions, tax reductions and regulatory relief would then just make the D-mark appreciate the more.

So, if investors expect a return to 'normalcy' it is rational for them to stay away from tradables, unless they feel that they have or will have an exceptionally strong market position. The individual enterprise can speculate that the favourable currency situation will continue, and expand its capacity in response to increasing foreign demand. But collectively this speculation would be self-defeating. Under these circumstances the creation of additional productive capacity only makes (collective) sense if it is oriented predominantly towards that part of the domestic market which is not exposed to foreign competition, that is, to the non-tradables sector. Later on, a restored balance of trade can be the basis of renewed export growth, as an increase in investment activity would lead to accelerated economic growth and hence to increasing import demand as well. However, investors would need a good reason to expect a lasting increase in sales. Yet the perspective of vigorously expanding demand for non-tradables has been conspicuously absent in the Federal Republic of the 1980s.[14]

Here then we have an explanation for the continuing weakness of investment activity which does not need the concept of a deteriorating industrial location West Germany. The particular macroeconomic configuration which prevailed in the 1980s has, in fact, immunised the country's locational quality (as far as overall profit chances are concerned) against changes in underlying competitiveness. Serious problems with profit chances arise only when currency adjustment does no longer work to the benefit of German exporters. This would be the case when production costs got out of hand in a context of excess demand (by consumers and investors). Such a context is typically characterised either by excess domestic money supply (which would be inflationary and cause the DM to appreciate in real terms, continuously outstepping the corrective devaluations) or by an 'orderly' increase in external indebtedness (which would cause nominal appreciation as it did in the USA). It would be essential then to restitute cost and spending discipline. Otherwise domestic tradables would be crowded out of the market.

There are other circumstances which endanger the effectiveness of the currency adjustment mechanism, making it difficult for enterprises to recuperate, with an adequate profit margin, their production costs in the unprotected open market. One is a structural shock which exposes in a relatively short period of time sizeable parts of the tradables sector to highly superior foreign competition – be it low-cost competition or be it high-quality competition. Exchange rate adjustments might then no longer serve as a remedy. Instead, a restructuring of the supply capacity may be required – which cannot be done overnight, of course. The West German economy, however, has maintained an industrial structure which has kept it pretty immune against such shocks (DIW, 1984; Gerstenberger, 1988b).

Like external structural shocks, internal disruptions (for example, because of labour conflicts) imply for each enterprise a threat of suddenly rising costs which are not neutralised by exchange-rate adjustment. In this respect again, the Federal Republic is generally considered as offering very favourable conditions.

Another obstacle to competitiveness maintaining currency adjustments is an institutional fixation of the nominal exchange rate, as it has been accorded to some degree within the European Monetary System and as it will perhaps be tightened further in the course of European unification. If corrective devaluation is difficult it could be a competitive advantage to have less inflation than the other countries within the monetary system, because this has the effect of a creeping devaluation of the own currency. In this respect, too, there has so far been no danger for the competitiveness of goods made in Germany, in fact quite the contrary.

Considering it all, it seems only logical that the overwhelming majority of German enterprises perceives the establishment of a truely unified European market by 1993 as a chance to boost sales rather than as a threat of losing market shares to cheaper foreign competitors (Gürtler, 1988; Franzmeyer, 1988). Was then the whole 'Standort' debate much ado about nothing? Not quite. For enterprises it is important that they can sell profitably what they produce in Germany. We have seen that international macroeconomics have made sure so far that this would be the case and that there is actually no danger in sight of an unfavourable turn of conditions. But for the country it is important in addition that high and growing incomes are earned in international trade, that sufficient goods are produced at the industrial location West Germany which achieve high prices in the international market. This is a matter of supply capacity which is facilitated by locational factors like human capital, social discipline or infrastructure, but which must be created, maintained and expanded by investments. Therefore, it must be a matter of concern for German competitiveness if enterprises abstain – for whatever reasons – from investing in productive capacity over a long period of time, as they have done during the 1980s. It leads to a degrading of the industrial location aspect of West Germany in the sense that an increasing part of the national workforce loses the chance of selling its labour services at a high price in the internationally exposed segments of the market. The high rate of unemployment in Germany substantiates this concern. Paradoxically, the continuing export success of the highly competitive installed industries made it the more difficult for those without the backing of high-productivity, high-quality capital equipment to stay in the market or to re-enter it.

THE POLICY RESPONSE

The challenge of international competition, as it presented itself with renewed force since the oil price explosions of the 1970s, left its mark on West German economic policy. The mark is deep, but it is nonetheless blurred. Deep it is because maintaining international competitiveness became again a consideration of the highest priority in policy-making after a short decade of a certain inclination towards domestic priorities. The very subtle 'macroeconomic mercantilism' that had been an important, albeit latent, feature of German economic policy until the later 1960s re-emerged in not quite such a subtle form in the late 1970s. 'Macroeconomic mercantilism' refers to the overriding goal of avoiding an interference of domestic absorption with German export chances. It implied a high priority for monetary stability, which, in turn, helped to maintain the D-mark slightly undervalued *vis-à-vis* countries with higher inflation rates. To achieve it, it was necessary to keep the growth of demand and production costs under tight control with the help of fiscal, monetary and incomes policies. The consequently export-oriented economy would derive much of its dynamic from the expansion of foreign demand and the investment-stimulating perspective of conquering additional world market segments. Domestic consumption would follow suit via rising real wages, putting a check on the growth of the export surplus and inducing a permanent shedding of less productive activities.[15]

Priorities began to be shifted away from external performance when the Social Democrats entered the government in 1966. And with the so-called social–liberal coalition of 1969 the strict stability-orientation which was an essential ingredient of the former export-led growth syndrome was definitely abandoned in favour of a strong expansion of welfare state programmes. This was done from a perceived position of economic strength in which the international competitiveness of the West German industry seemed to be solidly established. However, the increasing problems since the mid-1970s brought a turn-around back to 'macroeconomic mercantilism'. Securing the country's export chances became again a top priority.

But this response to the renewed challenge of international competition was embedded in a broader correction of economic policy (cf. Bundesminister für Wirtschaft, 1981). External threats were not the only problem that had to be addressed. In a way, the stagflation problem overshadowed everything by the end of the 1970s. Efforts to recuperate monetary stability cannot be seen only in function of the consolidation and improvement of export chances. Primarily, they responded to the general imperative of putting the economic house back in order. Also the specific policy goal of getting the budget deficit under control, which brought the Social Democrats' welfare statist reform programme to a halt, must, first of all, be seen as a tribute to the painfully rediscovered requirements of a well-functioning market economy.

Policy correction gained momentum when the Christian Democrats regained control of the Federal government in 1982 and set out to implement their long-announced 'turn-around' ('*die Wende*'). More drastic measures were taken to reduce the budget deficit, including several cuts in welfare state programmes. In addition, elements of supply-side reform – most importantly tax reductions – were put on the agenda. Again, the '*Wende*' was not primarily a programme to strengthen the international competitiveness of German industry. It was, similar to its much more thorough counterparts in the United Kingdom and the United States, conceived of as a programme to eliminate the excesses of state and interest group intervention into the market in order to re-establish the basis for sustainable economic growth.

Insofar it may appear inappropriate to speak of a return to export orientation in response to the escalating problems of the 1970s. Yet, there was, in fact, more to German macroeconomic policies in the 1980s than just prudency. They did have a slight 'mercantilistic' twist. It became most visible in the issue of international macroeconomic co-ordination as it evolved in the mid-1980s, with the USA facing more and more urgently the need to reduce its budget deficit and to retreat from its role as the main supporter of worldwide economic growth. The German economic authorities in the central bank and the government refused firmly then to give in to increasing international demands that the Federal Republic enact more expansionary monetary and/or fiscal policies in order to add support to global economic growth and to facilitate the necessary adjustments in the USA (cf. Kamppeter, 1988a). It was feared that compliance with these demands might re-fuel inflation in Germany, setting in motion a macroeconomic escalation process in which (a) profits in the tradables sector would be subjected to continuous pressure requiring repeated defensive devaluations; and (b) resources would be shifted to consumption and withdrawn from investment. The advantageous position which West Germany had *vis-à-vis* more inflationary competitor countries and which kept her competitiveness, macroeconomically seen, at the safe side was regarded to be at stake. And German authorities were not prepared to put at risk this safety as a service to the global economy.

It has to be seen that the strategy of ensuring competitiveness without recourse to currency devaluation made it mandatory that unit costs be kept from rising faster than abroad. A generally restrictive stance with regard to everything that would imply higher costs for enterprises was, therefore, essential. This affected wages, non-wage labour costs, regulative burdens (for instance on behalf of the environment) and taxes. In turn, everything that would reduce unit costs was to be welcomed, because it created an additional buffer against uncontrollable cost hikes like demographically conditioned increases in non-wage labour costs or the outcomes of 'irresponsible' collective bargaining. In other words, 'macroeconomic mercantilism', as it orientated West German foreign economic policy again since the late 1970s, required a direct approach to cost control. It could not rely on the balancing effects of macroeconomic mechanisms. It also left little room for the setting of societal priorities as far as they would result in higher D-mark prices of German-made goods. In recognition of the political system's limited capability of rational cost allocation (for example, wage restraint against additional regulative burdens) was the strategy's imperative rather to stem *any* rise of costs.

It should be noted, however, that in the 1980s 'macroeconomic mercantilism' with its austerity bias did not produce the same virtuous circle of creeping real devaluation, improving competitiveness, corrective nominal appreciation, higher real incomes and strengthened monetary stability as it did in the 1950s and 1960s. Instead, there was an increasing current account surplus related to a surplus of domestic saving over investment. Germany did not enjoy export-led growth but experienced export-alleviated stagnation and got into that very peculiar undervaluation trap which we referred to earlier. This difference had to do with the turmoils in the world currency and capital markets which followed the break-down of the old Bretton-Woods system of international economic relations, the oil price shocks and the tremendous American budget deficit of the 1980s.

The return to a competitiveness-oriented macroeconomic policy was meant to forestall a vicious circle of inflation, balance of payments problems and devaluation, which loomed as a threat in the 1970s. But an increasingly important policy goal was also to improve the supply-side conditions in the Federal Republic as compared with competitor countries and to ensure the attractiveness of the industrial location West Germany. The most important measure in this respect was the reduction of the corporate tax rate from 56 per cent to 50 per cent, which was decided in 1987 – not too spectacular a change.[16] The government faced a dilemma here: The competitiveness-oriented macroeconomic policy was hard to reconcile with an increasing budget deficit. Sizeable expenditure cuts, however, did not find sufficient political support. In other respects, the government's supply-side initiatives fitted very well into the strategy of 'macro-economic mercantilism'. Their primary objective was to reduce overall labour costs and to create conditions which would facilitate a higher productivity of installed capital equipment. As its most determined move into this direction the ruling coalition introduced in 1985 a legal amendment which relaxed several restrictions on employers' hiring and firing prerogatives (facilitating among other things temporary employment) and made strikes more expensive for the labour unions, thus weakening their bargaining power (cf. Adamy, 1988). But perhaps more effective in this regard was the *de facto* flexibilisation of employment relations which resulted from the continuous oversupply of labour throughout the 1980s. Employers simply could bypass much more easily the legal and union-imposed restrictions.[17]

Altogether, the steps which were taken into the direction of supply-side improvements must be qualified as rather timid, at least if measured at the rhetoric which preceded and accompanied the '*Wende*' of 1982. In part, this timidness, which radical supply-siders in business, academia and abroad have often reproached,[18] reflects the difficulty of obtaining majorities for drastic and painful policy measures in the political system of the Federal Republic. The ruling Christian Democratic Party itself is not an ideological *avant garde* troop of neo-conservative thinking, but is based on a broad spectrum of socio-economic interests. Radical deregulation would have meant for sizeable parts of the Christian Democrats' constituency an invasion of the market with its adjustment pressures into spheres of life which had long been protected from it. In this respect, West German society may be considered sclerotic indeed. But it would be too simple to say that affluent Germans just rejected anything that threatened their established comfort. It was important that the more radical deregulation proposals were widely regarded as an exaggeration of neo-liberal ideologists, as unnecessary and hence unjustified. There where it mattered, German enterprises and German labour had – according to the dominant image – proven over and over their extraordinary adaptiveness. The gloomy assessment of some, that sclerotic, lazy and comfort-loving Germany is destined to lose out against more dynamic competitors, was simply not shared by the majority of the population and was, therefore, not apt to underpin radical changes in a political system that depended heavily on consensus.

However, the polity lent support to a more traditional way of responding to the challenge of international competition. It consisted in the mobilisation of public resources for technological development: in the form of subsidies to private enterprises and in the form of publicly organised research. This line of competitiveness-oriented policy co-existed as a more or less unquestioned matter of fact with the consequently pursued 'macroeconomic mercantilism' and the half-hearted supply-side reforms. Established well before the 1970s it was given a new impetus by the threat of a widening expertise gap between Germany and the leading high-technology countries. In practice, resources were concentrated on aerospace which was considered a key industry.[19] In connection with the industrial policy line of response, mention should finally also be made of the covert export promotion which was stepped up by the conservative government in the areas of development aid for Third World countries and of East–West trade.

THE CASE OF THE AUTOMOBILE INDUSTRY

The production of motor vehicles has always been one of the most important industries of the Federal Republic of Germany. In the early 1970s it employed about 5 per cent of the labour force in manufacturing, in the early 1980s it was even more than 6 per cent. In 1987 motor vehicles headed with around 18 per cent the list of German export goods. The export surplus of the automobile branch amounted to more than half of West Germany's huge total trade surplus. Throughout the last two decades, roughly half of German-made cars, trucks and buses were sold abroad. Figure 6.1 shows how the German automobile industry compares internationally in the last two decades. If we considered only passenger cars the picture would be very similar. The rise of Japan would appear slightly less steep and its distance to Germany at the end of the period less large. On the other hand, Germany would be positioned more clearly ahead of France throughout the 1980s. In any case, the picture is ambivalent: the phenomenal success of the Japanese motor car industry overshadows everything else. Compared with Japan, the German industry has clearly fallen back. Compared with the rest of the world, West Germany's position has become stronger. Volume-wise the American automobile industry is far ahead of the German one, but its importance is confined to the American market. So, with regard to

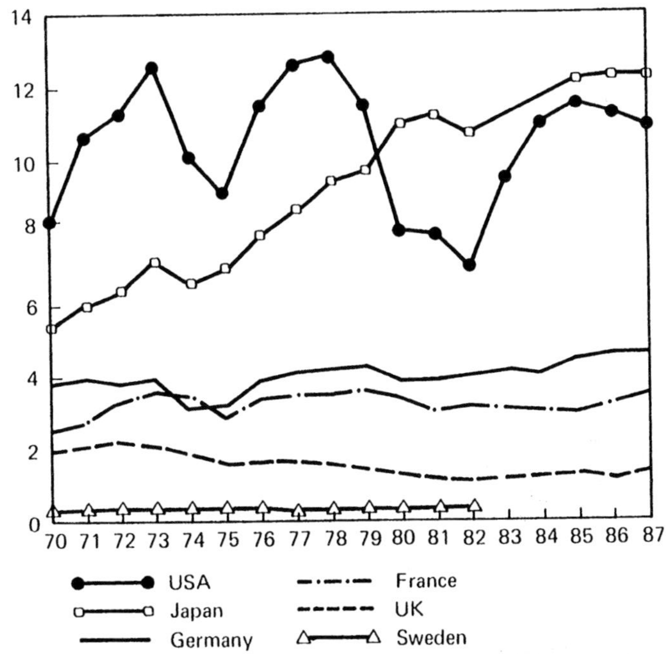

Sources: Globus Kartendienst, various issues: Zahlenbild-Pressedienst 30/88; *Financial Times*, 20 October 1983; Streeck & Hoff, 1983, Appendix One, Statistical Table IV

Figure 6.1 Number of motor vehicles produced in selected OECD countries, 1970–87 (thousands)

exports German automobiles are number two in the world, a position they have firmly maintained over the years (see Figure 6.2). The apparent comparative advantage indicator, which expresses the weight of automobiles in the German export basket as compared with their weight in the other car producing countries' export basket has gone up since the mid-1970s, when other European automobile industries, notably the British and the French, slid into crisis (OECD, 1985b).

Japanese competition has so far not put pressure on the German automobile industry to the point where it hurts. But one has to see that this relatively comfortable situation is owed in part to the protection of the EC market against large-scale Japanese imports. In the US market, where German and Japanese cars are competing on equal terms, the share of Japanese car imports has tripled to about

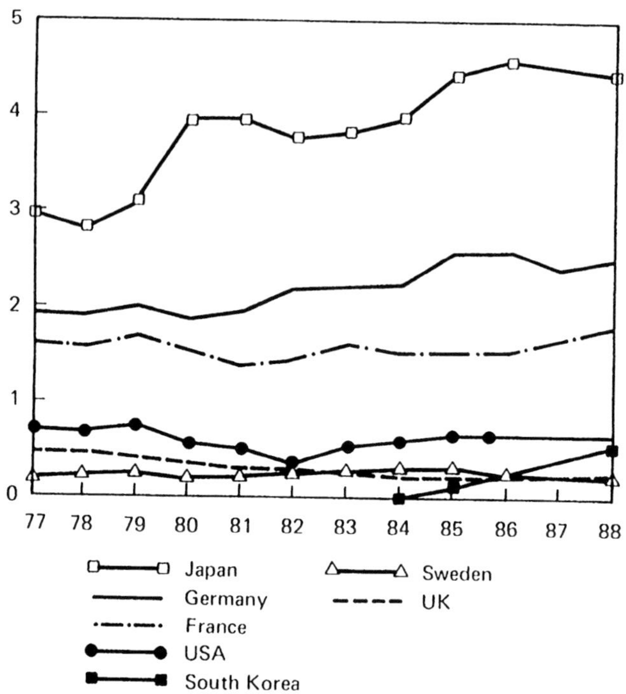

Sources: Globus Kartendienst, various issues; *Financial Times*, 20 October 1983, 22 October 1987

Figure 6.2 Car exports of selected OECD countries, 1960–87 (thousands of units)

20 per cent between 1970 and 1985 while the German share declined to less than 5 per cent (cf. Hild, 1981, p. 38). Japanese competition did constitute a very serious challenge indeed to the West German motor vehicle industry, a challenge which urgently demanded a response already by the early 1970s. Before the Japanese appeared on the international scene the strength of West German car makers had been quality, productivity and the relatively low real value of the D-mark. All three factors compensated for the ever increasing wages and non-wage labour costs in the Federal Republic. In fact, they constituted the economic basis of the high income of German automobile workers. It was at the wage front that the Japanese started attacking the German market position. They made high-quality vehicles at competitive levels of productivity with considerably cheaper manpower. The West German auto industry suffered its

first blatant defeat in a market where it had a decade ago experienced one of its most remarkable successes, the American small cars market. In the 1960s Volkswagens had become something like a myth in the United States, the symbol of an automobilistic counter-culture. But before shifting consumer priorities really revolutionised that most important auto market in the world and let the demand for Volkswagen-type fuel-efficient economy cars increase tremendously, the Japanese had secured for themselves the better chances. They simply were cheaper without being any the less good. Simultaneously with the American *debâcle* of Volkswagen, Japanese vehicles got to dominate many Third World markets and made the first major inroads into West European markets.

To prevent a further erosion of its market position German automobile manufacturers had to meet one of two conditions and preferentially both: (a) defend and extend the advantage they still had with respect to up-market quality standards and supreme engineering; (b) catch up with the Japanese cost advantage. The first condition implied two strategic elements, referring (i) to the consolidation and strengthening of their own position in those market segments where quality considerations dominate price considerations, (ii) to the expectation that these segments were going to gain weight, that is that an increasing number of people would be willing to pay a relatively high price for high quality. Abandoning the economy car markets entailed the risk of shrinking sales volumes for those car makers who had traditionally supplied these markets, in other words, to Volkswagen, Ford and Opel. Neglecting costs and going exclusively for engineering and performance would also turn out to be a fatal error if the competitors came out with equally good vehicles at lower costs, as the Japanese had done when they defeated Volkswagen in the USA.[20] Therefore, except for the most upmarket segments, the battle had to be waged simultaneously on the fronts of product technology and manufacturing costs.

On the latter front German producers were handicapped by high real wages and fringe benefits. Besides, the prolonged undervaluation of the West German currency had come to an end in the 1970s, whereas Japan still enjoyed that trade advantage. Under these circumstances, wages and non-wage labour costs (also under the aspect of working time) became an important competitive consideration in the motor vehicle industry of the Federal Republic (for the facts see Table 6.4).

But the German car makers also recognised that the cost advantage

Table 6.4 Hourly compensation for workers in the motor vehicles industries of selected OECD countries, 1975, 1981 and 1986 (USA=100)

	1975	*1981*	*1986*
USA	100	100	100
Germany	81	73	87
Japan	38	44	73
France	55	52	61
UK	42	45	48
Sweden	79	66	84

Sources: Streeck & Hoff 1983, Appendix One, Table X; and *Financial Times*, 28 August 1987; p. 4.

that could realistically be gained through wage discipline was rather limited, especially if compared with the magnitude of exchange rate effects. The auto industry had basically to accept that the Federal Republic was a high-wage country and was going to remain one at least for the years to come. True, the increasing challenge of foreign competition served to reinforce wage discipline, which had suffered a certain erosion since the late 1960s. Nonetheless, the key to controlling manufacturing costs had to be productivity.

And it was in the area of productivity that the Japanese challenge proved most serious. While the pure wage advantage it enjoyed during the 1960s was rapidly shrinking (and with regard to the European markets more and more being neutralised by transport costs) the Japanese automobile industry moved rapidly ahead of its German competitors in terms of productivity, as Figure 6.3 demonstrates. If one takes into account the different paces of working time reduction in the two countries, the comparison of productivity developments looks slightly less disadvantageous for the German motor vehicle industry. Yet even then Japan shows a productivity increase of 66 per cent during the 1970s and Germany only one of 4 per cent (Streeck and Hoff 1983, Appendix 1, p. 15). The picture can be brightened up somewhat by considering the German car makers' strategy of concentrating on high value added vehicles, whereas economy cars had been the major Japanese strength during that period. However, this could not blur the fact that productivity was no longer a competitive advantage of the German automobile industry by the end of the 1970s.

Both in order to stay ahead in product quality and to not fall back in productivity the German car makers had to step up investment (in

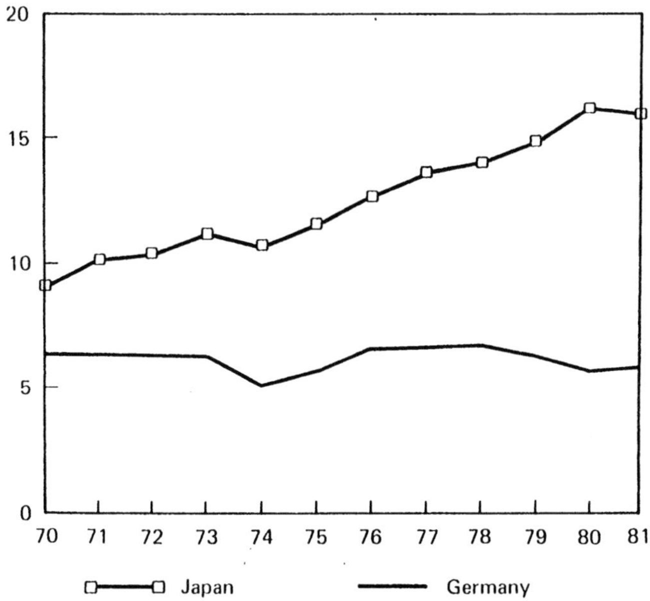

Source: Streeck & Hoff, 1983, Appendix One, Statistical Tables I and IV

Figure 6.3 Annual production of motor vehicles per employed person in the German and Japanese automobile industries, 1970–81

labour-saving machinery as well as in technological and managerial skills). The race for the development of ever better vehicles and ever faster production processes in expectation of a stagnating market required a tremendous financial effort. Between the mid-1970s and the mid-1980s investment outlays trebled (*Financial Times*, 26 March 1986). To spread the burden and also to diffuse some of the competitive pressure, the industry engaged in co-operative ventures of all kinds, from joint R&D to mutual sales arrangements and common ownership.

The need for stepped up innovation did not only apply to technology but also to organisation. Working processes had to be rationalised, unproductively spent time to be minimised. That meant that labour's position in the industry was to be affected in various ways. Labour-saving machinery constituted an immediate threat to employment. But so did foreign competition. To defend sales volumes and prevent involuntary unemployment at the same time workers had to be reallocated as flexibly as possible within the companies. This, in turn, required that labour would not insist in rigid job descriptions, seniority rules and the like. As the case would be, labour was even asked to consent to a degradation of skills and a deterioration of longer-term income chances (cf. Windolf, 1985).

By and large, the German automobile industry was able to go ahead with its modernisation plans without much effective resistance from the side of organised labour. The work councils, labour's representation at the plant and enterprise levels, supported the efforts of management to increase productivity as much as possible and opted for adjustment strategies which would protect employment for the existing personnel. Job flexibility was the price paid for that. Management, in turn, had to cede some terrain in the controversial area of co-determination (such as extended disclosure of information) in order to get labour's co-operation. Increased international competition with its adjustment pressure demonstrated the effectiveness of company-based mechanisms of protecting workers against economic adversity. And if anything, these mechanisms were consolidated as they were tested under strain. The old 'productivity coalition' between labour and capital was *de facto* confirmed at the enterprise level, even though the atmosphere had become more tense.

Of course, in times of high unemployment in the economy at large and a general downward trend of employment in the automobile industry the pragmatic understanding between the companies and their workforces neglected the interests of the outside job-seekers. Since labour also defended its remuneration, working time reductions without full pay were rejected by the metalworkers' union (IG Metall) which represents the German automobile workers. But raising hourly wages through less work with equal pay was, in turn, ruled out as incompatible with the requirements of international competitiveness. Thus unable (and partially unwilling) to do much about the large unemployment problem, organised labour at the enterprise level practised a policy of save-your-own-skin-first (cf. Windolf, 1985; and Streeck & Hoff, 1983, pp. 55ff.).

Altogether, the dominant adjustment pattern of the German automobile industry in view of mounting international (and that is mostly Japanese) competition has been accelerated product innovation and improved productivity. In this respect the old competitive formula 'high performance for high remuneration' was reconfirmed. But in the course of the 1980s another pattern gained importance, too. German companies began to relocate the production of smaller cars and parts to lower-wage countries, most of all Spain. Already in the 1970s Volkswagen had supplied certain markets from its Brazilian and Mexican plants, but mostly in response to export requirements which were imposed by the host governments (cf. Bennett & Sharpe, 1979). In the 1980s, however, the motive of saving labour costs became important. The former efficiency barriers which had made production in low-wage countries largely uncompetitive were no longer that unsurmountable and it became more and more difficult to offset high labour costs through superior productivity. On the other hand, the very concept of the standard technology economy car made the selling price the overriding criterion and set narrow limits to the price-for-quality approach, on which the success of German-made and Japanese-made automobiles alike had come increasingly to be based. In the economy class, outsourcing became the method with which the automobile multinationals tried to outbid each other as well as to defend themselves against the new wave of low-cost competition from Eastern Europe and from South Korea. This meant that at the prevailing wage level West Germany was losing international competitiveness as a place to produce small cars – for German as well as for foreign-based companies (*Financial Times*, 10 November 1988, p. 2). The decision of these companies to phase out small car production in the Federal Republic implied that the automobile industry would offer fewer jobs to German workers. But, of course, the lost jobs must be seen as a matter of the country's evolving *comparative* disadvantage for the production of small cars and not as a consequence of declining competitiveness. The increasing competitive strength of other German-made products just had to crowd out (with the help of the exchange rate) those disadvantaged products from the international market.

THE DEVELOPMENT OF THE WEST GERMAN WELFARE STATE[21]

The West German welfare state is conceptually deeply rooted in the history of Germany. It may suffice to recall the Bismarckian initiative for social security in the early 1880s and the rather coherent expansion of the welfare state system until 1914. In the years of the Weimar Republic certain parts of this system were improved dramatically (regulation of work relations, unemployment benefits, health insurance, and pensions). The Third Reich left the welfare state intact (Rimlinger, 1987). Although the labour unions and other organisations of the working class became illegal and their leaders were persecuted, the workers were considered to some extent as 'partners' of the productive German capital and they maintained rights with respect to working conditions, social security and health insurance.

After 1949 the first welfare state activities were mainly dealing with the integration of war victims and refugees. Another early feature of welfare statism in the Federal Republic was the concept of 'social partnership', which derived from the political and philosophical foundations of the post-war economic policy.

Its guiding principle, expressed in the term '*Soziale Marktwirtschaft*', required both a basically free market economy and the full integration of the working class into the economic community of the nation. Thus, already in 1951 labour's co-determination in the big coal mining and steel companies was established by law. A third important feature of welfare statism in the reconstruction period was the large-scale programme of public housing, which was initiated by the West German Parliament (the Bundestag) in the early 1950s.[22]

Then, within the three years from 1954 until 1957 the major steps forward to the modern West German welfare state were accomplished. The social security system was refounded on various laws, establishing indexed pension systems for workers, employees and farmers. Besides, the first law on child allowances was established in 1954. Later, from 1957 to 1965, reforms of social assistance ('welfare' in the meaning of everyday language) and of the obligatory insurance of occupational injuries were enacted. When the Social Democrats came into power in 1966 they reformed the entire educational system from pre-school education to the university. Access to higher education was broadened and many new schools and universities were founded.

1975 is the year which marks a drastic change in social policy. From then until now the welfare state system was no longer extended. On the contrary, there were several quantitative and qualitative reductions. The quantitative dimension of the welfare state development since 1970 is presented in Table 6.5. It should be noted that the impressive decline in the growth of social expenditure after 1975 occurred in the context of a prolonged economic crisis, which is, other things being equal, rather conducive to rising social expenditure due to the increased need for it (unemployment).

What caused the sudden halt in the development of West German welfare statism? The economic crisis in the wake of the first oil price

Table 6.5 The financial weight of the West German welfare state, 1970–85

	Ratio of taxes and social security contributions over GDP	*Ratio of social expenditure over GDP*	*Deflated growth rate of social expenditure out of federal, state, and local government budgets**
70	36.5%	23.5%	
(70–)75	40.9%	27.8%	85%
(75–)80	42.4%	26.6%	16%
(80–)85	42.2%	25.8%	– 1%
82–85			– 4%

* This excludes the semi-public legal health insurances (*Ersatzkassen*).
Deflated rate = nominal growth rate – cumulative yearly inflation rates
Sources: DIW 1986, OECD 1985a, p. 6 and 1988b, p. 81.

shock produced not only relative stagnation of output and income and accelerating inflation, it also brought a rapidly growing budget deficit. While government revenues stagnated, due to the recession, expenditure obligations went up because of the inflation and because of the entitlements created in the preceding period of reform enthusiasm. Budget consolidation became urgent for two reasons: firstly, increasing public indebtedness rapidly reduced the government's ability to use the budget as a meaningful instrument of economic and social policy; for debt servicing was going to absorb an ever-increasing share of it. Secondly, the budget deficit was itself an important (some say: the most important) factor in the inflation syndrome.

Of course one way to get the budget deficit under control would have been to raise government revenues. However, this was considered as highly undesirable, first because it was unpopular and therefore unwise to pursue for a government which was already under pressure because of mounting economic problems. But in addition, there was a widespread feeling, continuously reinforced by mainstream economists' public warnings, that the limits of state appropriation of economic resources that could be tolerated without considerable damage to the economy had been reached, if not already surpassed.

The government of Chancellor Schmidt not only stopped the expansionary reform process which had been the trademark (besides *Ostpolitik*) of the Social Democratic/Liberal government under Willy Brandt, it also introduced active measures designed to reduce the built-in dynamics of the previous social legislation. The process started with a Budget Consolidation Law in 1975. The obligatory health insurance was subjected to a 'Cost-rises Reducing Law' in 1977. In the same year, the adjustment of pensions to the increase in gross wage income was deferred. For the period of 1979–81 an upper limit for this adjustment was decreed, de-linking *de facto* the evolution of wages and pensions.

Budget consolidation was somewhat stepped up by the Christian Democrat/Liberal government under Chancellor Kohl, which took over from the Schmidt government in 1982. Some minor programmes where drastically reduced, as, for instance, non-repayable income support for high school and university students. Pensioners were required to contribute – in escalating steps – to their health insurance and the basis for calculating pensions was changed so as to render smaller imbursement sums for the social security system (DIW, 1986, p. 271). Unemployment benefits were reduced from 68 per cent to 63 per cent of the beneficiary's most recent wage income. In 1988 the public health insurance system was reformed in order to bring soaring health-care costs under control – with the consequence that the insured had to pay a considerably larger share of some treatments themselves. The subsidies for the provision of low-cost housing, which had played a very important role during the reconstruction years, were practically discontinued.

All these retrenchments of the welfare state fit under the heading 'financial consolidation of the system'. They were a tribute to the budget constraint at given tax and contribution rates, which made some cuts in entitlements mandatory if overall expenses were to be kept from growing excessively. All together, these cuts did not even come close to what could be called a dismantling of the welfare state – with the two minor exceptions perhaps of student income support and subsidised housing. But even with regard to the latter, the more significant aspect is that new needs emerged to which the welfare state did not respond adequately. On the other hand, the Kohl government also introduced some extensions of the welfare state system. They were to benefit – in the form of income support and pension rights – most of all women who forego, or have foregone in the past, income through work because of motherhood.

Nevertheless, the largely-kept-intact welfare state has not prevented a profound deterioration in material well-being and life perspectives for a significant segment of the West German population since the late 1970s. The reason is that it did not respond to the new

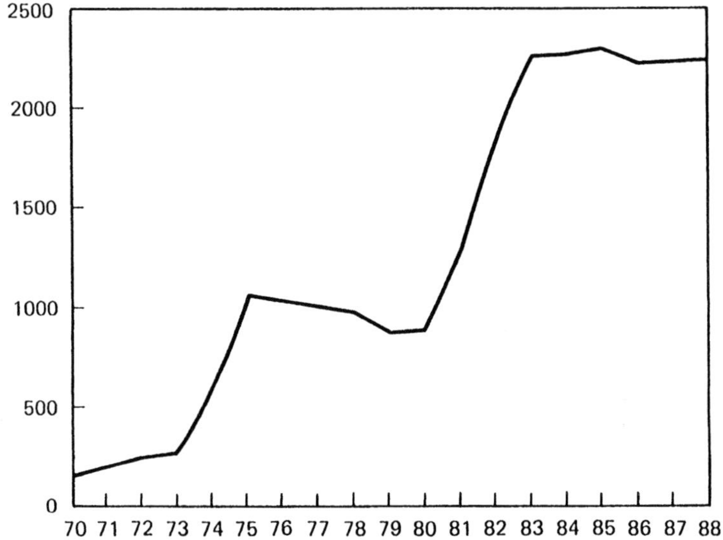

Source: Bundesanstalt für Arbeit, *Amtliche Nachrichten*, various issues

Figure 6.4 Persons registered as unemployed in West Germany, 1970–89 (thousands)

needs which emerged as the long post-war economic boom period came to an abrupt end. From 1980 to 1983 official unemployment shot up from 3.7 to 9.3 per cent. Thereafter, a change in the method of calculation rendered lower quotas. But the absolute number of officially unemployed persons did not really retrocede any more until the end of the decade (see Figure 6.4).

In view of the dramatic increase in unemployment, policy proved helpless. In the late 1960s the German government had formally (as a law!) introduced an anti-cyclical full employment policy in line with Keynesian recipes. But the cyclical down-turn of the mid-1970s combined rising unemployment with rising inflation – a shock to economic policy-makers. Although the goal of full employment was not formally abandoned, priority was given to the fight against inflation. After a short respite, caused by the mild economic upturn of the late 1970s, the dilemma became even more painfully manifest in the deep recession of the early 1980s. And again the Schmidt government shied away from expansionary policies that might have further exacerbated the problems of inflation and the budget deficit. The same applies to the Kohl government, which refused, even with inflation rates down to almost zero, to do anything which entailed – in the government's and many mainstream economists' view – the danger of a return to stagflation. It chose relative stagnation with its high unemployment rates as the minor evil.

The existing programmes of income maintenance via redundancy payments were unable to cope with the new dimensions of the unemployment problem. And there was no adjustment of the social safety net which would have restored the *status quo* with regard to income security and income distribution. As a consequence, an increasing minority of the population got effectively barred from participating in their country's affluence. They had to accept a standard of living which was in several respects well below the one of the average worker. In the Federal Republic of the 1980s, poverty was no longer an occasional phenomenon, due to exceptional individual circumstances, as it had come to be during the 1960s. For an additional part of the workforce material well-being has become hostage to the vicissitudes of an unregulated second-tier labour market. For them, poverty has become a realistic threat and the price to be paid for escaping it is often a far-reaching disregard of private concerns like health or leisure (Möller, 1988; Eichner & Richter 1989, p. 84).

The Competitiveness Issue and the Development of Welfare Statism

We have seen that the economic crisis which broke out in the wake of the first oil price shock eventually brought to a complete halt the expansion of the West German welfare state. Thereby the struggle against the stagflation phenomenon coincided with a renewed emphasis on export performance. The pursuit of these twin objectives took on a definite anti-welfare state bias with the advent to power of the Christian Democrats in 1982. But in spite of the ideological noise which was produced the conservative government did not undertake any serious attempts at a substantive dismantling of the existing welfare state institutions. After some initial spending cuts in peripheral programmes, it even introduced some new benefits. The major adjustments in the social security and the public health insurance systems, which implied a certain trimming of benefits, responded to demographic pressure and system-immanent cost escalation. They were meant to contain the welfare state burden on the economy, but not to diminish it or to re-delegate health care and old-age income maintenance to the market.

The relative ineffectiveness of the neo-liberal ideological offensive, as far as the propagated revision of the welfare statist 'exaggerations' is concerned, indicates how firmly the welfare state is anchored in the political system of the Federal Republic. This should be seen as a matter of political power and political attitudes at the same time. The existing welfare state is associated with a network of vested interests that covers the vast majority of the population. To introduce major changes against these interests within a representative democracy amounts to an uphill fight which every political realist will shun – unless extraordinary circumstances change the terms of reference. The particular way of political decision-making of the Federal Republic with its strong influence of organised interest groups made drastic interference with established 'property rights' especially difficult.[23] On the other hand, one can say that the usual pattern of interest group-oriented policy-making prevailed because the public did not accept the extraordinary nature of the challenge as it was portrayed by the neo-liberal ideologists. This has to do with the continuing export strength of German industry, a circumstance which stripped the competitiveness issue of much of its urgency in the public perception. Neither the concern for more economic dynamism in accordance with the supply-siders' diagnosis nor the concern for the country's international competitiveness were strong enough to break the political and ideological resistance power of the welfare state.

However, the effectiveness of West German welfare statism was undermined considerably by the tremendous increase in unemployment, so that the question arises as to why this has been tolerated. The emergence of lasting mass unemployment has a ready explanation in the slow-down of economic growth from a yearly average rate of almost 5 per cent during the 1960s to about 2.3 per cent between 1976 and 1987. The labour-saving increase in average productivity outstripped the increase in output, but the supply of labour did not decrease in the same measure as the demand for it. The way the system worked, the result was that many people were left without a job and, as a consequence, excluded from the enjoyment of mainstream standards of living and social security. Let us assume that a prolonged slow-down of economic growth was unavoidable after 1973 (even if one thinks that more could have been done than the Kohl government did to stimulate economic activity). Then the welfare state principle of full economic citizenship would have demanded that the disintegrating social consequence be prevented, be it by ensuring full employment despite slow growth or be it by maintaining standards of living despite unemployment. We have to ask, therefore, why this has not been done and whether the answer has anything to do with the issue of international competitiveness.

To begin with, one could make the point that persistent slow growth during the 1980s was itself a consequence of the policy of 'macroeconomic mercantilism' as we described it above in section III. Such an argument implies that faster economic growth would have come forth if less emphasis had been laid on monetary stability and the avoidance of current account deficits. Much as can be said in favour of a more expansionary fiscal and/or monetary policy, we do not want to enter this debate here. Nor do we want to tie the consideration of fully effective welfare statism to the feasibility of high average economic growth rates. In any case, even the competitiveness-oriented macroeconomic policy which was the dominant one in the Federal Republic since the end of the 1970s did not include slow growth as the pre-planned price to be paid, but was rather confronted with it as a non-calculated complication.

Why then was slow growth allowed to lead to lasting mass unemployment? And why were quite a few of the unemployed dismissed into poverty in one of the richest countries of the world? Institutional inertia is certainly part of the answer. West German society was confronted with an unexpected problem for which its welfare state institutions were not designed, and the same pattern of vested interests that shielded the existing welfare state institutions against the ideological attack from the neo-liberal side, also resisted other sorts of quick adjustments. Without a generalised social-movement-type mood in favour of institutional innovation, *any* attempts to remodel the system and, thus, redistribute costs and benefits were politically unrealistic from the outset. Thinking up new solutions was against the polity's conservative 'instinct'.

In addition, there was cognitive inertia. The initial response to mass unemployment was to consider it a temporary problem and to hope for it to disappear soon with the recuperation of the former economic growth dynamic. In the logic of public perception, a hasty adjustment of labour market and/or welfare state institutions to the fact of slow growth would have implied the abandonment of the goal of regaining satisfactory growth rates. Until about the mid-1980s neither the labour unions nor the conservative camp favoured such a shift of priorities. Of course, both sides dissented sharply on the question of how to get back to higher growth rates. Nevertheless, there is a remarkable symmetry in their response to emerging ideas on the reduction of working time and job-sharing. Organised labour tended to regard them as a distraction from the really important task, that is to stimulate economic activity in good Keynesian manner by injecting additional demand into the economy. The conservatives, in turn, were set on revitalising the economy with anti-sclerotic supply-side medicine and considered job-sharing as a capitulation before the forces of economic stagnation and as a frivolous waste of economic potential.

Besides, their general recipe against stagnation implied the promise of a quick return to full employment even before healthy economic growth would be restored. For them, the key was the removal of labour market rigidities, so as to make the terms of employment responsive to supply and demand. As the conservatives defined the issue, it was not one of giving everyone a highly paid and highly protected job, but to reduce pay and protection as a means to get jobs (see for example Soltwedel & Trapp, 1988). In other words, declining welfare for a minority was clearly seen as a consequence of too much welfare for the majority. But, of course, the solution favoured by the conservatives would have not just amounted to the removal of the jobholders' 'privileges' (for which the conservatives lacked anyway the political power and probably the political will). It rather would have led to a different sort of societal dualism, with a proliferation of badly paid jobs without security at the fringes of the labour market (dualism US style!).

In sum, the conservative side was closed to a restoration of effective welfare statism altogether. Even beyond the initial neglect of the issue, derived from the futile hope of a quick return to high growth rates, they envisaged – halfheartedly though – a more definite dismantling rather than a positive adjustment. The very idea of welfare state extension ran counter to the tenets of 'macroeconomic mercantilism' and of supply-side economics. It was, therefore, up to labour and the political left to redefine the issue as one of extending to the unemployed minority the income guarantees which were enjoyed by the employed majority. And it was the task of the left to develop solutions which would take into account the constraints imposed by the requirements of a well-functioning open economy.

What were the available options? Apart from solving a large part of the unemployment problem with the help of accelerated growth, an idea which still figured prominently in the economic policy programme of the Social Democratic party towards the end of the 1980s, there are two basic possibilities to extend welfare statist income guarantees without affecting accumulation and competitiveness. Both take care that the costs of additional benefits will not result in a squeeze on the profits of enterprises.

One option would rely on the established pattern of financing welfare state expenditure. It would increase the tax and contribution rates in order to provide funds for the additional spending needs. But it would use devaluation to neutralise the additional costs this would imply for enterprises. These costs would then be passed on to the consumers of imported goods (finished goods and inputs into finished goods) and would mean a reduction of their real disposable incomes. There are several problems with such a strategy. Firstly, it does not fit at all into the long-practised German policy pattern of 'macroeconomic mercantilism'. Secondly, the exchange rate should be seen as a mechanism which tends to correct *ex post* lasting imbalances that result from changes in competitiveness. But it is of questionable use nowadays as an instrument for securing *a priori* external competitiveness. Thirdly, even if purposeful exchange rate manipulation were feasible it would require a general acquiescence of wage earners in face of the devaluation-induced price increases. Otherwise the whole exercise would become inflationary. There was no serious suggestion in the West German debate to restore full welfare state effectiveness this way.

The other possibility to reconcile welfare state extension with the requirements of economic performance consists in the direct allocation of costs to households in general and to labour in particular rather than to enterprises. This can be done in various ways:[24]

(1) Government finances fully remunerated public employment, preferentially for useful social services with relatively small capital outlay per job. This way demand flows would be rechannelled so as to incorporate more persons (on a fully paid basis) into the market economy. It implies that average labour productivity would be reduced. Depending on political preferences and on macroeconomic considerations, the additional finance needed (part comes from saved redundancy payments) can come from cuts in other public expenditures, from additional public borrowing and from additional taxes levied on household incomes or consumption. From a purely financial point of view not very different from stepped up transfer payments, this option met with little sympathy on the conservative side because it runs counter to the goal of reducing the economic weight of the public sector.

(2) Wage formation is left to the market which re-incorporates excess labour by depressing its price (the wage) the way it has done it in the USA. But to keep working class incomes from falling below present standards they are supplemented by a sufficiently high transfer income, which is financed along the lines of option (1). However, this option is so different from the institutional reality in the Federal Republic that it has maintained a highly utopian character in the public debate. It has not been seriously considered in the political arena.
(3) The cost of hiring an additional worker is lowered for employers so that they have more incentive to do so. But the incomes of the additionally hired workers are topped with a solidarity contribution by the already employed, whose real incomes shrink by the amount of this contribution. Such redistribution could be organised by dividing workers' remuneration into a fixed basic wage and a profit dependent bonus. Then only the basic wage would constitute the price to be paid by the employer for having an additional person on the payroll. The bonus part would be paid by that person's colleagues whose share of the total bonus sum becomes smaller (Weitzmann, 1980). Like option (2), this option would amount to revolutionising West German labour market institutions. So far, there is no political force which could be expected to support it.
(4) The amount of remunerated work and the sum of wages plus fringe benefits paid for it are distributed more evenly among the members of the labour force. This means a shorter (daily, weekly, yearly, lifelong) working time and lower wages for those who are currently employed – a sacrifice which funds the employment of those who would otherwise remain jobless.

The German debate has concentrated on the third option. After several years of scepticism the unions have adopted it as their preferred strategy to regain full high-wage employment. But the pertinent discussion has been fundamentally flawed. The unions' demand for a reduction in working time was tied to the condition that wages would not be allowed to fall. In other words, it was presented as a way to absorb the *ongoing* rise in average productivity: instead of getting higher wages, labour would (partially) benefit in the form of more leisure time. This would make sure that as many workers are needed as before, since output somehow would not rise sufficiently.

However, the need to employ *additional* manpower would only arise if output grew beyond that what the old employed labour force can produce with the new productivity. Yet the difficulty is that the wage sum is itself an important determining factor of overall demand and hence of output growth. If productivity gains are passed on into more leisure rather than into more pay, unit labour costs remain unchanged, but the wage sum will grow insufficiently for consumers' demand to absorb the new output potential. As a consequence, less working hours altogether (not just per person) will be needed and the reduction of individual working time will, therefore, not leave a gap which would have to be filled by the employment of additional manpower. In other words, it is an illusion to see the reduction of working time as an adjustment to a *given* rate of output growth, because it reduces itself this growth rate.

The demand which lets output grow sufficiently to create the need for additional workers would have to come from elsewhere, that is, from abroad, from investors and/or from additional consumers (the state, for instance). A reduction of individual working time in response to productivity gains just transposes the whole problem to a lower level of aggregate sums without really tackling the decisive gap between output potential and actual output. Such a move may be a meaningful response to a general preference for more leisure and an important pre-condition for a more thorough emancipation of women, but it does not serve as a means to restore full employment.

Social Democrat vice-chairman Lafontaine heated up the debate in 1988 by suggesting that the employed members of the workforce would – while working less time – have to sacrifice part of their wage, so as to enable enterprises to employ additional people without incurring additional costs. Reduced working time not as a means to absorb 'excessive' increases in productivity, but as a direct redistribution of available work opportunities among the members of the workforce! This advance by a prominent political figure of the left shifted almost abruptly the discussion to different grounds. The unions had presented working-time reduction as a demand of labour directed to the address of the employers – as another issue in the ongoing struggle over distribution between labour and capital. In turn, Lafontaine made it explicit that it was an issue of redistribution within the working class: from jobholders to the unemployed. Accordingly, what was required was the solidarity of the wage earners rather than the responsiveness of the employers. The unions did not deny the solidarity aspect of the issue, but they had kept it muted. Confronted with Lafontaine's – their presumed ally's –

intervention, they felt induced to stress the class conflict aspect and to underline the limits of what (employed) labour would tolerate.

The unwillingness of the unions to follow the shift in focus and to approach the issue of shorter working time clearly as one of internal working class solidarity, up to the point where absolute sacrifices are called for, is symptomatic for the resistance of the existing structures to real welfare state adjustment. But it is not sure whether it really blocked an otherwise promising way back to high wage full employment and, thus, to the full restoration of economic citizenship rights. What has been said above on the negative demand effect of an incomplete adjustment of the wage sum to the increase in average productivity applies also to a reduction of the wage sum: shorter working time cum lower wages risk very much to lead to a fall in output, thus spoiling the hoped-for employment effect.

With regard to this problem, a tax financed wage subsidy has been proposed. This would enable enterprises to pay old wages despite a shorter new working time, thus preventing simultaneously the demand level to fall and labour unit costs to rise (Scharpf & Schettkat, 1984; Scharpf, 1988). The employed members of the workforce would be relieved from wage sacrifices, but in their role as taxpayers they would be asked for financial contributions. So, the proposal might point to a solution of the economic problem, but it shifts the political problem back to the sphere of fiscal policy, where it meets with the objections of the dominant supply-side philosophy. On more technical grounds, wage subsidies are bedevilled with the problem of how to exclude in practice large-scale substitution of subsidised for fully paid labour. Such technical problems are easily fatal for innovative and at the same time highly conflictive policy proposals. They are simply not pushed sufficiently.

It seems that the one approach to re-establish, in the context of slow economic growth, full economic citizenship rights which was seriously pursued in the West German debate turned out to be a largely sterile one. Was it just bad luck in a trial-and-error process? Or was there something in the political system which *a priori* excluded more promising approaches from serious consideration? It is striking how much care was taken not to step into certain taboo zones. One of these taboo zones is circumscribed by the 'social property rights' of those which were not dispossessed by the events in the market, that is, the majority of the population. Another taboo zone has been marked by the supply-side philosophy, which in the Federal Republic was strongly orientated towards international competitiveness. That the most straightforward approach to the restoration of effective welfare statism, tax financed public employment, was not a politically acceptable option, should be seen in connection with this double taboo.

The concluding thesis seems supportable that in the Federal Republic the concern for the country's international competitiveness has (a) contributed to the erosion of effective welfare statism (demand restraining policy of 'macroeconomic mercantilism') and (b) obstructed the return to it. But with equal truth we could say that solidarity within the West German society was too weak to push the search for effectived solutions with sufficient impetus into politically more difficult terrain. Objectively, the intensive debate on working time reduction has so far been an alibi for the avoidance of unpleasant decisions.

7 Sweden

Göran Therborn

In 1986–1987, the Social Democratically governed Swedish welfare state appeared as a strange, fascinating paradox to an international opinion of business journalism and liberal economics. This new picture took off in the 4 August 1986 issue of the American *Business Week*, featuring an article on 'How Sweden became Europe's industrial powerhouse', subtitled, 'Ten years ago it was "the sickest of sick men", now it's the envy of the continent'.

The liberal American think tank, the Brookings Institution, was invited by a Swedish business organisation to make a report on the Swedish economy. The head of the former, Barry Bosworth, described his first impression: 'When first presented with a description of an economic system with average tax rates near 60 per cent, a set of social welfare programmes far in excess of those of the United States, and an extremely narrow distribution of relative wage rates, one's first impression is that such an economy cannot work, or that it would work very inefficiently – sacrificing a high level of incomes to assure equality. The Swedish economy is a supply-side economist's version of a nightmare' (*Inside Sweden*, no. 1, 1987).

The report that came out (Bosworth & Rivlin, 1987) was so positive, that the Swedish hosts added a long critical comment to the Swedish version of it (Rivlin, 1987). Then, on 7 March 1987, *The Economist* added, 'Sweden is an economic paradox. It has the biggest public sector of any industrial economy, the highest taxes, the most generous welfare state, the narrowest wage differentials, and powerful trade unions. According to prevailing economic wisdom, it ought to be suffering from an acute bout of "eurosclerosis", with rigid labour markets and arthritic industry. Instead, Sweden has many large and vigorous companies, and one of the lowest unemployment rates in Europe.'

The Swedish case, then, brings us to the frontline of the controversies of the economic performance in general of extended welfare states, and of their competitiveness in particular.

THE SWEDISH SET-UP

Capitalist Vigour . . .

As any reader of the international business press knows, there can be no doubt of the vigour of Swedish capitalist enterprise. The expansion, acquisitions, and other moves of Electrolux, Asea, Ericsson, Volvo, Saab, SKF, and other Swedish corporations supply a not insignificant part of the news of the *Financial Times* and similar publications. Sweden has the world's biggest number per inhabitant of domestic private corporations among the *Fortune* list of the world's largest non-US industrial corporations, 17 in 1986 with a population of 8.4 million. The closest competitors, Switzerland, UK and Japan, all have a ratio of a good deal less than two big domestic corporations per million inhabitants, West Germany less than one (calculated from *Fortune*, 3 August 1987). The capitalisation of the Swedish economy has no match on the European continent, with the possible exception of Switzerland, for which data have not been found.

Table 7.1 The sum of stock exchange values as % of GDP in selected OECD countries, 1984

Japan	47
UK	44
US	41
Canada	36
Sweden	29
Netherlands	22
Belgium	14
West Germany	12
France	7
Italy	6

Source: Söderström, 1986, p. 79.

Sweden has for a long time been a good place for capital investment. This has been heavily underlined in the 1980s. In no other country would a million dollars invested in 1937 in an average stock market portfolio have yielded as much by 1984 as in Sweden. In current common dollar currency stock market values increased annually by 5.97 per cent in Sweden for 1937–1984, in USA by 5.46 per cent, in Canada by 4.75 per cent, in Switzerland by 4.41, and in the UK by 3.01 per cent. Starting in 1950, a stock market investor would have made more dollars in Germany, with an annual growth of 9.26 per cent, than in Sweden, 7.87, but less in the USA, 6.75 per cent annually. An investment in 1959 would by 1984 have become most profitable if made in Japan (for which earlier figures are missing), annual yield 12.26, but more in Sweden (7.22) than in USA (4.38) and in West Germany (4.11). An inspection of the tables reveals that this 'golden egg' basket of the Stockholm stock exchange is not due to the soaring values of the 1980s. The Swedish lead over other countries holds for most of the 47-year period investigated (TCO, 1985).

The crash of October 1987 hit the Stockholm stock exchange more than those of London, New York, and Tokyo, all somewhat above the end 1986 index of 100. Stockholm ended 1987 at point 90, better than Frankfurt (65), Hong Kong (81), and Paris (83) (*Svenska Dagbladet*, 4 January 1988). Swedish stockjobbers' spring in 1988 was flourishing.

Swedish capital has traditionally been industrially oriented, spearheaded by investment goods manufacturing corporations linked to and grouped around likewise industrially oriented banks. But the turn from highly to spectacularly profitable yields on the stock exchange has not been matched by any corresponding development of returns to real capital. For the period 1960–1985 gross operating surplus as a percentage of gross value added in manufacturing was 26.3 per cent in Sweden, higher than in the UK (25.0) and the US (25.7), and in Belgium. It was lower than in most OECD countries, however, than in the FRG, for example, 32.1 per cent, and a number of other countries around that figure, not to speak of Japan, with an operating surplus almost half of the value added (49.4 per cent). The lacklustre Swedish surplus dates from the 1960s and was further weighed down by the most severe profit squeeze of the OECD world in 1977–1978. In the 1980s Swedish manufacturing has again become respectably profitable (OECD, 1987d, 74).

. . . on the World Market

As a developed, small economy, Sweden is open to and dependent upon the world market. This dependence is an old, long-stable phenomenon. Apart from the period of the two World Wars and the Depression, goods exports constituted just below 20 per cent of the national product from the beginning of the modern economy, around 1880, till the end of the 1960s (Bunte & Jörberg, 1977, p. 102). Then it started to grow considerably. By 1985, the export of goods and services made up of 35.2 per cent of GDP (OECD 1987d, p. 67). That was about equal to the dependence of West Germany (32.5) and higher than that of the other big countries. In spite of some very early successes in engineering, Swedish exports had until about 1960 a predominantly traditional character, with more than half consisting of either primary commodities or, increasingly, of products out of national primary commodities: timber products, paper and pulp, iron ore, iron and steel (Bunte & Jörberg, 1977, p. 104). Since then, more competition exposed manufacturing has dominated Sweden's sales abroad. By 1985, 46 per cent of Swedish manufacturing production was sold for export, an increase from 29 per cent in 1970 (Flam 1987, p. 190)

Sweden is of old a free trade country, and scores among the very highest in international business opinion with regard to its openness to foreign imports (European Management Forum 1984, p. 56). Import-weighted manufacturing tariffs are generally lower than those of EC, a rate of 5.4 per cent in 1975 for total manufacturing as against an EC rate of 7.5 per cent. Footwear and textiles, but not wearing apparel, were then given somewhat more protection in Sweden (Lewis, 1986, p. 26).

On the other hand, Sweden's well-known openness has its special characteristics. First of all, in comparison with the other highly developed small European countries, Sweden is actually the country *least* dependent on the world market, after Finland.

Table 7.2 Exports of goods and services as % of GDP in small developed European economies, 1980–5

Austria	38.2
Belgium	72.3
Denmark	36.0
Finland	31.5
Netherlands	58.8
Norway	40.8
Sweden	33.1
Switzerland	37.0
For comparison:	
Japan	14.5
Germany	29.6
UK	27.8

Source: OECD, 1987d, p. 67.

In contrast to Norway (even before the oil), Sweden is not a seaboard economy of international shipping as well as ordinary exports; in contrast to the Netherlands it is not a transit economy, nor, in contrast to the Low Countries in general and to Belgium in particular, an important base of re-exports by foreign multinationals. Sweden receives very little foreign direct investment. The proportion of the latter in gross capital formation around 1980 was 0.65 per cent, after Japan and Finland the lowest of all developed countries (European Management Forum, 1984, p. 157). There has been a significant increase, though, of foreign investment and ownership in Sweden. From 2.5 per cent in 1962, foreign-owned companies comprised 9 per cent of the employment in Swedish manufacturing industry at the turn of 1986–1987 (Riksdagstrycket, 1986–1987, Proposition 74, p. 950. However, from a Swedish vantage point, multinational enterprise is above all Swedish corporations operating abroad. In 1985, employment in producing daughter companies abroad corresponded to 30 per cent of manufacturing employment in Sweden. (Riksdagstrycket, 1986–1987, Proposition 74, p. 88). This is a relative advantage to governments and workers of Sweden, since multinationals so far have tended to keep their home bases and to be much more mobile in foreign countries. Sweden is also outside both the EC and the European Monetary System, and the country plays no particular part in the international financial community, as Switzerland or the UK does.

Swedish foreign trade does not link the country very closely to one particular greater power. Around a quarter of Swedish exports go to an area, in which Sweden itself is, in fact, the major power – to the Nordic countries. About one-tenth each goes to Germany and Britain; Belgium and the Netherlands together buy slightly less than a tenth of Sweden's exports. Since the Industrial Revolution, the other Nordic countries have constituted an important training ground for Swedish enterprise with a view to world market, in terms of direct investment as well as with regard to exports (see further Therborn, 1989). Currently, incoming foreign investment is mainly Nordic, and Finnish above all (Riksdagstrycket, 1986–1987, Proposition 74, p. 95).

All this gives Swedish domestic, political and economic actors a leeway, a margin of manoeuvre, that is often veiled behind the frequent cliché of 'a small open economy', although that expression certainly contains an important kernel of truth.

In terms of income per head, the Swedes are among the most successful – or if you like, lucky – in the world. Sweden has had to leave its former position as the richest country of Europe to Norway, but for the rest the country is still surpassed only by the two classical top scorers in the international income league, USA and Canada (Blades & Roberts 1987, p. 188 reporting an OECD comparison of 1985 in terms of purchasing power parities).

Sweden operates in the world market as a high-wage economy, and has done so for a long time. In 1930, at the time of what enthusiastic Swedish industrialists called 'Sweden's second big power era', referring to the industrial boom of the second half of the 1920s and comparing it to the times of the country's military glory in the 17th century, Sweden had the highest wages in the engineering industry in Europe, after Denmark and Norway, which did not have very much of an engineering industry. True, this situation changed drastically with the 1931 devaluation of the crown (Verkstadsföreningen, 1933). Table 7.3 gives an overview of the more recent conditions.

The figures for 1966 and 1970, before the breakdown of the Bretton-Woods system of fixed exchange rates, are particularly noteworthy. By then, Sweden had by far the highest labour costs (wages and social security contributions) in Europe. The relatively low wages in

Table 7.3 Indices of total labour costs for manufacturing workers in selected OECD countries, at current exchange rates, 1966–85 (Sweden=100)

	1966	*1970*	*1979*	*1985*
Austria	52	51	70	76
Belgium	69	69	102	94
Canada	115[1]	115	69	111
Denmark	82	79	94	88
Finland	65	53	60	85
France	62	56	68	76
Germany	75	81	98	100
Italy	58	62	71	78
Japan	28	37	55	75
Netherlands	65	71	98	91
Norway	79	83	90	108
Switzerland	70	66	(109)[2]	(123)[3]
UK	64	56	50	66
US	157	141	77	132

Notes: [1] 1967. [2] Wages only. [3] Wages only, 1982.

Source: SAF, 1978, p. 41 and appendix, SAF, 1984, p. 38 and appendix, and SAF, 1986, appendix, provisional figures for 1985.

Switzerland at that time, before the strong appreciation of the franc, are remarkable. On the whole, except for the period after the September 1982 devaluation, Swedish industry has constantly operated with higher labour costs than those of its major export competitors (US domestic producers normally excepted).

... With Extensive Egalitarian Welfare

The welfare state pushed into top gear in Sweden only in the 1960s, but has now become second only to the Netherlands in its extensiveness. In 1960 Swedish social expenditure was virtually equal to that of Britain (Flora, 1987).

Since 1976 public income transfers to Swedish households have been above the sum of the operational surplus of unincorporated enterprise and property income received by households. Save for one recession year in Norway (and an OECD miscalculation of medical services into transfer payments) this overtaking of property and entrepreneurial income by public welfare has taken place only in one other country, in the Netherlands (since 1975) (OECD 1987e, National Tables 1 and 8). Public transfers to households amounted in 1986 to 19 per cent of GDP in Sweden (Finansdepartementet 1987, p. 152; 1988, p. 19). Taxes constituted about 52 per cent of GDP (Finansdepartementet, 1987, pp. 45–7; 1988, p. 19), the highest among the OECD countries, (OECD 1986c, p. 82).

Table 7.4 Social expenditure[1] in Western Europe in % of GDP, 1980

Austria	32.6
Belgium	36.0
Denmark	32.8
Finland	24.8
Germany	31.0
Ireland	29.0
Italy	27.0
Netherlands	40.2
Norway	26.1
Sweden	37.9
Switzerland	19.7
UK	24.5

Note: Includes public education, labour market policy expenditure, and housing benefits as well as income maintenance, and health and social care.
Source: Flora, 1987, vol. 4.

But the Swedish welfare state is a service state, rather than a transfer paymaster. Whereas for the EC as a whole the ratio of public consumption to social security transfers in 1980–1985 was 1:1, the Swedish was 1.6:1, in that respect similar to the British (OECD, 1987d, pp. 62–3). As such the Swedish (local as well as national) state is a major employer, of 38 per cent of the labour force in 1985, providing about 33 per cent of the labour volume according to the labour market surveys. Those are the highest figures of the capitalist world (see further Therborn, 1987, p. 17). Social service employment is particularly high.

Table 7.5 Public social services employment in selected OECD countries as % of the population between 15 and 64 years, 1985[1]

Belgium	6.3
Canada	4.4
Denmark	18.4
France	6.5
Germany	3.8
Norway	14.7
Sweden	19.6
UK	8.2
USA	5.3

Note: Employment in education, health care, and welfare services.
Source: Cusack *et al.*, 1987, p. 4.

The Scandinavian type of welfare state is distinctive, centred as it is on the public provision of education and care, care for the elderly, for the sick and the handicapped, for the children of working parents. The tiny public social sector of West Germany, a country with a proportion of old people similar to Sweden, is striking. The Scandinavian pattern of social service is mainly a product of the late 1960s and the 1970s.

For a long time, Sweden has been a relatively egalitarian country (see further Therborn *et al.*, 1978), and in the 1970s equality received a further push (Finansdepartementet, 1987, p. 193). The functioning of the Swedish welfare state in the (re)distribution of income is well shown by the specially gathered income survey data of the so-called Luxemburg Income Study. The Swedish, the West German, and some other data are from 1981, the Anglo-Saxon and the Norwegian ones from 1979.

State interventions have a major impact on the distribution of income. Market income is surprisingly similarly distributed between

Table 7.6 Distribution and redistribution of income in selected countries, around 1980 (family equivalent income as distributed among persons, Gini coefficients)[1]

	Market income[2]	*Gross income*[3]	*Disposable income*[4]
Canada	0.398	0.327	0.299
Germany	0.505	0.363	0.355
Israel	0.459	0.382	0.333
Norway	0.400	0.289	0.243
Sweden	n.a. (<0.400)	0.249	0.205
UK	0.414	0.297	0.273
USA	0.440	0.371	0.326

Notes: [1] The coefficient ranges from 0 to 1. The lower the value, the greater equality. [2] Earnings, capital income, occupational pensions. [3] Ditto plus public and private transfers. [4] Gross income minus taxes.
Source: Ringen, 1986, p. 31.

so seemingly different countries as Canada, Norway, UK, and Sweden (Ringen, 1986, p. 49). Transfer payments are everywhere more important redistributors than taxes. The difference is largest in West Germany, where transfers reduce market income inequality by 28 per cent while taxes leave 98 per cent per of the gross income inequality unchanged. From a comparable Swedish study (Gustafsson, 1987, p. 34) we know, that in 1980 40 per cent of the inequality of the factor income distribution in Sweden was done away with by transfers, and 22 per cent of that of gross income through taxation. The total redistributive effect was 53 per cent.

If the net assets of households are taken into account, redistribution is not quite as impressive. A Gini coefficient of 0.418 for factor income in Sweden in 1981 was then found to be reduced by 30 per cent through transfers and taxes, to 0.291 (Gustafsson, 1984, p. 60).

The public services are also redistributive. A study of Swedish married households in 1970 divided into six income groups found that the range of relative disposable income (that is, after taxes and transfers) was reduced from 0.43 to 1.85 to 0.87–1.59 in terms of relative standard with the inclusion of the effects of public services (Franzén *et al.*, 1975). Since the late 1970s equalisation has stopped in Sweden. In terms of disposable income as well as of wealth distribution there has even been a certain reversal in the 1980s (Vogel *et al.*, 1987, pp. 109ff; Finansdepartementet, 1987, pp. 93ff). The latter is certainly connected with the stock market boom noticed above.

Table 7.7 Relative disposable income per consumption unit[1] in Sweden, 1984–5 (all manual workers=100)

Farmers	68
Parents with 3 children or more	86
Recipients of social assistance[2]	87
Unemployed	88
Old-age pensioners	93
Self-employed	94
Foreign citizens	94
Pre-retired and long-term unemployed	97
Unskilled and semi-skilled workers	99
Single mothers	100
Skilled workers	101
Entrepreneurs with employees	113
Lower white-collar employees	114
All white-collar employees	121
Higher managers in private enterprise	149
Professionals	153
Private and public executives	164

Notes: [1] This means the same thing as what the Luxembourg Income Study called family equivalent income, although the calculation of equivalents between households of different size is not exactly the same. That is, the incomes analysed are all re-calculated with a view to taking the age and the number of persons of the same household into account.
[2] Broadly defined as persons living in a household, of which at least one member has received social assistance for some part of the year.
Source: Vogel *et al.*, 1987, p. 136.

A more concrete picture of the Swedish income distribution after transfer and tax corrections of market incomes is given in Table 7.7. By tough international standards, this is clearly an egalitarian distribution. The big exception are the farmers, many of whom are old with small holdings and very low cash income. Many farmers' wives are housewives, and the Swedish current high taxation–equal wages economy is strongly punitive to one-income families. On the other hand, the welfare state takes care of disadvantaged individuals. Most remarkable in an international perspective is probably the ordinary working class living standard of single mothers. This is due mainly to three factors: relatively good employment opportunities for women, priority access to public daycare for children of single parents, and the fact that the state pays for the upkeep of the child(ren) if and when the absent father does not pay.

One important reason why this egalitarianism goes along with vigorous capital accumulation is the taxation system, which levies a heavy toll on labour and consumption but little on capital and property. Whereas Sweden has the highest total tax ratio in the world, above 50 per cent of GDP, taxes on property are the second lowest in the OECD area, after Portugal (OECD 1986c, pp. 83, 93).

ECONOMIC PERFORMANCE AND COMPETITIVENESS

The Long-term Trajectory

Sweden rose to affluence and to relative international economic pre-eminence slowly but solidly during the period from about 1870 to around 1950. According to the calculations of Angus Maddison (1982, p. 67) per capita economic growth in Sweden in 1870–1913 was the highest in the world, although with USA and Canada perhaps not more behind than within the margin of error. Sweden was lucky in the decades of ensuing disaster – outside both World Wars and relatively little hit by the Depression of the 1930s. By 1938, Sweden was the second or third richest country in Europe. Swedish per capita GDP was 19 per cent higher than that of Germany and France and only 3 per cent lower than that of the UK (Bunte & Jörberg, 1977, p. 55). Comparable data for Switzerland have not been available, the country that in 1950 was Europe's richest, by a small margin (1.9 per cent) ahead of Sweden, which in turn was 7.0 per cent above Britain. The USA, Canada, and Australia were still more affluent (Maddison, 1982, p. 21).

The development during the post-war boom is given by Table 7.8. The losers of the war were clearly the winners of the peace. Except for unemployment, the Swedish performance is below the average, and even Sweden's unemployment record is far from outstanding. However, if we compare Sweden with the other five of the six richest countries in 1950 (USA, Canada, Australia, Switzerland, UK), Sweden turns out to have done quite well. Only Switzerland then appears more successful, having together with Sweden the highest growth, the best export performance, with Sweden and Canada the second-lowest inflation, and the lowest unemployment. With regard to inflation, Sweden is the worst performer of all the six richest countries, although the distance to Britain and Australia is negligible.

Let us now look at the evidence for the crisis period of the two oil shocks.

Table 7.8 Sweden's economic performance 1950–73 in international comparisons

	Growth/capita annual (%)	*Export volume growth %/year*	*Inflation index* 1950=100	*Unemployment*[1] *average 1964–73*
Sweden	3.1	7.0	285	1.9
Australia	2.5	5.8	280	1.8
Austria	5.0	10.8	280	1.7
Belgium	3.6	9.4	192	2.3
Canada	3.0	7.0	188	4.7
Denmark	3.3	6.9	294	(1.3)
Finland	4.2	7.2	351	2.2
France	4.1	8.2	310	2.3
Germany	5.0	12.4	187	0.8
Italy	4.8	11.7	243	5.4
Japan	8.4	15.4	321	1.2
Netherlands	3.5	10.3	250	1.2
Norway	3.1	7.3	296	1.7
Switzerland	3.1	8.1	198	(<0.5)
UK	2.5	3.9	284	2.9
USA	2.2	6.3	185	4.4
Unweighted Average	3.8	8.6	259	2.5[2]

Notes: [1] Internationally standardised rates, non-standardised ones within parenthesis. [2] Standardised rates only.

Sources: Unemployment: OECD, 1987d, p. 41; the rest: Maddison, 1982, pp. 67, 86, 318.

Sweden's pattern of relative performance in the crisis is rather similar to its location in the 1950s and 1960s. That is, below the average, except for unemployment, but doing well in relation to the Anglo-Saxon countries and Switzerland, save with regard to inflation. Canada is doing better this time, however. The recent superior growth and export record of most of the other European countries is more significant, since the countries were much more in a comparable situation in 1973 than in 1950. But Sweden has not received a blow comparable to what has happened to the Swiss and the Dutch, and Sweden's maintenance of almost full employment is remarkable (on the latter point see further Therborn, 1986).

Unemployment rates alone are very crude and sometimes misleading measures of labour market developments. International standardisation can at best provide us with comparable methods of defining

Table 7.9 Sweden's economic performance during the 1974–85 crisis in international comparisons

	Growth/capita annual (%)	*Export volume growth/year* %	*Inflation annual* %	*Unemployment*[1] *annual* %
Sweden	1.6	3.3	9.8	2.4
Australia	1.5	4.2	10.4	6.3
Austria	2.4	5.7	5.7	2.5
Belgium	1.6	3.3	7.7	8.8
Canada	2.1	5.1	8.6	8.6
Denmark	1.8	4.0	9.7	(7.6)
Finland	2.4	4.4	10.9	4.8
France	1.6	5.0	10.5	6.4
Germany	2.0	4.8	4.5	4.8
Italy	1.7	5.9	15.5	7.9
Japan	2.9	9.5	6.8	2.2
Netherlands	1.1	3.0	5.9	7.5
Norway	3.7	4.8	9.0	2.2
Switzerland	0.7	3.4	4.1	0.5
UK	1.3	3.2	12.3	7.8
USA	1.4	3.0	7.7	7.4
Unweighted Average	1.9	4.5	8.7	5.3[2]

Notes: [1] Standardised rates, non-standardised within parenthesis.
[2] Standardised rates only.

Source: OECD, 1987d, pp. 41, 44, 55, 83.

and counting the unemployed and the labour force. What the former leaves as it is, is the determination of labour force entry and exit. The unemployment rate can, then, be kept down by two means, by keeping the number of unemployed low, and by keeping the labour force small. The latter can, of course, be brought about in different ways: by expelling foreigners, by encouraging, for example, older males and married females to leave the labour force, by discouraging women and young people in general from entering it. For that reason, a better measure of what happened in labour markets during the crisis is what we may call the *labour market performance measure*, defined as the change of the number of people in employment minus the change of the number of unemployed, and the ensuing rest expressed as a percentage of the number of employed at the beginning of the period. The LMPM is a measure of the net employment change during a certain period. A negative sign means declining net employment.

Table 7.10 Labour market performance in Sweden and OECD countries 1973–84 (employment change net of unemployment growth in % of the number of employed in 1973)

Sweden	8.7
Australia	2.7
Austria	−0.2
Belgium	−16.1
Canada	15.2
Denmark	−10.1
Finland	6.4
France	−7.5
Germany	−13.2
Italy	2.5
Japan	7.9
Netherlands	−8.7
Norway	17.0
Switzerland	−5.6
UK	−13.7
USA	17.3

Source: OECD, 1986d.

We should look simultaneously at the unemployment column of Table 7.9 and at the LMPM in Table 7.10. Norway then appears as an outstanding labour market performer, managing to maintain more or less full employment together with vigorous net job creation. Sweden comes second, with low unemployment and important, though not spectacular growth of net employment, better than Japan. The size of the labour market decline in Germany is striking, in that respect very similar to the British. In Austria and in Switzerland, a low rate of unemployment has been maintained only with a stagnant or a contracting labour force, respectively.

The End of the 1980s

Sweden is likely to end the 1980s in a rather lacklustre way economically. Economic growth in 1986, 1.2 per cent, was less than half the OECD average. While it picked up in 1987, 2.8 per cent, it stayed below the OECD average, then at 3.1. There it is expected to remain for the rest of the decade. In 1988 Swedish growth was well below the West German, British and American rates. In 1989 the distance to the British rate narrowed, but to most other competitors, including Switzerland, it remained considerable. Inflation in

Sweden is and will stay higher than in most of the other Western countries. Exports grew slightly more than OECD exports in 1986, remained basically on par in 1987 and fell off slightly in the last years of the decade. The trade balance has remained positive also in 1988 and 1989. But the balance on current account changed from a small surplus to a small deficit in 1987, and it has grown since then, albeit not dramatically, remaining around one per cent of GDP. (OECD, 1988a; Statens Industriverk, 1988; TCO, 1988; Finansdepartementet, 1989, p. 13.)

Unemployment in Sweden is still and is most likely to remain among the very lowest in the world, 2.2 per cent in 1986, 1.9 per cent in 1987, 1.6 per cent in 1988. In early June 1988 the Swedish Labour Market Board and Statistics Sweden reported that the number of unemployed in May 1988 was lower than the number of vacant jobs, 66 000 and 76 000, respectively. On a year basis the last times the vacancy rate was higher than the unemployment rate were in 1970 and 1965 (Furåker, 1976, p. 61 and Åberg, 1984, p. 226). Sweden is back to the situation of labour scarcity prior to the international crisis, although employment is growing, by 1.4 per cent in 1988, in terms of persons, by 2.6 per cent in terms of hours (Finansdepartementet, 1989).

Competitiveness: a Conceptual Clarification ...

The often but very differently used concept of competitiveness seems to require a certain amount of clarification, before we can bring in meaningful evidence and before we can have a chance to put offered explanations to a relevant test. There appear to be at least three different meanings which either can be or *de facto* have been given to 'competitiveness'. One refers to world market location. Countries are exposed to the world market to vastly different extents. One kind of competitiveness is manifested, when a country enjoys a relatively high amount of prosperity – operationalised in GDP per capita and in levels of wages and salaries, for instance – while being relatively strongly exposed to foreign competition and balancing its trade with the world. This we may call a *structural competitiveness*. It is the most important kind, because competitiveness is here clearly only a capacity or resource whereby a population is able to enjoy a relatively high standard of living. Underlying this structural competitiveness are a number of structural features and capacities of and in the economy (OECD, 1986d, pp. 90ff). In recent years, particular interest has been paid to innovative capacity in science and technology and in scientific–technical infrastructure, R&D expenditure, size of high-technology sectors, qualitivative indicators of innovativeness.

A second sort of competitiveness is more tied to market performance *per se*. *Performing competitiveness* is usually measured in market shares, shares gained expressing high competitiveness, shares lost declining or non-competitiveness. It is often tacitly assumed that performing competitiveness is a pre-condition for maintaining what we have here termed structural competitiveness. That is not necessarily true. If the world market grows, exports may grow with declining market shares. More importantly for the welfare of the population what export development is needed depends on import needs. To the extent that domestic labour and consumers' markets are satisfied in an open economy, backsliding performing competitiveness does not diminish structural competitiveness.

Granting its importance, to measure performing competitiveness is not without problems. One important step is to separate some basic aspects of a 'market share'. The market is composed of other countries importing different commodities, and one analytical procedure is to single out market share effects of the exporter's country orientation and its commodity package. In the long run, a successfully competitive exporter should be expected to be able to re-orient itself to the most expanding import markets and to the most demanded import commodities, but in the short run market destination and product line may be taken as given. But what is left, when you correct market share changes for the country and commodity mix of exports? Logically, there remain two different elements. One is competitive capacity on given international markets. That is obviously a pure case of performing competitiveness. However, there is also the possibility of a chosen switch to the domestic market, which is not *per se* a manifestation of failing competitiveness. (If import penetration is the market share indicator used, then the possibility of a chosen turn away from the domestic market has to be taken into account.)

The most commonly used sense of competitiveness is *cost competitiveness*. Conceptually this is somewhat strange, as cost competitiveness is one means to performing competitiveness, which in turn is one means to maintaining structural competitiveness. Cost competitiveness is usually measured in unit labour costs, or in some other labour cost indicator. But the actual cost structure of competing firms is most often neglected in macroeconomic statistics and modelling (see for example Durand & Giorno, 1987). We will look a little into that aspect below.

In brief, there is no one concept of competitiveness, much less any one adequate measure of it. Available evidence should be related to this complexity, and the latter should be borne in mind when explanations are assessed.

. . . and Some Evidence

The fact, noticed above, that Sweden has been able to achieve and to maintain a top position in terms of GDP per capita and of wages paid in conjunction with an increased openness to international competition is an important indication of a successful structural competitiveness in the world economy. This capacity has further been maintained with a positive trade balance for the 1960–1985 period, including a clearly positive balance in the 1980s (OECD, 1987d, p. 68 and the previous section above). However, we have also seen some tendencies that might be interpreted as signs of an incipient erosion of this location, slower relative growth and a decline of relative wages after a series of devaluations. This is no conclusive evidence, however.

The scientific–technological position of Sweden is relatively strong. After Switzerland and the Federal Republic of Germany, Sweden has the largest proportion per capita of foreign patents in the US (Pavitt & Soete, 1982, p. 109). Sweden is (1983 figures) second to none in R&D expenditure per capita, closely followed by USA and, at a greater distance, France and Germany. Calculated as a proportion of value added in manufacturing industry the USA was still ahead in 1980, although Sweden had the most rapid growth of R&D expenditure in the 1970s (OECD, 1986e). In the 1970s Sweden had a balanced trade in licenses, patents, and such like, with a clear surplus since 1983 (Ohlsson & Vinell, 1987, p. 133). Among the OECD countries only the USA, UK, and probably Switzerland for which exact data are lacking, have a consistently positive trade balance of licences and patents. All the others, except Sweden, are running constant deficits (OECD, 1986e, pp. 52–3, this data set ends in 1983). However, in spite of all effort, the high-tech sector is not very prominent in Swedish employment, nor in Swedish exports. In both respects Sweden occupies a medium-rank position in the Western world. The big countries dominate, also in relative terms (OECD, 1986d and e). Whereas Sweden's total high-technology trade is evenly balanced, the country has a constantly growing deficit in its high-tech trade with the USA, Japan and the FRG (Ohlsson & Vinell, 1987, p. 128). On the other hand, in terms of research scientists and engineers per 1000 manufacturing employees Sweden comes third, with just above eight, after the USA at just above 18 and Japan just above 12, FRG close behind Sweden (Ergas, 1984, p. 57, data from 1979).

With regard to the first type of competitiveness, we are left with a strong structural position with a question mark after it. We have seen already that Swedish export growth has not quite kept pace with the rest of the OECD world. In this section we shall probe somewhat more deeply into the evidence concerning performing competitiveness.

The international market shares of Swedish export industry exhibit a long-term falling trend since the early 1960s. If the Swedish share of the manufacturing and mining imports of 14 major OECD countries, adjusted for the commodity composition and the country mix of Swedish exports, in 1963 is put to 100, by 1985 it had gone down to 73 (calculations in value terms from the indices presented in Statens Industriverk, 1982, p. 53; and Riksdagstrycket, 1986–1987, Proposition 74, p. 295). After the devaluation of 1982 market shares in this sense increased significantly in 1983 and 1984, but thereafter they have recommenced their descent, although exports are still growing in absolute terms (Statens Industriverk, 1987 and 1988). Imports started to grow strongly in 1983 and 1984, in volume as well as in value, beginning a new upward trend after the relative stagnation 1975–1981 (Konjunkturinstitutet, 1986, p. 51).

On an aggregate level at least, the downward trend is mainly the product of very heavy losses in 1969, 1976, 1977 and 1980, of which the three former were never regained. In those years Sweden lost 3.6, 6.2, 4.6 and 4.6 per cent, respectively, of its OECD market shares after controlling for the commodity and country distribution of Swedish exports (calculated from Horwitz, 1981, p. 8; and Horwitz, 1986, p. 9). Remarkably enough, these years of severe market share losses are *not* years of any particular growth of import penetration (OECD, 1985b, p. 173), although the trade balance deteriorated then, while it improved greatly in 1983–1984 (OECD, 1987d, p. 68).

Although there is no full explanation available for the loss of market shares, it seems clear enough that it largely expresses a decline of what we have called performing competitiveness. Since there is no downward trend of trade balance or GDP nor one of per capita growth (nor one of growth *tout court* deviating from OECD as a whole) (OECD, 1987d, pp. 44, 68), this development is not (yet?) very serious. A possible interpretation might be, that this nondisruptive decline of performing competitiveness, at least in part, signifies a maturing affluent economy.

Without calling a diminished performing competitiveness into doubt, we may ask whether there is any indication that the adjusted market shares lost may have been lost in some part also by choice. There is some circumstantial evidence. One has to do with public policy choice and its effects on the behaviour of firms. In 1971–1973 the declining trend of market shares was stopped, in value terms reversed. This coincided with and seems to have been partly determined by a restrictive macroeconomic policy. The trade balance improved considerably, but unemployment rose. In 1975–1976 the government was highly concerned with keeping employment up, in the face of the international crisis. This effort included subsidies of firms' production for their stockpile. In other words, non-exports were stimulated (Statens Industriverk, 1982, p. 49). Secondly, the upward turn of market shares in current prices was related to a significant increase of the relative prices of Swedish exports. In 1975 there was again a big rise of Swedish relative export prices. Export shares in value terms were kept up fairly well in 1975, with a precipitous decline in volume, and profitability also maintained itself almost. But this time the market could not bear it. In 1976 and 1977 markets were lost, and profits plummeted. Market share loss might here be due in part to a miscalculation by Swedish exporters, having chosen to gain by higher prices rather than by larger volume (Statens Industriverk, 1982, p. 51ff; Erixon, 1982, pp. 117–18; Erixon, 1987, p. 184).

Sweden has lost market shares over a quarter of a century at least, however market shares are calculated – be it as part of world imports, of the imports of Sweden's major trade partners in the OECD, in value or in volume terms, corrected for product and country mix or not – albeit the picture for individual years differs according to method. The devaluation of 1982 broke the trend, but in mid-1988 there are no strong reasons against believing that what happened in 1982 was only a temporary change rather than a secular turn, to a levelling off. By the turn of 1988–1989 Swedish export shares are back to their position in 1980 (Finansdepartementet, 1989). If adjusted for the distribution of Swedish exports over individual national markets and over the commodity range, the current tendency looks more like a resumption of the declining trend than like a break. The effects of this trend are difficult to gauge. The trade balance has seldom been negative, and not since 1982 (Finansdepartementet,

1989, p. 13). Even in the crisis years of 1976–1977 and 1980 Sweden's trade deficit, 1.9 per cent of GDP in 1980, 1.7 per cent in 1976–1977, was significantly lower than what most OECD (1987d, p. 68) countries have experienced in difficult times in the 1970s and 1980s. We have taken notice of some indications to the logical conceivability, that a loss of export market shares may be due to a deliberate choice. This has some probable connection with empirical reality. But on the whole, it is clear that Sweden has not for a long time been a star-performing international competitor. That proposition holds for the Swedish economy as a whole, but not for Swedish multinationals. Of them there is quite a number in proportion to the population, as was noticed above, and all of them have tended to do well in competitive arenas. We will look a bit more closely at a few of them below.

The most common indicator of cost competitiveness is unit labour costs. The relationship of the latter to competitiveness indicated by market shares is far from completely clear. Major losses of shares have been associated with rising unit labour costs in common currency, and gains with a decline of relative ULC. So far so good. The problem is that the relationship is asymmetrical in a remarkable way, which has led the two variables to end at almost the same index number for the 1970–1987 period. With 1970 = 100, unit labour costs in Swedish manufacturing industry relative to OECD and expressed in US dollars stood in 1987 at 86 and in Swedish crowns at about 79, while the Swedish share of OECD imports had the index 85 (calculations from diagrams in Riksdagstrycket, 1986–1987, Proposition 74, pp. 289, 295, and from Statens Industriverk, 1988). If there was a symmetrical inverse relationship, one of the indices should be around 120 when the other was 80.

The immediate reason for this unexpected relationship is the following pattern. For 1970–1976 ULC and market shares co-varied in inverse direction, but then when ULC decreased in 1977 and more strongly in 1978 market share losses continued. In 1979–1981, relative ULC was about equal to what they were in 1974, but a good 20 per cent market shares had gone. The more than 20 per cent decline of relative ULC between 1981 and 1983 had an immediate market share impact of about two per cent only. Markets shares have grown a few more per cent since 1983, but so have relative ULC. A full clarification of the relationship between unit labour costs and market shares remains to be done. But that much is clear, cost competitiveness measured by ULC is not a very reliable predictor, not to speak of proxy for performing competitiveness.

Even if not enough, unit labour costs are in themselves complex phenomena, determinable in different ways. A good illustration hereof is the composition of the ULC rise in Sweden between 1974 and 1976.

Table 7.11 Decomposition of the change of unit labour costs in Swedish manufacturing industry relative to ten OECD countries (cumulative % change between 1974 and 1976)

Relative ULC total	*Components of ULC*			
	Currency	*Productivity*	*Direct labour costs*	*Non-wage labour costs*
24.6	5.7	8.7	2.5	7.4

Notes: Effects of rounding off and cumulation makes the sum of the parts 24.3.
Source: Statens Industriverk, 1982, p. 32.

The effects of collective bargaining and wage drift were quite secondary. The productivity decline is mainly the effect of provisions for job security in the crisis, a variant of so-called labour hoarding. A significant increase in employers' social security contributions raised non-wage labour costs. The government and the national bank let the crown appreciate. In brief, there are four different variables to manipulate if something is to be done about relative unit labour costs.

Swedish experience of the 1980s appears to show that manufacturing firms set their prices in close association with movements in total variable costs, but not in labour costs alone. Input costs, for raw materials or semi-finished products, and energy, are much better predictors than labour costs. In the most important export sectors of Swedish manufacturing, labour costs amounted in 1985 to 34 per cent of total costs.

Table 7.12 Relative costs, prices, and margins per produced unit in Sweden related to OECD competitors, in common currency (1980=100)

	1981	*1982*	*1983*	*1984*	*1985*	*1986*
Input costs	100	94	88	93	96	93
Labour costs	101	89	75	79	83	81
Total variable cost	100	93	85	90	93	91
Product price	100	93	87	92	94	92
Margins	100	100	102	102	101	101

Source: Riksdagstrycket, 1986–1987, Proposition 74, p. 291.

In the course of 1986, the cost competitiveness of Swedish industry declined clearly, however. Unit labour costs in common currency increased by three percentage points more than in Sweden's main competitor countries. In 1986–1989 the market shares of Swedish exports are back at what they were before the devaluation of 1982. The tight labour market has its effects in spite of the co-operativeness of the unions. Almost half, 45–50 per cent of wage increases in 1987 and 1988 was wage drift (Finansdepartementet 1989, Bil. 1.1., pp. 18–21 and 41, respectively.)

Sectoral Competition: Auto and Telecommunications

From the point of view of international competition, the Swedish auto and telecommunications industries consist of three corporations, Ericsson, Saab–Scania, and Volvo, all three very much native multinationals, native in ownership, top management, technological edge and corporate culture. Televerket is a major enterprise in telecommunications too, but it is a public quasi-monopoly, subject to some recent but marginal competition, running the Swedish telephone system. A small domestic competitor to both Televerket and Ericsson in some segments of their services/products range exists, Cornvik, but will be left out of the picture here.

Sweden is the only small country of the OECD world to have a domestic car industry, with two prosperous car makers. Volvo is the larger of the two. It is Sweden's largest and socially leading corporation, its sales in 1987 corresponding to 9.2 per cent of Sweden's GDP. By international standards they are small. In 1987 Volvo produced 423 000 cars and Saab 134 000, which together makes up between one and one and a half per cent of the world market (a great deal of information in this section has been gathered from the information departments of the corporations). Volvo is about the same size as BMW and Saab not much smaller than Alfa Romeo.

Both of them started in the industry as domestic family car producers, besides important truck divisions. Saab was originally a military aircraft maker, and still is, although with very limited success outside the Swedish air force market. In the mid-1970s both took the decision, that with mounting international competition, small production capacity, and high labour costs, the product line and orientation had to change, drastically. In the 1980s both have become producers of very competitive upmarket cars. For both of them USA is the largest market, taking about a third of total sales for each. In the 1980s, demand for Volvo and Saab cars have exceeded production capacity, with waiting lists as a result. In 1988, however, both have had a setback on the American market, affected by the declining dollar and the malaise after the stock market crash in October 1987. While Volvo nevertheless still has a very profitable personal car division, the official Saab figures for 1988 showed a significant loss for its personal cars. By late spring 1989 serious doubts have been raised in the Swedish press about the future viability of Saab as an independent producer of personal cars (*Dagens Nyheter*, 31 May 1989; *Dagens Industri*, 1 June 1989).

Competition in the upmarket segments, whereto Saab and Volvo cater, has increased and is likely to increase strongly in the near future, with Japanese car makers competing on a large scale. Saab, and in the longer run perhaps even Volvo, may turn out to be too small a producer on its own to have sufficient capacity for competitive cost cutting and quality development. An agreed upon merger between Saab and Volvo before the late 1970s expansion of both was in the end blocked by the executives of Saab, which has left significant barriers for a new attempt. Clouds hang over the future of Saab and of Swedish personal cars, but so far the competitive record of both Saab and Volvo over the past 15 years has been impressive.

In the heavy trucks business Volvo and Saab are big. In the heaviest class, above 16 tons, Volvo is the world's third largest producer, after Mercedes/Freightliner and Renault/MAC, Saab–Scania the sixth. In a declining world market in the 1980s the Swedish producers have increased their market shares, and in 1985 Saab–Scania was the world's most profitable heavy trucks producer (*Svenska Dagbladet*, 13 August 1986, *Financial Times*, 24 November 1986). Seven or 8 per cent of the world market for heavy trucks are covered by the Swedish producers (Riksdagstrycket, 1986–1987, Proposition 74, p. 368). The export of vehicles did not follow the bulk of Swedish manufacturing in losing market shares below the 1978 point. In spite of a slight setback in 1980–1981 market shares stayed significantly above that level, and then grew again (Horwitz, 1986, p. 31).

These exclusive car makers retain a deep anchorage in Swedish society and Swedish politics. With their relations to Swedish business they have created a probably uniquely large upper-end market. In the industry, the market is divided into segments A to H. G–H are the most exclusive, those of the largest Mercedes, Porsche and Jaguar.

Saab and Volvo now have their cars in the E–F segment, together with BMW, Mercedes 190, Audi, and Ford Scorpio. Of the world market this segment constitutes about 5 to 8 per cent, in West Germany 23 per cent, in Sweden 45 per cent. The difference is the size of the lower end of the upper middle class, the E segment. It comprises (in 1987) 41 per cent of the Swedish car market, but only 17 of the West German (O. Wallén, Information Department, Saab Personal Cars). About half of Saab's Swedish sales are business cars, about a third of Volvo's. Their domestic market makes up between a fourth and a fifth of Volvo's and Saab's sales. Saab and Volvo have both chosen to concentrate on exports rather than on domestic sales, and in spite of the large business car market, imports cover today about two-thirds of the Swedish car market, to compare with 60 per cent in 1980 and 57 per cent in 1970 (*Bilstatistik*, various years).

Sweden is more important to the car companies as a production site. Two-thirds of the Saabs are made in Sweden, one-third in Finland. 45 per cent of the Volvos are made domestically, about 30 per cent in Holland, and the rest in Belgium, Canada and some other sites. With subcontractors and other related firms, the Swedish auto industry comprises 13–15 per cent of the country's manufacturing employment (Riksdagstrycket, 1986–1987, Proposition 74, pp. 367–9).

Saab and Volvo, in particular, are playing important parts in the relatively smooth restructuring of Swedish industry. The virtual end to the once very important shipbuilding industry has been significantly eased by the expansion of the car companies. In Göteborg, Volvo's headquarters and once the centre of Swedish shipbuilding, this occurred in a spontaneous expansion of the former, but after the closure of the shipyards in Uddevalla and Malmö, Volvo and Saab, respectively, are stepping in building new car plants with considerable economic incentives offered by the central as well as the local state. Starting with the opening in 1974 of its Kalmar works – also built with public incentives – Volvo has become an internationally renowned pacesetter for new and richer job relations, doing away with the assembly line. A further step at job expansion and job enrichment is meant to be taken with the new Volvo Uddevallia plant, to begin production in autumn 1988. It has been designed jointly by the corporation and by representatives of the trade unions (Bergman, 1987, p. 119ff). This is not pure idealism. Labour scarcity is a major problem for Swedish industry, and labour turn-over in the car assembly plants is very high, about 33 per cent in Volvo's Torslanda plant in Göteborg (Bergman, 1987, p. 141).

Telecommunications has been a very particular industry, based on a symbiotic relationship between a private corporation producing equipment and a public monopoly buying and running the latter. Competition has been mainly in small and/or less developed countries without a domestic telecommunications corporation. New productive forces of telecommunications, more suitable to private ownership, have recently begun to develop fast, and political deregulation has added to a new era of international competition in this industry.

Swedish Ericsson, whose founder first learnt the trade at Siemens in Berlin and who started on a small scale by out-competing a Bell concession in Stockholm in the late 1880s, is one of the world's four or five largest corporations in this field. AT&T and ITT-Alcatel are much larger, Siemens somewhat, and Canadian Northern Telecom, which grew up with Bell Canada, is about equal. Ericsson's market share is about 7 per cent of all telecommunications sales. In public switching equipment, the core of the industry, Ericsson's share is slightly larger. It has kept and tended to improve its position since the early 1970s, in very turbulent times. Only Northern Telecom has been clearly more successful in relative terms (Dang Nguyen, 1986; *Financial Times*, 4 December 1985; Roobeek, 1988). The European telecommunications market is dominated by the French–American Alcatel, 43 per cent, followed by Siemens, 15, and Ericsson 13 per cent (Ericsson Information Department). About half of Ericsson's employment is outside Sweden.

Given the background of the current market and given the still important relationships to public buyers, Ericssons' size is rather impressive for a company with such a small home market. But it remains a small company in view of the line-ups of Alcatel, AT&T–Philips, NEC–Fuijitsu–Hitachi, and also of Siemens, which in contrast to Ericsson is much more than a telecommunications company. Ericsson has opted for a go-it-alone strategy in production, but it is taking part in the new European research programme RACE, together with all the other major producers in Europe. Ericsson's venture into the computer business turned out an expensive flop, and its computer division was sold in late 1987 to the expanding Finnish electronics concern Nokia.

The future of Ericssons' competitiveness will depend mainly on the firm's capacity to keep its technological edge, when the race for technology of the 1990s is beginning, with huge development costs. It will also depend upon political factors. In autumn 1987, for instance,

US authorities were threatening to bar Ericsson from the USA or at least make business very difficult for them, unless it was satisfactorily demonstrated that public Televerket gave no subsidies or other favours to Ericsson (*Svenska Dagbladet*, 12 September 1987).

WHERE DO WELFARE AND COMPETITIVENESS MEET OR COLLIDE?

Social security and international competitiveness are not always major concerns of the same actors the same day. Rather, each concern tends to have its constituency, of professionals and amateurs, and they may very well talk by each other. In other words, if and in what form the relationship between welfare statism and world market competitiveness is a matter of public debate is an empirical question that this part of the study first has to answer. In order to do that properly, some kind of systematicity is called for. This is facilitated by the institutionalised character of most Swedish politico–economic discussion. In the usual triangle of government and the major interest organisations of capital and labour, systematic coverage will here be made of the first and the second. The assumption is, that the trade unions should not be expected to raise issues concerning welfare statism and competitiveness. A check of the major reports to the 1986 union congress, one of which dealt with the welfare state, confirms that assumption. Three institutions are noteworthy for their absence. There is in Sweden no official body of non-bureaucratic economic experts, such as the Council of Economic Advisors in USA or the German *Sachverständigenrat*. There is no special governmental planning and prognosis apparatus, like the *Commissariat du Plan* in France and the *Centraal Planbureau* in the Netherlands. (Previously, *Konjunkturinstitutet* had some such functions on a modest scale, but in the period under study here, it is no more than a watcher of the ups and downs of the business cycle.) Thirdly, in contrast to USA, Germany, and Holland, the central bank in Sweden is a secondary institution with a low profile, in practice obliged to follow and carry out government policy.

The central journal for economists' discussion (*Ekonomisk Debatt*) has been scanned, and found not to pay much attention to our issue. A special check of independent economists' arguments has been made, however. Electoral polemics, from the opposition in particular, in the elections of 1976–1985 have been checked, and found not to be focused on the issue.

This leaves us with two major sources, governmental and business. In both cases conclusions of analyses rather than ideological statements have been looked at. From the government side, we have used the annual budget statements and their attached economic analysis, and also paid attention to the Mid-Term (in Swedish Long-term) Economic Surveys made by Treasury officials, and other public reports dealing with general problems of economy and welfare. From September 1976 to September 1982 the three *bourgeois* parties governed Sweden, in different combinations, and since then the Social Democrats with Communist support. As far as business is concerned, the output of its two major units for the production of general socio-economic analysis has been investigated. One is the Research Institute of Industry (IUI), the other is the annual report on the Swedish economy by what started as the educational outfit of Swedish business, the Business and Society Study Association (SNS).

Governmental Interpretations of and Coping with the Crisis

The beginning of the international crisis was slow to affect Sweden. The country had had its domestic recession in 1971 and confronted the world with a largely internally generated upturn. Swedish growth rates in 1974 and 1975 were well above the OECD average, while inflation was lower. Unemployment actually went down in 1974 and 1975, from 2.5 to 2.0, to 1.6 per cent, where it remained also in 1976. In spite of the country's heavy dependence on oil imports, the balance on current accounts was less negative than for the OECD minus USA (OECD, 1985b, pp. 9, 44, 69, 83).

Consistently expansionary fiscal and monetary policies were pursued, apparently with great success. This impressive economic record notwithstanding, the electorate ousted the Social Democrats in 1976, after 44 years in office, a result due to an environmentalist opposition to nuclear energy, which tipped the even balance between the two blocs of Swedish contemporary politics into the favour of the *bourgeois* (Petersson, 1977).

Since the 1930s the Swedish Parliament has housed five parties. On one side there are the Social Democrats with about 45 per cent of the votes and the Communists with about 5 per cent, those two in the unicameral Parliament since 1970 officiously making up the 'socialist bloc', meaning that the latter constitute a necessary and recognised part of the parliamentary basis of the government of the former. On the other are three parties officially called '*bourgeois*': the Moderates, previously frankly calling itself 'the Right', the liberal People's party, and the ex-Farmers' League revamped into the Centre party.

The electoral support of each of these three parties of the *bourgeois* bloc moves up and down between ten and 25 per cent. In 1976 the Centre was the largest party, and the crucial one, as it was its environmentalism that had decided the election. The nuclear issue was, however, going to divide, demoralise, and ultimately discredit the *bourgeois* bloc. The three parties were also divided on economic policy. The Moderates were with some delay following international *bourgeois* opinion into a more aggressive neo-liberal stance, while the Centre and the Liberals were still firmly committed to Keynesianism and to maintaining the welfare state. It was the latter who set the course of the new government. Hopefully, the above gives the barely necessary background to an understanding of what ensued.

The Unlucky Bourgeois

The Government Declaration of Seden's first *bourgeois* government since 1932 (save for a Farmers' League caretaker government during the holiday months of 1936) refrained from proclaiming any new economic policy. A tax reform with lower marginal rates, inflation-indexed tax rates, and 'measures to restrain the municipal tax increases' were promised, no more. There was no crisis statement and therefore no crisis policy announced, though it was piously declared: 'The goal is in reasonable time to restore the balance of foreign payments and gradually to reduce the need for borrowing abroad.' In fact, the internal policy documents of the new government show that a new international boom was expected in a short time (Bergström, 1987, pp. 188ff). Much emphasis was laid on the intention to continue social reforms and to implement the recently passed industrial legislation, which significantly strengthened the position of labour at the point of production. In brief, the welfare state is safe in our hands, was the main message (Riksdagstrycket, 8 October 1976).

The new government's first budget statement, of January 1977, signed by the Moderate party leader Bohman as Minister of the Economy, stressed the necessity of 'endurance' in 'continued support of domestic demand in order to maintain employment', in the face of the still-not-happening international upswing. The Minister further referred to the Solomonic conclusion of Parliament's Finance Committee, that between the two alternatives presented by the 1975 Long-term Economic Report of an expansion of public or private consumption, one should choose a 'middle way' of equal expansion. 'Certain tax increases' were deemed necessary to dam up private consumption. As a cloud in a still basically clear sky, there was, true, the prices and cost development, which did threaten competitiveness. Therefore, 'all groups in society' must 'show restraint' (Riksdagstrycket, 1976–1977, Proposition, 100, appendix 'Finansplanen', pp. 12–18). Without reservation, this was still a Keynesian world. There was also nothing basically wrong with 'the Swedish model'.

In 1979, the budget statement of the then Liberal minority government – after the fall of the three-party coalition over nuclear energy – regarded the crisis as over. The business cycle had turned 'decisively' in 1978, the groundwork for which had been laid by governmental policy in 1977, by devaluation and by leaving the international currency 'snake' (Riksdagstrycket, Regeringens budgetförslag, 1979–1980, p. 12). But continued expansionist policy had led to a budget deficit that was beginning to snowball, and in its revised budget of 1979, the government stressed the necessity to bring it down, without proposing any drastic measures. In the elections of 1979, nuclear energy again turned out to be the pivotal issue, in *bourgeois* favour (Holmberg, 1981), and the three-party coalition returned. The 1980 budget was low-keyed, centred around the necessity to reduce the deficit, but still without a bite, and the revised budget only set the short-term goal of not further to increase the deficit. A modest 'bill of savings' was presented and carried in September 1980, and an unambitious view of the budget deficit continued in the 1981 budget.

The last *bourgeois* budget, of 1982, marked a cautious ideological turn in its veiled criticism of the expansionist policy of the 1970s. (Riksdagstrycket, Regeringens budgetförslag 1982–1983, Finansplanen, p. 20) Disequilibria had developed in the Swedish economy, manifested in the deficits on current account and in the state budget. However, no principled critique of the welfare state is provided. The picture given is one of a sombre international environment and a pre-decided expansion of public social expenditure, while public revenue stagnated because of the international crisis. The strategy proposed was two-pronged. Firstly, measures to strengthen the competitiveness of the Swedish economy, measures which included the 10 per cent devaluation in 1981, the reduction of marginal taxes – which had also taken place the year before, in the form of a deal between the two *bourgeois* parties in the middle and the Social Democrats, whereafter the Moderates had left the government – and various measures to better the functioning of labour, capital and primary commodities markets. The second prong was to 'restrain the resources claims which are financed by the public budget'. (Riksdagstrycket, Regeringens budgetförslag 1982–1983, Finansplanen, pp. 20–21).

However, expansion is built into the budget of a welfare state of an aging society, and the Swedish *bourgeois* parties in the middle remained parties of the middle road. In their revised budget, presented in April 1982, the aim was set no higher than 'to restrain the public budget expansion'. Only as a test balloon was it added, that the OECD Secretariat in its survey of Sweden had proposed a cut of the absolute level of public expenditure (Riksdagstrycket, 1981–1982, Proposition 150, appendix 1, p. 18)

The Swedish *bourgeois* parties and their four governments 1976–1982 were more unlucky than inept. They had no mandate for a change of a, till then, reasonably successfully socio-economic policy of capital accumulation, social security, and full employment. That policy complex still enjoyed high legitimacy, also among at least two of three *bourgeois* parties. They had come into office after 44 years, and remained in office in 1979, due to the marginally decisive issue of nuclear energy, an issue which *de facto* more divided the *bourgeois* parties among themselves than separated them from the Social Democrats. Sweden was out of step with the international business cycle, so the international crisis hit late, in fact mainly after the change of power. But it did hit, the most severe international crisis since the *bourgeois* parties had been in power the last time, in the early 1930s. The *bourgeois* governments received little credit for their tenacious, successful, and, as we can see now, historically decisive commitment to full employment, which favourably distinguished them from West German Social Democracy and British Labour. That duty was simply regarded as self-evident. The Swedish welfare state was set on a course of expansion, based on a broad political consensus after the *bourgeois* challenge to it in the elections of 1960 had suffered a severe beating, while GDP stagnated, and even fell. Net foreign debt turned from a credit of 0.9 per cent of GDP in 1976 to a debt of 21.9 per cent of GDP in 1962 (Jakobsson *et al.*, 1985, p. 87). The unions were at the height of their power, a power used with Swedish circumspection and moderation true, but they were no friends of the government to be called upon. Rivalry among the triad of *bourgeois* parties, with the constant temptation of the smaller one(s) of which to defect and strike a better deal with the Social Democrats, also contributed to collective weakness.

Fate Sides with the Resourceful: the Return of the Social Democrats

The Social Democrats rode back to power on four solemn promises of welfare state restoration, against the last minute cuts proposed by the *bourgeois* government: to reinstate full indexation of old-age pensions; to abolish the decided upon introduction of waiting days in the sickness insurance; to do away with the new stricter regulations of the unemployment insurance; to do away with the new cuts in state contributions to municipal daycare (Askling, 1982). These promises turned out more popular than the unpopularity of the wage earners' funds proposal, of public shares funds with capital levied on private enterprise, which the union and party cadre had forced the sceptical party leadership to stick to.

But what turned out to be the crucial, and eminently successful, economic strategy of the new Social Democratic government was not decided upon till after the elections. It had been prepared, in deep secrecy, by a group of economists in the entourage of the former, and later, Finance Minister since the spring of 1982. In the internal discussion of the government party leadership after the successful election three alternatives were presented: (1) demand expansion to bring down unemployment, at 3.1 per cent in 1982; (2) a restrictive alternative geared to cutting inflation and the current account and budget deficits; (3) a big, competitive devaluation of 20 per cent, combined with anti-inflationary measures with a view to boosting competitiveness and profitability of Swedish export industry and thereby to get the whole economy going again. It was the last alternative that the economists had been preparing, and that won the day. Thereafter the LO (trade union) leadership was informed and acquiesced. When the decision was taken the new Finance Minister told the head of the central bank, and the finance ministers of the other Nordic countries. Upon the latters' protests, Sweden's devaluation was limited to 16 per cent. Then, after a government decision at the Social Democratic party office, the formal decision was taken by the parliamentary executive board of the central bank (Bergström, 1987, pp. 193ff).

The Swedish Social Democrats, drawing upon previously accumulated capital of trade union and popular confidence, could have it both ways. They got into office as denouncers of the unsocial and unfair *bourgeois*. They brought about massive redistribution of income and wealth to capital and assetholders, at the expense of ordinary wage and salary earners, having their backs covered by the trade unions and the Social Democratic Pensioners' Organisation, not without crumblings true. The white-collar as well as the manual workers' confederations declared through their leaders that they would not seek compensation for the redistributive effects of the devaluation, undertaken in the economic interest of the nation. The Social Democratic pensioners accepted not to demand immediate compensation for the devaluation, in spite of the electoral promise of the Social Democrats. The devaluation was further flanked by some tax increases and one-off fiscal rearrangements beginning to reduce the budget deficit, without any major cuts (Riksdagstrycket, Regeringens budgetförslag, 1982–1983.)

On the whole, the operation was a big success, aided by international luck. The Swedish Social Democrats got back into office just before the international conjuncture was turning upward, and they were further helped by the collapse of the oil market in 1986. Exports, profits, wages and salaries, and tax revenues increased, and the budget deficit declined from 13 to 1 per cent of GDP (Riksdagstrycket: Regeringens budgetsförslag 1988–1989, p. 48). The international homages cited in the introduction to this paper express well the general perception of the outcome.

This does not mean that all visible problems have been solved. Swedish inflation remains well above OECD average, and economic growth stays below. Market shares lost in the 1970s have not been regained, in spite of an extraordinary reduction of unit labour costs. The regressive distribution effects are not uncontroversial in a still very egalitarian country.

Views of the Enlightened Bourgeoisie

Sweden is a country of thorough official or officious investigations. We should expect serious and considered opinion related to the interests of capital to be particularly concerned with issues of the compatibility of the welfare state with capital accumulation and world market competitiveness. The fact is, I think I am warranted to say after an extensive though hardly exhaustive survey, that this is not or remarkably little the case. The Swedish welfare state seems to have an uncontestable legitimacy, and business concerns therefore tend to be expressed in other ways.

In 1978 an American consulting firm, the Boston Consulting Group, presented an analysis of the Swedish economy, invited and sponsored by Volvo, the Ministry of Industry, the public investment bank, and some other private and public bodies (Boston Consulting Group, 1978). Its main conclusion was that Sweden's long-term economic problems derived from a necessary change from an old industrial structure largely based on natural comparative advantages, made necessary by the entry of new low-cost competitors. In other words, an industrial structure argument, easy to hand for a private industry consulting firm.

More official status was given to the Bjurel Commission, consisting of senior civil servants, which handed over its analysis of the 'Road to Increased Welfare' in 1979. The adaptation of labour costs to the international environment, the functioning of markets and the motivation of market actors were at the centre of the conclusions (Justitiedepartementet, 1979). Neither the Boston Group nor the Bjurel Commission had in the end much influence, although their reports were received with much attention and controversy. More official still was the Mid-Term Economic Survey of 1980, drawn up by the Economy Ministry. A sustained argument for the reduction of the public deficits was given, as well as a critique of rigid labour markets, with low mobility and high public sector demand, both affecting the labour supply of industry negatively (SOU, 1980, p. 52).

The Mid-Term Economic Surveys of 1984 and 1987 were drawn up by Social Democratic Treasury officials. The former underlined the necessity to deal with the public sector deficits and with the process of wage and salary formation, which tended to yield outcomes above those of competing countries (SOU, 1984, p. 4). The 1987 investigation singled out three major problems of the Swedish economy: (1) negative public sector saving and too low saving in the economy as a whole; (2) the current account balance is very sensitive to small changes in private consumption and investment; (3) wages and prices tend to grow faster than in competing countries (SOU, 1987:3, p. 214).

An alternative mid-term economic survey was presented by the Research Institute of Industry in 1979. As explanations for the 1970s crisis of the Swedish economy the following were offered; (a) international disturbances inadequately met by Swedish policies;

(b) further inefficiency of the Swedish economic system in a technical sense; (c) a loss of competitiveness due to new competition to traditional raw materials-based basic industries (of wood and iron) as well as to Sweden's technical advantage (IUI, 1979, p. 78).

The latest major publication in the field from the Industry Association and its researchers is a perceptive investigation into the resources, problems, and strategies of major industrial sectors in Sweden (Ohlsson & Vinell, 1987). The welfare state does not figure in their analysis either. Instead, they emphasise the following, in their view, important aspects of the social milieu: a stable decision environment, a wage structure more inegalitarian so as to give more incentives to structural change, a tax structure more favourable to venture capital, the need for stable owner-control, particularly in the construction of an enterprise, more decentralisation and higher capacity utilisation of the educational system (Ohlsson & Vinell, 1987, Ch. 10).

The annual reports of the business study association, SNS, give perhaps the best expression to independent-minded but institutionally attached and weighty collective *bourgeois* expert opinion. The group of authors varies from year to year, which loosens constraints of consistency. In these contexts the reports of 1983–1984 to 1988 have been studied.

The SNS report of November 1983 is entitled *The Debt Trap* (*Skuldfällan*), the gist of which is that expansive budgets have led the state into a debt trap, that perhaps in the long term is the most serious threat to employment. As a major reason for existing problems the centralisation of social benefits and social finance is offered. A system of more individualised payments is therefore suggested (SNS, 1983, pp. 84ff). Readers of the 1985 report are offered 'the road to a more stable Sweden'. The road recommended is 'a norm-based economic regime', with a low and constant inflation as its central goal. Keynesianism is bid farewell, but still prevailing politics is bowed to by underlining that the intention is not to fight inflation with unemployment, although a good deal of the responsibility for full employment is proposed being shifted from the state to the labour market actors (SNS, 1984–1985). The welfare state stays outside the shooting range.

The 1986 report called for 'new game rules for growth', in practice for deregulation, lower taxes, wage differentiation, and price stabilisation norms. The normative policy demanded in this and the previous report intended a return to the rules of the Bretton-Woods system, that is, a refusal to accommodate 'cost disturbances' by currency devaluations. The thrust of the argument is clearly neo-liberal, but in this context it is noteworthy, that it is *not* an explicit argument about the welfare state. The authors of the report also stated, that 'We can then unambiguously conclude that Sweden's international competitiveness currently is very good indeed' (SNS, 1986, p. 135).

For 1987 the US Brookings Institution was invited to provide the annual SNS report (Rivlin, 1987). The Brookings team was basically very positive in their evaluation. They found no signs of any long-term decline of competitiveness in Swedish industry (Rivlin, 1987, p. 100). In other words, the Swedish political economy was basically sound. They did see a contradiction betwen growth promotion and inflation mastering, and their recipe was that inflationary pressures should be dealt with through flexible exchange rates. Both their conclusion and their policy recommendation invoked a public critique by their hosts, reasserting previously mentioned arguments (Rivlin, 1987, pp. 113ff). In this context an open attack on the welfare state was mounted, *not* on the basis of its effects for Sweden's international competitiveness but because of its negative effects on the labour supply and because of its distortive effects on the allocation of labour time, due to tax wedges between labour costs and labour revenue (Rivlin, 1987, pp. 119–24).

The 1988 report is concentrated on an analysis of the redistributive effects of the Swedish welfare state. Egalitarianism is basically taken as given, and policy recommendations limit themselves to ones of redistribution with lower marginal tax rates and less regulated markets.

A similar – for the right-of-centre of Swedish debate very characteristic – mode of argumentation was put forward by a group of economists of the Swedish Employers' Confederation. Similar in the sense that Social Democratic goals are taken as premises of the debate, in which liberal means are proposed for those ends. This book is called *The Unemployment Trap* and argues that Sweden 'appears to have got into the same unemployment trap as the rest of Western Europe' (Jakobsson *et al.*, 1985, p. 20). The reason is said to be that because the tax ceiling has been reached public employment can no longer compensate for the shake-out of the private sector. The remedy is privatisation of the welfare state.

Voices of Individual Economists

No claim can be laid here to a full coverage of the Swedish economic debate, but the conclusion which seems to follow from major contributions of institutional economists should at least be checked with what has been said by two individual voices. The two most distinguished Swedish economists of the 1970s and 1980s have been the late Erik Lundberg, a universally respected focal figure of right-of-centre post-war liberal economics, and Assar Lindbeck, a pugnacious ex-Social Democrat turned major critic of the welfare state.

A perusal of the prolific writings of Lindbeck on the welfare state and a study of some key pieces of Lindbeck and Lundberg on the welfare state and on the Swedish economy sustain the conclusion coming from the previous two sections. The welfare state and international competitiveness has *not* been a major theme of debate in this open economy with one of the world's most extensive welfare states. Lindbeck's main points of issue with the welfare state are its tax wedges, their distortive effects on the functioning of market allocation and the negative tax effects on labour supply. He also sees negative effects on the freedom of individual choice (Lindbeck, 1984, 1986, 1988). Lundberg (1985) makes a subtle and complex enumeration of a number of factors through which the ambitious application of the welfare state ideology has made the Swedish economy more vulnerable to the external shocks of the 1970s and 1980s, but he never clinches welfare and competitiveness.

The Brookings economist Robert Lawrence merits special attention. In an updated version of his contribution to the Brookings study of Sweden. Lawrence (1987, pp. 329ff) has supplied an econometric argument about the negative effects of government expansion upon Swedish competitiveness 1972–1978. In Lawrence's equation the expansion of government expenditure comes out as the second most important determinant of the development of the Swedish foreign trade balance, after market growth. The effect should have been both to decrease exports and to increase imports. While there are visible mechanisms whereby exports may have been discouraged (referred to above), Lawrence provides no very plausible argument why government expansion, distinguished from expanding domestic demand, should have led to increased imports. Lawrence's argument, which refers only to 1972–1978, implies a crowding-out process, but he offers nothing more than some general guesses about how it could have happened, from undermining the work ethic to stimulating firms to switch from tradables to non-tradables. There is in fact no hard evidence of any crowding-out process (cf. Erixon, 1984).

Meeting on the Labour Market

The major themes of the Swedish politico-economic debate do not bring the welfare state and competitiveness into focus. But from the arguments about the Swedish economy and the Swedish welfare state it is possible to see where the two would meet first of all, that is on the labour market. Wage formation and its inflationary pressure has been a major ingredient in the SNS analyses of the problems of the Swedish economy as well as of the governmental assessments by *bourgeois* and Social Democratic Ministers of Finance alike (Riksdagstrycket, Regeringens budgetförslag, 1982–1983, p. 20 and 1988–1989, pp. 28–9), and by Treasury officials investigating the medium to long-term problems and prospects of the Swedish economy (SOU, 1984:4, p. 459; SOU 1987:3, p. 237). Welfare state effects on labour supply and labour allocation have also been a central target of criticism by liberal economists, such as Lindbeck.

Welfare and competitiveness meet on the labour market over four basic issues: labour supply, labour allocation, labour cost, and labour motivation. What we will do in this section is to structure each issue and to bring some evidence into light, not for final assertions but for indicating provisionally in what direction the available evidence seems to lead us.

The labour supply problem is primarily that the high taxation required by an extensive welfare state discourages labour supply, secondarily that generous income replacement ratios of social insurance reduce labour supply. In the Swedish discussion, it is mainly the former argument which has been used. The Brookings report presented some unfavourable comparisons of Sweden and the United States in this respect, and econometric models can also be called in to sustain the thesis (SOU, 1987:3, p. 168).

However, the picture changes if the frame of comparison is broadened, and if it is acknowledged that marginal changeabilities are *de facto* located in different institutional structures. After 1978, a long-term decline in the volume (hours) of paid work per year, going back at least to 1929, was *reversed* and started slowly upwards again. Such a reversal took place also in Finland and Norway, but in no other country of Western Europe. In West Germany, France, and in Britain, for example, an accelerated decline in the number of paid hours of work set in (see further Therborn, 1987b). It is also rational to expect that high but individual taxation combined with an ample supply of social service jobs should encourage married or cohabitating women to take a job. In comparison with most other countries, labour supply has developed favourably in Sweden. The comparison with USA is misleading, due to a century-old difference between New and Old World labour markets.

The allocation of labour may be distorted, impeding economic efficiency, both through the effect of tax wedges between labour revenues and labour costs, and because of rigidity due to labour entitlements and job rights. The working of taxation may sometimes look rather absurd. So, for example, in 1986 a Swedish industrial worker had a (couple of per cent) *lower* wage net of taxes than in 1965 (in 1980 prices), although labour costs had increased by two-thirds (SOU, 1987:3, p. 39). But there is little hard empirical evidence about distortive effects. With regard to labour flexibility/rigidity, the Swedish labour market fares well in international comparisons. Real wage sensitivity to unemployment is higher than in other European countries – in part due to the important role of wage drift alongside central agreements – and labour mobility, as measured by quit rates, was as high as in the USA in 1969–1977. Sweden was also found to have a better match of unemployed and vacancies than USA (Åberg 1984). It is true, though, that there is a tendency towards decreasing mobility (SOU, 1987:3, pp. 182–3). The positive attitude of Swedish unions to technological change is generally known and acknowledged. Again, the evidence points in the direction of concluding: there may very well be welfare state-related imperfections of the Swedish labour market when compared with an ideal market, but in relation to actually existing labour markets the Swedish one seems to be functioning better than most.

Labour costs and inflation are problems to the Swedish economy. Measured in local currency Sweden's labour costs in the 1980s are again running ahead of those of foreign competitors, and inflation is doing likewise. To some extent this is a price paid for full employment, a price all major political actors in Sweden are prepared to pay, if necessary, but it is also linked more directly to the welfare state, and not only through employers' social security contributions. The large public sector with their powerful unions in a low productivity growth sector, and a centralised and highly visible system of wage bargaining, where every collective is comparing itself with others, do create problems of wage pressure in an open economy (Elvander, 1988). As we have seen, however, the relationship between labour costs and competitiveness is more complex and unclear than is often assumed. Matters are further complicated by the fact that the rate of exchange can make or break wage moderation.

Results from a questionnaire in 1986 to 125 responding Swedish manufacturing firms underline the multifacetedness of competitiveness at the microlevel. The cost structure of 'a typical final product' of Swedish manufacturing was found to be the following:

Direct materials	44.4 per cent
Direct wages	13.2 per cent
Manufacturing costs	24.7 per cent
Overhead	19.0 per cent (Lindberg *et al.*, 1987, p. 41).

Labour costs were not mentioned among the ten biggest problems of the firms, nor did their reduction figure in the most popular competitive strategies of the firms. These strategies included the following items, in descending order of importance: reduction of putting away time; reduction of conduction time; motivation of direct personnel; better quality of suppliers; education of foremen; develop new processes for new products; better maintenance of new products; limitation of variants, standardisation; give workers job enrichment; better management–worker relations (Lindberg *et al.*, 1987, p. 37).

Social security is not always seen as something negative by employers and employers' organisations. Otherwise their readiness to extend legal social entitlements with additional social insurance by collective agreements could not be explained. Since the mid-1960s, the Swedish Employers' confederation, SAF, has been positive to an equalisation of the social rights of workers and white-collar employees. The reason has been a long-term strategy in view of a fear of separate conflicts with the white-collar unions while having to pay workers' wages. Abolishing differences between manual and white-collar workers would create a more manageable bargaining situation, and for that better social benefits for workers would be worth paying (SAF chief economist K.O. Faxen, oral communication).

In sum, the welfare state has not made the cost problem of international competitors easier, and Sweden has its own problematic process of wage formation, in which the public sector employees and their unions have played an extra complicating part since the early 1970s. The 1960s Swedish wage formation model, in which the competitive situation of the internationally competing sector defined 'the margin' for wage increases, has been broken up by the addition of the public sector unions as powerful independent actors. On the other hand, the connection between labour costs and competitiveness is neither direct nor straight. The welfare state does not seem to pose any direct noteworthy problems to Swedish firms and to their employers' organisation.

The fourth issue where welfare and competitiveness meet on the labour market concerns labour motivation. If the microeconomic theory of economic incentives is correct, we should expect that in a country with a high-level egalitarian distribution and broad-based social rights, ordinary workers and employees would put in greater effort, commitment and sense of responsibility, than in a more inegalitarian and authoritarian country. On the other hand, again if the theory is correct, managers and specialists should be expected to put in *less* effort in the former example. The net effect on welfare and competitiveness would depend on which effect was stronger.

With regard to the effect on managers and specialists, there is to my knowledge no systematic evidence available. The technical and managerial acumen of Swedish multinationals gainsays it, though. As far as workers and employees are concerned we do have evidence, from an international work attitude study. In this study, done in the early 1980s with large national samples in Sweden, FRG, UK, USA, Israel, and Japan, Swedish workers and employees were found to have the highest commitment to their employing organisation and to their job. Table 7.13 gives the figures for FRG, Japan, and Sweden.

Table 7.13 Commitment to one's job and to the organisation where one works in selected OECD countries, early 1980s (survey answers in %)

	Full commitment	*Limited commitment*	*Don't know*
Sweden	81	14	5
Japan	59	39	2
Germany	56	32	12

Source: Zetterberg *et al.*, 1983, p. 5.

An egalitarian welfare state can, then, make a positive contribution to competitive capacity. It also looks plausible, that the mobility and the openness to technical change which characterise the Swedish labour market is largely due to a sense of security among workers and employees because of mobile (because general) social entitlements and reliable government commitment to full employment. The welfare state may be a part of structural competitiveness. In other words, the encounters on the labour market of welfare and competitiveness are not always collisions and conflicts. They may also constitute confluence.

The paradox of an extensive Social Democratic welfare state and vigorous private capitalism, which has so baffled or impressed perceptive foreign observers makes sense, when the possibility of a confluence of welfare and international competitiveness is acknowledged. It has been built on four pillars: (A) a tradition of broad popular social entitlements – coming from the force of an independent peasantry – instead of segmented corporatist rights or charity concerns with poverty, (B) a sharp differentiation between high personal and low corporate taxation, (C) cautious and competent state management, and (D) employer–union co-operation. This is not a transcendence of social conflict, nor a definite solution to basic social problems. It is exposed to the storms of the world market, to the creeping dangers of ageing affluence in a changing environment, to the complexity of conflicting human concerns. However, contrary to much conventional wisdom, competitive welfare statism is a viable, actually existing social formation.

8 Welfare Statism and International Competition: The Lesson of the Case Studies

Alfred Pfaller, with Ian Gough and Göran Therborn

DOES INTERNATIONAL COMPETITION THREATEN THE WELFARE STATE?

Responses to the Challenge of International Competition Have Affected the Welfare State to Differing Extents . . .

In the past decade, international competitiveness has become a major public concern in Britain, France, Germany, the USA, but much less so in Sweden. A pervasive perception has evolved in Britain and in France that their national economy was or is falling behind the leading industrialised nations in terms of productivity and technological competence and that in many important markets national products cannot openly compete with foreign ones. There is no such unanimity in the United States, but the public debate has become more and more dominated by the theme that the country has lost its former technological leadership position and will fall further behind its foreign competitors if remedies are not devised quickly. In Germany the ever-present fear that the country might lose its international competitiveness has not so far turned into a generalised belief that this is actually happening. But by the end of the 1980s warnings about the decreasing attractiveness of the Federal Republic as an industrial production site have gained considerable weight in the public debate.

In all these four countries, concrete demands were made for policy measures to strengthen national competitiveness in the international market place. And in all four countries the central governments have come to accept, to varying degrees, the need for such policy measures. In the United States and Britain the policy imperative to do something for the country's competitiveness was somewhat blurred by the more explicitly formulated broader policy goal to revitalise the national economy, to overcome a deep-seated economic malaise.

A coherent policy programme to achieve the goal of competitive strengthening or of economic revitalisation was carried out only in Britain (though it also had other, at times contradicting goals). In the USA an equally thoroughgoing policy design was watered down considerably when it came to implementation. France, on the other hand, witnessed over the same period a sequence of two comprehensive policy programmes which explicitly intended to improve the country's international competitiveness, but which were in several respects contradictory. The later policy undid various measures which were central to the preceding one. However, in other respects they amounted to a cumulative effort to remove deep-rooted obstacles to a better competitive performance. In Germany there was much more discussion than policy change, which corresponds to the fact that in a way international competitiveness has always been a priority consideration in West German economic policy-making. Nevertheless, here, too, a few steps have been taken in a new direction since the end of the 1970s. The same may be said about Sweden, even though competitiveness never became there nearly as big a public issue as in the Federal Republic of Germany.

Table 8.1 presents a comparative summary of the measures taken in the five investigated countries in order to strengthen national competitiveness. The table features two blocks of policy measures: the first one includes the recipes of that school of thinking which in the course of the 1970s gained influence under the label of 'supply-side economics'. Their common denominator is the freeing of private enterprise from onerous burdens of various kinds. The second block of measures corresponds to the 'industrial-policy' school (in the broadest meaning of the term) and aims at mobilising public resources to supplement the efforts of private enterprise. There are two residual policies which cannot readily be attributed to either block, even though one, exposure to foreign competition, has some affinity to the 'supply-side' block.

It is this first block of policies which has obvious implications for welfare statism. Emphasis on tax restraint means a tighter budget situation and, thus, less financial leeway for social expenditure. Even if actual tax reductions are fully compensated by a broadened tax

Table 8.1 Policies introduced in the 1970s and 1980s in five industrialised countries in order to strengthen national competitiveness

	USA	*Britain*	*France*	*Germany*	*Sweden*
Lower taxes on personal and corporate income	*	*		(*)	
Remove regulatory rigidities	*	*	*		
Remove labour rigidities	*	*	*		
Impose labour discipline	(*)	*			
Lower labour costs	*	*			*
Increase public R&D expenditure			*	(*)	
Subsidise key investments in important branches			*	*	
Increase state control of investment			*		
Improve human capital			*		
Support access of national producers to foreign markets	*				*
Expose national producers to foreign competition		*			
Stabilise/reset macroeconomics	*	*	*	*	*

* indicates a major policy shift
(*) indicates a policy move of minor importance
a blank space indicates that the policy did not apply *or* that the opposite policy was carried out.

base or by increases in other (typically indirect) taxes, the approach to all expenditures is more than ever: avoid them if at all possible. The pressure to reduce expenditure increases and additional expenditure proposals face very high legitimacy barriers. Emphasis on deregulation implies that considerations of income security, protection against health hazards, environmental conservation and non-commercially provided quality of life in general have less weight *vis-à-vis* considerations of entrepreneurial freedom.

Likewise, a reduction of labour rigidities and labour costs tends to be pursued at the expense of job security and of fringe benefits like pensions, health insurance, sick payment, paid vacation days etc. Besides, the emphasis on market flexibility implies restrictions on union influence and hence on the political backing of the welfare state cause. On the other hand, cuts in welfare state security serve as a means to weaken labour and make it more 'flexible'. The fight against disruptive labour practices has in part the same implications. However, more discipline in labour relations has also been sought in some countries via an increased involvement of labour in the running of enterprises or even in the management of the national economy, which implies rather more income security and more generous fringe benefits – for those who have a job in the 'regulated' sector of the labour market.

The other set of measures, to which we attached the 'industrial policy' label, does not evince a general anti-welfare state bias. On the contrary, it is rather associated with those aspects of welfare statism like universal education which have an investment function.

It is striking to see in Table 8.1 that one of the investigated countries, France, concentrated its efforts to improve national competitiveness on that second block of policies, while the two Anglo-Saxon countries have relied so far predominantly on the prescriptions of the so-called supply-side economics school. The considerably lower scores of Germany and Sweden in either field of policies correspond to the lower degree of preoccupation with competitive inferiority in these countries, although new policies have tended to be of the 'industrial policy' sort.

In accordance with these preliminary considerations, we should expect that among the five countries it is Britain and the United States where there has been the clearest retrenchment of welfare statism. Table 8.2, which schematically summarises our pertinent findings, confirms this expectation, albeit very roughly so. The centrepiece of modern welfare statism, public transfer payments to households, suffered the heaviest cuts in the United States, where the scope of such transfers was the most restricted to start with. Otherwise, the table shows a retrenchment of welfare statism on the broadest front in the United Kingdom. However, the scores of France and the Federal Republic of Germany are also quite high. In particular the second mechanism on which the modern welfare society depends, the full-employment economy, has lost much of its effectiveness in both countries, as it did in Britain.

Of course, Table 8.2 cannot be read separately from the qualitative information provided by the case studies. And we cannot base on a comparison of the two tables a generalised statement concerning the consequences competitiveness-oriented policies have for welfare statism. A qualitatively enriched supplement to the schematic

Table 8.2 Retrenchments in welfare statism in five industrialised countries in the 1970s and 1980s

	USA	*Britain*	*France*	*Germany*	*Sweden*
Tax cuts	*	*	(*)	(*)	
Regressive shifts in the tax load	*	*	(*)	*	(*)
Reduced benefits for recipients of state transfers	*	(*)	(*)	(*)	(*)[1]
Reduced eligibility for state transfers	*	*	(*)		
Reduced social services		*			
Residualisation of benefits and services to the poor	(*)	*		(*)	
Reduced formation of social capital		*	*	(*)	
Reduced coverage of occupational benefits	*				
Reduction of public in favour of private provision		*			
Rising unemployment		*	*	*	
Rising inequality	*	*	(*)	(*)	

* indicates a policy shift
(*) indicates a policy move of minor importance
a blank space indicates that the policy did not apply *or* that the opposite policy was carried out
[1] temporary measure

information entailed in the two tables may be provided by a series of stylised summaries of developments in the five countries.

USA

The worsening performance of the American economy since the 1960s paved the way to political influence for the fundamentalist back-to-the-market philosophy which has shaped US economic policy in the 1980s. Even though declining American competitiveness was not the concern of the supply-side reformers, theirs were *eo ipso* also recipes for an internationally more competitive economy. At the same time, an intense public debate has been focusing specifically on the decline of US productivity and innovativeness in international comparison. But this debate has remained without much consequence for government policy. In effect, President Reagan's programme to reduce state influence in the economy brought with it several cuts in welfare benefits for specific target groups, mostly among the poor, as well as some tightening in eligibility criteria, while opposition by the Congress prevented more severe measures. However, labour market developments have been much more significant in diluting the essence of welfare statism. Apart from the recession years, wage flexibility prevented the emergence of long-term mass unemployment in spite of a huge increase in the labour force. But many people have acquired jobs with a wage insufficient to keep them out of poverty. Besides, since a large part of the social security benefits of the 'typical' employed American is provided by the employer and not enjoyed universally, the decline of several industries under the pressure of foreign competition and the ensuing structural recomposition of the US economy left many persons with considerably lower levels of protection. The sectoral and regional limitation of union influence was responsible for this consequence of structural change, which was further reduced by deliberate management and government policies. Altogether, a significant segment of the population has, thus, become much more vulnerable to adverse market conditions – a result which corresponds by and large to the free market ideal of the supply-side reformers. Initiatives to make the welfare state more responsive to the new poverty symptoms were successful only in some relatively affluent states. On the federal level, they encountered a formidable obstacle in the budget deficit which had resulted from the mismatch of soaring defence expenditure and decreasing tax rates.

United Kingdom

Since the mid-1960s the country's long-term competitive decline went along with more and more macroeconomic instability. After several governments had failed to get the worsening situation under control, the Conservatives under Mrs Thatcher set out in 1979 with a radical attack on the presumed causes of that instability. In sum their policies aimed at a thorough restoration of market discipline. These policies were understood to lay at the same time the basis for an internationally more competitive British economy, even though this was not the government's direct objective. By its very nature, Mrs Thatcher's back-to-the-market policy had a strong anti-welfare state bias. Yet, expenditure and benefits within the existing transfer system were reduced only in a very selective way. The central income maintenance mechanisms stayed intact, even though they were changed somewhat into the direction of less universality and more incomes-related benefits. The most significant development towards an erosion of welfare statism was the emergence of persistent mass unemployment. This was basically the result of reduced economic growth with non-adapting labour market institutions. The situation was exacerbated by the policy of the government which led the country into a particularly deep recession – for the sake of restoring market discipline. Monetarist restrictiveness was compounded with an unaccommodating stance *vis-à-vis* the currency appreciation which resulted from the soaring oil exports and which left a large part of British industry unable to compete. For an extension of welfare statist arrangements in order to maintain full employment despite slower growth and manufacturing decline, the free market-oriented Thatcher strategy had no room.

France

Long before the onset of the worldwide economic crisis in the 1970s France has been pre-occupied with catching up with the leading industrialised countries. It has also been a long-established function of the state to modernise the economy, making up for the shortcomings of the private enterprise sector. This traditional state-led approach to international competitiveness remained the dominating one throughout most of the crisis years until the mid-1980s. In a way, the development of a full-scale welfare state was considered part of the overall modernisation of the relatively backward French society. Thus, the public concern for international competitiveness did not have an implicit anti-welfare state bias. The perceived roots of the competitiveness problem (outdated structures) simply predated the arrival of full-scale welfare statism. However, the impetus to extend and complete the French welfare state encountered serious difficulties which were due to the economic crisis. The ill-fated expansionist and redistributive economic policy of the socialist government in the early 1980s was followed by a corrective austerity period which among other things reduced the scope for government expenditure. More important, it let unemployment swell to magnitudes which could no longer be compensated by the existing mechanisms of social protection. A problem of 'new poverty' emerged – not because of a retrenchment of welfare statism, but because the welfare state was ill-equipped to cope with the new problems. Entitlements to transfer income proved completely insufficient *vis-à-vis* the increased number of casualties from the market economy. There were initiatives to develop active employment policies to supplement the no longer adequate transfer mechanisms. But they were implemented half-heartedly, due not least to considerations of competitiveness, which imposed fiscal limits. By the mid-1980s, even large parts of the political left had become convinced that enterprises should not be burdened any further with taxes and social contributions, that there was rather a need for some relief. This conviction reflected the country's ongoing balance of payment difficulties within the context of monetary stabilisation as well as the dominant international trend towards tax cutting. Generalised anti-welfare statism has not gained much political ground yet, but several transfer programmes have been cut back financially for the sake of budgetary discipline.

The Federal Republic of Germany

The very high export dependence of the West German economy is reflected in the sensitiveness with which public opinion responded to recurrent signs of decreasing international competitiveness. Comparatively high non-wage labour costs, which have their origin in a highly developed system of social protection, have for a long time been under attack as harming competitiveness. However, the country's obvious export strength throughout most of the crisis period since the mid-1970s has counterbalanced this charge in the political debate. Until recently the view was widely shared in Germany that the high level of workers' education and skills coupled with the co-operative relations between organised labour and business management provide a solid basis for the high wages and social benefits – that the elaborate welfare state system is part and parcel of that high-efficiency syndrome which makes for the country's competitive strength. In fact, macroeconomic cost discipline, which has been an outstanding feature of German economic policy's pronounced competitiveness orientation, was fully restored in the 1980s. The more important danger was seen for a while in an increasing high-technology deficit *vis-à-vis* Japan and the United States, a fear which reinforced industrial policy tendencies, geared especially towards R&D. Since the mid-1980s, however, there has been a growing concern that despite her impressive export performance Germany is losing attractiveness as a place in which to invest for the future. This has been attributed to a combination of high labour costs, high taxation and increasing social rigidities, which make it difficult and expensive for enterprises to adjust to market changes. This charge entails a comprehensive attack on German welfare statism. Under the Christian Democratic government it has been inspiring a series of policy moves aiming at social deregulation and the restriction of union power. Disproportionate tax relief for the higher income strata has increased income inequality. However, the extensive system of social security and redistributive transfers, which had been built up until the mid-1970s, has so far remained basically intact. Cuts in the benefits of several programmes corresponded to the need to contain increasing expenditures when further significant tax increases were ruled out as highly undesirable – not least for reasons of international competitiveness. They were more a tribute to the limits of redistribution than a distributive rollback. In effect the most important break with past welfare statism was, as in Britain and France, the emergence of large-scale unemployment after the end of the 1970s, a problem which the existing social security system could not adequately cope with. Serious steps to reintegrate the jobless at comparable income levels into the market economy were not undertaken. In part, this can be attributed to a deficit of organisational innovation, but more important is the unwillingness of taxpayers and wage-earners to finance the demand for additional labour. In fact, mass unemployment provided the basis for the emergence of a second-tier labour market segment with much more flexibility and much less economic security.

Sweden

In the wake of the second oil crisis Sweden ran into serious balance of payment problems which were resolved through a package of macroeconomic adjustment measures, the most drastic of which was a 16 per cent devaluation. These measures implied a significant redistribution of income away from labour to capital. But the country's very extensive welfare state system was not the slightest bit questioned. On the contrary, general welfare state security and the government's strong commitment to it greatly facilitated the social discipline required successfully to implement the stablisation programme. Once the balance of payments problems of the early 1980s had been overcome, the Swedish economy performed sufficiently well to endorse politically the country's long-standing welfare-cum-efficiency formula of economic organisation, especially since some corrections in favour of efficiency were made. Part of the formula is an active, tax-financed employment policy which has enabled Sweden to maintain close-to-full employment throughout the 1980s in spite of her unimpressive growth. Voices who blame the extensive welfare state with its high tax-load for Sweden's below-average long-term growth rate and denounce it as a handicap for future competitiveness are as yet too feeble to have political effect. A more immediate threat to the welfare-cum-efficiency formula is posed by the possible erosion of corporatist wage discipline and the ensuing inflationary pressure.

... But a Common Trend Towards Social 'Dualism' has Emerged in Four of the Five Countries

The comparison of the five country stories reveals one recurrent cause-effect relationship which was not brought out by the comparative tables: economic changes diminished the effectiveness of the old welfare state arrangements even without any budget cuts or other restrictive measures. The reason for this is that a smaller part of the population could earn a 'decent' income (that is, one which is not too far below the national average) by working and that compensatory transfer payments were not sufficiently stepped up to cope with the new needs. In France, Germany and Britain this development towards more widespread poverty within affluent societies became manifest in significantly increased rates of unemployment. In the USA it took the form of growing low-wage employment. Of the five investigated countries, only Sweden was able so far to avoid either kind of incipient 'dualism', if we may attach this simplifying label to the syndrome of new poverty and reduced social security in an otherwise affluent society. As the only country it has been employing an active egalitarian labour market policy geared towards the explicit goal of maintaining high-wage full employment regardless of the economic growth rate.

The common immediate cause of large-scale mass unemployment in France, Germany and Britain was insufficient economic growth to keep up with the growth of average productivity. In the 1970s the United States also suffered a tremendous slow-down of economic growth which was only partly reversed during the mid-1980s. As a consequence, there, too, output growth did not match productivity growth in many branches of the economy, especially in manufacturing, and hence there, too, many jobs were lost. However, unlike in the other countries, the flexibility of the American labour market with regard to wages and working conditions allowed other branches (mostly services) with stagnating or very modestly growing productivity to expand and compensate for those job losses.[1] But it is precisely this compensation which gave rise to the US version of social 'dualism'.

We can only speculate how fare changes in international competition have contributed to the dissolution of the post-war high-growth syndrome, which constituted the economic basis of the modern Western welfare state.[2] Increasing instability in international economic relations is certainly part of the post-1960s crisis syndrome. So are adjustment problems of industries that were once pillars of the expanding Western economies and have since come under increasing pressure from newly emerging competitors. An argument can be made that growing concern for competitiveness in the international market place has an inherent austerity bias and has, thus, weakened the concern for demand maintenance.[3] We must leave it an open question whether international competition is linked causally in this way to the decline of effective welfare statism which we observed in our case studies. What we can safely establish is the immediate importance of slower economic growth.

In the United States and, to a lesser degree, in Britain international competition affected the tendency towards social 'dualism' also in a more directly observable way. In the USA the equivalent of welfare statism was based to a large extent on a specific structure of industrial production because it rested on the power organised labour had in specific industries. By effecting a structural change away from the highly unionised towards much less unionised industries, foreign competition weakened an important element of US welfare statism. This effect persisted well into the period of renewed economic growth in the mid-1980s. In the United Kingdom declining manufacturing competitiveness went along with (and was partly caused by) the expansion of the highly productive petroleum sector. This new kind of incorporation into the international division of labour increased the discrepancy between aggregate output growth and average productivity growth and, thus, exacerbated the employment problem. But these were special conditions, superimposed on the general and more essential problem.

Concern About Economic Performance Prevented Remedial Action

The reappearance of widespread poverty (including the threat of poverty) in the affluent Western countries poses the question, why has this been tolerated? With the governments of President Reagan and of Prime Minister Thatcher the answer is straightforward. Their programmes aimed explicitly at scaling down welfare statism and reinforcing the link between market chances and life perspectives. They ruled out the possibility of keeping in check with appropriate welfare state arrangements the tendency towards social 'dualism'. These governments were disposed to accept less equality and more widespread individual hardship, which were the consequences of their policies. One might even see in this new explicit acceptance of poverty the most significant aspect of welfare state erosion in the two Anglo-Saxon countries.

In France and Germany the position of the various governments reflected less ruthless determination and more helplessness. Rather than attacking the welfare state outright they just failed to adjust to the new situation. As the chance looked very remote that there would be a return in the foreseeable future to the high growth rates of the time before the oil crisis, only significant policy innovations could have dealt effectively with the new social problems. Either very different labour market policies were needed to maintain full high-wage employment in view of the discrepancy between output and productivity growth or transfer payments had to be increased considerably to cover the income deficits experienced by ever larger segments of the unemployed population. But there were powerful coalitions to veto such innovations in France as well as in Germany. Large parts of the middle income strata and those who aspired to represent them politically regarded the tax load (including social security contributions) as close to the limits of acceptability. Additional charges to finance more transfers or Swedish-style public employment would certainly have been extremely unpopular. In this respect, a new social contract would have been needed first to explicitly extend the limits of legitimate redistribution.[4]

But it is not only that the 'haves' refused to give more to the 'have-nots'. In addition there were those who advocated Anglo-Saxon style social deregulation for the good of the economy as a whole. In fact, more redistribution has generally come to be seen as harmful for the national economy, harmful especially in view of foreign competition.

The case studies show that this belief has gained considerable ground in four of the five investigated countries. It put those who were concerned about the welfare state – for altruistic or for egoistic reasons – into a defensive position. Not only would they have had difficulties getting majorities for the cause of higher taxes and social security contributions, increasingly they were impressed themselves by the perceived need to subordinate redistributive goals to the functional requirements of the capitalist economy. Thus, the German Social Democrats as well as, after a while, the French socialists were very careful to give priority to what was generally considered a 'responsible' economic policy. Responsibility in this sense did not allow welfare statism to expand to cope with the increasing number of casualties from the market economy. It rather required benefits to be adjusted downwards with the reduced availability of finance.

The rise of the 'limits-to-redistribution' theme to a widely-held belief has been established as an empirical fact. But to explain it we can only present arguments with a claim to plausibility. To start with: we cannot simply say, that the point has been reached where higher taxes do in fact harm the economy. These Laffer-curve economics cannot explain why, in countries with very different levels of taxation after decades of fiscal expansion further expansion was ruled out more or less simultaneously as economically dysfunctional. And it can explain even less why this dysfunctionality belief was particularly pronounced in the USA with its relatively low level of taxation and least so in Sweden, the country with the highest level.

When there is a general change in what people consider as functional or dysfunctional this must reflect a generalised new experience. Now, we have seen that with regard to competitiveness the five countries had rather diverging experiences. Therefore, on a comparative level, there is not much which would support the notion of a direct causal relationship between new intensities or qualities of international competition and the new scepticism about redistribution. The most obvious new common experience of our five countries has been the stagflation of the 1970s and early 1980s combined with the failure of the once effective Keynesian policy recipes – a very traumatic experience indeed. This was followed by a conspicuous differentiation: in the USA and Britain, who have both applied an outspoken policy of cutting back the government sphere and expanding the private sphere in the economy, economic growth has accelerated again – albeit at the cost of high balance of payments deficits.

In other countries growth has remained very modest. We should assume, therefore, that the rise of the limits-to-redistribution belief is primarily a response to the traumatic slow-down of economic growth. It is in line with this assumption that the basic intellectual argument which backs the new economic belief does not refer to changes in the international economic scene but to the fundamental preconditions of a well-functioning economy.[5]

But, of course, the concern for the performance of the economy combines with a comparative outlook – in some countries more, in others less. For those countries, like West Germany, who see their prosperity linked to their performance in the international market place, many things which concern the good functioning of the economy turn automatically into a matter of competitiveness. For them, the belief, for instance, that a higher tax load weakens entrepreneurship implies the fear of competitive decline if taxes should in fact be increased. The competitive logic also turns the superior performance of other countries into a threat to their own country's market position. In this sense, the neo-liberal revolutions in Britain and the USA with their apparent success in terms of growth and productivity have appeared increasingly as a challenge to other countries, setting new international standards of taxation and deregulation. Maybe one does not love them, but it would be unwise to neglect them! The German public debate on the country's endangered competitiveness as an industrial location has revealed this concern most clearly. In the pro-welfare camp (unions, social democrats and others) the view is unwillingly reflected by a widespread fear that too unrestricted competition, say within the European Community after 1992, might lead to a progressive erosion of welfare statist achievements.

The stagflation induced concern about too much state, thus, took on a competition oriented dimension. But in the light of our comparative evidence, this is a secondary phenomenon. The same eclipse of the post-war high-growth period which diminished the effectiveness of the existing welfare state arrangements and caused the need for additional welfare statism was also at the origin of the spreading concern about 'too much welfare state'. International competition served as a mechanism to propagate this concern. This is in essence the story told by the comparative evidence. The evidence of each case study adds to it country-specific experiences of declining or endangered competitiveness which make for variations on the main common theme.

Sweden has Avoided Social 'Dualism' Without Impairing Economic Performance

Like France and, until a few years before, Britain, Sweden faced mounting problems with external economic performance by the beginning of the 1980s. And as in other countries cost consciousness experienced a boost. Drastic steps indeed were taken to strengthen the country's international competitiveness. But in marked contrast to the other four countries, welfare statism was hardly affected. The system was supplied with sufficient finance to compensate the economic slow-down with an active labour market policy and, thus, prevent the emergence of individual economic hardship on a large scale.

The Swedish experience suggests that competition oriented cost consciousness is not necessarily incompatible with the extension of welfare statism in order to cover the needs which arise out of a protracted economic slow-down. What then are the conditions under which the two become compatible? We might be tempted to say: 'The Swedish governments or the Swedish public simply did not subscribe to the belief that a high tax load is bad for a private enterprise based economy. They just neglected the warnings of the supply-side prophets.' Depending on our own conviction, either we might conclude that the Swedish example shows the inappropriateness of the other countries' tax load worries, or we might want to predict that the Swedes will sooner or later have to pay the bill for their frivolous welfare statism.

But a closer look at the limits-to-redistribution argument itself should stipulate a more differentiated comment. This argument refers to at least two mechanisms of economic dysfunctionality, which ought to be kept apart. One mechanism is the disincentive to economic efforts – to work, to entrepreneurship and to saving – which results from the taxing away of adequate rewards (as well as from diluting economic sanctions through income guarantees). Another mechanism is the profit squeeze which results from excessive labour costs and excessive taxation of capital in a situation of international price competition. The second mechanism demands attention early on, whereas the first one could be neglected for quite a while before negative consequences become visible. Obviously Sweden must somehow have taken care of the problem of price competitiveness, the problem that for the Germans and later also the French constituted an important – though not the exclusive – aspect of the limits to welfare statism. And Sweden has found ways to step up welfare state expenses without triggering the second of the two mechanisms while only selectively testing the first one.

The country has for a long time relied heavily on the taxation of households to finance its expensive welfare state while capital has been taxed rather modestly in international comparison. Thus, by its very design, Swedish welfare statism has entailed less redistribution from capital to labour and more 'solidarity' among wage earners than it has been the case in other countries. The proposed tax reform, which intends to shift the burden radically from direct to indirect taxes, would even go one step further towards securing the non-interference of welfare state solidarity with economic efficiency. Among other things it would respond to the charge that excessive income taxes destroy the motivation to earn money. Still, with all its provisions Sweden could not completely avoid that rising labour costs endangered the country's competitiveness and macroeconomic stability. But then again, unlike France, Sweden was able to carry out a drastic competitive devaluation and make it stick in real terms. That is to say, the Swedish population, most of all Swedish wage earners, had to accept the loss in real income which was the necessary consequence of higher import prices. In particular, they had to abstain from compensating for this loss through higher wages, thus fuelling inflation and eroding the competitive effect of the devaluation. Swedish business, in turn, benefited from higher profit margins on the markets which are exposed to international competition.

The Strategy for Labour: More Solidarity, Less Redistribution

If Sweden showed the way to maintain a highly effective – and therefore expensive – welfare state while at the same time paying tribute to the requirements of a well-functioning and internationally competitive capitalist economy, why did other countries not emulate her example? How could the idea dominate in other countries that the economy would invariably suffer from that additional welfare statism which would be needed to cope with the social consequences of the economic slow-down?

A rather strong argument has been advanced that the maintenance of full employment (the decisive element in the maintenance of effective welfare statism) in some industrialised countries during the 1970s and 1980s was a result of political priorities and not of favourable economic conditions.[6] Taking up this argument, we should consider Sweden as the only one of our five investigated countries where sufficient importance was attributed to the participation of every citizen in the nation's prosperity. Why this is so, must ultimately be explained historically, something which we cannot seriously undertake here.[7] But, of course, we have to note that Sweden had already laid the institutional rails, so to speak, of its active labour market policy well before it was confronted with the slow-down of the 1970s. Sweden just had to stick to them like other countries stuck to their, less effective, systems. Thus, Swedish welfare effectiveness had institutional inertia on its side: it hardly required any political energy. To get the same results as Sweden, other countries would have had to come up with major institutional innovations at a time which was not at all propitious to them. The Swedish welfare state responded under stress in a different way because some time in its history it had acquired an institutional disposition to do so.[8]

We could accept this explanation and resign ourselves to the fact that the stress situation of the 1970s and 1980s was indeed not conducive to innovative welfare state expansion. But things do not stop evolving. If the trend towards social 'dualism', which has originated in the worldwide slow-down of economic growth and which is transmitted and reinforced by international competition, remains unchecked an essentially fluid situation emerges. It is a situation which opens up perspectives of far-reaching changes in the relationship between capital and labour. In such a situation further evolution will depend very much on the strategies deployed by the various collective actors.

The decline of effective welfare statism favours strategies by capital to dislodge labour from the position of relative power it has achieved in the post-war welfare state and to promote a society where weights are distributed quite differently. This is not just a matter of wage levels and the costs of fringe benefits, but of restrictions which labour can impose on the employers' freedom of manoeuvring (from limitations to hiring and firing to co-determination in questions of investment). The key to such a profound redistribution is the labour market. The relative power of labour rests on the control it exerts – via organised and thus disciplined collective action – over the supply of labour power to enterprises. Essential here is the ability to withhold the supply if certain conditions are not met. Permanently insufficient demand for manpower undermines this ability unless welfare state arrangements provide for adequate income maintenance. Therefore, social 'dualism' is not only disadvantageous for that minority of the workforce which is immediately excluded from the prevailing levels of mass prosperity. It provides employers with a means to erode organised labour's monopoly supply of labour power. Moreover, 'dualism' in the form of a split labour market in which the bulk of labour does maintain a position of power *vis-à-vis* capital (the US model in the post-war period) is directly advantageous for capital. The informal sector of the labour market provides a flexible buffer and, thus, makes the rigidity of the formal sector less costly. In this way, 'dualism' could constitute the basis for an armistice between capital and organised labour, an armistice at the expense of the workforce in the informal sector. Nonetheless, it is also the basis for a more far-reaching attack by capital on labour's position, with the objective of informalising as much as possible the formal, rigid segment of the labour market. To settle for a dualist arrangement is, to say the least, dangerous for organised labour.[9]

What is the scope for strategy in this situation? From the point of view of labour it would be decisive to reverse the trend towards social 'dualism' and to re-institute effective welfare statism. The Swedes have shown how it could be done. But as we have seen, in four of our five countries this would require major institutional innovations. Labour would not only have to overcome social inertia. Most important, it would have to break out of the circle of ideological barriers which keeps it paralysed and helpless in face of the new adversities.

It was to be expected that the conservatives in Britain, the USA, Germany and France would propagate the notion of economic sclerosis fostered by too much welfare statism. It may be considered as their natural ideological tendency, fitting the distributive interests of their political constituency. But, unfortunately for the political left, there is more to that notion than pure conservative propaganda. As Lindblom (1977) observed, the distributive interests of capital have a fundamental structural advantage *vis-à-vis* labour because they are associated with the efficiency requirements of the capitalist economy – in reality and not only in ideology. Therefore, economic responsibility forces the political representatives of labour, when in power, to cater more than they would like to the distributive interests of capital. It was economic responsibility that made the German Social Democrats and the French socialists (as well as eventually also the British Labour party) respect – more or less reluctantly – the limits-to-redistribution principle. The Swedish Social Democrats had *de facto* long accepted these limits and taken them into account when constructing their welfare state. But to the Germans as well as to the French and lately the British renouncing more redistribution meant renouncing the further expansion of the welfare state. In political reality welfare statism has been strongly associated with a specific pattern of distribution of the financial burden. This pattern implies that any extension of coverage and benefits would in fact put additional strains on enterprises, which, in turn, falls under the veto of the limits-to-redistribution dogma.

In order to avoid these unwanted effects, the pattern of burden sharing would have to be changed. However, this would constitute a socially regressive act to those whose political outlook is firmly rooted in the struggle-for-redistribution paradigm. Demands for extended welfare state protection have been introduced into the political system by those who see themselves or their political clientele as the beneficiaries in that general ongoing redistribution which is to create or facilitate a just society. Ideologically, these demands have been embedded in the struggle of the working class for its share of the national income. Their fulfilment has been regarded as social conquest. This approach assigns, of course, to the rich in general and to the adversary in the class struggle in particular the role of those who have to give. Their resistance against extended welfare statism then perfectly mirrors the redistributive attitude of the supporters.

This pattern of political cleavages does not leave much room for the cause of extended solidarity among the wage earners. To let the masses pay for additional welfare state programmes does not fit very well as a rallying cry into a political scene which is shaped by the conflict over distribution. As a consequence welfare statism stays trapped in the conflict between containment of public expenditure and excessive redistribution. The socially desirable extension of welfare statism is nailed down on the side of economically dysfunctional redistribution and therefore becomes the victim of supply-side caution. The combination of supply-side caution and welfare state extension, in turn, is opposed simultaneously to further redistribution from top to bottom or from capital to labour and to the containment of public expenditure. As such it links in neither with the conservative nor with the prevailing labour ideology.

These observations do not imply that more solidarity based welfare statism Swedish-style is unfeasible in other countries. After all, Sweden has demonstrated its feasibility. But it should have become clear that a profound political redefinition of the issue would be required. The worldwide slow-down of economic growth and the mediation and propagation of the ensuing adjustment pressure via international competition have marked the limits of traditional welfare statism, which has been embedded to a great extent in class conflict over distribution. Depending on the further evolution of economic growth and of competitive pressure, we might well see a more far-reaching erosion in the future, leading to more pronounced social 'dualism'. The relatively well integrated European countries might slide into American-style disparities. Subsistence oriented income maintenance schemes, as they are favoured by conservative welfare state models, could block off the rise of poverty and, thus, stabilise the emerging system of reinvigorated capitalism. But the position of organised labour would most likely be thoroughly weakened, manpower would become much more a commodity again and the segment of the labour force which enjoys full participation in the nation's general affluence would shrink considerably. Paradoxically, for the reasons given, traditional class based resistance to such a turn of events may prove ineffective. The working class may have to place much more emphasis on its internal solidarity while scaling down its redistributive claims *vis-à-vis* capital. Not an easy task in times of political and economic retreat!

DOES WELFARE STATISM IMPAIR A COUNTRY'S COMPETITIVENESS?

Lack of Economic Discipline brings Welfare Statism in Conflict With Price Competitiveness . . .

Under the combined impact of slower economic growth and extended international competition the core principle of economic citizenship has suffered – as far as the outcome in terms of a secure 'decent' standard of living for everybody is concerned – a significant setback in four of our five investigated countries. We argued that it was not sheer economic necessity which demanded this sacrifice. It was rather the way the issue was projected into the political arena which let welfare state extension appear to be in conflict with economic imperatives in a competitive world. Not least it was the rigidity of established distributive structures which excluded an adequate adjustment of welfare statism from the politically feasible options.

But we also found a generalised perception that there existed an inherent conflict between welfare statism on the one hand and economic performance on the other. Even where established welfare state standards were not seriously questioned, there was a diffuse awareness that an economic price had to be paid for them and that it would be wise not to increase the burden on the economy any further.

What is the comparative evidence on the appropriateness of this perception? To answer this question we may, as a starting and reference point, present for our five countries in a summary fashion the information on competitiveness on which our analysis of chapter 2 is based. This is done in Table 8.3 which, in addition, contains some information that played a role in the case studies. However, we shall not repeat here, with the smaller sample, the search for statistical associations between indicators of competitiveness and welfare statism. It may suffice to recapitulate the basic finding that there is in the 1980s a suggestive, but by no means conclusive negative association between welfare statism and certain indicators of economic performance. But the qualitative information provided by the case studies suggests two additional broad conclusions:

A. In some of our five investigated cases, the costs of welfare state provisions have been an element in what might be called a syndrome of insufficient macroeconomic discipline. This syndrome, in turn, has been a permanent handicap for the countries' performing competitiveness and, hence, a source of external imbalances. In the context of insufficient discipline, welfare state expenses have added to the difficulties, but they cannot be seen as the origin of the problem.

B. The analysis of weaknesses in underlying competitiveness has in all cases pointed to the importance of corporate culture, structure and strategies; of industrial relations; and of the way capital (including human capital) formation is organised. Welfare statist arrangements appeared in this connection rather as a competitive asset.

The findings of Chapter 2 may be seen as a certain weak support for claims that welfare statism constitutes a competitive burden. Conclusion A above underpins this claim but qualifies it at the same time. The most common charge made in the public debate that the welfare state has negative economic consequences is that it makes production too expensive – because of excessive non-wage labour costs or an excessive load of taxes and contributions. But of course, in this simple form the argument cannot be valid. What matters for competitiveness is how national unit costs (which reflect the price *and*

Table 8.3 Some indicators of competitiveness for five industrialised countries

		USA	*Britain*	*France*	*Germany*	*Sweden*
Average balance on current account, as % of GDP/GNP	*1973–79*	*+ 0.07*	*− 1.06*	*+ 0.17*	*+ 1.09*	*− 0.84*
	1980–86	− 1.49	+ 1.19	− 0.63	+ 1.14	− 1.57
	1984–88	**− 3.04**	**− 0.6**	**− 0.22**	**+ 3.32**	**− 0.34**
Growth rate of manufactured exports (% deviation from OECD total)	*1974–80*	*+ 4*	*+ 12*	*+ 4*	*−17*	*− 24*
	1981–86	−80	−118	−60	+13	+ 21
	1985–87	**−54**	**+ 22**	**+16**	**+51**	**+ 23**
Change in % share of world exports of R&D-intensive manufactures	*1970–80*	*− 4.2*	*+ 1.3*	*+ 0.7*	*− 0.4*	*− 0.3*
	1989–84	+ 1.5	− 2.5	− 0.8	− 2.7	− 0.3
Growth of value-added per employed person in manufacturing (% deviation from mean value of 10 OECD countries)	*1973–79*	*−60*	*− 76*	*+62*	*+34*	*− 55*
	1979–85	+14	+ 7	−21	−24	− 5
Growth of value-added per hour worked in manufacturing (% deviation from mean value of 10 OECD countries)	*1973–79*	*−61*	*− 64*	*+47*	*+29*	*− 19*
	1979–85	+ 2	+ 12	+ 1	−11	− 8
Growth of total factor productivity in manufacturing (% deviation from mean value of 10 OECD countries)	*1973–79*	*−76*	*−133*	*+95*	*+79*	*−116*
	1979–85	+23	− 7	−41	−26	+ 18
Ratio of investment over GDP (% deviation from OECD total)	*1973–79*	*−16*	*− 14*	*+ 5*	*− 5*	*− 7*
	1980–85	−14	− 20	0	0	− 9
	1984–87	**−12**	**− 15**	**− 4**	**− 2**	**− 7**
Growth rate of GDP (% deviation from OECD total)	*1973–79*	*− 5*	*− 27*	*+ 1*	*−13*	*− 32*
	1980–86	− 2	− 32	−31	−39	− 27
	1984–88	**+10**	**− 9**	**−39**	**−31**	**− 34**
Growth rate of GDP per capita (% deviation from OECD total)	*1973–79*	*−22*	*+ 8*	*+23*	*+26*	*− 20*
	1980–86	−11	− 17	−32	−11	− 3
	1984–87	**+20**	**− 1**	**−52**	**−16**	**− 24**

Sources: OECD, 1988c and 1989b, GATT, 1988, and Englander & Mittelstädt, 1988.

the productivity of labour and other inputs) compare with foreign ones, and this depends on the exchange rate between the national and foreign currencies. Domestic costs are 'excessive' to the degree they are inadequately converted into international costs by means of the exchange rate. If this is the case the trade balance becomes negative.

All our investigated countries, with the exception of Germany, have had major problems in this respect over a longer period of time. But the underlying macroeconomic patterns were quite different. Britain before Thatcher and France were caught in a vicious circle of inflation and currency depreciation. A faster pace of price increases than in competitor countries (notably Germany) eroded domestic producers' competitiveness in exposed markets. But corrective exchange rate adjustments, which naturally increased the prices of imported goods, gave additional impetus to inflation. The reason was that several groups managed to fend off the deterioration in real incomes which would have been implied in a simple acceptance of the devaluation induced price increases. Under these conditions currency depreciation proved an inappropriate means of reconstituting price competitiveness beyond a temporary respite. Thus, anything which would raise unit costs as expressed in the domestic currency would add to the country's external economic difficulties. A permanent improvement in performing competitiveness would demand some sort of cost discipline. The lack of such discipline was a serious competitive handicap for Britain, France and, at times, Sweden.

Establishing or re-establishing cost discipline is basically a matter of changing the behaviour of relevant economic agents, as 'excessive' price, wage, tax etc. *increases* have to be ruled out. But it implies also an initial correction of cost *levels*. In such a context, a point can be made that non-wage labour costs, social security contributions, environmental requirements or whatever are in fact too high. And it also seems justified to consider, in the context of insufficient cost discipline, additions to any of these cost factors as anti-competitive.

However, it would be utterly distorting to attribute the trade problems of Britain and France to their excessive welfare state burden. The key to both countries' external economic difficulties was the 'system's' inability to establish a pattern of final real income distribution in a non-inflationary way. Spending entitlements of various kinds were (nominally) granted without the corresponding real resources being made available – be it by providing for additional value added or by reducing openly somebody else's entitlements.

Instead, inflation became the way resources were shifted from the weaker to the stronger contenders. And to the degree that the inflationary method of 'discrete' expropriation became established, exchange rate adjustment lost its effectiveness as an instrument of neutralising domestic cost increases in the international market place. At the same time the inflationary culture weakened the original resistance to cost increases. So it would be blurring the facts to blame excessive unit costs (with their share of welfare state burden) for the difficulties in price competitiveness faced by Britain and France. The real culprit was these countries' general deficiency of economic discipline which manifested itself in inflation and which prevented domestic cost levels from being adequately transformed into international ones.

Another pattern of pricing domestic products out of the market with the help of an overvalued national currency was demonstrated by the United States in the 1980s. Here the government spent more than it could finance domestically – be it with its own revenues or be it with money borrowed from the American public. The excessive claim to real product, which resulted from the fact that the government and the private sector together spent much more than they produced, was then met in a non-inflationary way by increasing imports. The mechanism to establish this 'solution' was the influx of foreign capital which was attracted by the high American interest rates (themselves the result of the excess demand of the American state for credits under the conditions of a non-accommodating monetary policy) and which caused the international value of the dollar to rise. Thus, American tradables became less and less competitive, freeing resources for an increasing production of non-tradables. The lack of spending discipline in this case lay with the executive and the legislative branch of the government: military expenditure was increased without sufficient solid finance being provided via increased revenues (on the contrary!) or adequate reductions of non-military outlays. The relative stickiness of welfare state expenditure (though some drastic cuts were indeed made) was part of the US budget deficit syndrome. But at its origin were the 'frivolous' decisions to raise military outlays and reduce taxes at the same time.

Whereas in the context of Reaganomics the deficiency of spending discipline was largely a problem of ideological rigidity and political stalemate in Congress, in France and pre-Thatcher Britain it derived from the uncontrolled behaviour of decentralised economic agents. Regardless of what were the ultimate causes of the inflationary creation of spending entitlements, the problem betrayed both the unwillingness of relevant groups to accept the distributive *status quo* and their ability to revise it at least temporarily. With several attempts to arrive at some voluntary discipline remaining ultimately unsuccessful, attention shifted to the enforcement of discipline. And as far as labour is concerned the freedom from market sanctions has been singled out as a decisive condition of lacking wage discipline. This implies that effective economic security, as it is provided by full employment cum welfare state protection, is conducive to the perpetuation of that inflationary syndrome which in some countries has been hampering performing competitiveness.

The experience of Britain and France, and indirectly also of West Germany, seems to confirm this view. The emergence of lasting mass unemployment, which means a drastic erosion of effective welfare statism, has led in these countries to an improvement of cost discipline. A less accommodating monetary policy has been a major step in bringing about this situation. But a less accommodating exchange rate policy was also part of the story – although price competitiveness was thus sacrificed (temporarily?) on the altar of price stability. Sweden, in turn, offers an example of a consensual restoration of cost discipline without the recourse to drastic economic sanctions. On this basis the government was able in 1982 to restore price competitiveness directly with a major devaluation without giving a new boost to inflation. A highly developed welfare state was an important ingredient of Sweden's success with consensual economic discipline. However, the re-emergence of wage drift during the 1980s indicates that the permanent taming of group egoism without economic sanctions in the background remains a difficult task.

Our findings do not allow, of course, a conclusive evaluation of the disciplinary effectiveness of corporatist consensus formation. But they point to the emergence of a crucial test. During the phase of post-war economic development when near full employment became established as the norm in the advanced capitalist countries, corporatist patterns of consensual policy-making were, in general, conducive to a better economic performance than patterns of more decentralised interest articulation with their high degree of disruptive conflict. But full employment and high welfare state security changed the situation. The decisive issue is no longer 'corporatism versus pluralism'. It is whether consensual discipline in the absence of economic sanctions can match the discipline which is enforced by economic compulsion.[10] Only to the degree and under the conditions that this is the case will fully fledged welfare states (providing full income security) be able to stay price competitive.

... But Productivity and Quality Rather Benefit From the Welfare State

But the competitiveness of a country refers to more than to the selling chances of national producers on exposed markets. It refers to the chance of earning high incomes in these markets ('underlying competitiveness' according to the distinction introduced in Chapter 1). And this brings us to conclusion B above. The USA, the UK and France exhibited serious problems with underlying competitiveness. But nowhere did the analysis of these problems point to the rigidities which some critics associate with excessive welfare statism. On the contrary, it appeared that the most complete welfare states in our sample, that is Sweden and West Germany, were most thoroughly successful in orientating the national economy to high-productivity and high-quality production.

That the relatively smooth co-operation between business and labour has been an important ingredient in their success is confirmed by the corresponding deficits which appeared in the British and the American cases. In fact, inappropriate industrial relations were singled out as a major competitive handicap in both countries. On the one hand, this referred to organisational aspects at the enterprise level and at the level of collective bargaining (rigid job structures, decentralised interest articulation). On the other hand, it referred to the absence of motivational factors which encouraged the integration of labour into their enterprises and their participation in enterprise affairs. Purely contractual relations between the buyer (the enterprise) and the seller of labour services (the employee) were largely recognised as an inferior means of achieving maximum collective performance with regard to productivity, quality and innovation. An essential element of the basic welfare state idea, the granting of membership rights in a collectivity which entitle the individual member to some sort of solidarity by that collectivity, was found badly missing in the typical British and American enterprises. While the dominant response to the mounting difficulties with labour aimed at the restoration of compulsory discipline (unemployment, union-bashing), at the corporate level serious efforts were undertaken to involve the workforce in a more positive way, to capture indeed their 'hearts and minds' (Weisskopf *et al.*, 1983).

Human capital formation appeared as another important advantage of West Germany and Sweden in comparison with the other investigated countries. This is a factor which is directly related to welfare statist organisation: the collective responsibility for the individuals' qualification for the job market was an essential social right but proved at the same time an investment in the country's productive potential. These factors aside, weaknesses in underlying competitiveness had to be attributed predominantly to patterns of entrepreneurial behaviour with practically no bearing on welfare statism.

With the results of our study at hand we are not in a position to offer a definitive judgement on the various hypotheses which have been advanced in the competitiveness debates of our five countries. But the analyses have rendered conspicuously little which would confirm the suspicion – which appears quite defendable on theoretical grounds – that welfare statism impairs a country's underlying competitiveness. They also failed to substantiate any of the suspicions expressed at the end of our survey in Chapter 2 with regard to alternative mechanisms which could establish a nexus between welfare statism and some sort of economic sclerosis. However, in Sweden we can see a certain deliberate decision in favour of a universally accessible high standard of social services at the expense of more commodified output.[11] Real conflicts have shown up, as we have already noted, with regard to performing competitiveness. But they are contingent on a country's inability to establish cost discipline in a consensual way without recourse to economic compulsion.

Notes

1 The Issue

1. The rise of the modern welfare state can, in some respect, be seen as a corollary of the Keynesian 'revolution' of macroeconomic policy, which itself may have reflected the emergence of a particular mode of production. The notion of the 'Fordist' model of capitalist accumulation refers to such a Keynesian welfare state syndrome (see for example Lipietz 1984a). With the political, institutional and technological basis of 'Fordism' eroding or its internal 'contradictions' growing out of control, the welfare state should then also become outdated. For a systematic discussion of the ambivalent relationship between the welfare state and the advanced capitalist economy see for example Abramovitz 1981 and Gough 1979.
2. Rosenbrock's concept of the 'colonisation' of the welfare state (1985) refers to the selective maintenance and expansion of its economically functional aspects.
3. On the perspectives of low-wage competition for high-wage countries see Pfaller 1983 and 1986, and Dauderstädt & Pfaller 1985.
4. The Japanese especially have challenged the other industrialised countries with a series of innovations with regard to firm organisation and firm strategy, each of which outbid the efficiency gains of the preceding one. Libraries can be filled with the pertinent literature. For a very brief overview of strategy innovations see Stalk, Jr. 1988.
5. See also Göran Therborn's chapter on Sweden in this volume.
6. Cf. for example Curzon & Curzon-Price 1979, Krauss 1978 and Scott 1985b.
7. For a more detailed discussion of the effects welfare statism has and could have on the various dimensions of competitiveness see Pfaller 1987 and the literature cited there. Assar Lindbeck has since published a comprehensive account of the dysfunctional economic consequences of the 'advanced' welfare state (Lindbeck 1988).
8. Wolfgang Hager (1981 and 1982) has referred to this civilisation as the 'anti-industrial' society.

2 The Competitivness of Industrialised Welfare States: A Cross-Country Survey

1. See the critical note of Saunders on the comparative studies which have been carried out with the purpose of discovering such a relationship and whose main contribution 'is to dismiss the claims of those who argue that the links between the size of government and economic

performances are straightforward, simple and self-evident' (1986, p. 58). Cf. also Wilensky *et al.* 1985.

2. We use here the social expenditure data published in OECD 1985a, which are available for all advanced capitalist countries from 1970 through 1979, with the exception of France for which data start in 1975. For 1980 and 1981, the last year covered, there are several gaps. In 1988 the OECD filled these gaps for 1980 and provided, in addition, a complete data series for 1985 (OECD 1988b). However, the new data deviate from the earlier ones. While they show for 1980 ratios of social expenditure over GDP which are in general about two percentage points below the ones published earlier, for Belgium, West Germany and the Netherlands the difference is about four percentage points. France, in turn, has in the new series a higher ratio.
3. See for example Cohen *et al.* 1984 on the central importance of manufacturing and the subordinated role of services for an industrial country's competitiveness.
4. Spain, Ireland, Portugal and Greece are not counted here among the "highly" industrialized countries, even though with Spain this exclusion becomes more and more debatable.
5. The various location-bound conditions which determine the productivity potential, so to speak, of a productive venture at a specific location (region, country) are referred to in the concept of the 'industrial fertility' of that location. See on this Kamppeter 1987.

3 The United States

1. Actually, the amount of American net foreign debts varies considerably with the method used to calculate it, with the major difference referring to the true value of US firms' foreign assets.
2. In reality, the 'Fed' deviated considerably from the narrow monetarist prescriptions with regard to money supply in the course of the 1980s. Thus, it reflected the changing relationship between money supply and price level, which contradicted the basic 'law' of the monetarist theory (cf. Friedman 1988). However, in a broader sense monetarist-type discipline was maintained.
3. See for this approach to the US balance of payments Bergsten & Cline 1985 and Lawrence 1984. For a discussion see Friedman 1985.
4. See for example Abernathy *et al.* 1983, Bolling & Bowles 1982, Baumol & McLennan 1985a, Lawrence 1984, Scott & Lodge 1985a, Thurow 1985, Zysman & Tyson 1983 and the reports listed in the Report of the President's Commission on Industrial Competitiveness (1985, pp. 52f.).
5. As Norsworthy & Malmquist (1985, p. 59) state: 'It is not so much the pattern of recent decline in US manufacturing productivity growth that raises concern as the US performance relative to that of manufacturing in other industrialised countries.'
6. See the discussion of productivity convergence in Baumol & McLennan 1985b and in Norton 1986, pp. 28ff.
7. Several of those who point to the competitive challenge stress the extra-economic ambitions of the USA which require a certain com-

petitive superiority (see for example Zysman & Cohen 1983 and Scott 1985a). In fact, there is no *a priori* reason why the mismatch of declining hegemonic capacity and continuing hegemonic obligations, which is sometimes seen as a central cause of American and international economic difficulties, can be better corrected by renouncing obligations than by restoring capacity.

8. This sort of problem can, if it exceeds certain dimensions, pose a challenge which cannot be adequately met by responses on the production side (cf. Pfaller 1986 and Elsenhans 1987).
9. In line with this picture of inferior American productivity in important medium-technology branches is a survey of the European Management Forum which ranks the USA only as number 12 in production techniques (as to be distinguished from product technology, where the US is very strong). See President's Commission on Industrial Competitiveness 1985, Volume II, p. 48.
10. Extremely revealing in this respect is a comparative study of American and Japanese-made air conditioners, by all accounts not a high-technology product (Garvin 1983).
11. As Brooks (1985, p. 334) says: 'The real question is whether what we are seeing is merely the inevitable closing of a gap or whether other countries, particularly in East Asia, are on a trajectory that is about to pass us and leave us in much the situation Britain now finds itself in.'
12. The term has been coined by Chalmers Johnson (1982). The idea is a common theme in the literature on the Japanese 'miracle' (for example Pempel 1982, Vogel 1979, Hofheinz & Calder 1982 and Cumings 1984). It has found entrance into several important analyses of US competitiveness (cf. Cohen *et al.* 1984, Zysman & Cohen 1983 and Scott 1985b).
13. See for example the contributions to the 1980 volume of the *American Economic Review*, Papers and Proceedings. For an overview see E. Wolff 1985.
14. See for example Brooks 1985 for the view that organisational deficiencies go much further than a supposed insufficiency of technological innovation in explaining the evolution of US productivity.
15. Cf. Hatsopoulos 1983, Hatsopoulos & Brooks 1986, Bernhein & Shoven 1986 and Wellons 1985.
16. Cf. Aho & Rosen 1980, The National Commission on Excellence in Education 1983, and Business-Higher Education Forum *et al.* 1986.
17. For the controversial debate on the spin-offs of military R&D see Tirman 1984, Melman 1974, Ramo 1980, Rosenberg 1986 and Schulze 1988.
18. Cf. Thurow 1984, McGarrah 1987 and, for a general discussion of enterprises' orientation towards their work forces, Mahon 1987.
19. See on the evolutionary dynamics of inter-firm configurations Nelson & Winter 1982, pp. 282ff. and 388ff.
20. This view is confirmed in a study, submitted in 1988, by the Industrial Bank of Japan. Into the same direction points the observation that American firms retroceded massively from tradables when the dollar rose in the early 1980s (*Financial Times*, 2 September 1987), whereas

Japanese firms successfully adjusted to the rising Yen after 1985 (Kamppeter 1988b). Cf. also McGarrah's (1987) distinction between profitability and productivity orientation.

21. For an elaborate formulation of this theme, which transcends, of course, the narrow field of industrial relations, see Etzioni 1983. In a more rudimentary form it can be found in various public lamentos on declining American competitiveness, such as Bolling & Bowles 1982 or the 1985 Report of the President's Commission on Industrial Competitiveness.
22. Cf. Piore & Sabel 1984, Yankelovich & Immerwahr 1983, Derber & Schwartz 1983, Hirschhorn 1981 and Kovach 1987.
23. An interesting variant of the 'control-versus-participation' theme has been presented by Lester Thurow (1987a) who has observed that with the surge of modern information technology the number of white-collar workers increased much more than the number of blue-collar workers shrank. He attributes this labour productivity diminishing tendency to the quest for maximum information-based control which is inherent in the American corporate culture with its emphasis on bosses' authority and intra-firm hierarchy.
24. The latter refers to issues like consumer safety and environmental protection. See Bowles *et al.* 1986 on the erosion of the post-war 'capital-citizen accord'.
25. See the evidence reported in Naples 1981.
26. Lester Thurow's point of decreasing white-collar productivity, to which we referred in note 23, links in neatly with this explanatory approach.
27. Reagan had proposed cuts about twice as large as the ones which were eventually enacted. See Mills 1984, p. 113 and, for a general assessment of the political process of budget decision-making, Stockman 1986.
28. An additional advantage of the Reagan budget measures might be seen in the stimulating effect which increased demand for military hardware has on technological innovation, opening up new profitable opportunities to business, and which would not apply if the same amount of money is spent for income support programmes. See in this respect John Miller's (1986) distinction between government expenditure that is conducive to capitalist accumulation and expenditure that is not. See, however, also the debate on the spin-offs of arms-related innovation to which we referred in note 17.
29. See for example the following legislative initiatives: Bill H.R. 2203: 'To improve the competitiveness of the United States in domestic and foreign markets, and for other purposes' of 1983; the High Technology Research and Scientific Education Act of 1985; the Technology Competitiveness Act of 1987; the Economic Competitiveness, International Trade, and Technology Development Act of 1987; the Trade, Employment, and Productivity Act of 1987; and the Education for a Competitive America Act of 1987.
30. We refer to this in more detail in the following section on the automobile industry. For an overview see Kochan & Piore 1984, for a more extensive discussion of the overall transformation of American industrial relations Kochan *et al.* 1987.

31. Cf. Salter *et al.* 1985, p. 200. The theme of non-adjustment to a changed environment is echoed in most analyses dealing with the declining competitiveness of the American car industry. Cf. also Lawrence & Dyer 1983 and Abernathy *et al.* 1983.
32. Cf. Jürgens 1986, p. 44. An additional element of shifting demand were government-imposed regulatory requirements like safety and exhaust standards, which foreign car makers were also better able to meet than the American companies. Cf. Leone 1984 and the comment by Woodrow Eckard.
33. For example, a major disadvantage for American firms was that competition squeezed their profits at a time when they needed a great deal of finance to invest in efficiency increasing machinery and in the development of competitive products.
34. See on this point Wright's (1979) insider account of General Motors.
35. Lawrence & Dyer 1983, p. 43. See also Rothschild 1973, Widick 1976, Abernathy *et al.* 1983, p. 90 and Flaherty 1987, p. 182.
36. In 1970 hourly earnings in the motor vehicle industry were 30 per cent above the American average for private industry production workers. By 1980 the premium had gone up to 55 per cent (Katz 1985, p. 153).
37. Government added very little to the industry's adjustment efforts. Its major sector specific measure was trade policy support to make the Japanese agree on 'voluntary' export restraint. But some claim that this rather slowed down adjustment and speeded up the transfer of Japanese production to the USA and their advance into the upmarket segments. On the regulation front, political resistance ruled out significant relief. But regulations were not further tightened either.
38. Ford seems to have succeeded in the mid-1980s with such a strategy, while General Motors managed to erode with stepwise wage and job reductions the morale of its work force (see *Business Week*, 7 March 1988, *Financial Times*, 23 September 1987, *Wall Street Journal*, 3 March 1987).
39. On the conflict between commitment-creating and union-weakening see Kochan & Piore 1984, Kornbluh 1984 and Katz & Sabel 1985.
40. For a detailed survey of QWL-type reforms in the American automobile industry see Katz 1985.
41. For the underlying conflict between management objectives and workers' aspirations with regard to QWL see Wood 1986 and Kornbluh 1984.
42. On outsourcing as a means to lower costs see Altshuler *et al.* 1984 and Dunn 1987, pp. 246ff.
43. NEC and Fujitsu are among the 12 leading manufacturers of telecommunications equipment.
44. See Barry 1987 for reports on further plant closures and lay-offs.
45. This section relies heavily on the information presented in Bawden & Palmer 1985.
46. For earlier ways of poverty relief see Patterson 1981.
47. For the development of the American welfare state in the 1960s see for example Sundquist 1968, Levitan & Taggart 1976 and Patterson 1981.
48. The complete picture can be found in Bawden & Palmer 1984: Table 6.1, pp. 185–6.

49. See Root 1985 on the relation between public and occupational welfare. For the costs of occupational welfare see Chamber of Commerce of the United States 1981.
50. Cf. AFL-CIO 1984 and 1986 and Harrington 1988.
51. 'Workfare' has become one of the new buzz-words in this debate. A good account of the specific problems of getting the hard-to-employ into the labour market can be found in the Work and Welfare Hearing 1987. For a polemic landmark of the public debate see Murray 1984.
52. Cf. AFL-CIO 1986, Council on International and Public Affairs 1986, Loveman & Tilly 1988, Bluestone & Harrison 1986 and 1987 (in response to intense criticisms of their 1986 paper, like for example the one of Kosters & Ross 1987).
53. See Gross 1987 for a critique of the official concept of unemployment.
54. Bluestone & Harrison 1986. In this context it seems symptomatic that the USA among other larger OECD countries had an exceptional decrease in the earnings ratio of unskilled to skilled manual occupations (OECD 1987a, 82f.)
55. This judgement is confirmed by many of the statements in the Senate Hearing on Work and Welfare of 1987, the Joint Economic Committee Hearing 'War on Poverty – Victory or Defeat?' (US Congress 1985a) and the House Hearing on Work and Poverty (US Congress 1986a). It conforms also to the conclusion reached by Moon & Sawhill (1984) in their analysis of the change in income distribution. Cf. also Kuttner 1984, Levitan & Shapiro 1987 and Harrington 1988.
56. As Bawden & Palmer (1984, p. 195) point out, poverty would have been less, if the demographic composition of the population had not changed. Instead, the number of persons living in circumstances which are especially conducive to poverty (families headed by single mothers) increased significantly. On the redistributive effectiveness of welfare state policies in the USA see also Reynolds & Smolensky 1977.
57. Cf. Auletta 1982, Levy 1987, pp. 209ff., Sawhill 1988a and 1988b and Harrington 1984.
58. Frank Levy (1987) develops a strong argument that much of what has been described as the 'pauperisation' of parts of the American working class is basically a transitory phenomenon, owed to the coincidence of profound structural change, the prolonged economic stagnation and adverse demographics (baby-boomers entering the job market). His analysis stipulates confidence in a rapid normalisation (which does not mean absence of any serious problems). Maybe he will be right. But if so then for one of two reasons: (A) Prolonged high economic growth combined with favourable demographics make labour a scarce commodity again all over the economy, so that the lack of protection against economic adversity simply does not matter. (B) Welfare statist arrangements are extended (again) so that in times of economic adversity wage dependent people are less immediately exposed to the forces of supply and demand on a free labour market.
59. Cf. Harrington 1988. On the decline of union power see also Kassalow 1984, Barbash 1984, Bluestone & Harrison 1982 and Kochan & Piore 1984.

60. Cf. for example Bowles *et al.* 1985. In the wider political arena, there are some dispersed proposals for fundamental reform: for instance, the Hayes-Conyers 'Income and Jobs Action Act' of 1984 or the 1984–85 pastoral letter of the Catholic Bishops of America on Catholic Social Teaching and the US Economy. Cf. also Gross 1987.
61. On the other hand, the so-called 'bread-and-butter unionism' of the post-war United States can be seen as a *consequence* of the thorough defeat the American labour movement had suffered before it got co-opted – from above – into the political project of the New Deal. Out of its own force it had only achieved limited sectoral successes.

4 The United Kingdom

1. A detailed sectoral analysis has corroborated this picture for British manufacturing, in contrast to agriculture and construction where it found the UK had comparable productivity levels to the US (Smith *et al.* 1982).
2. This is supported by case studies of individual industries and firms in Prais 1983; see also Manison 1978; House of Lords 1985, p. 24.
3. From 57 per cent to 28 per cent (Patel & Pavitt 1987, p. 72).
4. They include:
   - the major political parties;
   - the Confederation of British Industry (CBI), the Bank of England and the Trades Union Congress (TUC);
   - research and proselytising organisations such as, on the political Right the Institute of Economic Affairs, the Adam Smith Institute and the Centre for Policy Studies; on the Left the Labour Research Department and the (post-Keynesian) Cambridge Political Economy Group; and in the political centre the Policy Studies Institute, the Tawney Society, the 'Clare' group, the Institute for Fiscal Studies and the Employment Institute;
   - influential intellectuals (such as Friedrich Hayek), newspapers and journalists (such as Samuel Brittan and Peter Jay).

   Much useful material is extracted in the two volumes edited by Coates & Hillard (1986, 1987).

   The House of Lords Select Committee on Overseas Trade (1985) attracted a considerable volume of written and oral evidence which I shall also draw on.
5. Joseph 1978; also Hoskyns, Institute of Directors and Lawson in Coates & Hillard 1986 and 1987.
6. Joseph 1979, 103; Hayek 1984; *The Times*, 13 November 1979.
7. Holland 1975. Evidence of the Association of Scientific, Technical and Managerial Staff to the House of Lords Committee (1985). Whilst it has been disputed that this alone would lead to de-industrialisation or declining competitiveness, in combination with other factors this can generate a cumulative spiral of downward decline (Currie & Smith 1981). Also Beynon 1984.
8. Hudson Report 1975; Ingham 1984; Leys 1986.

9. See the Hudson Report 1975, Nairn 1983, Barnett 1986, Middlemas 1986, Anderson 1987; and the analyses of Sampson, Pollard and Blank, extracted in Coates & Hillard 1986 and 1987.
10. The view of many groups giving evidence to the House of Lords Select Committee, including the Confederation of British Industry and the London Chamber of Commerce. In an innovative study Posner (1978) found agreement amongst economists from a wide variety of different schools of thought that two crucial mistakes of earlier years had been the failure of the Labour government to devalue sterling in 1964 or 1966, and the high value of sterling set by the Heath government in 1971.
11. See the conclusion of this chapter for more detailed analysis and sources.
12. Fores & Glover 1978; Williams *et al.* 1983.
13. Rowthorn 1983. Until very recently, too, British membership of the EEC was accused of contributing to de-industrialisation, unemployment and the deteriorating manufacturing trade balance since 1973, especially by the Labour Party and the trades unions.
14. This points the finger at systematic policy mistakes, poor industrial relations and political polarisation itself. It has generated novel policy proposals which combine Keynesian demand-side policies with new Right supply-side policies (for example see Matthews & Sargent 1983).
15. OECD 1986b; Moseley 1984 – though see Begg 1987.
16. OECD 1988d, p. 65, see also Matthews & Minford 1987.
17. On the other hand, if the government had been more successful in attaining its public expenditure targets, the recession would have been much deeper than it turned out to be.
18. Steel & Heald 1985; Cable 1986; Kay & Thompson 1987; *The Economist*, 18 July 1987.
19. OECD 1985c, p. 27; Matthews & Minford 1987. On the other hand others argue that collective bargaining may reduce labour turn-over, improve morale and above all build up a consensus over wage increases, and thus that unions have a positive role to play in combining better efficiency with wage moderation (Tomlinson 1986).
20. Foreman-Peck & Manning 1986; OECD 1985c; *The Economist*, 14 February 1987, p. 62.
21. Yet, according to Layard & Nickell (1985), benefit replacement rates contributed only 0.4 of the 11.8 percentage point rise in male unemployment between 1956 and 1983. The contributions of other variables were as follows:

Employers' labour taxes	+1.0
Unions	+2.3
Demand factors	+6.4
Other variables	+0.8

22. See also Parry, 1986, section 2; Levitt & Joyce 1987; Atkinson *et al.* 1987.
23. As the aged move up the income scale and their place is taken by unemployed families. Thus the proportion of children in the lowest quintile has increased from 5.6 per cent in 1979 to 12.5 per cent in 1985 (O'Higgins 1987, Table 4.3).

24. Piachaud 1987, p. 25; O'Higgins 1985, Table 9.
25. For example Maynard, an economist generally sympathetic to the government, contends that 'whilst there was a strong case for reducing marginal tax rates, the case for reducing average tax rates was good deal less pressing' (1988, p. 172).
26. The research programme initiated by S. J. Prais at the National Institute for Economic and Social Research is a major source for this analysis. See for example Prais & Wagner 1985, 1988; Steedman 1988.
27. Steedman & Wagner 1987; Finegold & Soskice 1988; Worswick 1985.

6 The Federal Republic of Germany

1. Although the trade balance of the Federal Republic remained positive throughout the entire post-war period, the current account sometimes exhibited smaller deficits. But from 1979 to 1981 the deficits reached very high levels, peaking in 1980 at about 28.5 billion D-mark (at the time about 15.7 US dollars). Prior to 1980 no advanced capitalist country in the world had ever faced such a huge deficit.
2. A benchmark of the political debate was the discussion in the Bundestag in 1981, with the government presenting an elaborated reply to an inquiry by Parliament. See also Deutsche Bundesbank 1983, pp. 347–360 or Wetter *et al.* 1984.
3. Genscher 1984, p. 3. For the technology-oriented mercantilistic sentiment, which characterised a large part of public thinking at the time, see also Grewlich 1981 and 1985 and Rhein 1981.
4. See on the issue of Germany's technological competitiveness also Bundesminister für Wirtschaft 1984.
5. See Chapter 1 of this book, pp. 6ff.
6. See for example ifo-Schnelldienst 30/88, Franz Thoma in *Süddeutsche Zeitung*, 16–17 June 1988, Lagebericht Wirtschaft LW 1/1988 of the Westdeutsche Landesbank, and Franz-Josef Strauß at the Handelsblatt-Konjunkturforum 1988 in Hannover (reported in *Handelsblatt*, 21 April 1988).
7. See for example Boss 1988 and Leibfritz & Parsche 1988. The notion that there is an international competition of tax systems had, by the mid-1980s, become a dominant theme in the German discussion of fiscal reform. See for example the contributions of W. Leibfritz and R. Kurz to a symposium of the German economic research institutes in May 1986 in Bonn (reported in ifo-Schnelldienst 18/1986).
8. According to one estimate, the rentability of real capital throughout the whole West German economy was around 11 per cent in the years 1965–1970, around 6 per cent during 1971–1975, but only about 3 per cent during 1984–1986 (Dicke & Trapp 1987, pp. 56–57).
9. Westdeutsche Landesbank: Lagebericht Wirtschaft 1/1988, p. 15 and Bundesminister für Wirtschaft: BMWi Tagesnachrichten Nr. 9275 (9 August 1988).
10. Klaus Murmann in an interview with *Die Zeit* (15 July 1988).

11. In fact, part of the international financial press portrayed the Federal Republic as a highly sclerotic, immobile society where all the essential conditions of economic vitality and performance, as the neo-conservative creed would have them, are disregarded in the most blatant way (see for example two series of articles in the *Financial Times* in November 1987 and again in August 1988 or the *Wall Street Journal* of 31 May, 1988). There was also some German sponsored advertising against the location West Germany (as, for instance, by Deutsches Industrie Forum in *The Times* in June 1988; see also *Blick durch die Wirtschaft*, 24 March 1988: 'Direkt investitionen sind die Antwort' and *Süddeutsche Zeitung*, 29 June 1988, 'Thema des Tages').
12. For this theoretical perspective on locational factors and their interaction with enterprises see McDermott & Taylor 1982.
13. On the German part in the increasing global imbalances of the 1980s see Kamppeter 1988a.
14. In the mean time, one-sided growth of export demand has been providing a selective stimulus to investment which has increased the bias towards tradables in the country's production structure (cf. DIW 1988).
15. Cf. Riese 1978 on export-led growth in the Federal Republic of Germany.
16. Households got a much more substantial direct tax relief, but they were confronted with higher indirect taxes. For a description and evaluation of the 1987 tax reform see for example ifo-Schnelldienst 16–17/1987.
17. See on this whole flexibilisation syndrome Mückenberger 1985 and 1986 and Möller 1988.
18. See for example Dicke & Trapp 1987, p. 59, or the foreign press articles cited in note 11.
19. The bulk of other public R&D finance was actually devoted to the solution of prioritarian societal problems: energy supply, environmental conservation, public transport and defence (cf. ifo-Schnelldienst 26–27/1986).
20. In fact, many in the branch consider over-engineering a traditional weakness of German car manufacturers *vis-à-vis* the Japanese competition. The German industry, in turn, reckoned with an increasing consumer preference for high-performance vehicles towards the end of the 1980s and the time thereafter (cf. *Financial Times*, 26 March 1986).
21. This section draws heavily on the information provided by Alber 1986, Schmähl *et al.* 1986 and Lampert 1985.
22. See Lampert 1985, pp. 100f. for a table containing all the relevant laws between 1948 and 1985.
23. Douglas Webber's case study of German health reform efforts (Webber 1988) shows in an exemplary fashion how multiple vetos have been forestalling any major change in the corporatist German system of interest articulation and representation.
24. Cf. Scharpf 1988 on the following list of alternative options. See also Eichner & Richter 1989, pp. 98ff.

8 Welfare Statism and International Competition: The Lesson of the Case Studies

1. This is not to deny that some service branches with fast advancing productivity (for example financial services) grew, too. But their growth does not account for the bulk of the new jobs which neutralised the job shedding in manufacturing. Put differently, the sector with non-stagnating productivity, be it manufacturing or be it services, did, as a whole, not grow fast enough to maintain employment rates.
2. See for example Anell 1987 for a 'syndrome' approach to the explanation of high post-war economic growth.
3. Such an argument is presented by Hager (1987).
4. This is forcefully argued by Rosanvallon (1981).
5. Of course, the relationship between collective experiences and generalised beliefs is not a direct one. The formation of new beliefs passes through the filters of already existing ideological predispositions and of structural conduciveness or aversion (Cf. Wilensky *et al* 1986 and, on the changing ideological predisposition to corrective state intervention in the economy, Friedman & Friedman 1989).
6. Cf. Therborn 1986, M. Schmidt 1987 and Brown & King 1988.
7. See on this for example Therborn 1986, pp. 101ff. For a general discussion of welfare state roots in comparative perspective see Wilensky *et al.* 1986.
8. This explanation corresponds to Göran Therborn's thesis (1986), that institutionalised commitment to full employment made the decisive difference, and not for example neo-corporatist ways of policy-making, as Manfred Schmidt (1982 and 1987) would have it.
9. For a more elaborate exposition of the relationship between social dualism, alternative welfare state concepts and classist strategies see Myles 1988.
10. Cf. Tarantelli 1986. The question links in with the debate on the effect of unemployment on the productive performance of labour, as it has been advanced, in particular, by neo-Marxian political economists (cf. Weisskopf 1986 and the literature cited there).
11. This observation is in line with Cameron's (1978 and 1985) generalised finding on the trade-off between increased tax-based redistribution and a dwindling availability of resources for capital accumulation.

Bibliography

AARON, H. J. (1982) *Economic Effects of Social Security* (Washington: Brookings).

ÅBERG, R. (1984) 'Market-independent income distribution: Efficiency and legitimacy', in J. Goldthorpe (ed.), *Order and Conflict in Contemporary Capitalism* (Oxford: Clarendon Press).

ABERNATHY, W. J., CLARK, K. B. and KANTROW, A. M. (1983) *Industrial Renaissance: Producing a Competitive Future for America* (New York, Basic Books).

ABRAMOVITZ, M. (1981) 'Welfare quandaries and productivity concerns', *American Economic Review*, 71 (March).

ADAMY, W. (1988) 'Deregulierung des Arbeitsmarktes. Zwischenbilanz des Beschäftigungsförderungsgesetzes', *WSI-Mitteilungen* 8/88.

AFL-CIO, Industrial Union Department (1984) *Deindustrialisation and the Two-tier Society. Challenges for an Industrial Policy* (Washington).

AFL-CIO, Industrial Union Department (1986) *The Polarization of America. The Loss of Good Jobs, Falling Incomes and Rising Inequality* (Washington).

AHO, M. and ROSEN, H. (1980) *Trends in Technology-intensive Trade: With Special Reference to US Competitiveness* (Washington, Bureau of International Labor Affairs, US Depertment of Labor) (mimeo).

ALBER, J. (1986) 'Germany', in P. Flora (ed.) *Growth to Limits: Western European Welfare States since World War II*, vol. 2: Germany, United Kingdom, Ireland, Italy (Berlin: De Gruyter).

ALTSHULER, A., ANDERSON, M., JONES, D., ROOS, D. and WOMACK, J. (1984) *The Future of the Automobile. The Report of MIT's International Automobile Programme* (Cambridge, MA: MIT Press).

ANDERSON, P. (1987) 'The figures of descent', *New Left Review*, 161.

ANELL, L. (1987) 'The breakdown of the postwar boom', *The Annals*, 492 (July).

ASKLING, L. (1982) Såvanns väljarna', *Tiden*, 7.

ATKINSON, A., HILLS, J. and LE GRAND, J. (1987) 'The welfare state', in R. Dornbusch and R. Layard (eds), *The performance of the British Economy* (Oxford: Oxford University Press).

AULETTA, K. (1982) *The Underclass* (New York: Random House).

BACON, R. and ELTIS, W. (1978) *Britain's Economic Problem: Too Few Producers* (London: Macmillan).

BARBASH, J. (1984) *The Elements of Industrial Relations* (Madison, Wisc.: University of Wisconsin Press).

BARNETT, C. (1986) *Audit of war* (London: Macmillan).

BARRY, J. J. (1987) *Testimony Before the Hearing of the Subcommittee on Telecommunications and Finance of the Committee on Energy and Commerce: U.S. House of Representatives, 10 March 1987* (Washington: US Government Printing Office).

BAUCHET, P. (1986) *Le plan dans l'économie francaise* (Paris: Fondation Nationale des Sciences Politiques).

BAUMOL, W. J. and McLENNAN, K. (eds) (1985a) *Productivity Growth and US Competitiveness* (New York: Oxford University Press).

BAUMOL, W. J. and McLENNAN, K. (1985b) 'US productivity performance and its implications', in W. J. Baumol and K. McLennan (eds), *Productivity Growth and US Competitiveness* (New York: Oxford University Press).

BAWDEN, D. L. and PALMER, J. L. (1984) 'Social policy: challenging the welfare state', in J. L. Palmer and I. V. Sawhill (eds), *The Reagan Record. An Assessment of America's Changing Domestic Priorities* (Cambridge, MA: Ballinger).

BEGG, D. (1987) 'Fiscal policy', in R. Dornbusch and R. Layard (eds), *The Performance of the British Economy* (Oxford: Oxford University Press).

BENNETT, D. and SHARPE, K. (1979) 'Transnational Corporations and the Political Economy of Export Promotion: the Case of the Mexican Automobile Industry', *International Organisation*, 33 (2) (Spring).

BERGMAN, Å. (1987) *Smeden såterkomst* (Stockholm: Tiden).

BERGSTEN, C. F. (1986) 'Gearing up world growth', *Economic Impact*, 56.

BERGSTEN, C. F. and CLINE, W. R. (1986) *The United States–Japan Economic Problem* (Washington: Institute for International Economics) (*Policy Analyses in International Economics*, 13).

BERGSTRÖM, H. (1987) *Rivstart?* (Stockholm: Tiden).

BERNHEIM, D. and SHOVEN, J. (1986) *Taxation and the Cost of Capital: An International Comparison*, paper presented to the American Council for Capital Formation.

BEYNON, H. (1984) *Working for Ford* (Harmondsworth: Penguin) 2nd edn.

BILSTATISTIK, various years, *Bilismen i Sverige* (Stockholm).

BLADES, D. and ROBERTS, D. (1987) 'A note on the new OECD benchmark purchasing power parities for 1985', *OECD Economic Studies*, 9.

BLANK, S. (1977) 'Britain: the politics of foreign economic policy, the domestic economy, and the problem of pluralistic stagnation', *International Organisation*, 31 (4) (Autumn).

BLUESTONE, B. and HARRISON, B. (1982) *The Deindustrialisation of America. Plant Closings, Community Abandonment and the Dismantling of Basic Industry* (New York: Basic Books).

BLUESTONE, B. and HARRISON, B. (1986) 'The great American job machine: The proliferation of low-wage employment in the US economy', a study prepared for the Joint Economic Committee, Washington.

BLUESTONE, B. and HARRISON, B (1987) 'The growth of low-wage employment 1963–1986', paper presented to the American Economics Association annual meeting in Chicago (28–30 December 1987).

BOLLING, R and BOWLES, J. (1982) *America's Competitive Edge. How to Get Our Country Moving Again* (New York: McGraw-Hill).

BOSS, A; (1988) *Unternehmensbesteuerung und Standortqualität – ein internationaler Vergleich* (Kiel: Institut für Weltwirtschaft an der Universität Kiel) (Kieler Diskussionsbeiträge, 145/146).

BOSTON CONSULTING GROUP (1978) *A Framework for Swedish Industrial Policy* (Stockholm: Industridepartementet).

BOSWORTH, B. and RIVLIN, A. (eds) (1987) *The Swedish Economy* (Washington: Brookings).

BOWLES, S., GORDON, D. and WEISSKOPF, T. E. (1985), *Beyond the Wasteland. A Democratic Alternative to Economic Decline* (London: Verso).

BOWLES, S., GORDON, D. and WEISSKOPF, T. E. (1986) 'Power and profits: The social structure of accumulation and the profitability of the postwar US economy', *Review of Radical Political Economics*, 18 (1/2) (Spring/Summer).

BRITTAN, S. (1977) *The Economic Consequences of Democracy* (London: Temple Smith).

BROOKS, H. (1985) 'Technology as a factor', in B. R. Scott and G. C. Lodge (eds), *US Competitiveness in the World Economy* (Cambridge, MA: Harvard Business School Press).

BROWN, A. and KING, D. S. (1988) 'Economic change and labour market policy: corporatist and dualist tendencies in Britain and Sweden', *West European Politics*, 11 (3) (July).

BUDD, A., SOLOW, A and VON WEIZSÄCKER, C. (1987) 'The conservative revolution: a roundtable discussion' *Economic Policy* (October).

BUNDESANSTALT FÜR ARBEIT (various issues) *Amtliche Nachrichten.*

DER BUNDESMINISTER FÜR WIRTSCHAFT (1981) *Wirtschaftspolitik bei defizitärer Leistungsbilanz*, Gutachten des wissenschaftlichen Beirats beim Bundesministerium für Wirtschaft (Bonn) (Studienreihe 31).

DER BUNDESMINISTER FÜR WIRTSCHAFT (1984) *Hochtechnologien und internationale Wettbewerbsfähigkeit der deutschen Wirtschaft* (Bonn) (Dokumentation 263).

BUNDESMINISTERIUM FÜR FINANZEN (1980) *Öffentliche Haushalte im internationalen Vergleich* (Bonn) (BMF Informationsdienst zur Finanzpolitik des Auslands, 2/1980).

BUNTE, R. and JÖRBERG, L. (1977) *Historia i siffror* (Lund: Liber).

BUSINESS–HIGHER EDUCATION FORUM, NORTHEAST-MIDWEST CONGRESSIONAL COALITION AND CONGRESSIONAL CLEARINGHOUSE ON THE FUTURE (1986) *An Action Agenda for American Competitiveness* (Washington).

CABLE, J. R. (1986) 'Industry', in M. Artis (ed.), *The UK Economy* (London: Weidenfeld and Nicolson) 11th edn.

CALMFORS, L. and DRIFFILL, J. (1988) 'Centralisation of wage bargaining', *Economic Policy* (April).

CAMERON, D. R. (1978) 'The expansion of the public economy: a comparative analysis', *American Political Science Review*, 72 (4) (December).

CAMERON, D. R. (1982) 'On the limits of the public economy', *The Annals*, 459.

CAMERON, D. R. (1985) 'Public expenditure and economic performance in international perspective', in R. Klein and M. O'Higgins (eds), *The Future of Welfare* (Oxford: Blackwell).

CAVES, R. E. (1980) 'Productivity differences among industries', in R.

Caves and L. Krause (eds), *Britain's Economic Performance* (Washington: Brookings).
CAVES, R. and ASSOCIATES (eds) (1968) *Britain's Economic Prospects* (Washington: Brookings).
CAVES, R. and KRAUSE, L. (1980) *Britain's Economic Performance* (Washington: Brookings).
CENTER FOR NATIONAL POLICY (1987) *Work and Welfare: The Case for New Directions in National Policy* (Washington) (Alternatives for the 1980s, 22).
CENTER ON BUDGET AND POLICY PRIORITIES (1987a) *1986 Poverty Tables and Graphs: A Collection of Time Series Data on Poverty and Income Distribution* (Washington).
CENTER ON BUDGET AND POLICY PRIORITIES (1987b) *Unemployment Insurance Coverage in October is Lowest Recorded in Program's History* (Washington).
CENTRAL STATISTICAL OFFICE (1987) *Social trends* 17 (London: HMSO).
CHAIGNEAU, Y. (1981) 'Work and society in the 1980s', in *The Welfare State in Crisis* (Paris: OECD).
CHAMBER OF COMMERCE OF THE UNITED STATES (1981) *Employee Benefits 1980* (Washington).
CHASSARD, P. and CONCIALDI, P. (1989) *Les revenus en France* (Paris: La Découverte).
COATES, D. and HILLARD, J. (eds) (1986) *The Economic Decline of Modern Britain* (Brighton; New York: Harvester-Wheatsheaf).
COATES, D. and HILLARD, J. (eds) (1987) *The Economic Revival of Modern Britain* (Aldershot: Edward Elgar).
COHEN, S., TEECE, D., TYSON, L. and ZYSMAN, J. (1984) *Competitiveness* (Berkeley, CA: Berkeley Roundtable on International Economy (BRIE), University of California at Berkeley).
COMMISARIAT GÉNÉRAL DU PLAN (1985) *Les industries de la télecommunication*, Rapport du commisariat Général du Plan (Paris).
COMMISARIAT GÉNÉRAL DU PLAN (1987a) *La situation de l'économie française* (Paris: La Documentation Française).
COMMISARIAT GÉNÉRAL DU PLAN (1987b) *Prospectives 2005* (Paris: Economica).
COMMISSION NATIONALE DE L'INDUSTRIE (1984) *Rapport sur l'industrie automobile française* (Paris: CGP).
COUNCIL ON INTERNATIONAL AND PUBLIC AFFAIRS (1986) *The Underbelly of the US Economy: Joblessness and Pauperization of Work in America* (New York).
CUMINGS, B. (1984) 'The origins and development of the Northeast Asian political economy: industrial sectors, product cycles, and political consequences', *International Organisation*, 38 (1) (Winter).
CUNEO, P. and ZAKIA, B. (1987) 'L'effritement des échanges industriels', *Economie et Statistiques*, 205 (décembre).
CURRIE, D. and SMITH, R. (1981) 'Economic trends and crisis in the UK economy', in D. Currie and R. Smith (eds), *Socialist Economic Review 1981* (London: Merlin).

CURZON, G. and CURZON-PRICE, V. (1979) 'The Undermining of the world trade order', *Ordo*, 30.

CUSACK, T., NOTERMANS, T. and REIN, M. (1987) *Political–Economic Aspects of Public Employment* (Berlin: WZB).

DANG NGUYEN (1986) 'Telecommunications: a challenge to the old order', in M. Sharp (ed.), *Europe and the New Technologies* Ithaca NY: Cornell University Press).

DANZIGER, S. and GOTTSCHALK, P. (1986) 'Families with children have fared worst', *Challenge* (March–April).

DAUDERSTÄDT, M. (1983) *Social Consensus and International Competition. A German View* (Bonn: Friedrich-Ebert-Stiftung) (Analysis and information series).

DAUDERSTÄDT, M. (1986) 'Internationale Konkurrenz und Wohlfahrtsstaat. Überlegungen am Beispiel Portugal', *Konjunkturpolitik*, 32 (6).

DAUDERSTÄDT, M. and PFALLER, A. (1985) *The New Zero-sum World. International Competition and Global Economic Growth* (Bonn: Friedrich-Ebert-Stiftung) (Analysis and information series).

DEBONNEUIL, M. and DELATTRE, M. (1987a) 'Investissements et adaptation: les ressorts de la compétitivité-volume', *Economie et Statistiques*, 203 (octobre).

DEBONNEUIL, M. and DELATTRE, M. (1987b) 'La compétitivité prix n'explique pas les pertes tendancielles de parts de marché', *Economie et Statistique*, 203 (octobre).

DENISON, E. F. (1979) *Accounting for Slower Economic Growth. The United States in the 1970s* (Washington: Brookings).

DENISON, E. F. (1980) 'The contribution of capital to economic growth', *American Economic Review – Papers and Proceedings*, 70 (2) (May).

DERBER, C. and SCHWARTZ, W. (1983) 'Toward a theory of worker participation', *Sociological Inquiry*, 53 (1) (Winter).

DEUTSCHE BUNDESBANK (1983) *Geschäftsbericht für das Jahr 1983* (Frankfurt).

DEUTSCHES INSTITUT FÜR WIRTSCHAFTSFORSCHUNG (DIW) (1983) *Erhöhter Handlungsbedarf im Strukturwandel. Analyse der strukturellen Entwicklung der deutschen Wirtschaft. Strukturberichterstattung 1983* (Berlin: Duncker & Humblot) (DIW-Beiträge zur Strukturforschung, 79).

DEUTSCHES INSTITUT FÜR WIRTSCHAFTFORSCHUNG (DIW) (1986) 'Ausgabenanstieg bei sozialen Leistungen stark gebremst', *Wochenbericht*, 22/86.

DEUTSCHES INSTITUT FÜR WIRTSCHAFTSFORSCHUNG (DIW) (1988) *Exportgetriebener Strukturwandel bei schwachem Wachstum. Strukturberichterstattung 1987* (Berlin) (DIW-Beiträge zur Strukturforschung, 103).

DEVINE, P. LEE, N. JONES, R. M. and TYSON, W. G. (1986) *An Introduction to Industrial Economics* (London; Boston: Allen & Unwin) (4th edn.).

DICKE, H. and TRAPP, P. (1987) 'Zur Rentabilität der Investitionen in der Bundesrepublik Deutschland,' *Die Weltwirtschaft* 1987, 2.

DONGES, J. B., SCHMIDT, K.-D., DICKE, H. *et al.* (1988) *Mehr*

Strukturwandel für Wachstum und Beschäftigung. Die deutsche Wirtschaft im Anpassungsstau (Tübingen: J. C. B. Mohr) (Kieler Studien, 216).
DUNN, J. A. Jr. (1987) 'Automobiles in international trade: regime change or persistance?', *International Organisation*, 41 (2) (Spring).
DURAND, M. and GIORNO, C. (1987) 'Indicators of international competitiveness: Conceptual aspects and evaluation', *OECD Economic Studies*, 9.
THE ECONOMIST (1985) 'A survey of the world's motor industry' (2 March).
THE ECONOMIST (1988) 'Company brief: Rover group' (16 January).
THE ECONOMIST (1989) 'The end of the beginning: a survey of business in Britain: (20 May).
EICHNER, H. and RICHTER, S. (1989) *Bedrohung für Millionen. Mit der Arbeitslosigkeit ins nächste Jahrtausend* (Bonn: Dietz Nachf.).
EISNER, R. (1980) 'Total income, total investment, and growth', *American Economic Review – Papers and Proceedings*, 70 (2) (May).
ELSENHANS, H. (1987) 'Absorbing global surplus labor', *The Annals*, 492 (July).
ELVANDER, N. (1988) *Den svenska modellen* (Stockholm: Publica).
ENGLANDER, S. and MITTELSTÄDT, A. (1988) 'Total factor productivity: macroeconomic and structural aspects of the slow-down', *OECD Economic Studies*, 10 (Spring).
ERDMANN, G. (1957) *Die Entwicklung der deutschen Sozialgesetzgebung* (Göttingen; Berlin; Frankfurt: Musterschmidt-Verlag).
ERGAS, H. (1984) *Why do some countries innovate more than others?* (Brussels: Centre for European Policy Studies).
ERIXON, L. (1982) 'Varför har Sveriges industri klarat krisen sämre?, *Skandinaviska Enskilda Bankens Kvartalstidskrift*, 4.
ERIXON, L. (1987) *Profitability in Swedish Manufacturing* (Stockholm: Almqvist and Wiksell).
ERIXON, L. and FRASER, N. (1984) 'Tränger den offentliga sektorn ut den privata?', *Häften för kritiska studier*, 3–4.
ETZIONI, A. (1983) *An Immodest Agenda: Rebuilding America Before the Twenty-first Century* (New York: New Press).
EUROPEAN MANAGEMENT FORUM (1984) *EMF's Report on International Industrial Competitiveness* (Geneva: EMF).
EUVRARD, F. (1987) *Les expériences locales de revenu minimum garanti en France* (Paris: CERC).
FELDSTEIN, M. S. (1980) 'International differences in social security and saving', *Journal of Public Economics*, 19.
FINANSDEPARTEMENTET (1987) *Långtidsutredningen* (Stockholm).
FINANSDEPARTEMENTET (1988) *Regeringens budgetförslag 1988/89* (Stockholm).
FINANSDEPARTEMENTET (1989) *Finansplanen* (Stockholm).
FINEGOLD, D. and SOSKICE, D. (1988) 'The failure of training in Britain: analysis and prescription', *Oxford Review of Economic Policy*, 4 (3).
FISCHER, S. (1987) 'Monetary policy', in R. Dornbusch and R. Layard (eds), *The Performance of the British Economy* (Oxford: Oxford University Press).
FLAHERTY, S. (1987) 'Strike activity and productivity change: The US auto industry', *Industrial Relations*, 26, (2) (Spring).

FLAM, H. (1987) 'Ökat utlandsberoende på gott och ont', *Ekonomisk Debatt*, 3.

FLORA, P. (ed.) (1987) *Growth to Limits: Western European Welfare States Since World War II*, vol. 4, (Berlin: De Gruyter).

FOREMAN-PECK, J. and MANNING, D. (1986) 'Liberalisation as an industrial policy: the case of telecommunications manufacturing', *Natwest Bank Review* (November).

FORES, M. and GLOVER, I. (eds) (1978) *Manufacturing and Management* (London: HMSO).

FRANZÉN, T., LÖVGREN, K. and ROSENBERG, I. (1975) 'Redistributional effects of taxes and public expenditure in Sweden', *Swedish Journal of Economics*, 77.

FRANZMEYER, F. (1988) *EG-Binnenmarkt – Integrationskonsequenzen für die Bundesrepublik* (Bonn: Friedrich-Ebert-Stiftung) (mimeo).

FRIEDMAN, B. M. (1985) 'Saving, investment, and government deficits in the 1980s', in B. R. Scott and G. C. Lodge (eds), *US Competitiveness in the World Economy* (Cambridge, MA: Harvard Business School Press).

FRIEDMAN, B. M. (1988) 'Lessons on monetary policy from the 1980s', *Journal of Economic Perspectives*, 2 (3) (Summer)

FRIEDMAN, M. (1980) *Memorandum to the House of Commons Select Committee on the Treasury and the Civil Service: Monetary policy* (HC 720).

FRIEDMAN, M. and FRIEDMAN, R. D. (1980) *Free to Choose* (London: Secker & Warburg).

FRIEDMAN, M. and FRIEDMAN, R. D. (1989) 'The "Tide in the affairs of men"', *Economic Impact*, 1989/1.

FURÅKER, B. (1976) *Stat och arbetsmarknad* (Lund: Arkiv).

GALLAWAY, L. and VEDDER, R. (1986) *Poverty, Income Distribution, the Family and Public Policy*, a study prepared for the use of the Subcommittee on Trade, Productivity, and Economic Growth of the Joint Economic Committee, Congress of the United States (Washington: Government Printing Office).

GARVIN, D. A. (1983) 'Quality on the line', *Harvard Business Review* (September–October).

GATT (1988) *International Trade 1987–1988*, vol. II (Geneva).

GENSCHER, H.-D. (1984) 'Die technologische Herausforderung', *Außenpolitik*, 35 (1).

GERSTENBERGER, W. (1988a) 'Entwicklung der Wettbewerbsfähigkeit der deutschen Industrie', *ifo-Schnelldienst*, 7/88.

GERSTENBERGER, W. (1988b) 'Wettbewerbsfähige Strukturen gestatten Expansionspolitik', *ifo-Schnelldienst*, 1. 88.

GIERSCH, H. (1984) 'Die Bundesrepublik und die USA – Wirtschaftssysteme und Zukunftschancen', *Jahrbuch für Sozialwissenschaft*, 35.

GLENNESTER, H. (1985) *Paying for Welfare* (Oxford: Basil Blackwell).

GORDON, D. M., EDWARDS, R. and REICH, M. (1982) *Segmented Work, Divided Workers. The Historical Transformation of Labor in the United States* (Cambridge: Cambridge University Press).

GOUGH, I. (1979) *The Political Economy of the Welfare State* (London: Macmillan).

GREFFE, X. (1987a) *Politique économique: programmes, instruments et perspectives* (Paris: Economica).
GREFFE, X. (1987b) *Décentraliser pour l'emploi: les initiatives locales de développement* (Paris: Economica).
GREFFE, X. (1987c) 'En déclinant le déclin', *Le Monde* (25 September).
GREFFE, X. (1989) 'La tentation de l'oubil', *Le Monde* (21 February).
GREWLICH, K. W. (1981) 'Technologie – die Sicherheit Europas', *Außenpolitik*, 32 (3).
GREWLICH, K. W. (1985) 'Informationstechnologie – Europas Antwort', *Außenpolitik*, 36 (2).
GROSS, B. (1987) 'Toward global action', *The Annals*, 492 (July).
GÜRTLER, J. (1988) 'Erwartete Auswirkungen des Europäischen Binnenmarktes auf die deutsche Industrie', *ifo-Schnelldienst*, 16/88.
GUSTAFSSON, B. (1984) *Tranfereringar och inkomstskatt samt hushållens materiella standard* (Stockholm: Finansdepartementet) (DS FI 1984:17).
GUSTAFSSON, B. (1987) *Den offentliga sektorn – fördelningsaspekter* (Stockholm: Finansdepartementet) (Langtidsutredningen bil. 20).
HAGER, W. (1981) 'Protectionism in the 1980s: the managed coexistence of different industrial cultures', in N. Noelke and R. Taylor, *EEC Protectionism: Present Practice and Future Trends*, vol. I (Brussels: European Research Associates).
HAGER, W. (1982) 'Protectionism and autonomy: How to preserve free trade in Europe', *International Affairs*, 58 (3) (Summer).
HAGER, W. (1987) 'The neomercantilist constraint', *The Annals*, 492 (July).
HANS-BÖCKLER-STIFTUNG and DEUTSCHER GEWERKSCHAFTSBUND (1988) *Der Industriestandort Bundesrepublik. Deutschland in der Weltwirtschaft. Materialien zur aktuellen Debatte* (Düsseldorf).
HARRINGTON, M. (1984) *The New American Poverty* (New York: Penguin Books).
HARRINGTON, M. with M. LEVINSON (1988) *The Future of American Labor* (Bonn: Friedrich-Ebert-Stiftung) (International Economics series).
HARVARD BUSINESS REVIEW in cooperation with the Harvard Business School (1987) 'Competitiveness: 23 leaders speak out', *Harvard Business Review* (July–August).
HATSOPOULOS, G. N. (1983) *High Cost of Capital: Handicap of American Industry* (Waltham, MA: Thermo Electron).
HATSOPOULOS, G. N. and BROOKS, S. (1986) *The Gap in the Cost of Capital: Causes, Effects and Remedies* (Cambridge, MA: Ballinger).
HAYEK, F. A. (1984) *1980s Unemployment and the Unions* (London: Institute of Economic Affairs).
HILD, R. (1981) 'Tendenzen und Perspektiven des PKW-Marktes', *ifo-Schnelldienst*, 7/81.
HILLS, H. (1987) 'What happened to spending on the welfare state?' in A. and C. Walker (eds), *The Growing Divide: A Social Audit 1979–1987* (London: Child Poverty Action Group).
HIRSCHHORN, L. (1981) 'The post-industrial labor process', *New Political Scientist*, 7 (Fall).
HMSO (1979) *The Government's Expenditure Plans* (London) (Cmnd 7746).
HMSO (1984) *Public Expenditure: the next ten years* (London).

HMSO (1988) *The Government's Expenditure Plans 1988/89 to 1990/91* (London) (Cm 288).
HOFHEINZ, R. Jr and CALDER, K. E. (1982) *The Eastasia Edge: Why an Entire Region is Overtaking the West in Technology, Exports and Management* (New York: Basic Books).
HOLLAND, S. (1975) *The Socialist Challenge* (London: Quartet).
HOLMBERG, S. (1981) *Svenska Väljari* (Stockholm: Liber).
HORWITZ, C. (1981) *Swedish Export Performance 1963–1979* (Stockholm: Industrial Institute for Economic and Social Research).
HORWITZ, C. (1986) *Marknadsandelar för svensk export 1978–84* (Stockholm: Kommerskollegium).
HOUSE OF LORDS SELECT COMMITTEE ON OVERSEAS TRADE (1985) *Report on Overseas Trade* (London: HMSO).
HUDSON REPORT (1975) *The United Kingdom in 1975* (London: Associated Business Programmes).
INDUSTRINS UTREDNINGSINSTITUTET (IUI) (1979) *Att välja 80-tal* (Stockholm: Almqvist and Wiksell).
INGHAM, G. (1984) *Capitalism Divided? The City and Industry in British Social Development* (London: Macmillan).
INSEE (various years) *Les comptes de la nation* (Paris).
JACKSON, P. (1985a) 'Policy implementation and monetarism,' in P. Jackson (ed.), *Implementing Policy Initiatives: The Thatcher Administration 1979–1983* (London: Royal Institute of Public Administration).
JACKSON, P. (1985b) 'Perspectives on practical monetarism', in P. Jackson (ed.), *Implementing Policy Initiatives: The Thatcher Administration 1979–1983* (London: Royal Institute of Public Administration).
JAKOBSSON, U., CARLSSON, B., DANEMAR, O., DU RIETZ, G. and FRANZHÉN, T. (1985) *Arbetslöshetsfällan* (Stockholm: SAF).
JAY, P. (1986) 'The future that doesn't work', in D. Coates and J. Hillard (eds) *The Economic Decline of Modern Britain* (New York; Brighton: Wheatsheaf).
JOHNSON, C. (1982) *MITI and the Japanese Miracle: The Growth of Industrial Policy, 1952–1975* (Stanford, CA: Stanford University Press).
JONES, D. (1983) 'Technology and the UK automobile industry', *Lloyds Bank Review*, 148 (April).
JONES, D (1985) *A revolution in automobile manufacturing? Technological change in a mature industry* (Brighton: Science Policy Research Unit, University of Sussex).
JONES, D. (1986) 'The dynamics of the world motor vehicle industry: issues for analysis', paper for the research meeting of the international motor vehicle programme in Boston, MA (14–18 September 1986) (Brighton: Science Policy Research Unit, University of Sussex).
JOSEPH, K. (1986) 'Solving the union problem is the key to Britain's recovery' in D. Coates and J. Hillard (eds), *The Economic Decline of Modern Britain* (New York; Brighton: Wheatsheaf).
JÜRGENS, U. (1986) *Entwicklungstendenzen in der Weltautomobilindustrie bis in die 90er Jahre* (Berlin: WZB) (IIVG/pre 86–218).
JUSTITIEDEPARTEMENTET (1979) *Vägar till ökad välfärd* (Stockholm) (Ds Ju 79:1).

KAHN, A. J. and KAMERMAN, S. B. (1983) *Income Transfers for Families with Children: An Eight-Country Study* (Philadelphia: Temple University Press).

KALECKI, M. (1943) 'Political aspects of full employment', *Political Quarterly*, 14.

KAMPPETER, W. (1987) 'The distribution of production and incomes in the world economy. An explanation based on differential rent theory', paper presented at the research seminar of the Institute of Economics, Yokohama National University (19 January 1987).

KAMPPETER, W. (1988a) 'The double deficit of the USA and disequilibria in the world economy', *Intereconomics*, 23 (4) (July/August).

KAMPPETER W. (1988b) *Endaka – die japanische Wirtschaft nach der Aufwertungskrise* (Bonn: Friedrich-Ebert-Stiftung) (mimeo).

KASSALOW, E. (1984) 'The future of American unionism: a comparative perspective', *The Annals*, 473 (May).

KASSALOW, E. (1988) 'Concession bargaining: towards new roles for American unions and managers', *International Labour Review*, 127 (5).

KATZ, H. C. (1985) *Shifting Gears: Changing Labor Relations in the US Automobile Industry* (Cambridge, MA: MIT Press).

KATZ, H. C., KOCHAN, T. A. and GOBEILLE, K. R. (1983) 'Industrial relations performance, economic performance and the effects of Quality of Working Life: an inter-plant analysis', *Industrial and Labor Relations Review*, 37 (1) (October).

KATZ, H. C. and SABEL, C. F. (1985) 'Industrial relations and industrial adjustment in the car industry', *Industrial Relations – A Journal of Economy and Society*, 24 (3) (Fall).

KATZENSTEIN, P. J. (1985) *Small States in World Markets: Industrial Policy in Europe* (Ithaca, NY: Cornell University Press).

KAY, J. and THOMPSON, D. (1987) 'Policy for industry', in R. Dornbusch and R. Layard (eds), *The Performance of the British Economy* (Oxford: Oxford University Press).

KENDRICK, J. W. (1980) Discussion of the articles on 'A General View of Capital Formation and Economic Growth', *American Economic Review – Papers and Proceedings*, 70 (2) (May).

KOCHAN, T. A., KATZ, H. C. and McKERSIE, R. B. (1987) *The Transformation of Industrial Relations* (New York: Basic Books).

KOCHAN, T. A. and PIORE, M. J. (1984) 'Will the new industrial relations last? Implications for the American labor movement', *The Annals*, 473 (May).

KONJUNKTURINSTITUTET (1986) *Konjunkturläget December 1986* (Stockholm).

KORNBLUH, H. (1984) 'Work place democracy and Quality of Work Life: problems and prospects', *The Annals*, 473 (May).

KORPI, W. (1985) 'Economic growth and the welfare state: leaky bucket or irrigation system', *European Sociological Review*, 1.

KOSKELLA, E. and MATTI, V. (1983) 'Social security and household saving in an international cross-section', *American Economic Review*, 73.

KOSTER, M. H. and ROSS, M. N. (1987) 'The influence of employment shifts and new job opportunities on the growth and distribution of real wages', in P. Cagan (ed.), *Deficits, Taxes and Economic Adjustments* (Washington: American Enterprise Institute).

KOVACH, K. A. (1987) 'What motivates employees? Workers and supervisors give different answers', *Business Horizons* (September/October).

KRAUSS, M. (1978) *The New Protectionism. The Welfare State and International Trade* (New York: New York University Press).

KRIEGER, J. (1986) *Reagan, Thatcher and the Politics of Decline* (Cambridge: Polity).

KUTTNER, R. (1984) *The Economic Illusion* (Boston: Houghton Mifflin).

LAMPERT, H. (1985) *Lehrbuch der Sozialpolitik* (Berlin).

LAWRENCE, P. R. and DYER, D. (1983) *Renewing American Industry* (New York: Free Press).

LAWRENCE, R. Z. (1984) *Can America Compete?* (Washington: Brookings).

LAWRENCE, R. Z. (1987) 'Trade performance as a constraint on European growth', in R. Z. Lawrence and Ch. Schulze (eds), *Barriers to European Growth* (Washington: Brookings).

LAYARD, R. (1986) *How to beat Unemployment* (Oxford: Oxford University Press).

LAYARD, R. and NICKELL, S. (1985) 'The causes of British unemployment', *National Institute Economic Review* (February).

LEIBFRITZ, W. und PARSCHE, R. (1988) 'Steuerbelastung der Werkzeugmaschinenindustrie im internationalen Vergleich' *ifo-Schnelldienst*, 9/88.

LEONE, R. A. (1984) 'Regulatory relief and the automobile industry', in E. C. Eads and M. Fix (eds), *The Reagan Regulatory Strategy. An Assessment* (Washington: The Urban Institute).

LEVITAN, S. A. and SHAPIRO, I. (1987) *Working but Poor. America's Contradiction* (Baltimore: Johns Hopkins University Press).

LEVITAN, S. A. and TAGGART, R. (1976) *The Promise of Greatness* (Cambridge, MA: Harvard University Press).

LEVITT, M. and JOYCE, M. (1987) 'Public expenditure: trends and prospects', in M. S. Levitt (ed.), *New Priorities in Public Spending* (London: Gower).

LEVY, F. (1987) *Dollars and Dreams. The Changing American Income Distribution* (New York: Russell Sage Foundation).

LEWIS, D. (1986) 'Sweden's manufacturing sector: A success story', *Australian Quarterly*, 58 (1).

LEYS, C. (1986) 'The formation of British capital', *New Left Review*, 160.

LINDBECK, A. (1984) 'Internationella och inhemska förutsättningar för ekonomisk stabilitet', *Skandinaviska Enskilda Bankens Kvartalstidskrift*, 2.

LINDBECK, A. (1986) 'Limits to the welfare state', *Challenge*, 28.

LINDBECK, A. (1988) 'Consequences of the advanced welfare state', *The World Economy*, 11 (1).

LINDBERG, P., TUNÄLV, C. and HÖRLE, S.-A. (1987) *Tillverkningstrategier* (Göteborg: Institute for Management of Innovation and Technology).

LINDBLOM, C. E. (1977) *Politics and Markets. The World's Political–economic Systems* (New York: Basic Books).

LIPIETZ, A. (1984a) *La mondialisation de la crise générale du Fordisme: 1967–1984* (Paris: CEPREMAP) (No. 8413).

LIPIETZ, A. (1984b) *L'audace ou l'enlisement* (Paris: La Découverte).

LLOYDS BANK (1987) *Economic Bulletin*, 105 (September).

LODGE, G. C. and CRUM, W. C. (1985) 'The pursuit of remedies', in B. R. Scott and G. C. Lodge (eds), *US Competitiveness in the World Economy* (Cambridge, MA: Harvard Business School Press).

LOVEMAN, G. W. and TILLY, C. (1988) 'Good jobs or bad jobs? Evaluating the American job creation experience', *International Labour Review*, 127 (5).

LUNDBERG, E. (1985) 'The rise and fall of the Swedish model', *Journal of Economic Literature*, 23.

MACGREGOR, S. (1985) 'Social security', in P. Jackson (ed.), *Implementing Policy Initiatives: The Thatcher Administration 1979–1983* (London: Royal Institute of Public Administration).

MACKENZIE, I. and HESSELMAN, L. (1984) 'European electronics in an era of US–Japanese competition', background paper for a conference (22–23 November 1984), Royal Institute of International Affairs, London.

MADDISON, A. (1982) *Ontwikkelingsfasen van het kapitalisme* (Utrecht: Spectrum).

MADDISON, A. (1987) 'Growth and slowdown in advanced capitalist economies: techniques of quantitative assessment', *Journal of Economic Literature* 25 (2) (June).

MAGAZINER, I. C. and REICH, R. B. (1982) *Minding America's Business: the Decline and Rise of the American Economy* (New York: Harcourt, Brace, Jovanovich).

MAHON, R. (1987) 'From Fordism to?: New technology, labour markets and unions', *Economic and Industrial Democracy*, 8.

MANISON, L. (1978) *Some factors influencing the UK's economic growth performance*, IMF Staff Papers, 25 (Washington: IMF).

MARQUAND, D. (1988) *The Unprincipled Society*, (London: Fontana).

MARSDEN, K. (1983) *Links Between Taxes and Economic Growth: Some Empirical Evidence* (Washington: World Bank) (World Bank Staff Working Paper, 605).

MARSDEN, D., MORRIS, T., WILMAN, P. and WOOD, S. (1985) *The Car Industry* (London; New York: Tavistock).

MATHIS, J. and MAZIER, J. (1987) 'Niveaux des couts de production et performances extérieures des grands pays industrialisés, *La note de l'IRES*, 12.

MATTHEWS, K. and MINFORD, P. (1987) 'Mrs Thatcher's economic policies 1979–1987', *Economic Policy* (October).

MATTHEWS, R. and SARGENT, J. (1983) *Contemporary Problems of Economic Policy: Essays from the Clare Group* (London: Methuen).

MAYES, D. (1987) 'Does manufacturing matter?', *National Institute Economic Review* (November).

MAYNARD, G. (1988) *The Economy under Mrs Thatcher* (Oxford: Basil Blackwell).

McCALLUM, J. and BLAIS, A. (1984) 'Government, special interest groups and economic growth' (Montreal: Departemente de Science Economique, Université de Quebec à Montréal) (Working Paper).

McDERMOTT, P. and TAYLOR, M. (1982) *Industrial Organisation and Location* (Cambridge: Cambridge University Press).

McGARRAH, R. E. (1987) 'The decline of US manufacturers: causes and remedies', *Business Horizons* (November/December).

MELMAN, S. (1974) *The Permanent War Economy. American Capitalism in Decline* (New York: Simon & Schuster).

METCALF, D. and RICHARDSON, R. (1986) 'Labour', in M. J. Artis (ed), *The UK Economy*, (London: Weidenfeld & Nicolson) 11th edn.

MIDDLEMAS, K. (1986) *Power, Competition and the State. Vol.I: Britain in Search of Balance 1940–1961* (Stanford: Hoover Institution Press, Stanford University).

MILEWSKI, F. (1989) *Le commerce extérieur de la France* (Paris: La Découverte).

MILLER, J. A. (1986) 'The financial crisis of the state reconsidered: two views of the state and the accumulation of capital in the postwar economy', *Review of Radical Political Economics*, 18 (1/2) (Spring/Summer).

MILLS, G. B. (1984) 'The budget: a failure of discipline', in J. L. Palmer and I. V. Sawhill (eds), *The Reagan Record. An Assessment of America's Changing Domestic Priorities* (Cambridge, MA: Ballinger).

MILLS, D. Q. and LOVELL, M. R. Jr (1985) 'Competitiveness: the labour dimension', in B. R. Scott and G. C. Lodge (eds), *US Competitiveness in the World Economy* (Cambridge, MA: Harvard Business School Press).

MINFORD, P. (1983) *Unemployment: Cause and Cure* (Oxford: Blackwell).

MÖLLER, C. (1988) *Flexibel in die Armut. Empirische Untersuchung und theoretische Verortung prekärer Arbeitsverhältnisse* (Hamburg: Hamburger Institut für Sozialforschung) (Forschungsbericht Bd. 3).

MOON, M. and SAWHILL, I. V. (1984) 'Family incomes: gainers and losers', in J. L. Palmer and I. V. Sawhill (eds), *The Reagan Record. An assessment of America's Changing Domestic Priorities* (Cambridge, MA: Ballinger).

MORAN, M. (1987) *Thatcherism and the Constitution: The Case of Financial Regulation in the 1980s* (unpublished).

MORGAN, K. and WEBBER, D. (1986) 'Divergent paths: political strategies for telecommunications', in K. Dyson (ed.), *The Politics of the Communications Revolution in Western Europe* (London: Frank Cass).

MOSELEY, P. (1984) *The Making of Economic Policy* (New York: Harvester-Wheatsheaf).

MÜCKENBERGER, U. (1985) 'Deregulierendes Arbeitsrecht. Die Arbeitsrechtsinitiativen der Regierungskoaliation', *Kritische Justiz*, 18 (3).

MÜCKENBERGER, U. (1986) 'Zur Rolle des Normalarbeitsverhältnisses bei der sozialen Umverteilung von Risiken', *Prokla*, 64 (16 (3)).

MURARD, N. (1989) *La protection sociale* (Paris: La Découverte).

MURRAY, C. (1984) *Losing Ground. American Social Policy, 1950–1980* (New York: Basic Books).

MYLES, J. (1988) 'Decline or impasse? The current state of the welfare state', *Studies in Political Economy*, 26 (Summer).

NAIRN, T. (1983) *The Break-up of Britain*, (London: Verso) 2nd edn.

NAIRN, T. (1988) *The Enchanted Glass* (London: Radius).
NAPLES, M. J. (1981) 'Labor militance and the end of the postwar truce', *American Economic Review – Papers and Proceedings*, 71 (2) (May).
NATIONAL ASSOCIATION OF MANUFACTURERS (1986) *US trade balance at a turning point: Can we eliminate the trade deficit by 1990?* (Washington).
THE NATIONAL COMMISSION ON EXCELLENCE IN EDUCATION 1983. *A nation at risk: the imperative for educational reform* (Washington, Government Printing Office).
NELSON, R. R. and WINTER, S. G. (1982) *An Evolutionary Theory of Economic Change* (Cambridge, MA: Harvard University Press).
NORSWORTHY, J. R. and MALMQUIST, D. H. (1985) 'Recent productivity growth in Japanese and US manufacturing', in W. J. Baumol and K. McLennan (eds), *Productivity Growth and US Competitiveness* (New York: Oxford University Press).
NORTON, R. D. (1986) 'Industrial policy and American renewal', *Journal of Economic Literature*, 24 (March).
OECD (1983) *Economic Outlook*, 33 (Paris).
OECD (1984) *Economic Outlook*, 36 (Paris).
OECD (1985a) *Social expenditure 1960–1990 – problems of growth and control* (Paris).
OECD (1985b) *Competitive position indicators of manufacturing industries* (Paris) (DSTI/SPR/85.14).
OECD (1985c) *Economic Survey: the UK* (Paris).
OECD (1986a) *Science and technology indicators II: R&D, invention and competitiveness* (Paris).
OECD (1986b). *Economic Survey: the UK* (Paris).
OECD (1986c) *Revenue statistics of OECD member countries 1965–1985* (Paris).
OECD (1986d) *Labor force statistics 1964–1984* (Paris).
OECD (1986e) *STI Review*, 1.
OECD (1987a) *OECD employment outlook* (Paris).
OECD (1987b) *National accounts: supplement* (Paris).
OECD (1987c) *Rapport sur la France* (Paris).
OECD (1987d) *Historical statistics 1960–1985* (Paris).
OECD 1987e) *National accounts 1975–1985. Vol. II* (Paris).
OECD (1988a) *National accounts 1960–1986. Main aggregates. Vol. I* (Paris).
OECD (1988b) *Social expenditure trends and demographic developments* (Paris).
OECD (1988c) *Economic Outlook*, 44 (Paris).
OECD (1988d) *Economic Survey: the UK* (Paris).
OECD (1989a) *Economies in transition. Structural adjustment in OECD countries* (Paris).
OECD (1989b) *National accounts 1960–1987. Main aggregates. Vol. I* (Paris).
O'HIGGINS, M. (1985) 'Inequality, redistribution and recession', *Journal of Social Policy*, 14 (3).
O'HIGGINS, M. (1987) 'The distribution and redistribution of income in the UK, 1971–1984', in M. S. Levitt (ed.), *New Priorities in Public Spending* (London: Gower).

OHLSSON, L. and VINELL, L. (1987) *Tillväxtens drivkrafter* (Stockholm: Industribundets förlag).
OLSON, M. (1982) *The Rise and Decline of Nations: Economic Growth, Stagflation, and Social Rigidities* (New Haven, Conn.: Yale University Press).
OLSON, M. (1988) 'The productivity slowdown, the oil shock, and the real cycle', *Journal of Economic Perspectives*, 2 (4) (Fall).
PALMER, J. L. and SAWHILL, I. V. (1984) 'Overview', in J. L. Palmer and I. V. Sawhill (eds), *The Reagan Record. An Assessment of America's Changing Domestic Priorities* (Cambridge, MA: Ballinger).
PARRY, R. (1986) 'The United Kingdom', in P. Flora (ed.), *Growth to Limits: Western European Welfare States Since World War II*, vol. 2 (Berlin: De Gruyter).
PATEL, C. and PAVITT, K. (1987 'The elements of British technological competitiveness', *National Institute Economic Review* (November).
PATTERSON, J. T. (1981) *America's Struggle Against Poverty, 1900–1980* (Cambridge, MA: Harvard University Press).
PAVITT, K. and SOETE, L. (1982) 'International differences in economic growth and the international location of innovation', in H. Giersch (ed.), *Emerging Technologies: Consequences for Economic Growth, Structural Change, and Employment* (Tübingen: J.B.C. Mohr).
PEMPEL, T. J. (1982) *Policy and Politics in Japan: Creative Conservatism* (Philadelphia: Temple University Press).
PETERSSON, O. (1977) *Väljarna och valet 1976* (Stockholm: Liber).
PFALLER, A. (1983) *Trade Restrictions Against Low-cost Imports: What is at Stake*? (Bonn: Friedrich-Ebert-Stiftung) (Analysis and Information Series).
PFALLER, A. (1986) 'The changing North–South division of labour', *Kyklos*, 39 (1).
PFALLER, A. (1987) 'Are the Western welfare states still competitive?', *Intereconomics*, 22 (3) (May/June).
PIACHAUD, D. (1987) 'The growth of poverty', in A. and C. Walker (eds), *The Growing Divide: A Social Audit 1979–1987* (London: Child Poverty Action Group).
PIORE, M. J. and SABEL, C. (1984) *The Second Industrial Divide: Possibilities for Prosperity* (New York: Basic Books).
POSNER, M. (ed.) (1978) *Demand Management* (London: Heinemann).
PRAIS, S. J. (1983) *Productivity and Industrial Structure* (Cambridge: Cambridge University Press).
PRAIS, S. and WAGNER, K. (1983) 'Some practical aspects of human capital investment: training standards in five occupations in Britain and Germany', *National Institute Economic Review*, 105.
PRAIS, S. J. and WAGNER, K. (1985) 'Schooling standards in England and Germany: some summary comparisons bearing on economic performance', *National Institute Economic Review* (May).
PRAIS, S. J. and WAGNER, K. (1988) 'Productivity and management: the training of foremen in Britain and Germany', *National Institute Economic Review* (February).
THE PRESIDENT'S COMMISSION ON INDUSTRIAL COMPETITIVE-

NESS (1985) *Global Competition. The New Reality. The Report of the President's Commission on Industrial Competitiveness* (Washington: Government Printing Office) 2 vols.
QUICK, P. D. (1984) 'Businesses: Reagan's industrial policy', in J. L. Palmer and I. V. Sawhill (eds), *The Reagan Record. An Assessment of America's Changing Domestic Priorities*, Cambridge, MA, Ballinger).
QUINET, E. and TOUZERY, L. (1986) *Le Plan français, mythe ou nécessité*, (Paris: Economica).
RAMO, S. (1980) *America's Technological Slip* (New York: Wiley).
RAY, G. F. (1987) 'Labor costs in manufacturing', *National Institute Economic Review* (May).
RAY, J. C., DUPUIS, J. M. and GAZIER, B. (1988) *Analyse économique des politiques sociales* (Paris: Presses Universitaires de France).
REICH, R. B. (1983) *The Next American Frontier* (New York: Times Books).
REICH, R. B. and MANKIN, E. D. (1986) 'Joint ventures with Japan give away our future', *Harvard Business Review* (March–April).
REYNOLDS, M. and SMOLENSKY, E. (1977) *Public Expenditures, Taxes and the Distribution of Income* (New York: Academic Press).
RHEIN, E. (1981) 'Europa, Japan und die internationale Arbeitsteilung', *Europa Archiv*, 36 (7).
RIESE, H. (1978) 'Strukturwandel und unterbewertete Währung in der Bundesrepublik Deutschland. Bemerkungen zur theoretischen Position des Instituts für Weltwirtschaft Kiel', *Konjunkturpolitik*, 24.
Riksdagstrycket (various years) (Stockholm).
RIMLINGER, G. V. (1987) 'Social policy under German fascism', in M. Rein, G. S. Esping-Andersen and L. Rainwater (eds), *Stagnation and Renewal in Social Policy. The Rise and Fall of Policy Regimes* (Armonk, NY: Sharpe).
RINGEN, S. (1986) *Difference and Similarity: Two Studies in Comparative Income Distribution* (Stockholm: SOFI) (Report No. 2).
RIVLIN A. (ed.) (1987) *Den Svenska economins Framtid Sutsikter* (Stockholm: SNS).
ROBINSON, R. (1986) Public expenditure 1979/80–1984/5, *Journal of Social Policy*.
ROOBEEK, A. (1988) 'Telecommunications: an industry in transition', in H. W. de Jong (ed.), *Structure in the European Industry* (Amsterdam: Martinus Nijhoff) 2nd edn.
ROOT, L. S. (1985) 'Employee benefits and social welfare: complement and conflict', *The Annals*, 479 (May).
ROSANVALLON, P. (1981) *La crise de l'Etat-providence* (Paris: Seuil).
ROSENBERG, N. (1986) *Civilian 'Spillovers' From Military R&D Spending: the American Experience Since World War II* (Stanford, CA: Stanford University) (unpublished).
ROSENBROCK, R. (1985) *Die Kolonialisierung des Sozialstaats – Ein Essay* (Berlin: WZB) (IIVG/pre 85–213).
ROTHSCHILD, E. (1973) *Paradise Lost: The Decline of the Auto-industrial Age* (New York: Random House).
ROWTHORN, BOB (1989) 'The Thatcher revolution', in F. Green (ed.), *The Restructuring of the UK Economy*.

ROWTHORN, R. and WELLS, J. (1987) *De-industrialisation and Foreign Trade* (Cambridge: Cambridge University Press).

SACHVERSTÄNDIGENRAT ZUR BEGUTACHTUNG DER GESAMTWIRTSCHAFTLICHEN ENTWICKLUNG (1987) *Jahresgutachten 1986/87* (Bonn).

SACHVERSTÄNDIGENRAT ZUR BEGUTACHTUNG DER GESAMTWIRTSCHAFTLICHEN ENTWICKLUNG (1989) *Jahresgutachten 1988/89* (Bonn).

SAF (1978) *Wages and Total Labour Costs for Workers 1966–1976* (Stockholm).

SAF (1984) *Wages and Total Labour Costs for Workers 1972–1982* (Stockholm).

SAF (1986) *Wages and Total Labour Costs for Workers 1973–1983* (Stockholm).

SALTER, M. S., WEBBER, A. M. and DYER, D. (1985) 'US competitiveness in global industries: lessons from the auto industry', in B. R. Scott and G. C. Lodge (eds), *US Competitiveness in the World Economy* (Cambridge, MA: Harvard Business School Press).

SAUNDERS, P. (1985) 'Public expenditure and economic performance in OECD countries', *Journal of Public Policy*, 5 (1).

SAUNDERS, P. (1986) 'What can we learn from international comparisons of public sector size and economic performance?', *European Sociological Review*, 2 (1) (May).

SAUNDERS, P. and KLAU, F. (1985) *The role of the public sector. Causes and consequences of the growth of government* (Paris: OECD).

SAWHILL, I. V. (1988a) 'Poverty in the US: Why is it so persistent?', *Journal of Economic Literature*, 26 (September).

SAWHILL, I. V. (1988b) 'What about America's underclass?', *Challenge* (May–June).

SAWHILL, I. V. and STONE, C. F. (1984) 'The economy: the key to success', in J. L. Palmer and I. V. Sawhill (eds), *The Reagan Record. An assessment of America's Changing Domestic Priorities* (Cambridge, MA: Ballinger).

SCHARPF, F. W. (1987) *Sozialdemokratische Krisenpolitik in Europa* (Frankfurt: Campus).

SCHARPF, F. W. (1988) 'Vollbeschäftigung kostet Geld', *Die Zeit* (1 July 1988).

SCHARPF, F. W. und SCHETTKAT, R. (1984) *Verkürzung der Wochenarbeitszeit: Nur der Staat kann den beschäftigungspolitischen Handlungsspielraum erweitern* (Berlin: WZB) (Diskussionspapier IIM/LMP 84–5).

SCHMÄL, W., CONRADI, H., JACOBS, K., MEIERJÜRGEN, R. and PRINZ, A. (1986) *Soziale Sicherung 1975–1986. Verteilungswirkungen sozialpolitischer Maßnahmen in der Bundesrepublik Deutschland* (Frankfurt: Peter Lang).

SCHMIDT, M. G. (1982) *Wohlfahrtsstaatliche Politik unter bürgerlichen und sozialdemokratischen Regierungen. Ein internationaler Vergleich* (Frankfurt: Campus).

SCHMIDT, M. G. (1987) 'The politics of full employment in western democracies', *The Annals* 492 (July).

SCHULZE, P. W. (1987) 'Shifts in the world economy and the restructuring of economic sectors: increased competition and strategic alliances in the

information technologies', *Vierteljahresberichte – Problems of International Cooperation*, 109 (September).
SCHULZE, P. W. (1988) 'Die Auflösung der dualen Technologie-Konzeption', *Vierteljahresberichte – Problems of International Cooperation*, 114 (December).
SCOTT, B. R. (1985a) 'US competitiveness: concepts, performance, and implications', in B. R. Scott and G. C. Lodge (eds), *US Competitiveness in the World Economy* (Cambridge, MA: Harvard Business School Press).
SCOTT, B. R. (1985b) 'National strategies: key to international competition', in B. R. Scott and G. C. Lodge (eds), *US Competitiveness in the World Economy*, (Cambridge, MA: Harvard Business School Press).
SCOTT, B. R. and LODGE G. C. (eds) (1985a) *US Competitiveness in the World Economy* (Cambridge, MA: Harvard Business School Press).
SCOTT, B. R. and LODGE, G. C. (1985b) 'Introduction', in B. R. Scott and G. C. Lodge (eds) *US Competitiveness in the World Economy* (Cambridge, MA: Harvard Business School Press).
SEIDMANN, B. (1976) 'Pensions: the public–private interplay', *American Federationist*, 83 (19) (July).
SHAPIRO, I. (1987) *No escape: the minimum wage and poverty* (Washington: Center on Budget and Policy Priorities).
SMITH, A. D., HITCHENS, D. M. and DAVIES, S. W. (1982) *International Industrial Productivity. A Comparison of Britain, America and Germany* (Cambridge: Cambridge University Press).
SMITH, K. (1984) *The British Economic Crisis* (Harmondsworth: Penguin).
SNS (various years) *Konjunkturrådsets rapport* (Stockholm).
SOCIAL SECURITY CONSORTIUM (1987) *Of little benefit: a guide to the social security act 1986* (London).
SÖDERSTRÖM, H. T. (ed) (1986) *Nya spelregler för tillväxt* (Stockholm: SNS).
SOLOW, R. (1987) 'The conservative revolution: a roundtable discussion', *Economic Policy* (October).
SOLTWEDEL, R. and TRAPP, P. (1988) 'Labor market barriers to more employment: Causes for an increase of the natural rate? The case of West Germany; in H. Giersch (ed.), *Macro and micro policies for more growth and employment. Symposium 1987* (Tübingen: J. C. B. Mohr).
SOU (various years) (Stockholm: Allmänna).
STALK, G. Jr (1988) 'Time – the next source of competitive advantage', *Harvard Business Review* (July–August).
STARK, T. (1988) *A New A to Z of Income and Wealth* (London: Fabian Society).
STATENS INDUSTRIVERK (1982) *Produktivitet och konkurrenskraft* (Stockholm: Liber).
STATENS INDUSTRIVERK (1988) *Konkurrensläget 1988* (Stockholm).
STEEDMAN, H. (1988) 'Vocational training in France and Britain: mechanical and electrical craftsmen', *National Institute Economic Review* (November).
STEEDMAN, H. and WAGNER, K. (1987) 'A second look at productivity, machinery and skills in Britain and Germany', *National Institute Economic Review* (November).

STEEL, D. and HEALD, D. (1985) 'The privatisation of public enterprises 1979–83', in P. Jackson (ed.), *Implementing Policy Initiatives: The Thatcher Administration 1979–1983* (London: Royal Institute of Public Administration).

STOCKMAN, D. A. (1986) *The triumph of Politics* (New York: Harper & Row).

STREECK, W. (1982) 'Neo-korporativistische Kooperation und weltwirtschaftliche Konkurrenz', in Friedrich-Ebert-Stiftung, *Pluralismus unter Konkurrenzdruck* (Bonn: Friedrich-Ebert-Stiftung) (Analysen, Nr 101/102).

STREECK, W. and HOFF, A. (1984) *Manpower Management and Industrial Relations in the Restructuring of the World Automobile Industry* (Berlin: WZB) (IIM/LMP 83–55).

SUNDQUIST, J. L. (1968) *Politics and Policy: the Eisenhower, Kennedy and Johnson Years* (Washington: Brookings).

TARANTELLI, E. (1984) 'The generation leap hypothesis: Can unemployment go down in industrialized (and less developed) countries?', paper presented to a conference on 'Global Unemployment: a Challenge for Policy-makers', organised by the Friedrich-Ebert-Stiftung and the Democratic Planning Project (4 and 5 December) (Bonn).

TARANTELLI, E. (1986) 'The regulation of inflation and unemployment', *Industrial Relations – A Journal of Economy and Society*, 25 (1) (Winter).

TARSCHYS, D. (1986) 'Curbing public expenditure: current trends', *Journal of Public Policy*, 5 (1).

TCO (1985) *Aktiekursernas utveckling i Sverige och 15 andra industriländer* (Stockholm).

TCO (1988) *TCO-ekonomernas vårrapport* (Stockholm).

THERBORN, G. (1985) 'The coming of Swedish social democracy', in E. Collotti (ed.), *L'Internazionale Operaia e Socialista tra le due guerre* (Milan: Feltrinelli).

THERBORN, G. (1986) *Why Some Peoples are More Unemployed Than Others. The strange paradox of growth and unemployment* (London: Verso).

THERBORN, G. (1987a) 'Den svenska välfärdsstatens särart och framtid', *Lycksalighetens halvö* (Stockholm: FRN-Framtidsstudier).

THERBORN, G. (1987b) 'Tar arbetet slut? – och post-fordismens problem', in U. Björnberg and I. Hellberg (eds), *Sociologer ser pa arbete* (Stockholm: Arbetslivscentrum).

THERBORN, G. (1989) *Borgarklass och Byräkraty i Sverige* (Lund: Arkiv).

THERBORN, G., LUND, M., KJELLBERG, A. and ÖHLUND, U. (1978) 'Sweden before and after social democracy', *Acta Sociologica* (ISA Congress Supplement Issue).

THUROW, L. C. (1984) 'Jobs versus productivity: the Euro-American dilemma', *Technology Review* (October).

THUROW, L. C. (1985) *The Zero-sum Solution. Building a World-class American Economy* (Greenville, N.C.: Simon & Schuster).

THUROW, L. C. (1987a) *Economic Paradigms and Slow American Productivity Growth* (Cambridge, MA: MIT) (mimeo).

THUROW, L. C. (1987b) 'A surge in inequality', *Scientific American*, 256, (5) (May).

TIRMAN, J. (1984) *The Militarization of High Technology* (Cambridge: Cambridge University Press).
TOMLINSON, J. (1986) *Monetarism: Is There an Alternative?* (Oxford: Blackwell).
TYSON, L. and ZYSMAN, J. (1983) 'American industry in international competition', in J. Zysman and L. Tyson (eds), *American Industry in International Competition* (Ithaca, NY: Cornell University Press).
UHLMANN, L. (1986) 'Kosten und Leistung in der Industrie', *ifo-Schnelldienst*, 29/86.
UNEMPLOYMENT UNIT (1987) *Briefing* (August).
US CONGRESS (1985a) *War on Poverty – Victory or Defeat*, hearing before the Subcommittee on Monetary and Fiscal Policy of the Joint Economic Committee, 99th Congress, 1st session (20 June 1985) (Washington: Government Printing Office).
US CONGRESS (1985b) *Telecommunications Trade*, hearings before the Subcommittee on Telecommunications, Consumer Protection and Finance and the Subcommittee on Commerce, Transportation, and Tourism of the Committee on Energy and Commerce, House of Representatives, 99th Congress, 1st session (27 and 28 March 1985) (Washington: Government Printing Office).
US CONGRESS (1986a) *Work and Poverty: the special problems of the working poor*, hearing before the Subcommittee of the Committee on Government Operations, House of Representatives, 99th Congress, 1st session (12 December 1985) Washington: Government Printing Office).
US CONGRESS (1986b) *Poverty, Hunger, and the Welfare System*, hearing before the Select Committee on Hunger, House of Representatives, 99th Congress, 2nd session (5 August 1986) (Washington: Government Printing Office).
US CONGRESS (1987) *Work and Welfare*, hearings before the Committee on Labor and Human Resources, United States Senate, 100th Congress, 1st session on reviewing the extent of long-term poverty and dependence, focusing on job training and employment services provided by the Government (21 January; 3 and 4 February 1987) (Washington: Government Printing Office).
VERKSTADSFÖRENINGEN (1933) *Verksamhetsberättelse* (Stockholm: Verkstatdsföreningens arkiv).
VOGEL, E. F. (1979) *Japan as Number One. Lessons for America* (Cambridge, MA: Harvard University Press).
VOGEL, J., ANDERSSON, L.-G. DAVIDSSON, U. and HÄLL, L. (1987) *Ojämlikheten i Sverige* (Stockholm: SCBI).
WEBBER, D. (1988) 'Krankheit, Geld und Politik: Zur Geschichte der Gesundheitsreformen in Deutschland', *Leviathan*, 16 (2).
WEISSKOPF, T. E. (1987) 'The effect of unemployment on labor productivity: an international comparative analysis', *International Review of Applied Economics*, 1 (2) (July).
WEISSKOPF, T. E., BOWLES, S. and GORDON, D. M. (1983) *Hearts and Minds: A Social Model of US Productivity Growth* (Washington: Brookings).
WEITZMAN, M. L. (1984) *The Share Economy. Conquering Stagflation* (Cambridge, MA: Harvard University Press).

WELLONS, P. A. (1985) 'Competitiveness in the world economy: the role of the US financial system', in B. R. Scott and G. C. Lodge, *US Competitiveness in the World Economy* (Cambridge, MA: Harvard Business School Press).

WELZMÜLLER, R. (1988) 'Personalzusatzkostengefahr für die Wettbewerbsfähigkeit oder Nebenschauplatz im Verteilungskonflikt?', *Soziale Sicherheit*, 3.

WETTER, W., LANGER, C., JUNGNICKEL, R. and RESZAT, B. (1984) *Die Wettbewerbsposition der deutschen Wirtschaft. Wechselkurs und internationale Wettbewerbsfähigkeit* (Hamburg).

WIDICK, B. J. (ed.) (1976) *Autowork and its Discontent* (Baltimore: Johns Hopkins University Press).

WILENSKY, H. L. (1976) *The 'New Corporatism', Centralization, and the Welfare State* (London: Sage).

WILENSKY, H. J. (1981) 'Democratic corporatism, consensus and social policy', in OECD, *The Welfare State in Crisis* (Paris).

WILENSKY, H. J. (1982) 'Ideology, education, and social security', in I. Garfinkel (ed.), *Income-tested Transfer Programs: The Case for and Against* (New York: Academic Press).

WILENSKY, H. J. (1983) 'Political legitimacy and consensus: missing variables in the assessment of social policy', in S. E. Spiro and E. Yuchtman-Yaar (eds), *Evaluating the Welfare State: Social and Political Perspectives* (New York: Academic Press).

WILENSKY, H. L., LUEBBERT, G. M., REED HAHN, S. and JAMIESON, A. M. (1986) *Comparative Social Policy. Theories, Methods, findings* (Berkeley, CA: Institute of International Studies, University of California at Berkeley) (research series, 62).

WILKS, S. (1985) 'Conservative industrial policy 1979–83', in P. Jackson (ed.) *Implementing Policy Initiatives: The Thatcher Administration 1979–1983*, (London: Royal Institute of Public Administration).

WILLIAMS, K., WILLIAMS, J. and THOMAS, D. (1983) *Why are the British Bad at Manufacturing?* (London: Routledge).

WILSON COMMITTEE (1980) *Report of the Committee to Review the Functioning of the Financial Institutions* (London: HMSO) (Cmnd. 7937).

WINDOLF, P. (1985) 'Industrial robots in the German automobile industry: new technology in the context of industrial relations', in W. Streeck (ed.), *Industrial Relations and Technical Change in the British, Italian and German Automobile Industry. Three Case Studies* (Berlin: WZB) (IIM/LMP 85–5).

WOLFF, E. N. (1985) 'The magnitude and causes of the recent productivity slowdown in the United States: a survey of recent studies', in W. J. Baumol and K. McLennan (eds), *Productivity Growth and US Competitiveness* (New York: Oxford University Press).

WOLFF VON AMERONGEN, O. (1981) 'Leistungsbilanzdefizit – eine Herausforderung der nächsten Jahre', *Zeitschrift für Wirtschaftspolitik – Wirtschaftspolitische Chronik*, 30 (1).

WOOD, J. P. (1986) 'The cooperative labour strategy in the US auto industry', *Economic and Industrial Democracy*, 7 (4) (November).

WORSWICK, G. D. (1985) *Education and Economic Performance* (London: Gower).

WRIGHT, J. P. (1979) *On a clear day you can see General Motors. John Z. De Lorean's look inside the automotive giant* (Grosse Point, Mich.: J. Patrick Wright Enterprises).

YANKELOVICH, D. and IMMERWAHR, J. (1983) *Putting the Work Ethic to Work* (New York: Public Agenda Foundation).

YPSILANTI, D. and MANSELL, R. (1987) 'Reforming telecommunications policy in OECD countries', *OECD Observer*, 148 (October/November).

ZETTERBERG, H., BUSCH, K., CRONA, G., FRANKEL, G., JORNSSON, B., SÖDERUND, I. and WINANDER, B. (1983) *Det osynliga Kontrakter* (Vällingby: SIFO).

ZYSMAN, J. (1983) *Governments, Markets, and Growth: Financial Systems and the Politics of Industrial Change* (Ithaca, NY: Cornell University Press).

ZYSMAN, J. and COHEN, S. S. (1983) 'Double or nothing: open trade and competitive industry', *Foreign Affairs* 61 (5) (Summer).

ZYSMAN, J. and TYSON, L. (eds) (1983) *American Industry in International Competition* (Ithaca, NY: Cornell University Press).

Index

Aaron, H. J., 16
Åberg, R., 148, 243, 266
Abernathy, W. J., 75, 76, 300 (note p. 50), 303 (notes pp. 76 and 77)
absenteeism, *see* work discipline
Abramovitz, M., 299 (note p. 2)
Adam Smith Institute, 305 (note p. 114)
Adamy, W., 207
AFL-CIO, 46, 304 (notes pp. 88 and 89)
Aho, M., 52, 301 (note p. 62)
Aide à toute détresse, 184
air conditioners, comparison of US and Japanese production, 301 (note p. 54)
Altshuler, A., 303 (note p. 80)
American Telephone & Telegraph Company (AT&T), 82ff., 134
Anderson, P., 306 (note p. 119)
Anell, L., 42, 309 (note p. 281)
anti-collectivism, *see* individualism
anti-industrial culture, 120
anti-industrial society, 299 (note p. 11)
anti-Keynesianism, 124
anti-welfare statist attitudes/ programme, 86, 94, 96, 102–3, 135, 175, 220–1, 223, 276, 278, 282
apprenticeship, 126
arms exports, 109
Askling, L., 259
Atkinson, A., 139, 140, 144, 146, 306 (note p. 140)
Attlee, Clement, 134
Auletta, K., 304 (note p. 92)
Auroux Laws, 169, 180
Austin-Rover, *see* Rover
automobile industry
  France, 171–3
  in selected OECD countries, 209–10
  Japanese challenge, 74ff., 172, 208ff., 251
  Sweden, 250
  United Kingdom, 109, 129–32
  USA, 74–81
  West Germany, 208–15

Baker, James, 71
balance of payments
  and competitiveness 4, 5, 7, 18–19, 48–9, 94, 293
  France, 153, 155, 159, 161, 168, 278
  Japan, 49
  macroeconomic conditions of, 48–9, 95, 192, 200ff.
  Sweden, 243, 245ff., 257, 261, 264, 279
  United Kingdom, 103, 106ff., 119, 122, 130, 133
  USA, 45ff., 53–4, 71–2, 82, 83
  West Germany, 187, 189, 192, 194, 200ff., 206, 208
Bank of England, 305 (note p. 114)
banks, importance for investment patterns, 60, 119
Barbash, J., 304 (note p. 97)
Barnett, C., 306 (note p. 119)
Barre, Raymond, 168
Barry, J. J., 82, 83, 303 (note p. 84)
Bauchet, P., 167
Baumol, W. J., 300 (notes pp. 50 and 51)
Bawden, D. L., 86, 303 (note p. 85), 304 (note p. 90)
Begg, D., 123, 306 (note p. 122)
Bell Operating Companies, 82
Bennett, D., 215

Bergman, Å., 252
Bergsten, C. F., 50, 300 (note p. 49)
Bergström, H., 256, 259
Bernheim, D., 301 (note p. 59)
Beveridge/Butler/Beven welfare state, 135, 146
Beveridge Report, 134
Beynon, H., 305 (note p. 118)
Bilstatistik, 252
Bismarck, Otto von, 215
Bjurel Commission, 261
Blades, D., 234
Blais, A., 15
Blank, S., 306 (note p. 119)
Blick durch die Wirtschaft, 308 (note p. 199)
Bluestone, B., 48, 73, 304 (notes pp. 89 and 97)
Bohman, 256
Bolling, R., 59, 300 (note p. 50), 302 (note p. 65)
Boss, A., 307 (note p. 196)
Boston Consulting Group, 261
Bosworth, B., 229
bourgeois bloc, 255ff.
Bowles, J., 59, 300 (note p. 50), 302 (note p. 65)
Bowles, S., 65, 302 (note p. 66), 305 (note p. 98)
Brandt, Willy, 217
British Aerospace, 132
British disease, 114, 116, 121, 147
British Motor Corporation, 131
British Telecom, 132ff.
Brittan, S., 115, 117, 305 (note p. 114)
Brookings Institution, 229, 263, 264, 265
Brooks, H., 54, 59, 301 (notes pp. 55 and 58)
Brown, A., 309 (note p. 287)
Budd, A., 123
Budget Consolidation Law, 218
budget deficit
  Sweden, 257, 260ff.
  United Kingdom, 121
  USA, 48, 58, 68ff., 97, 205–6, 276, 294
  West Germany, 204, 206, 217–8
Bundesanstalt für Arbeit, 219
Bundesminister für Wirtschaft, 204, 307 (notes pp. 193 and 198)
Bundesministerium der Finanzen, 22, 36, 38
Bundestag, 307 (note p. 192)
Bunte, R., 231, 232, 239
bureaucracy, 119 (*see also* state)
Bush, George, 72
Business and Society Study Association (SNS), 255
business climate, 58, 71
Business Higher Education Forum, 301 (note p. 62)
Business Week, 74, 229
Butler's Education Act, 134

Cable, J. R., 113, 127, 129, 306 (note p. 128)
Cable & Wireless, 133
Calder, K. E., 301 (note p. 57)
Callaghan, James, 102
Calmfors, L., 148
Cambridge Political Economy Group, 305 (note p. 114)
Cameron, D. R., 15, 309 (note p. 297)
capital
  costs of, 59
  division of, 118–19
  inflow of, 23–4, 48, 71, 134, 199, 233, 294
  outflow of, 106–7, 119, 198, 200, 233
  social, spending on, 138–9
capital market, organisation of, 60–1
capital–citizen accord, 302 (note p. 66)
capital–labour accord, 98 (*see also* post-war labour truce)
capital-output ratio, 113
capitalisation
  of state enterprises, 168–9
  of the economy, 230
Carter, Jimmy, 45, 71, 72, 86, 97
Catholic Bishops of America, 305 (note p. 98)

Caves, R., 103, 116
Center for National Policy, 98
Center on Budget and Policy
Priorities, 87, 91
Centraal Planbureau, 254
Central Statistical Office (CSO), 106, 125, 144, 146
Centre for Policy Studies, 305 (note p. 114)
Centre Party, 256
CGE, 173
Chaigneau, Y., 1
Chamber of Commerce of the United States, 304 (note p. 88)
charity as substitute for welfare statism, 183
Chassard, P., 175
child labour, 87
children, situation of, 92, 143, 238
Chirac, Jacques, 169, 171, 179
choices of society, 4, 7–8, 10, 63, 247–8, 286–7, 297
Christian Democrats, 204, 207, 218, 220
Chrysler, 74, 79, 81
Churchill, Winston, 134
Civil Rights Act, 87
citizens' power *vis-à-vis* business, 66
City (of London), 107, 118, 120, 127
Clare group, 305 (note p. 114)
class conflict, *see* distribution of income: struggle over; industrial relations; post-war labour truce; two-tier society: effect on labour power
Cline W. R., 300 (note p. 49)
Coates, D., 305 (notes pp. 114 and 116), 306 (note p. 119)
co-determination, 214, 216, 287
Cohen, S., 300 (notes pp. 50 and 51), 301 (note p. 57)
Colbert, Jean-Baptiste, 185
collective bargaining, *see* industrial relations; labour unions
Commissariat Général du Plan, 157, 162, 254
commitment of workers and employees, 9, 58, 65–6, 73, 77, 79, 98, 150, 267–8, 296, (*see also* work discipline)
  in selected OECD countries, 268
communality of interest, 9, 79 (*see also* industrial relations: adversarial *v.* cooperative pattern)
Communists, 255
Community Programme (CP), 137
comparative advantage, 77
  of Sweden, 261
  of the British automobile industry, 130
  of the West German automobile industry, 209, 215
  profile of, 53
competition, international
  adjustment to, 3–4, 7–8, 10, 284
  and inter-firm dynamics, 64, 76
  and limits to redistribution, 283
  as external shock, 202
  as zero-sum game, 4
  challenge of, 2ff., 12ff., 284; France, 153–167, 271; Sweden, 261; United Kingdom, 101–34, 271; USA, 45–85, 271; West Germany, 187–215, 271
  changes in, 3ff.
  effect on economic growth, 281
  effect on industry structure, 94, 281
  effect on public perception of priorities, 97–8, 284
  effect on the pattern of accumulation, 94
  effect on welfare statism, 5ff., 95, 182ff., 228, 281, 284
  exposure to, 3–4, 19, 94, 232, 243
  in tax-cutting and deregulation, 196, 284
  low-wage, 4, 54, 84, 215, 261 (*see also* relocation of production)
  strategic, 83–4
competition policy, 127, 128, 170
competitiveness
  and disruption of production, 202
  and domestic demand, 162, 264

competitiveness *cont.*
and organisation of the production process, 57, 75ff., 267
and specialisation, 164–7
and the relation of cost and non-cost advantages and disadvantages, 164–5
as policy focus, 3, 68, 72, 187, 203, 222, 272, 278, 284, (*see also* exports: importance attributed to; mercantilism, macroeconomic)
as policy focus and demand maintenance, 281
as pretext for particularistic interests, 195
concept of, 5ff., 17ff., 195, 203, 243ff.
confidence in 194, 204, 278
cost or price, 110ff., 157, 164–5, 187, 192, 197–8, 211, 215, 244, 250, 285, 293ff.
embodied in enterprises, 198–9
France, 153–7, 161ff.
importance of, 3, 5
indicators of, 17ff.; for OECD countries, 21ff., 292; France, 154; United Kingdom, 110
national debates on, 12ff., 114; France, 161–7, 278; Sweden, 254–5, 260ff.; United Kingdom, 101ff., 114–21; USA, 56–67, 94, 97, 275; West Germany, 191–203, 221, 278–9, 284
non-cost or non-price, 112ff., 120, 164–5
of enterprises, *see* enterprise
of locations, 3, 34ff., 41–2, 61, 84, 131, 134, 195ff., 215, 278, 284
performing, 6ff., 18, 189–91, 195, 244, 246–7, 291, 295, 297
policies to improve, 272ff., implications for welfare statism, 272–3, 276; France, 167–71, 277; Sweden, 259, 279; United Kingdom, 121–9, 276; USA, 67–74; West Germany, 203–8
requirements of, 4–5, 34, 153
structural, 243ff.
Sweden, 245–54, 257, 263
underlying, 6, 18, 19, 50, 110, 190–1, 195, 296
United Kingdom, 101–14, 123, 129ff.
USA, 47–85
West Germany, 188–215
complacency as cause of competitive decline, 56–7, 68, 193
concession bargaining, 73, 81, 88
Concialdi, P. 175
Confederation of British Industry (CBI), 305 (note p. 114), 306 (note p. 119)
consensus, social, 16, 42, 148, 207, 295 (*see also* industrial relations; work discipline; welfare statism furthering consensus)
Conservative Party, 140, 148
Manifesto, 121, 144, 146
conservative revolution, 71
consumer safety, 302 (note p. 66)
consumption, social preference for, 60–1
consumption-led growth, 58
containment, culture of, 119
Cornvik, 250
corporate citizenship, 73–4, 98–9
corporate culture, *see* management pattern
corporatism, 16, 60–1, 148, 150, 295, 308 (note p. 221), 309 (note p. 287)
cost discipline, 278, 285, 293, 295, 297
Council of Economic Advisors, 254
Council on International and Public Affairs, 304 (note p. 89)
craftsmanship, importance for competitiveness, 190
credits, availability to investors, 119
crowding out of investors, 47, 49, 59, 71, 118, 200

crown, *see* exchange rate, Sweden
Crum, W. C., 59
Cumings, B., 301 (note p. 57)
Cuneo, P., 162, 165, 172
currency
  appreciation, 111, 123, 201–2, 277
  depreciation, 19, 71, 111, 202–3, 205, 234, 245, 247, 257ff., 279, 286; and inflation, 7–8, 293ff.; as a means of spreading welfare costs, 7, 224
  overvalued, 23–4, 50, 54, 71–2, 77, 95, 110, 119, 294
  undervalued, 187, 189, 200ff., 206, 210
  see also exchange rate
Currie, D., 305 (note p. 118)
Curzon, G., 299 (note p. 8)
Curzon-Price, V. 299 (note p. 8)
Cusack, T., 236

Dagens Industri, 251
Dagens Nyheter, 251
Dang Nguyen, 253
Danziger, S., 90, 92
Dauderstädt, M., 194, 299 (note p. 4)
Debonneuil, M., 162, 165
decline of the country, concern about, 50, 51, 56ff., 68, 97–8, 101ff., 114, 148, 153
defence expenditure
  effect on technology, 62, 84, 302 (note p. 71)
  United Kingdom, 119
  USA, 48, 58, 59, 62, 70, 302 (note p. 71)
de-industrialisation
  United Kingdom, 104–5, 129, 305 (note p. 118), 306 (note p. 121)
  USA, 48, 95
Delattre, M., 162, 165
Delors plan, 150
demand
  expansion of, 167–8
  shift in, 75ff., 211
de-maturity, 75
Denison, E. F., 58, 61
dependence, culture of, 118
Derber, C., 302 (note p. 65)
deregulation
  asymmetric, effect on competitiveness, 83, 134
  opposition against, 207
  see also regulation
Deutsche Bundesbank, 188, 307 (note p. 192)
Deutscher Gewerkschaftsbund (DGB), 195
Deutsches Industrie Forum, 308 (note p. 199)
Deutsches Institute für Wirtschaftsforschung (DIW), 202, 217, 218, 308 (note p. 201)
developmental state *v.* regulatory state, 57
Devine, P., 127, 128
DHSS, 141
Dicke, H., 207, 307 (note p. 197)
dismissal, 73, 77
  protection against, 87, 126, 170, 183, 207
distribution of income
  and investment, 160–1, 167, 309 (note p. 297)
  France, 157–8, 175–6
  in selected OECD countries, 237
  orientation towards, as opposed to performance orientation, 56, 58, 61
  struggle over, 226–7, 289–90, 293, 295
  Sweden, 229, 236ff., 260, 279
  United Kingdom, 101, 141ff.
  see also limits to redistribution
distributional coalitions, 10, 67
D-mark, *see* exchange rate, West Germany
dollar, *see* exchange rate, USA
Donges, J., 197
Driffil, J., 148
dualism *see* labour market: two-tier; two-tier society
Dunn, J. A. Jr., 75, 303 (note p. 80)
Dupuis, J. M., 175

Durand, M., 244
Dyer, D., 74, 76, 303 (notes pp. 76 and 77)

East Asia: challenge for the West, 1, 56–7, 84, 301 (note p. 55) (*see also* Japan)
Eckard, W., 303 (note p. 76)
economic citizen rights, 7, 9, 88, 98, 99, 221, 227, 290
Economic Competitiveness, International Trade, and Technology Development Act, 302 (note p. 72)
economic growth
  and economic efficiency, 37
  as basis of the modern welfare state, 281, 284
  as indicator of competitiveness, 36ff.
  as stake in international competition, 5, 195
  of OECD countries, 38ff., 240–1
economic performance
  and economic weight of government, 283–4
  priority of 1, 11, 219–20
Economic Recovery Tax Act (ERTA), 58, 69
economies of scale, *see* standardised mass production
Economist, The, 107, 131, 132, 138, 141, 144, 229
education, 62, 87, 137, 173 (*see also* human capital)
  and social inequality, 184
  as competitive disadvantage, 131
  government expenditure on, 141, 145, 169, 177–8
  free, 134
Education Act, 145
Education for a Competitive America Act, 302 (note p. 72)
Edwardes, Sir Michael, 131
Edwards, G., 119
efficiency of production
  and economic growth, 37
  and financial capacity, 303 (note p. 76)
  and locational conditions, 198–9
  organisation for, 4, 58, 75ff., 213, 291
  Sweden, 262
  USA, 58, 76ff.
Eichner, H., 220, 308 (note p. 224)
Eisner, R., 61–2
Ekonomisk Debatt, 254
elites
  administrative, outlook of, 119ff.
  role in investment, 60–1
Elsenhans, H., 301 (note p. 54)
Elvander, N., 266
Employee Retirement Income Security Act, 87
Employees Involvement Program, 79
employment
  active policy of, 280 (*see also* employment: creation of public)
  and wages, 89, 95, 223, 225, 266, 295
  and working time, 179, 214, 222–3, 225ff.
  and economic growth, 221ff., 280–1
  as ingredient of welfare statism, 1, 2, 17, 88–90, 118, 135, 143, 147, 218ff., 274, 277
  creation of public, 178–9, 224, 228, 236
  effect on unionisation, 126
  France, 179–81, 277, 280
  government commitment to, 135, 137, 219, 247, 258, 262, 266, 268, 286–7
  in OECD countries, 240–1
  low-wage, 89–90, 92–5, 180, 276, 280
  non-standardised, 126, 180, 207, 220
  policy debate on, 222ff.
  security *v.* job security, 81, 214
  subsidies to enterprises, 127, 179, 227
  Sweden, 243, 255, 280
  United Kingdom, 103–5, 123, 135ff., 277, 280–1

USA, 45ff., 88–90, 95
West Germany, 203, 207, 219ff., 279–80
see also labour market performance measure; labour-shedding; non-accelerating inflation rate of unemployment
Employment Institute, 305 (note p. 114)
engineers, number of, 62, 174, 246
Englander, S., 33, 292
enjoyment of life, 2, 197
enterprise(s)
alliance between, 78, 84–5, 131, 213
goal of, 64
international mobility of, 3, 196, 198, 233
measures to improve competitiveness, 267
organisation of, 58, 76ff., 296 (*see also* efficiency of production: organisation for)
performance and cultural context, 199
response to market opportunities and challenges, 64, 75ff., 96, 161, 197
strategic capacity of, importance for competitiveness, 83–4
strategies of, importance for competitiveness, 57, 63–4, 75ff., 156, 211, 250
Sweden, 230, 248, 250ff., 267, 291
United Kingdom, 118ff.
USA, 63–4, 72–4, 82ff.
see also management
Enterprise Allowance Scheme, 137
entitlement mentality, 8, 194, 197 (*see also* distribution: orientation towards)
entrepreneurship, financial, 63, 64, 72–3, 118–19, 199 (*see also* enterprise; rent-seeking)
Entreprises Intermédiaires, 179
environmental protection, 302 (note p. 66)
Erdmann, G., 191
Ergas, H., 246
Ericsson, 250, 253–4
Erixon, L., 247, 264
Etzioni, A., 302 (note p. 65)
European Community, 121, 284, 306 (note p. 121)
technological initiatives of, 128
European integration, 203
European Management Forum, 34ff., 232, 233, 301 (note p. 54)
European Monetary System, 119, 166, 202, 233
Euvrard, F., 175, 176, 177
exchange controls, 127
exchange rate
as adjustment mechanism, 4, 202, 206, 215, 224, 262–3, 266, 291–3, 295 (*see also* currency)
France, 162–3, 166
relativising wage effects, 212
Sweden, 234, 245, 247, 249, 259–60, 279, 286, 295
United Kingdom, 10–11, 119, 122, 124
USA, 23–4, 49, 50, 54, 71–2, 77, 83, 95, 294
West Germany, 187, 200ff., 206, 210–11
exit, option for, 145–7
export-led growth, 19, 37, 204, 206
export restraint agreement, 74–5, 303 (note p. 78)
export(s)
and the distortion of the production structure, 308 (note p. 201)
as indicator of competitiveness, 19ff.
growth in OECD countries, 20ff., 240–41
importance attributed to, 187–8, 191–2, 203ff. (*see also* mercantilism, macroeconomic)
market destination of, 156, 164–5, 174, 233, 244, 250ff.
share of GDP, 188, 231ff.

export(s) *cont.*
  supply structure of, 19, 157, 159, 165, 232, 244

Fair Labor Standards Act, 87
families, situation of, 92–3, 238, 306 (note p. 143)
Farmers' League, 256
Faxen, K.-O., 267
Federal Reserve Bank, 47
Feldstein, M. S., 15
Financial Services Act, 127
Financial Times, 69, 82, 83, 209, 210, 212, 213, 215, 230, 251, 253, 308 (notes pp. 199 and 211)
Finansdepartementet, 235, 236, 237, 243, 247, 250
Finegold, D., 307 (note p. 149)
fiscal welfare, 139–140
Fischer, S., 123
Flaherty, S., 303 (note p. 77)
Flam, H., 232
Flora, P., 235
Ford, Gerald, 45
Ford Motors, 79, 81, 130, 131, 211, 303 (note p. 79)
Fordism, 57, 102, 299 (note p. 2)
foreign debt
  France, 153
  Sweden, 258
  USA, 45, 59, 71
Foreman-Peck, J., 133
Fores, M., 306 (note p. 120)
Fortune list of world's largest corporations, 230
France, economic policy, 167ff., 277
Franzén, T., 237
Franzmeyer, F., 203
free-market philosophy, 187, 207, 275–6 (*see also* individualism; supply-side economics; Thatcherism)
Friedman, B. M., 59, 300 (note p. 47)
Friedman, M., 115, 123, 309 (note p. 284)
Friedman, R. D., 309 (note p. 284)
fringe benefits, *see* occupational welfare
Front Populaire, 174
Fujitsu, 303 (note p. 84)
Furåker, B., 243

Gallaway, L., 93
Garvin, D. A., 301 (note p. 54)
Gazier, B., 175
GEC, 132–33
General Agreement on Trade and Tariffs (GATT), 21, 22, 23, 25, 292
General Motors, 77, 79ff., 132, 303 (notes pp. 76 and 79)
Genscher, Dietrich, 193
Gerstenberger, W., 190, 193, 202
Giersch, H., 197
Giorno, C., 144
Globus Kartendienst, 25, 35, 36, 38, 191, 209, 210
Glover, I., 306 (note p. 120)
Gordon, D. M., 65
Gottschalk, P., 90, 91, 92, 93
Gough, I., 150, 299 (note p. 2)
government
  economic intervention of, 68ff., 102, 115ff., 166, 276
  economic weight of, 15, 69ff., 97, 121–2, 125, 181, 217, 229, 276, 283, 299–300 (note p. 16) (*see also* economic performance and economic weight of government; taxes)
  links with financial capital, 120, 148
  promoting competitiveness, 57, 118, 167–8, 185, 193, 208, 277
  promoting exports, 187
  spending: effect on inflation, 97, 115; effect on the balance of trade, 264
  see also state
grass-root organisations, 184
Great Society programme, 59, 85ff.
Greenstein, 92
Greffe, X., 153, 167, 173, 175, 179, 185
Grewlich, K. W., 307 (note p. 193)

Gross, B., 304 (note p. 89), 305 (note p. 98)
Gürtler, J., 203
Gustafsson, B., 237

Hager, W., 299 (note p. 11), 309 (note p. 281)
Hans-Böckler-Stiftung, 195
Harrington, M., 73, 304 (notes pp. 88, 90, 92 and 97)
Harrison, B., 48, 73, 304 (notes pp. 89 and 97)
Harvard Business Review, 61
Hatsopoulos, G. N., 59
Hayek, F., 116, 123, 305 (note p. 114)
Hayes-Conyers Income and Jobs Action Act, 305 (note p. 98)
Heald, D., 306 (note p. 128)
health insurance
  France, 178
  United Kingdom, *see* National Health Service
  USA 87–8 (*see also* Medicaid; Medicare),
  West Germany 218
Health Services Board, 146
Heath, Edward, 102, 114
hegemony, *see* leadership position
Hermes, 187
Hesselman, I., 82, 83
High Speed Train, 156
high technology, strength in, 51ff., 82, 156, 190, 192–3, 245, 278
High Technology Research and Scientific Education Act, 302 (note p.72)
Hild, R., 210
Hillard, J., 305 (notes pp. 114 and 116), 306 (note p. 119)
Hills, H., 139, 140, 150
Hirschhorn, L., 302 (note p. 65)
HMSO, 124, 125, 128
Hoff, A., 209, 212, 213, 214
Hofheinz, R. Jr., 301 (note p. 57)
Holland, S., 305 (note p. 118)
Holmberg, S., 257
Honda, 131
Horwitz, C., 246, 251
Hoskyns, 305 (note p. 116)
House of Lords Select Committee on Overseas Trade, 107, 109, 117, 119, 120, 305 (notes pp. 113, 114 and 118), 306 (note p. 119)
housing, public, 141, 143, 216
  and labour mobility, 144
Hudson Report, 305 (note p. 119), 306 (note p. 119)
human capital, 9–10, 291, 297
  and inflation, 149
  France, 172, 174, 185
  United Kingdom, 118, 120, 149
  USA, 61–2, 72, 77, 98
  West Germany, 194

Iacocca, Lee, 74
ideological predisposition, 288–9, 309 (note p. 284)
ifo-Institute for Economic Research, 190, 307 (notes pp. 196, 206, 208, 211)
IG Metall, 214
ILO Convention 26, 127
Immerwahr, J., 302 (note p. 65)
income security, 2, 81
  in old age, 91, 140, 145, 218
indexation of wages, 169
individualism, principle of, 86, 102, 147, 148, 282
Industrial Bank of Japan, 301 (note p. 64)
industrial culture, 66–7
industrial dispute, 117, 126
industrial divide, second, 65
industrial policy, 120, 127–8, 167–8, 208, 272, 274, 278
industrial relations
  adversarial/co-operative pattern of, 66, 79, 117, 131, 150, 194, 214, 252, 269, 306 (note p. 129)
  centralisation/decentralisation of 117
  effect on work discipline, 16, 66, 73, 79
  flexibility/rigidity of, 65, 73, 77, 79, 116–17, 213–14
  France, 172

industrial relations *cont.*
importance for competitiveness, 65–6, 77, 116–17, 150, 213–14, 269, 291, 296
Sweden, 252, 267
United Kingdom, 116–17, 126–7
USA, 65–7, 73–4, 77ff.
West Germany, 213–14
(*see also* commitment of workers; industrial dispute; labour unions; participation of workers in enterprise affairs; Quality of Work Life; work discipline)
industrial revolution, third, 193
industrins Utredningsinstitutet (IUI), 255, 261, 262
inertia, organizational, 64, 75–7
inertia, social/institutional, 96, 222, 287–8
inflation
effect on competitiveness, 115, 202
in OECD countries, 240–41
trade-off with economic growth, 45, 115, 263
see also monetary stability; currency depreciation and inflation
infrastructure, importance for competitiveness, 149–50
Ingham, G., 120, 305 (note p. 119)
innovation
and financial capacity, 303 (note p. 76)
effect on markets, 75ff., 82
importance for competitiveness, 75, 77, 84, 213, 243–4
incorporation into conventional goods, 190
organisation for, 4
INSEE, 155, 157, 158, 160, 161, 163, 165, 179
Institute for Economic and Social Research (IRES), 162, 164
Institute of Directors, 305 (note p. 116)
Institute of Economic Affairs, 115, 305 (note p. 114)
Institute of Fiscal Studies, 305 (note p. 114)
interest groups
and economic adjustment, 8, 10, 295
and welfare statism, 10–11, 42–3, 221–2, 227
in policy discourse, 114
(*see also* sclerosis, institutional)
interest payment on public debts, 70
inter-firm dynamics, 64, 76
international economic cooperation, 205
International Monetary Fund (IMF), 138
investment
abroad, *see* capital: inflow of; capital: outflow of
and domestic demand, 201
and interest rate, *see* crowding out of investors
France, 160–61, 166, 173
importance for competitiveness, 34, 55ff., 118, 120, 166, 203, 212–13
in selected OECD countries, 55
United Kingdom, 112–13, 118–19, 123, 133
USA, 57–61
v. consumption, 192, 205
West Germany, 198ff., 213
yield of, 230–31
invisibles, balance of, 106–7

Jackson, P., 115, 123
Jaguar, 132
Jakobsson, U., 258, 263
Japan
challenge to American leadership position, 52ff., 84
corporatist structure, 60
enterprises, 64
investment in the United Kingdom, 131
investment in the USA, 75, 80
management, 76ff.
see also automobile industry: Japanese challenge

Japanisation of the US automobile industry, 75
Jay, P., 115, 117, 305 (note p. 114)
Johnson, C., 301 (note p. 57)
Johnson, Lyndon, 59, 85
Jones, D., 75, 78, 130, 132
Jörberg, L., 231, 232, 239
Joseph, Sir Keith., 115, 117, 128, 131, 305 (note p. 116)
Joyce, M., 138, 140, 306 (note p. 140)
Jürgens, U., 303 (note p. 76)
Justitiedepartementet, 261

Kamppeter, W., 205, 301 (note p. 64), 308 (note p. 200)
Kassalow, E., 73, 88, 304 (note p. 97)
Katz, H. C., 77, 80, 81, 303 (notes pp. 77 and 79)
Katzenstein, P., 15
Kay, J., 127, 129, 306 (note p. 128)
Keith, L., 117
Kendrick, J. W., 60
Keynesianism, 115, 223, 256, 262, 283, 299 (note p. 2), 306 (note p. 121)
King, D. S., 309 (note p. 287)
Kochan, T. A., 66, 77, 302 (note p. 73), 303 (note p. 79), 304 (note p. 97)
Kohl, Helmut, 218–19, 221
Konjunkturinstitutet, 246, 254
Kornbluh, H., 303 (note p. 79)
Korpi, W., 15
Koskella, E., 15
Kosters, M. H., 304 (note p. 89)
Kovach, K. A., 302 (note p. 65)
Krause, L., 103
Krauss, M., 299 (note p. 8)
Kurz, R., 307 (note p. 196)
Kuttner, R., 304 (note p. 90)

labour, attachment to enterprises, 62
labour costs, 73, 94, 131, 153, 157, 162–5, 197, 210, 234 (*see also* unit labour costs; wages)
  and subcontracting, 163
  in selected OECD countries, 234
labour force, structure of, 73, 88, 89
labour market, and welfare state, 265ff. (*see also various subheadings under* welfare statism)
  deregulation of, 122, 126–7, 207
  flexibility/rigidity of, 62, 89, 95, 116, 127, 129, 138, 194, 223, 261, 266 (*see also* wage rigidity/flexibility)
  performance measure (LMPM) in OECD countries, 241–2
  position of labour in, 78ff., 85, 93, 95
  two-tier, 73, 93–5, 126, 141, 220
Labour Party, 117, 121, 125, 135, 138, 148, 258, 288
Labour Research Department, 305 (note p. 114)
labour scarcity, 243, 252, 261, 263ff.
labour-shedding as response to competitive pressure, 78ff., 173
labour supply, *see* labour scarcity; welfare statism: encouraging labour supply; welfare statism: sustaining labour market rigidities)
labour unions
  as culprits of competitive decline, 116ff.
  as promoter of the welfare state idea, 99
  power of, 72, 78ff., 87, 116, 126, 150 (*see also* two-tier society: effect on labour power)
  hostility towards, 66, 73, 94, 97, 126–7, 276, 296
  ideology of, 117, 288
  legislation against, 126, 207
  links with political party, 117
  public sector, 117, 266–7
  Sweden, 258ff., 266–7
  United Kingdom, 116ff., 126ff.
  USA, 72–3, 79ff., 87, 95, 99, 276, 281
  West Germany, 225
  see also industrial relations; unionisation
Laffer curve, 97, 116, 283

Lafontaine, Oskar, 226
Lawrence, P. R., 74, 76, 303 (notes pp. 76 and 77)
Lawrence, R. Z., 264, 300 (notes pp.49 and 50)
Lawson, Nigel, 124
Layard, R., 116, 306 (note p. 138)
leadership position
of USA, 51ff., 271
of Sweden in the Nordic region, 233
Leibfritz, W., 307 (note p. 196)
Leone, R. A., 303 (note p. 76)
Lever, H., 119
Levitan, S. A., 303 (note p. 86), 304 (note p. 90)
Levitt, M., 138, 140, 306 (note p. 140)
Levy, F., 304 (notes pp. 92 and 94)
Leys, F., 305 (note p. 119)
Liberal Democratic Party of Japan, 60
Liberals, 256–7
limits to redistribution, 279, 282ff., 288–9 (*see also* tax ceiling)
Lindbeck, A., 2, 41, 264, 265
Lindberg, P., 267
Lindblom, C. E., 288
Lipietz, A., 168, 299 (note p. 2)
Lloyds Bank, 136
LO, 259
Lodge, G. C., 56, 59, 300 (note p. 50)
London Chamber of Commerce, 306 (note p. 119)
Lordstown Syndrome, 77, 79
Lovell, M. R. Jr., 300 (note p. 50)
Loveman, G. W., 304 (note p. 89)
Lundberg, E., 264
Luxemburg Income Study, 236, 238

MacGregor, S., 144, 145
Mackenzie, I., 82, 83
Maddison, A., 159, 160, 239, 240
Magaziner, I. C., 57
Mahon, R., 98, 301 (note p. 62)
Malmquist, D. H., 300 (note p. 50)
management
attitude towards state intervention, 121
autonomy and workers' rights, 171, 199
pattern, 57, 63, 76ff., 171, 199, 291, 302 (note p. 65)
responsibility for competitive decline, 63–4, 75ff., 120, 297
training, 120
see also enterprise; efficiency of production: organisation for
Manison, L., 305 (note p. 113)
Mankin, E. D., 75
Manning, D., 133
Mansell, R., 133
manufacturing industry
competitive importance of, 20
exports in OECD countries, 20ff.
indicators for selected OECD countries, 105
see also de-industrialisation
market failure *v.* regulatory failure, 129
market shares
as indicator of competitiveness, 18–19, 244
as result of deliberate societal choice, 248
France, 155ff., 165–6, 172ff.
selected OECD countries, 51, 53
Sweden, 246–7, 251, 253, 260
United Kingdom, 101
USA, 48–51, 72, 74–5
West Germany, 190, 207ff.
Marquand, D., 148
Marsden, K., 15, 130
Mathis, J., 162, 163, 165
Matthews, R., 127, 150, 306 (notes pp. 121, 124 and 129)
Matti, V., 15
Maynard, G., 120, 124, 307 (note p. 149)
Mazier, J., 162, 163, 165
McCallum, J., 15
McDermott, P., 308 (note p. 199)
McGarrah, R. E., 64, 301 (notes pp. 62 and 64)
McLennan, K., 300 (notes pp. 50 and 51)
Medicaid, 87

Medicare, 70, 85, 86, 91
medium technology
  competitiveness of UK in, 108
  importance for US competitiveness, 53, 56
medium-term financial strategy (MTFS), 123–4
Melman, S., 301 (note p. 62)
mercantilism, 307 (note p. 193)
  macroeconomic, 204ff., 222ff., 228
Mercury, 133
Metcalf, D., 126
Middlemas, K., 146, 306 (note p. 119)
Mid-Term Economic Surveys, 255, 261
military, *see* defence
Miller, J. A., 302 (note p. 71)
Mills, D. Q., 300 (note p. 50)
Mills, G. B., 69, 70, 302 (note p. 70)
Minford, P., 116, 117, 123, 127, 150, 306 (notes pp. 124 and 129)
minimum wage, 1, 87, 89, 116
Mittelstädt, A., 33, 292
Moderate Party, 256, 258
Möller, C., 207, 220
monetarism, 46–7, 115, 122ff., 277
monetary stability, 4, 97, 115, 121ff., 170, 204, 206, 219, 222, 259–60, 262, 266, 278, 295 (*see also* inflation; stagflation)
  as competitive advantage, 192, 202ff.
Moon, M., 92, 304 (note p. 90)
Morgan, K., 132, 134
Moseley, P., 123, 306 (note p. 122)
motivation, *see* commitment
Mückenberger, U., 207
Murard, N., 176
Murman, K., 307 (note p. 199)
Murray, C., 304 (note p. 89)
Myles, J., 309 (note p. 288)

Nairn, T., 101, 306 (note p. 119)
Naples, M. J., 302 (note p. 66)
National Association of Manufacturers (NAM), 54
National Commission on Excellence in Education, 301 (note p. 62)
National Committee for Resistance, 174
National Health Service, 127–8, 134, 140–1, 146
National Income and Expenditure, 104
National Institute for Economic and Social Research, 307 (note p. 149)
National Insurance Scheme, 134
national priorities, public perception of, 96ff., 192, 203, 222
national purpose, 57, 68
nationalisation of enterprises, 167, 174
natural resources and export performance, 20
NEC, 303 (note p. 84)
negative income tax, 145, 177, 225
Nelson, R. R., 301 (note p. 64)
neo-liberal ideology, *see* free-market philosophy; monetarism; supply-side economics; Thatcherism
New Deal, 85, 186, 305 (note p. 99)
New Centrism, 121
New Left, 114, 120
New Right, 114ff., 120–1, 141, 147
Nickell, S., 306 (note p. 138)
Nissan, 131
non-accelerating inflation rate of unemployment (NAIRU), 116
non-economic objectives of society, 1, 2, 10, 11
non-wage labour costs, 77, 194, 196–7, 278, 291 (*see also* occupational welfare; social security contributions of employers)
  as incentive to increase productivity, 158–9
Norsworthy, J. R., 300 (note p. 50)
North Sea oil, 20, 23, 102, 106ff., 121, 125–6, 277, 281 (*see also* natural resources)

Norton, R. D., 67, 300 (note p. 51)
nuisance potential of labour, 66

Occupational Safety and Health Act, 87
occupational welfare, 73–4, 78, 87–8, 139–40, 146, 267
  and changes in the industry structure, 88, 276
  management initiatives to extend, 267, 274
  tax incentives for, 87 (*see also* corporate citizenship)
Office of Telecommunications (OFTEL), 133
O'Higgins, M., 142, 143
Ohlsson, L. 245, 262
Olson, M. 10, 43, 67
Opel, 211
order, maintenance of, 148
Organisation of Economic Cooperation and Development (OECD), 17, 21, 23, 28, 29, 30, 31, 32, 33, 38, 39, 46, 47, 53, 55, 56, 101, 103, 108, 112, 123, 124, 125, 126, 127, 128, 129, 154, 155, 157, 158, 172, 190, 209, 217, 231, 232, 235, 239, 240, 241, 242, 243, 245, 246, 248, 255, 258, 292, 300 (note p. 17), 306 (notes pp. 122 and 124)
outsourcing, 78, 80, 215
overcapacity, 74
overstaffing, 172

Palmer, J. L., 69, 86, 303 (note p. 85), 304 (note p. 90)
Parry, R., 134, 138, 306 (note p. 140)
Parsche, R., 307 (note p. 196)
participation of workers in enterprise affairs, 79ff., 98, 169, 171, 180–1, 296, 302 (note p. 65) (*see also* co-determination)
  as economic danger, 262
part-time work, 73, 126, 136, 180
party, political, 305 (note p. 114)
  competition furthering welfare state expansion, 117
Patel, C., 130, 133, 305 (note p. 113)
patents, 113, 130, 245
Patterson, J. T., 303 (note p. 86)
Pavitt, K., 130, 133, 245, 305 (note p. 113)
Pempel, T. J., 301 (note p. 57)
pensions, *see* income security in old age
Petersson, O., 255
Peugeot, 131, 171ff.
Pfaller, A., 6, 10, 299 (note p. 4), 301 (note p. 54)
Phillips curve, 115
Pichaud, D., 307 (note p. 143)
Piore, M. J., 66, 77, 302 (notes pp. 65 and 73), 303 (note p. 79), 304 (note p. 97)
Plessey, 132–3
policy discourse, 114
policy errors, as cause of declining competitiveness, 117, 119–20, 306 (note p. 121)
Policy Studies Institute, 305 (note p. 114)
political polarisation, 306 (note p. 121)
politics, economic theory of, 117
Pollard, S., 306 (note p. 119)
Poor Law, 135
Posner, M., 306 (note p. 119)
post-Fordism (*see* Fordism)
post-war labour truce, 65–6, 73, 77, 94
pound sterling, *see* exchange rate: United Kingdom
poverty
  and structure of the population, 304 (notes pp. 90 and 94)
  as general perspective for Western societies, 1, 282
  challenge of, 96
  France, 177, 184, 277
  relief, 85, 88, 90–3, 144–5, 176–7, 290
  culture of, 92

United Kingdom, 143, 276
USA, 90–3
West Germany, 220, 222
Prais, S. J., 305 (note p. 113), 307 (note p. 149)
President's Commission on Industrial Competitiveness, 50, 52, 56, 62, 67, 72, 301 (note p. 54), 302 (note p. 65)
price
controls, 168, 170, 172
discipline, 187, 189
priorities of society, *see* choices of society
privatisation 124, 127ff., 132–3, 169–70 (*see also* state enterprises and competitiveness)
vested interest in, 102
product cycle and strategic competition, 84
production costs, structure of, 267
productivity
and claims on its yields, 196
and economic growth, 105–6
and employment, 27–8, 105, 249
as condition for competitiveness, 6, 27ff., 54, 75, 212–13
coalition, 194, 214
convergence in, 51, 54
France, 158ff., 172, 173
in OECD countries, 28–33, 105, 111–12, 159–60
of capital, 32, 113, 160
Sweden, 249
total factor, 32–3
United Kingdom, 103, 105–6, 110, 111, 123–4, 131, 149
USA, 54, 57, 75
West Germany, 189–90, 196, 210, 212–13
profitability
of enterprises, 66, 73, 81, 111, 131, 150, 197–98, 231, 247 (*see also* taxes: effect on profits)
v. productivity orientation, 64
prosperity for all, 1, 86, 94, 287 (*see also* economic citizen rights)
protectionism
European, as advantage for German car industry, 209
foreign, as threat to own industry, 82ff., 254
see also trade policy
Public Expenditure White Paper, 124, 125
public sector borrowing requirement (PSBR), 122

quality of life, 1, 7, 9, 63
quality of products
as condition of competitiveness, 6, 164, 190, 210ff.
USA, 54, 75
West Germany, 196, 210
Quality of Work Life (QWL), 79–80
Quick, P. D., 71

RACE, 253
Ramo, S., 301 (note p. 62)
rational expectations, 115, 117
Ray, G. F., 110, 111
Ray, J. C., 175
Reagan, Ronald, 45ff., 68ff., 86, 90, 91, 97, 101, 276, 282
Reagonomics, 48, 95, 294 (*see also* USA: economic policy)
recession, 46, 47, 60, 89, 93, 95, 114, 123, 143, 147, 148, 217, 219, 277
redistribution, *see* distribution of income
regional disparities, as remedy against institutional sclerosis, 67
regulation of economic activities by the government, 63, 71, 82, 116, 118, 122, 127, 133, 168, 170, 194, 196–7, 262, 282, 303 (notes pp. 76 and 78)
Reich, R. B., 57, 75
relocation of production to low-wage countries, 78, 84, 214–5
Renault, 171ff.
rentier nation, 107
rent-seeking, 18, 161, 167 (*see also* entrepreneurship, financial)

research & development
  concentration in a few industries, 113, 208
  costs of, 83–4
  expenditure in OECD countries, 113, 191
  France, 161, 166, 169
  government funding for, 84–5, 208
  importance for competitiveness, 84, 113, 120, 193
  military, 62, 84
  Sweden, 245
  United Kingdom, 113
  USA, 56
  West Germany, 190–1, 193, 208
  see also innovation
Restaurants of the Heart, 183
Reynolds, M., 304 (note p. 90)
Rhein, E., 307 (note p.193)
rhetoric, importance of, 122
Richardson, R., 126
Richter, S., 220, 308 (note p. 224)
Riese, H., 308 (note p. 204)
Riksdagstrycket, 233, 246, 248, 249, 251, 252, 256, 257, 258, 260, 265
Rimlinger, G. V., 216
Ringen, S., 237
Rivlin, A., 229, 263
Roberts, D., 234
Robinson, R., 141
Rocard, Michel, 177
Roobeek, A., 253
Roosevelt, Franklin D., 85
Root, L. S., 88, 304 (note p. 88)
Rosanvallon, P., 309 (note p. 282)
Rosen, M., 52, 301 (note p. 62)
Rosenberg, N., 301 (note p. 62)
Rosenbrock, R., 299 (note p. 2)
Ross, M. N., 304 (note p. 89)
Rothschild, E., 303 (note p. 77)
Rover, 130ff.
Rowthorn, R., 102, 104, 105, 106, 108, 124, 150, 306 (note p. 121)

Saab-Scania, 250ff.
Sabel C. F., 302 (note p. 65), 303 (note p. 79)
Sachverständigenrat, 189, 254
SAF, 234, 267
Salter, M. S., 74, 75, 302–3 (note p. 76)
Sampson, A., 306 (note p. 119)
Sargent, J., 306 (note p. 121)
Saunders, P., 15, 299 (note p. 16)
savings
  incentives for, 60
  Sweden, 261
  USA, 49, 58–60
  West Germany, 200, 206
Sawhill, I. V., 45, 58, 69, 92, 304 (notes pp. 90 and 92)
scattergram, 16
Scharpf, F. W., 200, 227, 308 (note p. 224)
Schettkat, R., 227
Schmidt, Helmut, 217–19
Schmidt, M., 309 (notes p. 287)
Schulze, P. W., 85, 301 (note p. 62)
Schwartz, W., 302 (note p. 65)
sclerosis, institutional, 10, 23, 67, 119, 193–4, 197, 207, 229, 288, 297
Scott, B. R., 50, 51, 52, 53, 56, 299 (note p. 8), 300 (notes pp. 50 and 51), 301 (note p. 57)
Seidman, B., 87
self-interest *v*. common-goal orientation, 65
services
  employment in, 89, 105, 281
  importance for competitiveness, 129, 300 (note p. 20)
  see also invisibles
Shapiro, I., 89, 304 (note p. 90)
Sharpe, K., 215
Shoven, J., 301 (note p. 59)
Shreveport telephone plant, 84
Smith, A. D., 305 (note p. 111)
Smith, K., 113
Smith, R., 305 (note p. 118)
Smolensky, E., 304 (note p. 90)
SNS, 262, 263, 265
Social Democratic Pensioners' Organisation, 260

Social Democrats, 192, 204, 216–17, 223, 229, 255, 258ff., 282, 284, 288, 289
social discipline, 196, 203 (*see also* consensus, social; industrial relations: adversarial/co-operative pattern of; wage discipline)
social expenditure
and unemployment, 140
as indicator of welfare statism, 17, 20ff.
in OECD countries, 20ff., 235
United Kingdom, 138ff.
USA, 85ff.
West Germany, 217
see also transfer payments
social partnership, concept of, 216
social property rights, 221, 227
social security
and saving, 15
income replacement ratio of, 127, 265
linkage with earnings, 126–7
private provision of, 145–7, 183 (*see also* occupational welfare)
Social Security Act (United Kingdom), 135, 145
Social Security Act (USA), 85
Social Security Consortium, 145
social security contributions, 176, 182–3
as share of GNP, 69
effect on production costs, 182ff.
increases as a means to meet new welfare needs, 224
of employers, 163, 182, 249 (*see also* non-wage labour costs)
social services, 236–7, 297
social virtues, 65
socialism, 101
socialist bloc, 255–6
socialists, 283, 288
Söderström, H. T., 230
Soete, L., 245
solidarity
among wage earners, 225ff., 286, 289–90
within society, 92, 99, 228, 296
Solow, R., 101
Soltwedel, R., 223
Soskice, D., 307 (note p. 149)
SOU, 261, 265, 266
Soziale Marktwirtschaft, 216
specialisation, index of, 109
stagflation, 283–4
United Kingdom, 103–4, 115
USA, 45, 72
West Germany, 193, 204, 219–20
see also monetary stability
Stalk, G. Jr., 299 (note p. 4)
standardised mass production, declining importance of, 57, 75
Stark, T., 141, 142
state
archaic, 119–21
enterprises and competitiveness, 128–9, 182
state earnings-related pension scheme (SERPS), 135, 145
Statens Industriverk, 243, 246, 247, 248, 249
STC, 132–3
Steedman, H., 307 (note p. 149)
Steel, D., 306 (note p. 128)
Stockman, D. A., 302 (note p. 70)
Stone, C. F., 45, 58
Strauß, F.-J., 307 (note p. 196)
Streeck, W., 42, 209, 212, 213, 214
strike, *see* industrial dispute
student support, 87, 218
subcontracting as competitive disadvantage, 145
subsidies, 17, 128, 131, 194, 247, 254
for new plants, 252
Sundquist, J. L., 303 (note p. 86)
Supplementary Benefits Commission, 144
supplementary unemployment benefits, *see* unemployment compensation
supply-side economics, 47ff., 59, 68ff., 115ff., 138, 223, 227, 229, 272, 274, 285, 306 (note p. 121)
Svenska Dagbladet, 251, 254

Sweden
  economic performance, 15, 230ff., 237ff., 255
  economic policy, 256ff.
  fiscal policy, 255, 258, 260
  industry structure, 231, 261
  structure of foreign trade, 232–3
Swedish Employers' Confederation, 263
Swedish Labour Market Board, 243

Taggart, R., 303 (note p. 86)
Tarantelli, E., 66, 309 (note p. 295)
Tarschys, D., 144
Tawney Society, 305 (note p. 114)
Tax Equity and Fiscal Responsibility Act (TEFRA), 69
tax(es)
  as indicator of welfare statism, 17
  ceiling, 217, 263, 278–9, 282, 285 (*see also* government: economic weight of)
  cuts, 69–70, 121, 124, 170, 182, 195, 206, 258, 279
  effect on economic effort, 97, 116, 118, 121, 239, 283, 285–6
  effect on income distribution, 69, 70, 126, 145, 237, 279
  effect on labour supply, 265
  effect on production costs, 182
  effect on profits, 285
  effect on saving, 58, 116, 118
  expenditures, 139, 144
  France, 175–6
  importance for the supply of venture capital, 262
  increases, 260
  in OECD countries, 20ff.
  on capital *v.* consumers and households, 9, 239, 269, 286
  restructuring of, 125–6, 128
  Sweden, 229, 239, 258, 262, 269, 286
  United Kingdom, 125, 128, 307 (note p. 149)
  USA, 58, 69
  wedge between labour costs and labour revenue, 263–4, 266
  West Germany, 196, 198, 206, 217
Taylor, M., 308 (note p. 199)
Taylorism, 65, 77
TCO, 231, 243
technological capacity, 58, 82
  and capacity of exploiting it commercially, 156, 171
  and enterprise strategy, 84
  erosion because of foreign investment, 75
  government initiative to increase, 128
  government spending on, 128
  importance for competitiveness, 84, 253
  increase through military expenditure, 62, 302 (note p. 71)
  see also high-technology: strength in; research & development
Technology Competitiveness Act, 302 (note p. 72)
telecommunications sector
  France, 173–4
  Japanese challenge, 83ff.
  market size, 82, 83
  regulation of, 82, 133
  Sweden, 253–4
  United Kingdom, 132–4
  USA, 82–5
Televerket, 250, 254
terms of trade, 4, 166 (*see also* exchange rate)
  USA, 49, 54
Thatcher, Margaret, 101ff., 111, 115, 121ff., 132, 138–9, 143ff., 150, 196, 276–7, 282, 293
Thatcherism, 102–3, 120, 148
  political strategy of, 102–3
  political tactics of, 122
Therborn, G., 233, 236, 240, 265, 309 (notes p. 287)
think tanks, in policy discourse, 114
Third Reich, 215
Thoma, F., 307 (note p. 196)
Thompson, D., 127, 129, 306 (note p. 128)
Thomson, 173
Thurow, L. C., 62, 89, 94, 300 (note p. 50), 302 (notes pp. 65 and 66)

Tilly, C., 304 (note p. 89)
Tirman, J., 301 (note p. 62)
Titmuss, R. M., 140
Tomlinson, J., 122, 306 (note p. 129)
Total Incomes System of Account (TISA), 61–2
total costs, importance of, 163, 249
Toyota, 131
Trade, Employment, and Productivity Act, 302 (note p. 72)
trade policy, as response to problems with competitiveness, 72, 74, 84, 303 (note p. 78)
trade strategy, 18–19, 82ff.
trade union, *see* labour union
Trade Union Congress (TUC), 126, 305 (note p. 114)
training, *see* apprenticeship; education; human capital
transfer payments
  and wage flexibility, 89
  as ingredient of welfare statism, 1
  effects on poverty, 90ff.
  effects on income distribution, 237 (*see also* welfare statism: effects on income distribution)
  eligibility for, 86, 87, 127
  France, 175
  in relation to public consumption, 236
  Sweden, 235
  United Kingdom, 127, 134, 135, 138ff.
  USA, 69–70, 85–7, 90
Trapp, P., 207, 223, 307 (note p. 197)
Travaux d'Utilité Collective, 179
two-tier society, 95ff., 183–4, 223, 280–90
  effect on labour power, 287–8, 290
Tyson, L., 300 (note p. 50)

Uhlmann, L., 197
underclass, 92
unemployment
  compensation, 81, 85, 87, 116, 140, 180, 218, 220
  long-term, 137
  see also employment
Unemployment Unit, 136
unemployment trap, 263
unionisation
  United Kingdom, 126, 131
  USA, 73, 80–1, 89, 95
United Automobile Workers' Union (UAW), 80, 81
United Kingdom
  economic performance, 15, 38ff., 101, 103ff.
  economic policy, 115–16, 119, 121–9
  fiscal policy, 115, 122ff., 128
  monetary policy, 119, 122ff.
  state, 119ff.
unit labour costs
  and competitiveness, 161ff., 205–6, 244, 248
  France, 154, 158ff., 161ff.
  in selected OECD countries, 189
  Sweden, 248–9, 260
  United Kingdom, 110–11
  West Germany, 189, 197, 205–6
USA
  Congress, 68ff., 84, 86, 90, 91, 92, 93
  economic policy, 45ff., 68–72
  economic performance, 15, 38ff., 45–56
  fiscal policy, 48, 69–70
  monetary policy, 48

Vauxhall, 131
Vedder, R., 93
venture capital, 119, 262
Verkstadsföreningen, 234
Vinell, L., 245, 262
Vogel, E. F., 301 (note p. 57)
Vogel, J., 237–8
Volkswagen, 211, 215
Volvo, 250ff., 261

wage(s)
  and competitiveness, 6, 18, 50ff., 75, 77, 94, 98, 116–7, 131, 157ff., 162, 182, 190, 194, 210, 214, 250, 261, 267, 286
  and inflation, 265–6, 280, 286
  and macroeconomic demand, 226–7
  and market power, 76, 77–8, 89
  and transfers for income-support, 89, 116
  differentials, 229; and economic adjustment, 262
  discipline, 187, 189, 212, 280, 286, 294
  division into basic and bonus component, 225
  drift, 250, 266, 295
  flexibility/rigidity, 89, 95, 116, 129, 281
  France, 157ff.
  in selected OECD countries, 52, 105, 212
  public sector, 266–7
  restraint of, 78ff., 98, 168–70, 175, 182, 192
  Sweden, 234, 245, 261–2, 265ff.
  United Kingdom, 116–17
  United States, 50–2
  West Germany, 188–9
  see also minimum wage
wage earners' funds, 259
Wages Councils, 116, 127
Wagner, K., 307 (note p. 149)
Wagner Act, 87
Wallén, O., 252
Wall Street Journal, 308 (note p. 199)
War on Poverty, 88, 92, 94, 96
  - Victory or Defeat?, Hearing of the US Congress, 304 (note p. 90)
Webber, D., 132, 134, 308 (note p. 221)
Weimar Republic, 215
Weisskopf, T. E., 16, 30, 296, 309 (note p. 295)
Weitzman, M. L., 225
welfare-cum-efficiency formula, 279–280
welfare state
  colonisation of, 299 (note p. 2)
  consensus, 146
  integrated, 148
  reform, debate on, 98
  residual, 148
welfare statism
  adjustment of, 7ff., 94, 99, 182, 185, 222, 290
  as part of high-efficiency syndrome, 194, 278
  and budget deficit, 49, 68, 69–70, 98, 118, 204, 217–18, 278, 294 (*see also* tax ceiling; limits to redistribution)
  and civil rights considerations, 86
  and deregulation, 68
  and exposure to the market, 93, 276, 282, 304 (note p. 94)
  and macroeconomic discipline, 291ff.
  and vulnerability to external shocks, 264
  as tied to the struggle-for-redistribution paradigm, 289–90
  at the service of interest groups, 2, 117, 118, 221
  bureaucracy of, 144–5
  centralisation of, 146, 262
  conservative model of, 290
  costs of, 7, 42–3, 145, 153, 181, 224–5, 283, 291–3; allocation of, 7ff., 269, 289 (*see also* taxes on capital *v.* consumers and households)
  cuts in, 7–8, 10, 274–5; France, 180, 274–5, 278; United Kingdom, 121, 126–7, 135, 138ff., 274–5, 277; USA, 48, 59, 69–70, 86–7, 92, 97, 274ff.; West Germany, 205, 216ff., 274–5, 279
  decentralisation of, 86, 144, 183
  effectiveness of, 90–94, 143, 218, 277–90

effects on economic performance and competitiveness, 6ff., 16, 41–2, 98, 118, 148ff., 153, 159, 181ff., 194, 291–7
effects on income distribution, 175
effects on wages, 116, 266
encouraging labour supply, 265–6
eroding wage discipline, 295 (*see also* welfare statism sustaining labour market rigidities)
eroding work discipline, 9, 16, 30, 149, 285, 309 (note p. 295)
essence of, 2, 99, 276, 296
extension of, 174ff., 204, 218, 220, 277; institutional conduciveness to, 287
facilitating economic adjustment, 9, 148, 150, 182, 268
facilitating industrial modernisation, 185
France, 174–86
functionality for capitalist production, 2, 41–2, 149–50
furthering consensus and labour commitment, 9, 98, 150, 185–6, 194, 268, 279,m 295–6
impeding economic adjustment, 116, 181
indicators of 16–17; for OECD countries, 18ff.
inflationary effect of, 266
input dimension of, 17
opposition to cuts in, 68–9, 221, 259, 276
opposition to extension/ modernisation of, 186, 282, 289
output dimension of, 17 (*see also* welfare statism: effectiveness of)
philosophy of, 86
political basis of, 8, 221
political pressure on, 8, 12, 41, 182
pragmatism *v.* fundamental commitment to, 99
privatisation of, 263 (*see also* social security: private provision of)
public support for, 96ff., 258–9, 261
responsiveness to new needs, 13, 90ff., 141, 143, 177, 184, 218ff., 276–86; policies needed for, 223ff., 282, 286ff.
restricting individual freedom, 264
statistical association with competitiveness, 13, 15–42, 291
stifling private initiative, 118
stigma attached to, 145
sustaining labour market rigidity, 116, 118, 144–5, 181, 263ff.
Sweden, 235ff., 285–6
synthetic index of, 17–18, 21, 23, 29, 30
target group approach, 85–6, 92, 98
trade-off with individual consumption, 7–8, 9, 10
United Kingdom, 134–51
USA, 85–99
ways to ensure compatibility with competitiveness, 285ff.
weakening incentives for managers and specialists, 268
West Germany, 215–228
Wellons, P. A., 301 (note p. 59)
Wells, J., 104, 105, 106
Welzmüller, R., 197
Wende, 205, 207
Westdeutsche Landesbank, 307 (notes pp. 196 and 198)
Western -Electric, 82–3
West Germay
economic performance, 15, 38ff.
economic policy, 187, 203ff., 217ff., 222
fiscal policy, 217–18
image abroad, 199
political system, 207, 221
role of banks, 60
Wetter, W., 307 (note p. 192)
white-collar workers, increase of, 302 (note p. 65)
Widick, B. J., 303 (note p. 77)
Wilensky, H. J., 16, 96, 300 (note p. 16), 309 (notes pp. 284 and 287)

Wilhelm II, Emperor of Germany, 191
Wilks, S., 128
Williams, K., 306 (note p. 120)
Wilson, Harold, 101, 103, 114, 115
Wilson Committee, 119
Windolf, P., 214
Winter, S. G., 301 (note p. 64)
Wolff, E. N., 301 (note p. 57)
Wolff von Amerongen, O., 192
women
  equal pay for, 116
  welfare treatment of, 145, 180, 238
Wood, J. P., 80
work council, 214
Work and Poverty Hearing, 304 (note p. 90)
Work and Welfare Hearing, 304 (notes pp. 89 and 90)
work discipline, 9, 16, 30, 42–3, 47, 66, 77, 79, 264 (*see also* commitment of workers and employees; industrial relations)
  as a generational phenomenon, 66
work ethic, *see* work discipline
workfare, 137–8, 145, 304 (note p. 89)
work incentive programme, 87
working practices, 252 (*see also* industrial relations: flexibility/rigidity of; quality of work life)
working time, 169, 179–80, 212, 214, 265 (*see also* employment and working time)
Worswick, G. D., 307 (note p. 149)
Wright, J. P., 303 (note p. 76)

x-efficiency, 58 (*see also* efficiency of production)

Yankelovich, D., 302 (note p. 65)
Youth Training Scheme (YTS), 137, 149
Young Workers' Scheme, 127
Ypsilanti, D., 133

Zahlenbild-Pressedienst, 209
Zakia, B., 162, 165, 172
Zeit, Die, 307 (note p. 199)
Zetterberg, H., 268
Zysman, J., 60, 300 (notes pp. 50 and 51), 301 (note p. 57)